A PEACE READER

Essential Readings on
War, Justice, Non-Violence
and World Order.

EDITED BY

JOSEPH FAHEY & RICHARD ARMSTRONG

PAULIST PRESS
New York/Mahwah

To Ita Ford, M.M.
May her light end the darkness

Library of Congress Cataloging-in-Publication Data

A Peace reader.

    Includes bibliographies.
    1. Peace.   2. Nuclear arms control.   3. Pacific
settlement in international disputes.   4. International
relations.   5. Nonviolence.   I. Fahey, Joseph.
II. Armstrong, Richard, 1932–
JX1952.P345   1987   327.1'7   87-13673
ISBN 0-8091-2914-0 (pbk.)

Published by Paulist Press
997 Macarthur Boulevard
Mahwah, New Jersey 07430

Printed and bound in the
United States of America

Contents

SECTION THREE • Non-Violence: Philosophy and Strategy

SECTION FOUR • Other Forms of Conflict Resolution

SECTION FIVE • World Order

Acknowledgements

The articles reprinted in A PEACE READER first appeared in the following publications and are reprinted with permission: "The Causes of War" from the *Wilson Quarterly* by Michael Howard; "Arms Race and Escalation" from *Journal of Conflict Resolution*, March 1979, pp. 3–16; "Arms Race and Escalation— A Closer Look" from *Journal of Peace Research* Vol. 20, No. 3, 1983, pp. 205–212; "Military Policy and Economic Decay" in *The Political Economy of Arms Reduction*, Westview Press, 1982, pp. 1–26; "Militarism in America" from the *Defense Monitor*, 1986, #3; "Deep Roots of the Arms Race" from *Christianity and Crisis*, May 13, 1985, pp. 177–179; "Nuclear Terror/Moral Paradox" from *America*, 2–19–83 issue by James Finn; "Are You a Conscientious Objector?" from *CCCO*, April 1986; "Military Service: A Moral Obligation" in *The New York Times*, 12/4/83 by Donald Kagan; "ROTC Today and Tomorrow" from the *Military Review*, May 1986, Vol. LXVI, No. 5, pp. 36–39 by Robert F. Collins; "Investigating New Options in Conflict and Defense" from the *Teachers College Record*, Fall 1982 by Gene Sharp; "Inheritance, Extinction & Personal Honesty" in *The Social Studies*, May–June 1984 by Donovan Russell; *Pacem in Terris*, April 1963, #130–145 by Pope John XXIII; "The Arms Race and Its Consequences for Developing Countries," from *Asian Survey*, Vol 24, No. 11, November 1984; "The Perils of Intervention" from *Worldview*, March 1985, Vol. 28, No. 3, pp. 4–6 by Nicholas Berry; "The Costly Business of Arming Africa" from *African Business*, February 1985, pp. 12–14 by Patrick Fitzgerald and Jonathan Bloch; "Whose Development?: Women Strategize" from *Christianity and Crisis*, September 16, 1985, pp. 344–349 by Laurien Alexandre; "Seedlings of Survival" from *Christianity and Crisis*, September 16, 1985, pp. 177–179 by Sidney Lens; "The Case against Helping the Poor" in *Psychology Today*, Vol. 8, No. 4, 1974, pp. 38–43, 123–126 by Garrett Hardin; "Aims and Means of the Catholic Worker" from *The Catholic Worker*, May 1987, p. 2 and p. 4; "Gandhi's Nonviolence" from *Friends Journal*, November 1, 1983, 99, 12–14 by Haridas T. Muzumdar; "Letter from a Birmingham Jail" from *Why We Can't Wait*, Harper, 1963, pp. 76–95 by Martin Luther King, Jr.; "The Challenge of Peace:God's Promise and Our Response" from the *Pastoral Letter on War and Peace*, pp. 40–43, 1983 United States Catholic Conference, Washington, D.C.; "Murderous Evil: Does Nonviolence Offer a Solution?" from *Commonweal*, September 20, 1985, pp. 483–487 by John Garvey; "Identifying Alternatives to Political Violence: An Educational Imperative" in *Harvard Educational Review*, 55:1, 109–117 (c) 1985 by Christopher Kruegler and Patricia Parkman; "Is There a Future to Nonviolence in Central America?" from *Fellowship*, Oct./Nov. 1983, pp. 6,7,28 by Dan R. Ebener; "A Latin American Response" from *Fellowship*, Oct./Nov. 1983, pp. 28–29, by Mano Barreno; "The Precarious Road, Nonviolence in the Philippines," from *Commonweal*, June 20, 1986, pp. 364–367 by Peggy Rosenthal; "Communication and Conflict-Management Skills" from *National Forum*, Fall 1983, pp. 31–33 by Neil H. Katz and John W. Lawyer; "The Techniques of Nonviolent Action" from an article in *Exploring Nonviolent Alternatives*, 1970 by Gene Sharp; "You Be the Arbitrator" from a pamphlet by the American Arbitration Association; "Conflict Resolution: Isn't There a Better Way?" from an article in *National Forum*, Fall 1983, by Warren E. Burger; "The Coming Evolution in Court Administered Arbitration" from *Judicature*, Feb./March 1986, pp. 276–277 by Robert Coulson; "Arbitration vs. Mediation—Explaining the Differences" from *Judicature*, Feb./March 1986, Vol 65, No. 5, pp. 263–269 by John W. Cooley; "Mandatory Mediation of Divorce: Maine's Experience" from *Judicature*, Vol. 69, No. 5, Feb./March 1986, pp. 310–312 by Lincoln Clark and Jane Orbeton; "Arbitration: An International Wallflower" from *National Forum*, Fall 1983, pp. 18–19 by Robert Coulson; "Getting to 'Yes' in a Nuclear Age" from an article in *Getting to "Yes": Negotiating Agreement without Giving* by Roger Fisher; "Ideological Convergence of the U.S. and U.S.S.R." from *International Social Science Review* 1985 by Gordon L.

vii

Anderson; "Redefining National Security" from an article in *Nuclear Times*, June 1986 by Lester R. Brown; "Obtain the Possible: Demand the Impossible" from an article in *Indefensible Weapons*, Basic Books, 1982 by Robert Jay Lifron and Richard A. Falk; "The Lesser Evil over the Greater Evil" from *Commentary*, Nov. 1981, pp. 344–348 by Jeane Kirkpatrick; "America's Liberal Tradition" from *Commentary*, November 1981 by Charles William Maynes; "Scientists and the Peace Movement: Some notes on the Relationship from *The Bulletin of Peace Proposals*, #1, 1986 by Johan Galtung; "Why the U.N. is Worth Saving" from *The New York Times*, June 2, 1986 by Harvey J. Feldman; "The Establishment of a World Authority: Working Hypotheses" from *Alternatives—A Journal of World Policy*, Fall 1982 by Silviu Brucan.

SECTION ONE

War and the Arms Race

1

The Causes of War

Michael Howard

This article originally appeared in *Wilson Quarterly*, Summer 1984.

As far back as ancient Greece, historians have sought to discover the causes of war. In this essay, Michael Howard of Oxford University finds human psychology not very different from what it was in the days of the Greek historian Thucydides (400 B.C.) when Sparta acted out of fear of Athenian power. Through the centuries, other explanations have been offered: ignorance and immaturity, survival of the fittest (Social Darwinism) and pathological aberration.

As a student of the Prussian strategist von Clausewitz, Howard holds that states go to war to achieve specific ends—that war is a product of human reason. He sees it as an action undertaken to preserve or enlarge the power of a particular state, with all its political and cultural overtones. This derives from a "superabundance of analytic rationality." With modern technology, the scope of war has changed, but not its goals. "Arms races," in Howard's view, are the modern equivalent to dynastic marriages of an earlier day. England and Germany, for example, in their eagerness to strengthen their navies before World War II, were the modern counterparts of Athens and Sparta. Today, Russia seeks to be treated as an equal by the United States.

At the same time, Howard argues that some things have changed. The stakes are higher and a revulsion to war, though not universal, is far more widespread. But war will continue to be an instrument of policy, says the author, so long as nations think that they can achieve more by fighting than by remaining at peace. The advent of nuclear weapons, he concludes, is perhaps the best deterrent to this willingness to go to war, since it would mean suicide for the parties involved.

Since the mid-18th century, many European and American theorists have attempted to explain war as an aberration in human affairs or as an occurrence beyond rational control. Violent conflicts between nations have been depicted, variously, as collective outbursts of male aggression, as the inevitable outcome of ruling-class greed, or as necessary, even

3

healthy, events in the evolutionary scheme. One exception to the general trend was the 19th-century Prussian strategist Karl von Clausewitz, who declared, in an oft-quoted dictum, that war was the extension of politics "by other means." Here, historian Michael Howard argues further that war is one of Reason's progeny—indeed, that war stems from nothing less than a "superabundance of analytic rationality."

No one can describe the topic that I have chosen to discuss as a neglected and understudied one. How much ink has been spilled about it, how many library shelves have been filled with works on the subject, since the days of Thucydides! How many scholars from how many specialties have applied their expertise to this intractable problem! Mathematicians, meteorologists, sociologists, anthropologists, geographers, physicists, political scientists, philosophers, theologians, and lawyers are only the most obvious of the categories that come to mind when one surveys the ranks of those who have sought some formula for perpetual peace, or who have at least hoped to reduce the complexities of international conflict to some orderly structure, to develop a theory that will enable us to explain, to understand, and to control a phenomenon which, if we fail to abolish it, might well abolish us.

Yet it is not a problem that has aroused a great deal of interest in the historical profession. The causes of specific wars, yes: These provide unending material for analysis and interpretation, usually fueled by plenty of documents and starkly conflicting prejudices on the part of the scholars themselves.

But the phenomenon of war as a continuing activity within human society is one that as a profession we take very much for granted. The alternation of war and peace has been the very stuff of the past. War has been throughout history a normal way of conducting disputes between political groups. Few of us, probably, would go along with those sociobiologists who claim that this has been so because man is "innately aggressive." The calculations of advantage and risk, sometimes careful, sometimes crude, that statesmen make before committing their countries to war are linked very remotely, if at all, to the displays of "machismo" that we witness today in football crowds. Since the use or threat of physical force is the most elementary way of asserting power and controlling one's environment, the fact that men have frequently had recourse to it does not cause the historian a great deal of surprise. Force, or the threat of it, may not settle arguments, but it does play a considerable part in determining the structure of the world in which we live.

I mentioned the multiplicity of books that have been written about the causes of war since the time of Thucydides. In fact, I think we would find that the vast majority of them have been written since 1914, and that the degree of intellectual concern about the causes of war to which we have become accustomed has existed only since the First World War. In view of the damage which that war did to the social and political structure of Europe, this is understandable enough. But there has been a tendency to argue that because that war caused such great and lasting damage, because it destroyed three great empires and nearly beggared a fourth, it must have arisen from causes of peculiar complexity and profundity, from the neuroses of nations, from the widening class struggle, from a crisis in industrial society. I have argued this myself, taking issue with Mr. A. J. P. Taylor, who maintained that because the war had such profound consequences, it did not necessarily have equally profound causes. But now I wonder whether on this, as on so many other matters, I was not wrong and he was not right.

It is true, and it is important to bear in mind in examining the problems of that period, that before 1914 war was almost universally considered an acceptable, perhaps an inevitable and for many people a desirable, way of settling international differences, and that the war generally foreseen was expected to be, if not exactly brisk and cheerful, then certainly brief; no longer, certainly, than the war of 1870 between France and Prussia that was consciously or unconsciously taken by that generation as a model. Had it not been so generally felt that war was an acceptable and tolerable way of solving international disputes, statesmen and soldiers would no doubt have approached the crisis of 1914 in a very different fashion.

But there was nothing new about this attitude to war. Statesmen had always been able to assume that war would be acceptable at least to those sections of their populations whose opinion mattered to them, and in this respect the decision to go to war in 1914—for continental statesmen at least—in no way differed from those taken by their predecessors of earlier generations. The causes of the Great War are thus in essence no more complex or profound than those of any previous European war, or indeed than those described by Thucydides as underlying the Peloponnesian War: "What made war inevitable was the growth of Athenian power and the fear this caused in Sparta." In Central Europe, there was the German fear that the disintegration of the Habsburg Empire would result in an enormous enhancement of Russian power—power already becoming formidable as French-financed industries and railways put Russian manpower at the service of her military machine. In Western Europe, there was the traditional British fear that Germany might establish a hegemony over Europe which, even more than that of Napoleon, would place at risk the security of Britain and her own possessions, a fear fueled by the knowledge that there was within Germany a widespread determination to achieve a world status comparable with her latent power. Considerations of this kind had caused wars in Europe often enough before. Was there really anything different about 1914?

Ever since the 18th century, war had been blamed by intellectuals upon the stupidity or the self-interest of governing elites (as it is now blamed upon "military-industrial complexes"), with the implicit or explicit assumption that if the control of state affairs were in the hands of sensible men—businessmen, as Richard Cobden thought, the workers, as Jean Jaurès thought—then wars would be no more.

By the 20th century, the growth of the social and biological sciences was producing alternative explanations. As Quincy Wright expressed it in his massive *A Study of War* (1942), "Scientific investigators . . . tended to attribute war to immaturities in social knowledge and control, as one might attribute epidemics to insufficient medical knowledge or to inadequate public health services." The Social Darwinian acceptance of the inevitability of struggle, indeed of its desirability if mankind was to progress, the view, expressed by the elder Moltke but very widely shared at the turn of the century, that perpetual peace was a dream and not even a beautiful dream, did not survive the Great War in those countries where the bourgeois-liberal culture was dominant, Britain and the United States. The failure of these nations to appreciate that such bellicist views, or variants of them, were still widespread in other areas of the world, those dominated by Fascism and by Marxism-Leninism, was to cause embarrassing misunderstandings, and possibly still does.

For liberal intellectuals, war was self-evidently a pathological aberration from the norm, at best a ghastly mistake, at worst a crime. Those who initiated wars must in their view have been criminal, or sick, or the victims of forces beyond their power to control. Those who were so accused disclaimed responsibility for the events of 1914, throwing it on others or saying the whole thing was a terrible mistake for which no one was to blame. None of them, with their societies in ruins around them and tens of millions dead, were prepared to say courageously: "We only acted as statesmen always have in the past. In the circumstances then prevailing, war seemed to us to be the best way of protecting or forwarding the national interests for which we were responsible. There was an element of risk, certainly, but the risk might have been greater had we postponed the issue. Our real guilt does not lie in the fact that we started the war. It lies in our mistaken belief that we could win it."

The trouble is that if we are to regard war as pathological and abnormal, then all conflict must be similarly regarded; for war is only a particular kind of conflict between a particular category of social groups: sovereign states. It is, as Clausewitz put it, "a clash between major interests that is resolved by bloodshed—that is the only way in which it differs from other conflicts." If one had no sovereign states, one would have no wars, as Rousseau rightly pointed out—but, as Hobbes equally rightly pointed out, we would probably have no peace either. As states acquire a monopoly of violence, war becomes the only remaining form of conflict that may legitimately be settled by physical force. The mechanism of legitimization of authority and of social control that makes it possible for a state to moderate or eliminate conflicts within its borders or at very least to ensure that these are not conducted by competitive violence—the mechanism to the study of which historians have quite properly devoted so much attention—makes possible the conduct of armed conflict with other states, and on occasion—if the state is to survive—makes it necessary.

These conflicts arise from conflicting claims, or interests, or ideologies, or perceptions; and these perceptions may indeed by fueled by social or psychological drives that we do not fully understand and that one day we may learn rather better how to control. But the problem is the control of social conflict as such, not simply of war. However inchoate or disreputable the motives for war may be, its initiation is almost by definition a deliberate and carefully considered act and its conduct, at least at the more advanced levels of social development, a matter of very precise central control. If history shows any record of "accidental" wars, I have yet to find them. Certainly statesmen have sometimes been surprised by the nature of the war they have unleashed, and it is reasonable to assume that in at least 50 percent of the cases they got a result they did not expect. But that is not the same as a war begun by mistake and continued with no political purpose.

Statesmen in fact go to war to achieve very specific ends, and the reasons for which states have fought one another have been categorized and recategorized innumerable times. Vattel, the Swiss lawyer, divided them into the necessary, the customary, the rational, and the capricious. Jomini, the Swiss strategist, identified ideological, economic, and popular wars, wars to defend the balance of power, wars to assist allies, wars to assert or to defend rights. Quincy Wright, the American political scientist, divided them into the idealistic, the psychological, the political, and the juridical. Bernard Brodie in our own times has refused to discriminate: "Any theory of the causes of war in general or any war in particular that is not inherently eclectic and comprehensive," he stated, " . . . is bound for that very reason to be wrong." Another contemporary analyst, Geoffrey Blainey, is on the contrary unashamedly reductionist. All war aims, he wrote, "are simply varieties of power. The vanity of nationalism, the will to spread an ideology, the protection of kinsmen in an adjacent land, the desire for more territory . . . all these represent power in different wrappings. The conflicting aims of rival nations are always conflicts of power."

In principle, I am sure that Bernard Brodie was right: No single explanation for conflict between states, any more than for conflict between any other social groups, is likely to stand up to critical examination. But Blainey is right as well. Quincy Wright provided us with a useful indicator when he suggested that "while animal war is a function of instinct and primitive war of the mores, civilized war is primarily a function of state politics."

Medievalists will perhaps bridle at the application of the term "primitive" to the sophisticated and subtle societies of the Middle Ages, for whom war was also a "function of the mores," a way of life that often demanded only the most banal of justifications. As a way of life, it persisted in Europe well into the 17th century, if no later. For Louis XIV and his court war was, in the early years at least, little more than a seasonal variation on hunting. But by the 18th century, the mood had changed. For Frederick the Great, war was to be pre-eminently a function of Staatspolitik, and so it has remained ever since. And although statesmen can be as emotional or as prejudiced in their judgments as any other group of human beings, it is very seldom that their attitudes, their perceptions, and their decisions are not related, however remotely, to the fundamental issues of power, that capacity to control their environment on which the independent existence of their states and often the cultural values of their societies depend.

And here perhaps we do find a factor that sets interstate conflict somewhat apart from other forms of social rivalry. States may fight—indeed as often as not they do fight—not over any specific issue such as might otherwise have been resolved by peaceful means, but in order to acquire, to enhance, or to preserve their capacity to function as independent actors in the international system at all. "The stakes of war," as Raymond Aron has reminded us, "are the existence, the creation, or the elimination of States." It is a somber analysis, but one which the historical record very amply bears out.

It is here that those analysts who come to the study of war from the disciplines of the natural sciences, particularly the biological sciences, tend, it seems to me, to go astray. The conflicts between states which have usually led to war have normally arisen, not from any irrational and emotive drives, but from almost a superabundance of *analytic rationality*. Sophisticated communities (one hesitates to apply to them Quincy Wright's word, "civilized") do not react simply to immediate threats. Their intelligence (and I use the term in its double sense) enables them to assess the implications that any event taking place anywhere in the world, however remote, may have for their own capacity, immediately to exert influence, ultimately perhaps to survive. In the later Middle Ages and the early Modern period, every child born to every prince anywhere in Europe was registered on the delicate seismographs that monitored the shifts in dynastic power. Every marriage was a diplomatic triumph or disaster. Every stillbirth, as Henry VIII knew, could presage political catastrophe.

Today, the key events may be different. The pattern remains the same. A malfunction in the political mechanism of some remote African community, a coup d'état in a minuscule Caribbean republic, an insurrection deep in the hinterland of Southeast Asia, an assassination in some emirate in the Middle East—all these will be subjected to the kind of anxious examination and calculation that was devoted a hundred years ago to the news of comparable events in the Balkans: an insurrection in Philippopoli, a coup d'état in Constantinople, an assassination in Belgrade. To whose advantage will this ultimately redound, asked the worried diplomats, ours or theirs? Little enough in itself, perhaps, but will it not precipitate or strengthen a trend, set in motion a tide whose melancholy withdrawing roar will strip us of our friends and influence and leave us isolated in a world dominated by adversaries deeply hostile to us and all that we stand for?

There have certainly been occasions when states have gone to war in a mood of ideological fervor like the French republican armies in 1792; or of swaggering aggression like the Americans against Spain in 1898 or the British against the Boers a year later; or to make more money, as did the British in the War of Jenkins' Ear in 1739; or in a generous desire to help peoples of similar creed or race, as perhaps the Russians did in helping the Bulgarians fight the Turks in 1877 and the British dominions certainly did in 1914 and 1939. But, in general, men have fought during the past two hundred years neither because they are aggressive nor because they are acquisitive animals, but because they are reasoning ones: because they discern, or believe that they can discern, dangers before they become immediate, the possibility of threats before they are made.

But be this as it may, in 1914 many of the German people, and in 1939 nearly all of the British, felt justified in going to war, not over any specific issue that could have been settled by negotiation, but to maintain their power; and to do so while it was still possible, before they found themselves so isolated, so impotent, that they had no power left to maintain and had to accept a subordinate position within an international system dominated by their adversaries. "What made war inevitable was the growth of Athenian power and the fear this caused in Sparta." Or, to quote another grimly apt passage from Thucydides:

> The Athenians made their Empire more and more strong . . . [until] finally the point was reached when Athenian strength attained a peak plain for all to see and the Athenians began to encroach upon Sparta's allies. It was at this point that Sparta felt the position to be no longer tolerable and decided by starting the present war to employ all her energies in attacking and if possible destroying the power of Athens.

You can vary the names of the actors, but the model remains a valid one for the purposes of our analysis. I am rather afraid that it still does.

Something that has changed since the time of Thucydides, however, is the nature of the power that appears so threatening. From the time of Thucydides until that of Louis XIV, there was basically only one source of political and military power—*control of territory,* with all the resources in wealth and manpower that this provided. This control might come through conquest, or through alliance, or through marriage, or through purchase, but the power of princes could be very exactly computed in terms of the extent of their territories and the number of men they could put under arms.

In 17th-century Europe, this began to change. Extent of territory remained important, but no less important was the effectiveness with which the resources of that territory could be exploited. Initially there were the bureaucratic and fiscal mechanisms that transformed loose bonds of territorial authority into highly structured centralized states whose armed forces, though not necessarily large, were permanent, disciplined, and paid.

Then came the political transformations of the revolutionary era that made available to these state systems the entire manpower of their country, or at least as much of it as the administrators were able to handle. And finally came the revolution in transport, the railways of the 19th century that turned the revolutionary ideal of the "Nation in Arms" into a reality. By the early 20th century, military power—on the continent of Europe, at least—was seen as a simple combination of military manpower and railways. The quality of armaments was of secondary importance, and political intentions were virtually excluded from account. The growth of power was measured in terms of the growth of populations and of communications; of the number of men who could be put under arms and transported to the battlefield to make their weight felt in the initial and presumably decisive battles. It was the mutual perception of threat in those terms that turned Europe before 1914 into an armed camp, and it was their calculations within this framework that reduced German staff officers increasingly to despair and launched their leaders on their catastrophic gamble in 1914, which started the First World War.

But already the development of weapons technology had introduced yet another element into the international power calculus, one that has in our own age become dominant. It was only in the course of the 19th century that technology began to produce weapons systems—initially in the form of naval vessels—that could be seen as likely in themselves to prove decisive, through their qualitative and quantitative superiority, in the event of conflict. But as war became increasingly a matter of competing technologies rather than competing armies, so there developed that escalatory process known as the "arms race." As a title, the phrase, like so many coined by journalists to catch the eye, is misleading.

"Arms races" are in fact continuing and open-ended attempts to match power for power. They are as much means of achieving stable or, if possible, favorable power balances as were the *dynastic marriage policies* of Valois and Habsburg. To suggest that they in themselves are causes of war implies a naive if not totally mistaken view of the relationship between the two phenomena. The causes of war remain rooted, as much as they were in the preindustrial age, in perceptions by statesmen of the growth of hostile power and the fears for the restriction, if not the extinction, of their own. The threat, or rather the fear, has not changed, whether it comes from aggregations of territory or from dreadnoughts, from the numbers of men under arms or from missile systems. The means that states employ to sustain or to extend their power may have been transformed, but their objectives and preoccupations remain the same.

"Arms races" can no more be isolated than wars themselves from the *political circumstances* that give rise to them, and like wars they will take as many different forms as political circumstances dictate. They may be no more than a process of competitive modernization, of maintaining a status quo that commands general support but in which no participant wishes, whether from reasons of pride or of prudence, to fall behind in keeping his armory up to date. If there are no political causes for fear or rivalry, this process need not in itself be a destabilizing factor in international relations. But arms races may, on the other hand, be the result of a quite deliberate assertion of an intention to change the status quo, as was, for example, the German naval challenge to Britain at the beginning of this century.

This challenge was an explicit attempt by Admiral Alfred von Tirpitz and his associates to destroy the hegemonic position at sea which Britain saw as essential to her security, and, not inconceivably, to replace it with one of their own. As British and indeed German diplomats repeatedly explained to the German government, it was not the German naval program in itself that gave rise to so much alarm in Britain. It was the intention that lay behind it. If the status quo was to be maintained, the German challenge had to be met.

The naval race could quite easily have been ended on one of two conditions. Either the Germans could have abandoned their challenge, as had the French in the previous century, and acquiesced in British naval supremacy; or the British could have yielded as gracefully as they did, a decade or so later, to the United States and abandoned a status they no longer had the capacity, or the will, to maintain. As it was, they saw the German challenge as one to which they could and should respond, and their power position as one which they were prepared, if necessary, to use force to preserve. The British naval program was thus, like that of the Germans, a signal of political intent; and that intent, that refusal to acquiesce in a fundamental transformation of the power balance, was indeed a major element among the causes of the war. The naval competition provided a very accurate indication and measurement of political rivalries and tensions, but it did not cause them; nor could it have been abated unless the rivalries themselves had been abandoned.

It was the general perception of the growth of German power that was awakened by the naval challenge, and the fear that a German hegemony on the Continent would be the first step to a challenge to her own hegemony on the oceans, that led Britain to involve herself in the continental conflict in 1914 on the side of France and Russia. "What made war inevitable was the growth of Spartan power," to reword Thucydides, "and the fear which this caused in Athens." In the Great War that followed, Germany was defeated, but survived with none of her latent power destroyed. A "false hegemony" of Britain and France was established in Europe that could last only so long as Germany did not again mobilize her resources to challenge it. German rearmament in the 1930s did not of itself mean that Hitler wanted war (though one has to ignore his entire philosophy if one is to believe that he did not); but it did mean that he was determined, with a great deal of popular support, to obtain a free hand on the international scene.

With that free hand, he intended to establish German power on an irreversible basis; this was the message conveyed by his armament program. The armament program that the British reluctantly adopted in reply was intended to show that, rather than submit to the hegemonic aspirations they feared from such a revival of German power, they would fight to preserve their own freedom of action. Once again to recast Thucydides:

> Finally the point was reached when German strength attained a peak plain for all to see, and the Germans began to encroach upon Britain's allies. It was at this point that Britain felt the position to be no longer tolerable and decided by starting this present war to employ all her energies in attacking and if possible destroying the power of Germany.

What the Second World War established was not a new British hegemony, but a Soviet hegemony over the Euro-Asian land mass from the Elbe to Vladivostok; and that was seen, at least from Moscow, as an American hegemony over the rest of the world; one freely accepted in Western Europe as a preferable alternative to being absorbed by the rival hegemony. Rival armaments were developed to define and preserve the new territorial boundaries, and the present arms competition began. But in considering the present situation, historical experience suggests that we must ask the fundamental question: What kind of competition is it? Is it one between powers that accept the status quo, are satisfied with the existing power relationship, and are concerned simply to modernize their armaments in order to preserve it? Or does it reflect an *underlying instability* in the system?

My own perception, I am afraid, is that it is the latter. There was a period for a decade after the war when the Soviet Union was probably a status quo power but the West was not; that is, the Russians were not seriously concerned to challenge the American global hegemony, but the West did not accept that of the Russians in Eastern Europe. Then there was a decade of relative mutual acceptance between 1955 and 1965; and it was no accident that this was the heyday of disarmament/arms-control negotiations. But thereafter, the Soviet Union has shown itself increasingly unwilling to accept the Western global hegemony, if only because many other people in the world have been unwilling to do so either. Reaction against Western dominance brought the Soviet Union some allies and many opportunities in the Third World, and she has developed naval power to be able to assist the former and exploit the latter. She has aspired in fact to global power status, as did Germany before 1914; and if the West complains, as did Britain about Germany, that the Russians do not need a navy for defense purposes, the Soviet Union can retort, as did Germany, that she needs it to make clear to the world the status to which she aspires; that is, so that she can operate on the world scene by virtue of her own power and not by permission of anyone else. Like Germany, she is determined to be treated as an equal, and armed strength has appeared the only way to achieve that status.

The trouble is that what is seen by one party as the breaking of an alien hegemony and the establishment of equal status will be seen by the incumbent powers as a striving for the establishment of an alternate hegemony, and they are not necessarily wrong. In international politics, the appetite often comes with eating; and there really may be no way to check an aspiring rival except by the mobilization of stronger military power. An arms race then becomes almost a necessary surrogate for war, a test of national will and strength; and arms control becomes possible only when the underlying power balance has been mutually agreed.

We would be blind, therefore, if we did not recognize that the causes which have produced war in the past are operating in our own day as powerfully as at any time in history. It is by no means impossible that a thousand years hence a historian will write—if any historians survive, and there are any records for them to write history from—"What made war inevitable was the growth of Soviet power and the fear which this caused in the United States."

But times have changed since Thucydides. They have changed even since 1914. These were, as we have seen, bellicist societies in which war was a normal, acceptable, even a desirable way of settling differences. The question that arises today is, how widely and evenly spread is that intense revulsion against war that at present characterizes our own society? For if war is indeed now universally seen as being unacceptable as an instrument of policy, then all analogies drawn from the past are misleading, and although power struggles may continue, they will be diverted into other channels. But if that revulsion is not evenly spread, societies which continue to see armed force as an acceptable means for attaining their political ends are likely to establish a dominance over those which do not. Indeed, they will not necessarily have to fight for it.

My second and concluding point is this: Whatever may be the underlying causes of international conflict, even if we accept the role of atavistic militarism or of military-industrial complexes or of sociobiological drives or of domestic tensions in fueling it, wars begin with conscious and reasoned decisions based on the calculation, made by both parties, that they can achieve more by going to war than by remaining at peace.

Even in the most bellicist of societies this kind of calculation has to be made and it has never even for them been an easy one. When the decision to go to war involves the likelihood, if not the certainty, that the conflict will take the form of an exchange of nuclear weapons from which one's own territory cannot be immune, then even for the most bellicist of leaders, even for those most insulated from the pressures of public opinion, the calculation that they have more to gain from going to war than by remaining at peace and pursuing their policies by other means will, to put it mildly, not be self-evident. The odds against such a course benefiting their state or themselves or their cause will be greater, and more evidently greater, than in any situation that history has ever had to record. Society may have accepted killing as a legitimate instrument of state policy, but not, as yet, suicide. For that reason I find it hard to believe that the abolition of nuclear weapons, even if it were possible, would be an unmixed blessing. Nothing that makes it easier for statesmen to regard war as a feasible instrument of state policy, one from which they stand to gain rather than lose, is likely to contribute to a lasting peace.

Questions

1. What was the general European attitude toward war before 1914?
2. What occurred to change it?
3. Do you think wars result from pathological or "superrational" causes? Give your reasons.
4. What causes does Howard give for the underlying instability of U.S.– Soviet relations?
5. Do you agree with his contention that the elimination of nuclear weapons would make it easier to go to war? Identify other factors that may be taken into consideration.

2
Arms Races and Escalation

Michael Wallace

This article originally appeared in the *Journal of Conflict Resolution*, March 1979.

As Michael Howard depicted arms races as an instrument of policy, Michael Wallace of the Universities of Michigan and British Columbia sees them as powerful determinants of the likelihood of war itself. Using a mathematical model first constructed by others and refined by himself, Wallace studied ninety-six international conflicts and found a close association—perhaps even a causal one—between preparation for war and the actual outbreak of hostilities. Some advocates of military preparedness— both in the Pentagon and in the Kremlin—attribute wars to the failure to maintain a strong military posture. Others, in both camps, take the opposite view: that preparation for war makes its outbreak almost inevitable. Through the use of the social sciences, Wallace tries to resolve this disagreement.

He begins by giving his definition of "arms race." It involves an abnormal and simultaneous increase in military expenditures by two or more equal powers, arising from international and not domestic concerns. He regards spending increases of ten percent or more for three years prior to resolution of a conflict as "abnormal." By examining international disputes between the years 1816 and 1965 (later updated to 1970), he develops an "arms race index" against which he tests whether the degree of probability of war was accurate in predicting actual warfare.

Wallace finds that wars resulted from "arms races" in ninety percent of the cases, while wars seldom broke out in their absence.

This study lends fresh urgency to the efforts of the superpowers to curb their strategic arsenals.

Although major power arms races have been the subject of a great amount of mathematical modelling, there has been little data-based research concerning their impact on international war. This study attempts to determine whether or not these arms races affect the probability that a serious dispute between major powers will escalate to all-out war. To do this, an arms race index is constructed in the following manner: a curve-fitting technique is employed to calculate changes in

16

arms expenditures for each major power as a function of time. The smoothed rates of increase for each of the parties to a dispute are multiplied together, yielding an index whose values will be high only if the two powers have engaged in rapid and simultaneous military expansion prior to the dispute. It was found that disputes preceded by such an arms race escalated to war 23 out of 28 times, while disputes not preceded by an arms race resulted in war only 3 out of 71 times. It was concluded that at the very least, arms races are an important early warning indicator of escalation potential, and may well play a central role in the escalation process. The implications of this finding for the current debate over SALT II were noted.

INTRODUCTION

More than 30 years have passed since Lewis Fry Richardson began his pioneering treatise on the dynamics of arms races (Richardson, 1960), and nearly two decades have gone by since David Singer (1958) and Samuel Huntington (1958) staked out their positions on opposite sides of the "armaments-tensions" debate. In the intervening years, a great deal has been written concerning the onset and dynamic evolution of arms races,[1] and on the relationship between national capabilities and likelihood of violent conflict.[2] Yet, oddly enough, virtually nothing written to date has shed much light on the central question these pioneering works address: does the existence of an arms race between two states significantly increase their probability of going to war?

It is only necessary to peruse the current debate over the parturient SALT II negotiations to realize that the outlines of the controversy have remained essentially unchanged since classical times. On the one side, Vegetius's doctrine "si vis pacem, para bellum" finds its contemporary expression amongst the partisans of military expansion in both the Pentagon and the Kremlin. They argue that only a strong military posture can deter an opponent's military adventurism, which, unchecked, would lead to armed conflict. In other words, it is not arms races that lead to war, but rather a nation's failure to maintain its military capabilities vis-à-vis its potential rivals and adversaries.

On the other side of this debate are those who believe that military expansion per se contributes to the danger of war. It is argued, to begin with, that military expansion is self-defeating, in that it is likely to provoke a similar countervailing expansion by the other side. Moreover, the mutual threat posed by such competitive military growth intensifies other conflicts and contentions among nations, leading to additional uncertainty and insecurity, further pressures for military expansion, and so on in a vicious, escalating circle. In short, the partisans of the "arms race" school do not see the competitive acquisition of military capability as a neutral instrument of policy, still less as a means to prevent war, but rather as a major link in the complex chain of events leading to armed conflict.

Given the central role this debate has played in current policy discussions, and considering the magnitude of the stakes involved in the nuclear age, it is long past time that some direct scientific evidence were brought to bear on the matter. That is what I shall attempt here.

In order to address the question in a systematic manner, two preliminary conceptual matters must be dealt with. First, we must decide what is to be meant by an "arms race," and second, we must specify the process by which arms races may be thought of as influencing the probability of war.

THE DEFINITION OF AN ARMS RACE

Turning first to the definition of an arms race, the literature presents numerous alternatives.[3] While many of these differ in some respects, there are two elements common to all. First, arms races involve simultaneous abnormal rates of growth in the military outlays of two or more nations. Second, in an arms race these result from the competitive pressure of the military rivalry itself, and not from domestic forces exogenous to this rivalry.

Beginning with the second of these two components of a definition, it is clear that, at a minimum, we can only speak of an "arms race" between nations whose foreign and defense policies are heavily interdependent; the behavior and capabilities of each nation must be highly salient to the other nations. Thus, it is meaningless to speak of an "arms race" between nations with little contact with or interest in each other. But more than this is required. The capabilities of the putative military rivals must not only be mutually salient, but also roughly comparable. However great their mutual antagonism, and however rapidly their armed forces grow, it would make little sense to speak of an "arms race" between, say, the United States and Cuba, or the Soviet Union and Iran. In short, arms races can exist only amongst the great powers, or amongst local powers of comparable military standing within the same region.

The next question is, what are we to understand as the "abnormal growth" which constitutes an arms race? Clearly, not all competitive or simultaneous increases qualify. Throughout most of the nineteenth and twentieth centuries, a majority of nations, and virtually all of the great powers, have made continual qualitative and quantitative additions to their armed forces. More often than not, these have been undertaken in a spirit of rivalry—country X wishing to possess bigger battleships than Y or more armoured divisions than Z. Yet these competitive acquisitions are not "arms races"; the average annual rate of growth has not usually exceeded 4 or 5% in real terms, and an examination of historical accounts indicates that contemporary elites have worried very little about them.

At frequent intervals, however, this pattern of normal arms competition is transformed into a runaway arms race through some combination of domestic, diplomatic, and strategic pressures.[4] The competition now becomes a matter of great, perhaps paramount salience for both sides. The annual rate of growth in military capability occasionally climbs to a figure in excess of 10%, even as much as 20 or 25%. In short, the onset of an arms race is characterized by a sharp acceleration (significant increase in the rate of increase) in military capability. It is these "runaway accelerations" that we shall term "arms races" for purposes of this paper.

FROM ARMS RACE TO WAR

In specifying the impact which rapid military growth has upon the probability of war, two problems arise. First, how do we distinguish empirically between genuine competitive arms races as described above, and mere coincidental military "accelerations"? For example, between 1937 and 1939, both Britain and the United States increased the size and quality of their armed forces many times over, yet it would be absurd to speak of them as engaging in an arms race.

The second problem arises from the fact that military acquisitions by themselves are extremely unlikely to provoke military hostilities. Even in the era of "counterforce" and "flexible response," few responsible observers suggest that any nation would initiate violent hostilities with a power of comparable size solely to protect or enhance its military-strategic position. Some other factor or factors must lead nations into a dispute or confrontation of sufficient severity that the military dangers created by the arms race are transformed from chronic irritants into acute threats to national survival.

Both of these problems are easily solved by turning the central question on its head. Instead of asking whether or not bilateral or multilateral runaway arms growth enhances the likelihood of war, we can pose the problem this way: "do serious disputes between nations engaged in an arms race have a significantly greater probability of resulting in all-out war than those between nations exhibiting more normal patterns of military competition?" Presumably, if two nations are on opposite sides of a serious dispute, any military acquisition they might make will be directed towards each other at least in part. At the same time, such a dispute provides the theoretical preconditions for the transition from war preparation to war initiation.

THE DOMAIN

As is customary with studies using Correlates of War Project data, the test period for our hypotheses will extend from 1816 to 1965. In this paper we shall consider only great power disputes and wars occurring during this period, that is, those in which there was at least one great power on each side. There are two reasons for this. First, we noted that rough equivalence of capability was a crucial prerequisite for an arms race, ruling out consideration of "major vs. minor" wars and disputes. Although rough equivalence of capability often obtains among hostile lesser powers, these are often dependent upon great powers for weapons and political support to the extent that their decisional autonomy is open to question. A second difficulty is that data concerning the military capability of, and disputes concerning, lesser powers is far less reliable than the corresponding information for the majors.

In sum, it was felt that any major extension of the test population at this stage would muddy the waters, and possibly confuse the results. There is one important exception, however. In those cases where there occurs a dispute between a great power and a minor power bound in a military alliance to another great power, we consider this to be a great power dispute.

The population of "great powers" is that used by Singer and Small (1966), and comprises Britain from 1815 to 1965; France from 1816 to 1940, and 1945 to 1965; the United States from 1898 to 1965; Germany from 1816 to 1918, and 1923 to 1945; Austria-Hungary from 1816 to 1917; Russia from 1816 to 1917, and from 1920 to 1965; Japan from 1904 to 1945; and China from 1950 to 1965.

SERIOUS DISPUTES

As the data collected by the Correlates of War Project on serious international disputes have not yet appeared in print, a brief summary of the coding rules is in order here. Briefly, for our purposes a dispute is a military confrontation between two or more nations not deadly enough to qualify as a war defined by Singer and Small. However, it must be "serious enough for one of the parties involved to threaten to commit, or actually commit, significant military resources to resolve the dispute" (Levy, 1977). We consider this a commitment to have a specific series of acts initiated by the official representatives of a power and clearly a commitment directed towards another great power. This series of acts comprises the following: the act of blockade, declaration of war, seizure or occupation of territory, the use of military forces, the mobilization of armed forces, and the seizure of foreign personnel or materiel. In all, a total of 99 disputes between major powers met our criteria; a complete list will be found in Table 1.

THE WARS

Of these 96 serious dispute dyads, only 23 resulted in the outbreak of full-scale war as defined by Singer and Small (1972). Included are all military clashes in which at least one great power participated on each side, and which resulted in at least 1,000 battle-related fatalities. Only one departure is made from the Singer-Small codifications. In the case of those wars which involved more than two powers, each dyad is coded separately. Thus, for example, World War II is coded as an initiation of Franco-German and Anglo-German hostilities in 1939, an Anglo-Italian and Franco-Italian outbreak in 1940, and a Russo-German and Japanese-American conflict initiated in 1941. This was done to avoid the practical and conceptual difficulties of aggregating military capabilities of nations entering the conflict at different times.

THE MEASUREMENT OF MILITARY CAPABILITY

The next step in the operational test of our hypotheses is the development of an index of military capabilities. For present purposes, we shall use annual aggregate military expenditures. Included in this total are both regular and extraordinary expenditures for all regular armed forces, as well as proceeds from borrowings in aid of the military. Both metropolitan and colonial expenditures are included. However, we exclude unexpended appropriations, military pensions, and expenditures on police, frontier guards, and reserves.

At this point, a few words of justification are in order. Obviously, many will argue that expenditures for armed forces do not always reflect true military capabilities; to use expenditures as an index would be to assume that military "cost-effectiveness" remains constant through time and space. Obviously, this is not the case, and represents a major potential source of bias in the index. But, in mitigation, two points may be made.

First, while military efficiency varies widely, it tends to change fairly slowly. As we shall see, our measurement of the severity of an arms race is made with reference to a time-span of ten years. Within this time period, changing cost-effectiveness is unlikely to be a problem.

TABLE 1
Serious Disputes Between Major Powers, 1816–1965

Year	Nations Involved		Escalation to War	Arms Race Index
1833	UK	Russia	No	2.73
1833	France	Russia	No	0.17
1836	Russia	UK	No	1.00
1840	France	Russia	No	12.90
1840	France	Germany	No	0.66
1849	UK	Russia	No	1.02
1849	France	Russia	No	36.27
1850	Germany	Austria	No	9.54
1853	UK	Russia	Yes	0.06
1853	France	Russia	Yes	31.74
1854	Austria	Russia	No	53.80
1859	France	Austria	Yes	120.91
1861	UK	Russia	No	0.16
1866	Germany	Austria	Yes	148.61
1866	Italy	Austria	Yes	575.14
1867	France	Italy	No	55.00
1870	France	Germany	Yes	8.91
1875	France	Germany	No	1.19
1877	UK	Russia	No	3.22
1878	UK	Russia	No	0.88
1878	Austria	Italy	No	0.48
1885	UK	Russia	No	4.93
1887	Germany	France	No	1.07
1888	Italy	France	No	7.17
1888	Austria	France	No	8.35
1888	England	France	No	1.63
1893	Austria	Russia	No	0.23
1895	Russia	Japan	No	61.53
1897	UK	Russia	No	0.17
1898	UK	France	No	0.35
1899	UK	Germany	No	0.39
1900	Japan	Russia	No	53.17
1902	US	Germany	No	0.15
1902	US	UK	No	0.01
1903	US	UK	No	0.07

Year	Nations Involved		Escalation to War	Arms Race Index
1904	UK	Russia	No	0.07
1904	Russia	Japan	Yes	221.00
1905	Germany	France	No	0.04
1911	Germany	France	No	2.48
1911	Germany	UK	No	28.07
1912	Russia	Austria	No	0.02
1912	Austria	Italy	No	0.37
1913	Italy	France	No	43.39
1914	Germany	UK	Yes	133.20
1914	Germany	France	Yes	231.25
1914	Germany	Russia	Yes	205.35
1914	Austria	UK	Yes	90.00
1914	Austria	France	Yes	156.25
1914	Austria	Russia	Yes	138.75
1915	Italy	Germany	Yes	811.30
1915	Italy	Austria	Yes	912.38
1917	US	Germany	Yes	349.68
1923	UK	Russia	No	0.04
1931	US	Japan	No	0.53
1932	UK	Japan	No	0.85
1932	US	Japan	No	1.05
1934	Italy	Germany	No	14.58
1934	Russia	Japan	No	0.13
1935	Japan	Russia	No	106.13
1935	UK	Italy	No	38.21
1936	UK	Germany	No	112.68
1936	France	Germany	No	5.56
1937	Russia	Japan	No	51.47
1937	Japan	US	No	28.28
1938	Russia	Japan	No	14.96
1938	UK	Germany	No	90.06
1938	France	Germany	No	25.97
1939	Japan	France	No	11.49
1939	UK	Japan	Yes	261.23
1939	France	Germany	Yes	495.51

Year	Nations Involved		Escalation to War	Arms Race Index
1940	Italy	UK	Yes	559.65
1940	Italy	France	Yes	643.70
1940	Japan	UK	No	39.98
1940	Japan	France	No	11.49
1941	Germany	Russia	Yes	221.61
1941	US	Japan	Yes	314.58
1945	Japan	Russia	Yes	102.93
1946	US	Russia	No	0.03
1948	Russia	US	No	0.32
1948	Russia	UK	No	0.25
1948	Russia	France	No	10.01
1953	Russia	US	No	68.72
1953	Russia	UK	No	41.80
1954	China	UK	No	22.89
1956	China	US	No	25.03
1956	Russia	France	No	61.89
1956	Russia	UK	No	53.05
1958	China	US	No	65,.02
1958	UK	Russia	No	0.19
1960	US	Russia	No	6.34
1961	US	Russia	No	14.14
1962	US	China	No	103.73
1962	US	Russia	No	122.10
1964	US	Russia	No	30.70
1965	China	UK	No	81.43
1965	China	US	No	47.97

Moreover, we shall be concerned here not with the absolute level of military expenditures, but rather with their rates of change (deltas) from year to year. Thus, the problem of comparing absolute levels across nations does not arise.

We have now specified operational criteria for wars, disputes, and military capabilities. It remains to distinguish operationally between those instances of military growth which are to be characterized as "arms races," and those which are not. This is not quite as easy as it might seem at first blush, and to make a valid and useful distinction, we shall have to enlist the aid of some recent developments in applied mathematics that are unlikely to be familiar to most social scientists.

AN ARMS RACE INDEX

It is easier to set down the conditions which an operational definition of an arms race must satisfy than it is to meet them. First and foremost, the measure should distinguish clearly between the "normal" incrementation of arms levels and abnormal "runaway" growth. Second, it should be sensitive only to competitive growth, where both sides are increasing rapidly and simultaneously. Third, given the occasional problems of data accuracy which persist despite our best efforts, the measure should be founded on as solid a data base as possible. Finally, it should be relatively more sensitive to the situation immediately prior to the dispute or war, and relatively less sensitive to the rates of arms growth further away in time.

The application of these criteria rules out several initially plausible index construction procedures. Measures based upon mean rates of increase do not satisfy the first and fourth criteria, as they are likely to average together observations made before and after the onset of the arms race. Moving averages go a long way towards satisfying the fourth criterion, but are still likely to "average out" periods of fast and slow growth. Indices based upon growth immediately prior to the dispute are likely to involve only two or at most three data points, leaving themselves extremely vulnerable to error. Finally, indices based upon the direct measurement of the acceleration of the arms race also run into problems with criterion three, since more data points are required for an unbiased estimate of the rate of acceleration than for the simple rate of change.

In this paper, a completely different approach will be employed. Instead of detecting the existence of an arms race by measuring the rate of increase or acceleration in arms spending directly, the issue shall be determined by extrapolating from a polynomial function fitted to the arms expenditure data for ten years prior to the onset of the dispute or war.[5] This polynomial function shall be used to estimate the time rate of change (delta) for each nation for the year prior to the dispute. The existence of an arms race prior to the dispute or war shall be determined by obtaining the product of the national rates of change for each side, with higher values representing "arms-race" dyads. By calculating national rates of growth on the basis of a ten-year data series, and by constructing the final index in a multiplicative fashion, we ensure that only long-term, intense, bilateral growth in arms expenditures will score high on our arms race scale. The calculated arms race index values for each dyad are displayed in Table 1.

    5. The mathematically trained reader may be interested in the procedure used to derive the polynomial functions from which the time rates of change of national arms levels are calculated. Given a set of (m + 1) data observations, $y_o, y_1 \ldots y_m$ corresponding to evenly spaced points in time, let us express the value of y at time u as $Y(u) \approx \beta_o(u)y_o + \beta_1(u)y_1 + \ldots \beta_m(u)y_m$, where $\beta_o(u), \beta_1(u), \ldots \beta_m(u)$ represent

$$\beta_i(u) = \sum_{\lambda=i}^{p-2} a_i|u|^\lambda + \sum_{\epsilon=0}^{m} b_{i\epsilon}|u-\epsilon|^p$$

and p represents the specified degree of the polynomial function. Now it can be shown (Sard and Weintraub, 1971) that if p is a real, positive integer, there exist matrices A, B

$$A = \begin{vmatrix} {}^{a}0i & {}^{a}0m \\ {}^{a}i1 & {}^{a}im \end{vmatrix} \qquad B = \begin{vmatrix} {}^{b}01 & {}^{b}0m \\ {}^{b}i1 & {}^{b}im \end{vmatrix}$$

whose elements (the so-called "cardinal splines"), are unique, and define a unique approximation function $Y \approx F'(t)$, which is continuous with respect to the p–1th derivative. Sard and Weintraub have calculated the elements of A and B for p = 3, 4, 5, 6, and 10, and m = p, p + 1, . . . 20. Since our hypotheses are concerned only with the first and second derivatives (the rate of change and acceleration of arms expenditures), we take p = 3, and since we estimate the function on the basis of ten annual observations, m = 9. Using Sard and Weintraub's values, we can calculate that, for the year prior to a dispute,

$$\Delta y \approx \frac{k - y_9}{k + y_9}$$

where $k = .000025y_0 + .00014y_1 - .00059y_2 + .00317y_3 - .01929y_3 + .0307y_5 - .1148y_6 + .43097y_7 - 1.60773y_8 + 2.26581y_9$ and $y_0 \ldots y_9$ are the arms expenditure values for the ten years prior to the dispute.

THE RESULTS

    Given these values, how does our hypothesis fare? Even by inspection, it is clear that the mean arms race score for nation-dyads entering into full-scale warfare is much greater than the corresponding score for "no war" dyads—292.2 compared with only 23.0. The probability that this difference would occur by chance is less than one in 10,000.

In other words, pairs of nations which end up going to war are characterized by much more rapid military growth in the period immediately prior to the conflict than those which do not resolve their conflicts by other means. The predictive power of this relationship can be seen more clearly if we dichotomize the independent variable to produce a 2 × 2 table. In Table 2, we see that a high arms race score for a pair of nations correctly predicts the outbreak of war 23 out of 28 times, and conversely, a low score correctly predicts the nonescalation of a dispute 68 out of 71 times, for an overall "batting average" of 91 cases out of 99. For those addicted to correlational statistics, the overall strength of the relationship as measured by Yule's Q is .96; using the more conservative ø coefficient, it is .75.

As interesting as the strength of the relationship are the identities of some of the "incorrect predictions." Included among the five conflicts preceded by an arms race which did not result in war are the remilitarization of the Rhineland, the Munich Crisis, and the Cuban Missile Crisis. In each of these cases, the consensus of historians has it that war was averted only by the narrowest of margins.

TABLE 2

	Arms Race	*No Arms Race*
War	23	3
No War	5	68

INTERPRETING THE FINDINGS

The relationship between arms races and conflict escalation uncovered in this study is unusually strong. For this very reason, great caution must be exercised in interpreting its meaning. First, it is worth emphasizing that these findings do not imply that an arms race between the powers necessarily results in war. To prove this, it would be necessary to show not only that arms races lead to the escalation of conflicts, but also that they play an important role in the initiation of such conflicts. No such evidence has been adduced here.

Moreover, the findings do not provide incontrovertible proof of a causal link between arms races and conflict escalation; they establish only that rapid competitive military growth is strongly associated with the escalation of military confrontations into war. It is conceivable that this result is a spurious effect of the level of ongoing hostility and tension between powers. It is possible that, when they are very great, such tensions simultaneously stimulate military competition and induce a greater propensity to war. If such is the case (and this itself would have to be demonstrated by further research), then arms races, while remaining a valuable "early warning indicator" of war, could not be considered a causal factor in war onset.

But despite these caveats, it will not do to interpret the findings too conservatively. When two great powers engage in acts of military force or violence against one another, we cannot but assume that their relationship is characterized by a considerable degree of hostility and tension. Yet, in only 3 of 71 cases did such acts lead to war when not preceded by an arms race. Conversely, when an arms race did precede a significant threat or act of violence, war was avoided only 5 out of 28 times. It is difficult to argue, therefore, that arms races play no role in the process of leading to the onset of war.

The policy implications of this are obvious and immediate. The findings support with hard evidence the intuitive fears of those who argue that an intensification of the superpower arms competition could lead to a "hair-trigger" situation in which a major confrontation would be far more likely to result in all-out war. Thus, they underline the urgency of present efforts to curb the looming quantitative and qualitative expansion of superpower strategic arsenals.

Notes

1. Useful summaries and critiques of this extensive literature are to be found in Rapaport (1958), Busch (1970), Chaterjee (1974), Zinnes (1976), Gillespie et al. (1977), and Hollist (1978).

2. See, for example, Singer, Bremer, and Stuckey (1972); Wallace (1974); and Choucri and North (1974).

3. See Huntington (1958); Richardson (1960); Milstein and Mitchell (1968); and Busch (1970).

4. See Luterbacher (1975), and Wallace (1976; 1978).

Questions

1. Despite their many differences, what do the two superpowers appear to agree on?

2. How does Wallace define an "arms race"?

3. When does a competitive increase in armaments become an "arms race"?

4. Does the author claim that arms races play an essential role in the initiation of conflicts? Quote his words.

5. How convincing do you find the author's arguments?

3
Arms Races and Escalation:
A Closer Look

Paul Diehl

This article originally appeared in the *Journal of Peace Research*, #3, 1983.

One of Michael Wallace's most thoughtful critics on the relationship between "arms races" and war is Paul Diehl, his fellow professor at the University of Michigan. Diehl credits his colleague with raising an important question and calls his study "the most definitive to date." Diehl finds fault with Wallace's methods and claims that his conclusions would be vastly different with only a few changes in the coding procedure.

While the mathematical details are difficult to follow, the debate between the two academics is characterized by patient analysis and an objective tone. Diehl accepts Wallace's conclusions concerning the two World Wars of this century, but asserts that his thesis breaks down in most of the other wars studied. The reader is left to decide.

Diehl stresses the obligation of academics to give greater attention to research design and urges all his colleagues to "reveal all relevant information that impinges on the conduct of the study." He calls for sensitivity to the data and rigor in interpreting them. No less than Wallace, Diehl insists on the importance of further study of the relation between wars and arms races, so that "decision makers can avoid mistakes which could have unintended and disastrous consequences."

The relationship between arms races and war is a critical consideration in both peace research and strategic planning. This study reconsiders the work of Michael Wallace which has postulated that arms races significantly increase the probability of a serious dispute escalating to war. A critique of Wallace's coding procedures and arms race index precedes an attempt to replicate his findings. In the replication, serious disputes, taken from the Correlates of War Project, among major powers during the years 1816–1970 serve as the population to be tested. Adjustments in coding and index construction from the Wallace work are made. It was discovered that only 25% of those disputes preceded by a mutual military buildup escalated to war, while almost 77% of the wards in this population were preceded by periods lacking armaments competition. Controls for inter-century differences and unilateral military buildups failed to alter this apparent lack of a relationship between arms races and dispute escalation. Differences with Wallace's study are analyzed and the implications for peace research discussed.

Conventional wisdom has always presupposed a link between rapid military buildups and war. The old dictum "If you want peace, prepare for war" offers one perspective on the inter-relationship of military spending and the outbreak of conflict. The spiral model is indicative of a more dangerous connection between increasing weapons and war. Whether the effect is deterrence or provocation, a nation's decision to significantly increase its military capability could be an important factor in the understanding of interstate war.

Despite the central nature of military spending in national security decision-making, empirical researchers have generally ignored its possible effect on the initiation of war. This void in the academic literature noted by Singer (1979) in 1969 remains large today.

Nevertheless, some recent efforts have extended the pioneering ideas of Richardson (1960), studying the impact of arms races and military spending decisions on the outbreak of war. The most interesting work in this area has been that of Michael Wallace. He used early Correlates of War (COW) Project compilations on major power military expenditures and serious disputes to investigate nation behavior in conflict generated situations. In a widely quoted article, Wallace (1979) concluded that the presence or absence of an arms race between two rivals correctly predicted war/no war outcomes in over 90% of the serious disputes studied. Those results are summarized in Table I.

A later study by the same author (Wallace 1982), using the same data base, served to reinforce this strong association between arms races and war. The general paucity of alternative investigations makes Wallace's studies the most definitive to date.

If Wallace's findings are correct, the implications for policymaking on arms limitation are clear. The START negotiations must proceed with all deliberate speed, lest a clash between the superpowers should escalate to all-out war. However, certain methodological problems cast doubt on the

Table 1
Wallace's arms races and escalation

	War	No War
Arms race	23	5
No arms race	3	68
$\chi^2 = 62.99$	$\phi = .8$	$Q = .98$

validity of Wallace's conclusions. It is the purpose of this paper to detail these difficulties and retest the military buildup–war relationship with a modified set of assumptions and indicators.

A CLOSER LOOK

The Correlates of War treats multi-party serious disputes (three or more disputants) as one integrated dispute. Where there was a clear informal/formal partnership among the disputants on one side and where the subject matter of the dispute was the same for each partner, the dispute classification scheme served to reflect the interconnection of events and interests for all those involved. Wallace chose to code each dispute participant dyadically against those nations in opposition. Thus, the original 1914 dispute which escalated to World War I is analyzed as if it were six separate disputes and consequently six individual wars. Overall, 26 distinct wards are created where only 7 or 8 integrated ones occurred.[1] As a result, the strength of the arms race–war relationship stems not from an abundance of distinct cases of dispute escalation, but merely is a function of a coding decision. Wallace's (1980) response to this problem was to re-evaluate his results using only formal alliance patterns to combine certain sets of disputes. This only partly solved the difficulty of numerical inflation of disputes and wars. The follow-up analysis failed to consider situations which share similar characteristics to those involving formal alliances, but merely lack a signed instrument between the parties.

A related problem is Wallace's inclusion in his population of serious disputes those cases which were not independent of ongoing wars. In some ways, this explains the fact that the two World Wars account for over 80% of the explanatory capability in his study (Weede 1980). Serious problems are inherent in studying war-related disputes in this context. Wallace's purpose was to assess whether an arms race affected the probability of a serious dispute escalating to war. However in cases where one or both disputants are involved in a war, the probability of that war-related dispute escalating is greater than that of a dispute independent of an ongoing war. An inference about the effect of an arms race on a war-related dispute must be considered tentative at best. In Wallace's work, the arms race impact (if any) on dispute escalation is indiscernible from the effects of the ongoing war. Nevertheless, it is these cases of war-related disputes which enhance the confirmation of the hypothesis that arms races lead to war.

Wallace's results indicate the U.S.S.R.–Japan dispute of 1945 to be an instance of an arms race leading to the escalation of a dispute. Yet, it is difficult to believe that this brief war was anything but a result of the hostilities associated with World War II. To suggest that an arms race in the late 1930's exercised any influence on the outbreak of war in this dispute five years later is premature without additional research and runs contrary to accumulated historical opinion on the subject.[2]

Wallace (1979:8) justifies his choice of case and the dyadic coding method by stating: This explanation is open to criticism as the disputes involving different actors in different years are coded as separate disputes anyway according to COW criteria. If the disputants entered the dispute in the same year (thereby determining the same data points for military expenditures—the ten years prior to that year in the Wallace study), it is irrelevant if the disputants entered the war emanating from the dispute at different times. Furthermore, Wallace's explanation provides no justification for separating a dispute (such as the 1939 Poland crisis) in which all parties entered the dispute and the war at the same time.

Wallace's method of determining an arms race is not without conceptual problems. An arms race is conventionally described as a process involving competitive interaction, manifested by rapid increases in military spending and weaponry. In Wallace's analysis, it is only determined whether or not the disputants are rapidly arming themselves; there is no determination if this spending is directed against the dispute opponents. More properly, the process described by Wallace is a mutual "military buildup" rather than an "arms race" per se. A determination of the latter must await the completion of a more sensitive test of military spending decisions.

Beyond the absence of definitional rigor, the mutuality of rapid spending increases cannot necessarily be deduced from Wallace's arms race index. By multiplying the products of each side's cardinal spline estimate of military spending, a unilateral buildup by one side might be defined as an arms race. For example, if country A had a score of 100 (high) and country B had a score of 1 (low), the net index would be 100 and the situation classified as a Wallace arms race. Clearly, this instance is neither a mutual military buildup nor an arms race in any reasonable definition of the two terms.

Wallace also chooses a seemingly arbitrary threshold of a 90.00 index score to distinguish between arms races and their absence. No justification is presented and experimentation with alternative thresholds is not evident. Wallace's conclusions are substantially weakened if the threshold is lowered to 50.00. Then, ten additional cases would be contrary to the escalation model, while its strength would not be enhanced by even a single case.

While Wallace's striking findings have dominated this topic area over the past few years, it seems that criticisms associated with his work are sufficient to warrant a re-examination of the relationship between rapid military buildups and war.

A RE-EVALUATION

In retesting Wallace's conclusions, a number of modifications are made. The temporal domain is extended five years, now 1816–1970, to reflect the most complete listing of COW serious disputes. Since Wallace used only a preliminary draft of this same compilation, the disputes and the correction of coding errors would suggest that the set of cases used by this replication attempt is more accurate than that employed by Wallace.

Each serious dispute is treated as an integrated whole (non-dyadically) as is consistent with the original COW coding scheme. For example, the dispute leading to the outbreak of the Crimean War is coded: Russia v. Great Britain and France. Where it was clear that partnerships existed and the partners were inexorably tied up in the disposition of the dispute, it seems reasonable to consider allies together rather than separately in the dyadic scheme. Surely, the military calculus of the opposing side must consider the joint actions of those partners. Moreover, we need a good scientific, yet reasonable, set of cases. If Wallace's results are conclusive, they should be able to be reproduced under the conditions outlined here.

Certain factors dictated that some of the cases be eliminated from the study. Any dispute which was related to an ongoing major power war was dropped from the population.[3] As discussed above in the critique of Wallace, the escalatory effects of the ongoing war are indistinguishable from those of arms increases. To include those cases might yield a false indication of the real effects military buildups have on the initiation of war.

It is all but impossible to accurately estimate wartime military expenditures for a nation whose whole economy is devoted to the war effort. Accordingly, COW treats expenditures during the two World Wars as missing data. Due to this data limitation and the nature of the arms race indicator, cases independent of ongoing wars from 1915–1920 and 1940–1947 are necessarily eliminated.[4] Idiosyncrasies in the data set resulted in the elimination of another case.[5] Overall, the analysis here considers 86 separate disputes.[6]

A measure of mutual arms buildup must reflect significant military increases for both sides in a dispute and yet be able to detect instances where only a unilateral buildup is present. In addition, an appropriate threshold point must be chosen to differentiate between incremental spending patterns and those which are abnormally high. These two considerations were judged to be lacking in the original Wallace article.

With this in mind, an index of military growth for each side in a dispute will be constructed from the newly revised COW file on military expenditures (an earlier version was used by Wallace in his work). This index is the mean rate of change in military expenditures (expressed in common currency and controlled for price fluctuations) for each side in the three years prior to the initiation of the dispute.[7]

Only expenditures prior to the initiation of the dispute are analyzed. This precludes consideration of military spending which was reactive to the dispute itself. In this way, the index is able to isolate the effects of an arms buildup from the bias of dispute-induced spending. Disputed spending patterns tend to reflect significant spending increases whether war results or not. This is not surprising as nations seek to ensure security in a crisis situation.

Furthermore, the index measures only spending trends in the immediate past of the dispute. Military expenditures tend to show greater variation as one moves farther back in a time-series. Too often, studying a time period of five or ten years will cause an overlap into a war period or time frame in which other disputes influenced expenditure patterns. Focusing on the three years prior to the dispute allows consideration of behavior which is more perceptually important than comparable spending decisions ten years before. Rapid changes in military expenditures not only are warning signals for peace researchers, but are perhaps one of the indicators used by foreign policy elites to ascertain a large scale military buildup by an opponent.

In this study, I have chosen to designate any instance of both dispute sides increasing their military expenditures at a rate of 8% or greater for the three years before the dispute as a "mutual military buildup." This threshold was chosen because it most perfectly captured the dividing line between incremental increases in military outlays and abnormal spending increases. This coding decision allows the World War I dispute to be classified as a mutual military buildup as is the concerted opinion of most historians. In no case, however, are both sides in such a buildup below a 1% threshold often cited as an indicator of high level military spending increases.[8]

The operational definitions of a "major power," "serious dispute," and "war" developed by Singer & Small (1972) and used by Wallace are retained in this study.

RESULTS

The determination of a mutual military buildup or its absence for each dispute was combined with the outcome of that dispute and the aggregated results are presented in Table II.

No meaningful covariation exists here between mutual military buildups and dispute escalation. Only 25% of the disputes which were preceded by a mutual military buildup escalated to war, while almost 77% of the

Table II
Mutual military buildup and escalation

	War	No War
Mutual military buildup	3	9
No mutual military buildup	10	64

$\chi^2 = 1.06$ $\phi = .11$ $Q = .36$

major power wars constituting this sample population were preceded by periods in which there was no incidence of joint and rapid spending increases by the protagonists.

Of the three disputes which fit the escalation hypothesis, one is World War I and the other two led to the Second World War. However, even these cases raise questions about the impact of mutual arms buildup on the outbreak of war. There were five other disputes prior to World War II which were preceded by this type of buildup and yet did not escalate to war. This suggests that the cases which support the escalation model might only be the product of a spurious association.

Overall, it appears that most serious disputes do not involve previous dual military spending increases and most serious disputes do not escalate to war; but there does not seem to be any connection between these facts. The Yule's Q value is .36 indicating a much weaker positive relationship than Wallace reported. However, the more conservative ϕ coefficient is only .11 and the Chi-square value is not significant at any meaningful level.

It is possible that this analysis, aggregated over a two-century period, may hide a relationship that is present in only a portion of this time period. Other scholars have noted inter-century differences in studying international conflict. Therefore, the results were disaggregated, divided into 19th and 20th groups and the hypothesis retested. The findings were quite similar to the original results. Although the association was stronger in the 20th century, neither relationship was significant at the .10 level.[9] It is also important to consider the effect of a unilateral arms buildup on the outbreak of war. It may be that the absence of mutuality in arms increases causes one side or the other to consider war a more viable means of competition. In testing this possibility, cases in which there was no mutual military buildup are considered (N = 74). The proposition that a unilateral buildup (constituting a 10% or more increase in military expenditures by one and only one side using the same index construction as before) affects the probability of a dispute escalating to war is considered in Table III.

There seems to be no basis for concluding that a unilateral military buildup prior to a dispute increases the chances of war. A Yule's Q value of $-.35$ suggests a possible negative association between unilateral build-

Table III
Unilateral buildup and escalation*

	War	No War
Unilateral buildup	3	30
No unilateral buildup	7	34

$\chi^2 = .997$ $\qquad\qquad\qquad\qquad \emptyset = .12 \qquad Q = -.35$

*Table includes only those cases which fail to meet the criteria for a mutual military buildup.

ups and war but the Chi-square value indicates that the association is not statistically significant.

TOWARD A CONVERGENCE OF FINDINGS

The findings presented here are quite contrary to Wallace (1979). This lends itself to a number of possible explanations. Immediately the differences in arms indices come to mind. However, Wallace's cardinal spline function is heavily weighted toward changes in military expenditures in the three or four years prior to the dispute, much as the index used in this study. In applying the Wallace measure to the data set used in this study, similar findings can be reported where coding rules between the studies were not in conflict. Where differences did exist, the variation can be explained by reference to other factors besides index construction. Thus, I conclude that the differences are in the military spending indices.

Another hypothesis is that differences between the two studies' data sets led to divergent findings. Wallace's list of disputes was only in its early stages of completion when his article first appeared. The population of serious disputes used in this replication attempt represents a more recent and complete version of that list. In comparing the two versions (prior to any coding decisions), the disparities do not seem to be extraordinary, at least not to suggest radically different conclusions. The newer data set includes a few more cases of pre-World War II disputes which were preceded by dual arms increases but did not escalate to war. The Korean War, actually preceded by spending cutbacks, is another instance of a dispute not covered by Wallace. Most of the other changes in the new file are additions or deletions of "no buildup–no war" disputes. As a whole, the empirical validity of the escalation hypothesis is weakened when tested with the updated file, but the changes alone are insufficient to reject Wallace's conclusions.

Beyond simple changes in the number of cases, the new file contains some corrections. The Russo-Japanese War of 1904 had its dispute beginning in 1903 according to the latest file. This is an update from the Wallace report that the dispute began in 1904. Wallace considers spending increases in this dispute through the actual first year of the dispute (1903). It is not surprising then that he concludes that an arms race took place before the war. However, according to the corrected files, one might infer that spending in 1903 was reactive to the dispute and that the Wallace index would yield a false indication of prior military competition. Looking only at military spending patterns prior to the beginning of the dispute (pre-1903), this study finds no significant joint arms increases occurring.

Differences in military expenditure figures might account for opposite conclusions in a few cases. Wallace replaced some interpolated data points with his own estimates of military appropriations. This may explain why different results are obtained in the 1866 dispute war between Germany, Italy and Austria.[10]

While revision of research files is to some degree a continuing process, it is presumed (pending comparison) that the data used in this study are more complete and accurate than previous compilations.

Most of the remaining conflict in the aggregate findings of the two studies can be traced to differences in coding procedures. Then cases which were not independent of ongoing wars, yet exhibited covariation of spending increases and escalation, were eliminated in this study. In addition, the non-dyadic coding method used here resulted in the collapse of ten cases, which fit the escalation hypothesis into three integrated disputes. In each case, the two World Wars account for almost all the instances. In effect, the strength of the arms race–war relationship cited by Wallace rests heavily on the two World Wars. The relationship seems absent in any other circumstance and gains statistical significance only through an artificial division of an integrated situation.

CONCLUSIONS

This study retested Wallace's (1979) findings that a mutual military buildup between major powers increased the probability of a serious dispute escalating to war. Using a modified set of assumptions and indicators, it was discovered that only one-fourth of the disputes preceded by mutual military buildups resulted in war, while ten of thirteen wars occurred in the absence of joint arms increases by the dispute participants. Therefore, it was concluded that mutual military buildups did not exercise any general impact on the initiation of war under the limited conditions studied. This lack of a relationship between military spending and dispute escalation remained unchanged when controls were instituted for intercentury differences and when retested to ascertain the influence of a unilateral military buildup.

In considering the differences in findings between this study and Wallace's work, the importance of assumptions, coding decisions and data manipulation techniques in empirical research should be highlighted. Apparently significant research choices can collectively influence results in a profound way. We owe it to our colleagues and those in policy-making circles to be explicit and reveal all relevant information that impinges on the conduct of the study. This is not to imply that academics should retreat to merely debating semantics or methodological approaches. Rather, it means we must give greater attention to the research design of a study and consider the study and its utility in light of the validity of that design. The operative message is that creativity and rigor must coexist in research. Neither is a substitute for the other.

This paper does not in any way lay to rest the debate over the danger of rapid military spending increases. What is apparent, however, is that they do not constitute an explanation by themselves for the escalation of disputes. Future research should expand the scope of past studies to consider arms buildups beyond those which end in war. Incidences of compromise and capitulation resulting from arms acquisition may be just as significant as war outcomes. The relative mix of mutual and self-stimulatory processes driving each nation's spending increases may be an important key in predicting those outcomes.

A careful examination of the relationship of the arms races and war might yet provide guidance to foreign policy elites, such that at a minimum, those decision makers can avoid mistakes which could have unintended but disastrous consequences.

Notes

1. The number of separate wars in that study is variable, depending on how the analyst would treat the interrelationship of the European and Pacific theatres in World War II.

2. In cases which involved wartime disputes, Wallace studied the disputants' military expenditures in the nearest pre-war year instead of the year before the dispute.

3. The cases dropped are mainly those which occurred after the outbreak of World War I and World War II. Other cases eliminated were those associated with the Crimean War, and the 1866 war involving Germany, Italy and Austria. The Russo-Japanese conflicts in the 1930's are included as both temporally preceded the Polish crises and were distinct from tensions in Europe and elsewhere in Asia.

4. The most notable absence necessitated by data unavailability is the U.S.–Japan dispute of 1941. Unlike other disputes surrounding World War II, this dispute could justifiably be considered separate from the European War. There was also missing data for one side in two disputes: U.S.S.R.–Great Britain in 1923 and the dispute over Korea in 1950. However, there was calculation of a military buildup according to the criteria used in this study. Consequently, these cases remain included in the analysis. In addition, a 1948 dispute involving the Soviet Union and the three Allied Powers was not excluded despite the inclusion of only two (instead of three) years of military expenditure data in the military buildup indicator. Missing data for the war year 1945 were responsible for this alteration.

5. The dispute between France and Italy in 1860 is not considered. Prior to the dispute, Italy's military expenditures were coded as those only of Sardinia. With the advent of Italian unification, expenditure figures were derived from all of Italy. Consequently, an artificial jump in military spending occurs in the data set. This changeover occurs in one of the years under study for this case, and to avoid misconceptions, this dispute is eliminated from the sample.

6. Some wars which resulted from a major power serious dispute, but did not involve major power participation on both sides, are included in this study. These are: the 1863 war between Denmark on one side and Germany and Austria on the other; Italy's invasion of Ethiopia in 1934; and the Sino-Indian border war of 1962.

7. The formula for the index is: $\%\Delta \ (M_{+-2} \to M_{+-1}) + \%\Delta \ (M_{+-3} \to M_{+-2})/$ 2 where t is the year of the dispute and $M = m_1 + m_2 \cdots m_k$; where m represents the military expenditures of a major power on that side of the dispute.

8. Experimentation with other thresholds did not significantly affect the results reported here.

9. The ø value for the nineteenth century war .08 and Chi-square was a paltry .198. The twentieth century yielded a ø of .18 and a Chi-square value of 1.79.

10. These manipulations are not apparent in any of the Wallace articles. The disclosure of these transformations was graciously made to me in a personal conversation with Professor Wallace. However, analysis of the extent and validity of these changes cannot be assessed without a copy of the Wallace data base. Professor Wallace is attempting to reconstruct that file and results as of this writing are incomplete.

Questions

1. Why does Diehl doubt the validity of Wallace's data?
2. In Diehl's re-evaluation of Wallace's data, how widely do his conclusions vary from those of Wallace?
3. How much credence does Diehl give to Wallace's assertion that unilateral buildups increase the chances of war?
4. On which wars do Wallace's assertions mainly rest? Identify the major conflicts omitted from his data.
5. Who, in your opinion, gets the better of the argument?

4
Military Spending and Economic Decay

Lloyd J. Dumas

This article originally appeared in *The Political Economy of Arms Research*, Westnew Press, 1982.

Lloyd J. Dumas, Associate Professor of Political Economy at the University of Texas, Dallas, paints a distressing picture of U.S. military spending.

First of all, he labels as untrue the widely held belief that World War II brought about the end of the 1930's Depression. He contends that full employment of productive resources (as happens in wartime) is not enough, but that such resources must be used "in ways that contribute to the societal standard of living." Military spending, in contrast, diverts direct (food, clothing, etc) and indirect (industrial investment) production "away from ordinary contributive use." He concedes that defense production brings "the short-run appearance of prosperity" but says that, in the long run, it will be "a drain on the society."

Dumas attributes U.S. economic decline in recent years to more than three decades of neglect in replacing civilian facilities (railroads, mass transit systems, industrial equipment) and civilian-oriented technological development. Unemployment and inflation are the twin offspring of such military policies in the U.S., he says, while the same activities in the U.S.S.R. bedevil the Russian economy with shortages of goods and services. He goes on to explain why capitalist and communist economies ended up with different sets of problems.

To the argument that security—"protecting the nation and its people"—has been a good result of military spending, Dumas calls it at best a "necessary evil." He further contends that building weapons is "extremely costly and inefficient." The Vietnam War, the fall of Iran's Shah and the sharp rise in oil prices in the 1970's all show, he says, "the ineffectiveness of military force." He quotes a former member of the Defense Department to the effect that the arms race has actually reduced American security.

Besides the diversionary nature of military production, the author indicts the Pentagon for inefficient procurement practices, the balance of payments deficit and the negative impact of military spending on the development of civilian technology. In considerable detail, he documents these assertions.

Dumas gloomily predicts that the "horrific" rates of inflation and unemployment at the beginning of the 1970's "may well look like economic good times compared to what will be commonplace by the end of the 1980s." He cautions, however, that the transition to civilian production must be handled with care. His final plea to the U.S. and the U.S.S.R. is for "real, meaningful arms reduction."

INTRODUCTION

The terrible social and economic trauma of the Great Depression and the prolonged boom during and after the Second World War that finally laid it to rest, deeply imbedded an economic lesson in the American psyche: military spending stimulates production, creates employment and generally brings prosperity. The problem with this well-learned lesson is that it is based on a combination of shoddy empiricism and poor economics, and more importantly, it is absolutely untrue.

Ultimately, the degree of material well-being generated by any economy depends not only on its ability to fully employ the productive resources (labor, capital, materials, energy, etc.) available to it, but also on its ability to employ them in ways that contribute to the societal standard of living. The production of ordinary consumer goods and services, such as food, clothing, housecleaning, barbering, etc. clearly adds directly to the present material living standard. The production of producer goods and associated services, such as industrial machinery, rail transportation systems, factory buildings, supporting engineering consulting services, etc. is also contributive, but through a less direct route. This class of goods and services expands an economy's ability to produce, and by so doing enhances the supply of consumer-oriented output in the future. Hence it contributes not to the present, but to the future standard of living. There are also categories of mixed goods, i.e., both consumer and producer goods combined, the most prominent examples of which are probably education and health care. Resource use for the supply of mixed goods as well must therefore be considered productive since they augment both the present and the future standard of living.

Military oriented production however falls into a wholly different category. It does not add to the supply of consumer goods or to the supply of producer goods, and so contributes to neither the present nor future material standard of living. Resources put to this use can then be said to have been diverted, i.e., channeled away from ordinary contributive use. They are not, in and of themselves, adding to material well-being.

When resources which have been idle are put to work, whether or not that work is useful, unemployment will be reduced, income will be distributed and at least the short-run appearance of prosperity will be achieved. But if those resources have been used unproductively, they will in the long term be a drain on the society. Because resources are being wasted, things which need doing will not be done, and so the economy and the wider society will suffer.

The issue of the use to which resources are put is so fundamental and so overriding in its impact on the ability of an economy to efficiently generate economically useful goods and services that economic systems as distinct as those of capitalism and communism experience similar structural problems when resources are diverted from contributive use. This is particularly true over the long run.

During the half decade or so of heavy World War II military spending in the U.S., neglect of the renewal of various types of civilian oriented equipment and facilities (e.g., railroads, mass transit systems, industrial equipment), and neglect of civilian oriented technological development did not create major problems. Such capital equipment is long-lived, and sizeable technological leads do not typically disappear quickly. But as the substantial diversion of productive resources stretched from half a decade to three decades, severe strains and stresses did occur. And we see the effects of this sapping of our economic vitality all around us.

Neither capitalist nor socialist economies are capable of overriding negative economic effects of persistently high military spending. Differences in economic systems and circumstances, however, can and do influence the way in which the economic distress surfaces.

As will be discussed, the economic damage done by the military burden in the U.S. has surfaced mainly in the form of simultaneously high inflation and high unemployment, through the intervening variable of deteriorating productivity. In contrast, in the U.S.S.R., the damage has surfaced mainly in the form of chronic problems of supplying sufficient quantity and quality of goods and services—particularly consumer goods and services. There are two main reasons for these differences.

First, the military economy of the U.S. developed, post World War II, alongside a well developed and booming civilian economy. In fact, the U.S. was the only major industrial nation in the world not devastated by the horrors of that war. The Soviet military economy, on the other hand, developed alongside a civilian economy massively damaged by that conflict and itself struggling hard to develop. Thus, the Soviet civilian economy was never able to work on breaking its chronic supply problems with a major, systematic and sustained effort. On the contrary, shortages were continually made more severe by the demands of the military economy under the impetus of an escalating superpower arms race.

Second, the differences between the capitalist and communist economic systems make it easier for the latter to prevent unemployment and cope with inflation. A capitalist economy must rely on the voluntary actions of individuals seeking private economic gain (in present forms, with more or less government intervention) in order to provide employment, while relying on such private decisions, along with the impersonal mechanism of competition and governmental control of the money supply to control inflation; a communist economy, on the other hand, features direct government control of both employment opportunities and prices (though the latter tends to be somewhat more subject to external influence through rising import costs). On the other hand, incentive problems, along with ponderous bureaucratic and informational difficulties, tend to make adequate supply and coordination of supply with demand more difficult for a communist economy than for one operated by capitalist principles.

But doesn't the military contribute to the standard of living by protecting the nation and its people, i.e., by providing the consumption good "security"? Does it not therefore constitute a contributive resource use?

In the first place, the definition of "security" as a consumer good to be lumped in with all other consumer goods is yet another example of the tendency of economists to end run around sticky analytic problems by definitional manipulation, not unlike defining goods of differing quality to be different goods in order to avoid facing the difficult issues of quality measurement and competition. Security is, of course, necessary, but its production does not contribute to the material standard of living in quite the same way as does the production of cars, TV's, furniture, housing, machine tools, trucks, etc. It is, in a sense, a "necessary evil" type of activity, and as such is most usefully viewed as burden on the directly and indirectly contributive elements of the economy. And since it is an economically painful activity, common sense would indicate that it needs to be constantly scrutinized and reviewed with an eye toward keeping it as small as possible, consistent with real security needs.

Secondly, it is not difficult to demonstrate that the stockpiling and expansion of military forces is an extremely costly and inefficient means of generating "security" at best. The lengthy U.S. experience in the Vietnam War, the ineffectiveness of military force or threat of force in countering the vast international redistribution of income and economic power from the industrialized world to the nations of OPEC, the inability of the extremely well-financed and well-supplied army of the Shah of Iran to prevail over an aroused population armed with "sticks and stones"—all of these and more should have by now taught us something about the limits of military power in protecting security interests (rightly or wrongly perceived) abroad. Furthermore, it is an undeniable fact of the nuclear age that there is not a thing the U.S. or Soviet militaries can do to protect their countries against being turned into smoldering radioactive wastelands within a couple of hours if either launches an all out nuclear attack against the other. Is this security?

Finally, as I have argued in some detail elsewhere, the nuclear and associated forces beyond those necessary to constitute a minimal deterrent are not merely useless, but for military and technical reasons tend to substantially degrade security.[1] This is chiefly due to reliability problems interacting with excessive weaponry and associated systems to exacerbate problems of nuclear weapons accidents, accidental war, theft of weapons by hostile forces (including terrorists) and so on. Incorporating these effects into a theoretical arms race model centered on the desire of participants to maximize security further elaborates the security reducing character of an interactive arms race.[2] This view is corroborated by the observation and arguments of such participants in the dynamics of the real world arms race as Herbert F. York, former Director of Defense Research and Engineering in the Department of Defense, and of Livermore Laboratories.[3]

But the main focus of this present analysis is not on the issue of security *per se*, but rather on the particular economic effects of military expenditure. And it is that question to which attention is now directed.

The fullest explication of these effects will be in the U.S. context, not because the damage is greater there or more easily understood, but simply because the relative availability of data and analysis is presently so much greater than for the U.S.S.R. Some of the analysis, however, is fairly easily translatable into the Soviet situation.

There are essentially four reasons why the maintenance of high levels of military expenditure in the U.S. during the post-World War II period has massively contributed to the generation of both inflation and unemployment. These are: (1) the economic nature of military goods; (2) the way in which military procurement has been conducted; (3) effects on the international balance of payments; and (4) effects on civilian technological progress. Each of these is now considered in turn.

THE ECONOMIC NATURE OF MILITARY GOODS

Military goods are those products purchased by the military which are to some degree specialized to military use. Thus, tanks, rifles, bombs, fighter planes, etc. are military goods, while milk, meat, detergents, etc. purchased by the armed forces are not.

Despite the fact that military goods do not produce economic value in the sense of contribution to the material standard of living, as has been discussed, they do require valuable economic resources for their production, and therefore impose a real cost on society. This cost is best measured not purely in terms of money, but rather in terms of the sacrifice of the economically and socially useful goods and services that could have been produced with the labor, materials, energy, machinery, etc. which were instead devoted to military production.

Now, the money that flows to producers of military goods in exchange for their products is spent by the firms primarily on producer goods and by their workforces primarily on consumer goods. Thus these funds injected into the economy by the government call forth increased demand for consumer and producer goods without a corresponding increase in supply of either consumer or producer goods. The excess demand that tends to result, or put simply the situation of too many dollars chasing after too few goods, is a classic economic prescription for inflation. For example, during nearly all of the latter part of the decade of the 1960's, when the U.S. involvement in the Vietnam War was intensifying, the unemployment rate was under 4%.[4] Military spending was not offset, and between 1965 and 1969, the rate of inflation more than tripled.[5]

There were and are clearly no purely economic reasons for failing to offset expansions in military spending with higher taxation. Nor can this failure be explained by ignorance of the probably inflationary effects of failing to do so, since existing well accepted macroeconomic theory would predict this part of the inflationary effect. Rather, this policy (or lack thereof) seems more readily attributable to a political calculation that raising taxes for the express purpose of supporting increased military activity might have quickened and heightened public opposition, particularly during Vietnam, since the economic costs of this activity would be made more explicit. So a political sleight-of-hand approach was adopted, making the public pay through increased inflation that eroded their purchasing power, rather than through direct taxation. It was a strategy that relied upon the unlikelihood that the public would directly connect the war and subsequent military expansion with the growing inflation about which they grew more and more concerned. And by all appearances, this strategy has been and still appears to be politically effective.

MILITARY PROCUREMENT PRACTICES

Care has been taken, over the years, to develop a variety of payment formulas for military contracts to provide strong incentives for military industrial firms to produce efficiently, that is to produce products meeting the agreed upon performance specifications, adhere to agreed delivery schedules and hold costs down to a minimum. However, none of these payment formulas work. In practice, whatever the formulas formally written into major military procurement contracts, the contracts are effectively performed on a "cost plus" basis.[6]

A detailed analysis of this problem seems inappropriate here, but in essence there appear to be two main reasons why this is so. One seems to be in the fact that the formulas are designed to provide appropriate incentives for efficiency on the assumption that the firm involved is interested in maximizing profits. The incentives collapse to an essentially cost-plus situation in the case of a sales maximizing firm. The other reason seems to be a plain and simple failure of the government to enforce the terms of the contract, an explanation that admittedly raises more questions than it answers.[7]

In any case, operating under an effectively cost-plus system, the producing firm is paid an amount equal to its total cost of production (whatever that eventually turns out to be) plus a guaranteed profit. Thus, the firm involved not only has no risk, but also has no incentive to hold its costs down. In fact, to the extent that the firm wants to increase its sales revenue, it will have a very powerful incentive to run its costs up in order to achieve the highest possible payment for its product.

Combining this incentive system with the very large amounts of money made available for military procurement year after year by the Congress has created a situation in which military industry can and does pay whatever is necessary and then some for whatever resources it needs or wants. As a result, it has bid up the price of those resources—resources like machine tools, engineers and scientists, skilled machinists, etc. To the extent that other industries require these same resources, they now face increased costs and hence feel pressed to raise their prices. Thus a cost-push inflationary pressure is fed throughout not only the military sector, but the entire economy.

Aside from its direct inflationary effects on resource costs, the purchasing power of defense firms, backed by their rich customer (the Federal Government), has completely pre-empted a substantial amount of some of these resources, with serious long-term effects on the health of the civilian economy.

For example, by crude and conservative estimate nearly one-third of all the engineers and scientists in the United States were engaged in defense-related work (discussed below). This can be taken as a lower limit on the true figure. It seems more likely that the figure is higher, perhaps as high as one-half. Whether the actual figure is one-third or one-half, the crucial point is that a great deal of the nation's technological talent has been diverted to the development of military and military-related technology. The pre-emption by the military of such a large fraction of what we will subsequently see is a critical resource in a modern industrial society, cannot fail to have significant effects on the functioning of that part of the economy that produces goods and services which, unlike military goods, do contribute to the standard of living and the quality of life. Furthermore, it is important to understand that this magnitude or pre-emption of technological resources has been maintained for two to three decades or more. But full discussion of the implications of this pre-emption will be deferred for now.

Thus directly through its effects on bidding up certain resource costs and less directly though more powerfully by its pre-emption of key resources from the civilian economy, the free spending procurement practices of military industry have contributed importantly to the ongoing inflation.

INTERNATIONAL BALANCE OF PAYMENTS EFFECTS

From 1893 through 1970, year by year the U.S. had a *balance of trade* surplus, i.e. the U.S. exported a greater value of goods and services than it imported. Since exports bring foreign currency into the U.S., while imports send U.S. dollars abroad, if this had been the only aspect of the U.S. international transactions, there would have been a considerable accumulation of foreign currencies (or gold) in the U.S., and comparative shortage of U.S. dollars abroad. Consequently, by 1971 the U.S. dollar would have been one of the strongest (if not the strongest) currencies in the world. Instead, in 1971 the U.S. dollar was officially devalued, in formal recognition of its declining worth relative to key foreign currencies. How could this seeming paradox occur?

The *balance of payments*, the total net figure of international currency flows includes not only money flows related to trade, but all other international money flows as well (e.g. foreign investments in the U.S., profits flowing from U.S. subsidiaries abroad into the U.S., foreign aid, etc.). And the U.S. balance of payments has been in continuous deficit for decades now.

What role has U.S. military expenditure played in this situation? It has affected the U.S. international economic position directly through outflows of dollars for defense expenditures abroad, and indirectly through its effects on the balance of trade, chiefly via its influence on the competitiveness of U.S. civilian industries in domestic and foreign markets. This latter effect is extremely important and will be discussed in detail subsequently.

Table 1 presents some basic U.S. Department of Commerce data which bear on the direct effects of military expenditures abroad and on the U.S. international financial situation. We note that the entire cumulative balance of payments deficit for the period 1960–1970 (inclusive) was $35 billion, whereas over the same period, total direct defense expenditures (net after military sales abroad) were more than $30 billion. Hence, *U.S. military expenditures abroad accounted for 86.6% of the entire U.S. balance of payments deficit during that period.*

During the years 1966–1970 (inclusive) there was a huge inflow of foreign currencies into the U.S., represented by a cumulative balance of trade surplus of nearly $62 billion. But during those same years, net military expenditures abroad were responsible for an outflow of dollars from the U.S. amounting to more than $43 billion. *The outflow of U.S. currency owing to military spending abroad thus wiped out 69.9% of the balance of trade surplus, 1955–1970.*

These comparisons greatly understate the magnitude of U.S. defense expenditures abroad, because they do not include outright U.S. grants of military goods and services. Since they involve no international flows of currency, these gifts of military equipment and services are not involved in the balance of money flows. However, if included, the total of almost $34 billion worth of such grants recorded during the years 1960–1974 would increase the military expenditure figures given for that period by more than 80%.

It is clear from these data that direct outflows of dollars in the form of U.S. military expenditures abroad played a major role in destroying the favorable balance of trade surplus, and contributed to the severe weakening of the U.S. dollar. This substantially raised the price of imported goods (including oil) upon which the nation's business and consumers have become increasingly dependent in the past few years. Even when an imported product has not had a price increase in terms of its native currency, the declining value of the dollar relative to that currency will result in a rising dollar price. Insofar as consumer goods are directly imported then from countries against whose currency the dollar is weakening, this will contribute straight-forwardly to domestic inflation. When industrial goods and resources are imported, the effect of a failing dollar in raising their prices will result in a broad costpush pressure on all U.S. industries using these goods and resources (and there are many, many such industries). To the extent that this pressure cannot be offset (a phenomenon that will be discussed shortly), rising prices of these domestically produced goods will result, further exacerbating inflation. Thus, the massive outflow of military spending abroad has directly and substantially contributed to the generation of inflation within the domestic U.S. economy.

Table 1. U.S. military expenditures abroad and the international balance of payments.

Year[1]	Balance of Trade[2] ($millions)	Balance of Payments[3] ($millions)	Net Direct Defense Expenditures Abroad[4] ($millions)
1955	2,897	– –	2,501
1956	4,753	– –	2,627
1957	6,271	– –	2,466
1958	3,462	– –	2,835
1959	1,148	– –	2,503
1960	4,892	– 3,667	2,752
1961	5,571	– 2,252	2,596
1962	4,521	– 2,864	2,449
1963	5,224	– 2,713	2,304
1964	6,801	– 2,696	2,133
1965	4,951	– 2,478	2,122
1966	3,817	– 2,151	2,935
1967	3,800	– 4,683	3,226
1968	635	– 1,611	3,143
1969	607	– 6,081	3,328
1970	2,603	– 3,851	3,354
1971	– 2,268	–21,965	2,893
1972	– 6,409	–13,829	3,621
1973	955	– 7,651	2,316
1974	– 5,528	–19,043	2,159
TOTAL	48,703		54,263

Notes: 1. Problems of data availability and comparability complicate a more complete analysis over the entire post World War II period.
2. Exports-imports, merchandise, adjusted excluding military (minus implies deficit).
3. Net liquidity balance (minus implies deficit).
4. Direct defense expenditures - military sales (does not include military grants of goods and services).

Sources: Bureau of Economic Analysis, U.S. Department of Commerce, *Business Statistics* (1973), pp. 13–14, and *Survey of Current Business* (June 1975), pp. 26, 30.

But what of the huge increases in international oil prices in recent years? Has this, rather than the military, not been the major cause of the international weakening of the dollar and its corresponding inflationary effects?

A simple look at the sequence of events is sufficient to demonstrate that neither the international breaking of the value of the dollar nor the high inflation/high unemployment economy of the U.S. could have been initiated by the actions of the Organization of Petroleum Exporting Countries (OPEC). In the first place, the U.S. has been suffering from unprecedented simultaneous high inflation/high unemployment every year since 1969. Secondly, the dollar was officially devalued for the first time in modern U.S. history in 1971. But the OPEC oil embargo and the subsequent huge increases in oil prices did not even occur until late 1973!

That is not to say that the OPEC oil price escalation has not contributed significantly to the piling up of dollars abroad and to the U.S. general economic woes. Certainly, it has had an important exacerbating effect, particularly in conjunction with the progressive loss of cost offsetting capability by U.S. industries, a phenomenon clearly and importantly related to the military drain on the nation's civilian economy (as will be discussed in detail). But the chronology makes it obvious that it could not have been the fundamental cause of these problems.

IMPACT OF MILITARY SPENDING ON CIVILIAN TECHNOLOGY AND THE IMPLICATIONS THEREOF

Allocation of scientific and engineering resources to military-oriented activity. Since the beginning of the Second World War and with substantially more force since the latter half of the 1950's, the United States has channeled a large fraction of the nation's engineering and scientific resources into military-related research. Some of this has been direct, through priority allocation of Federal Government grants for these purposes; and some has been indirect, through the utilization of a considerable portion of the annual discretionary federal budget for purchase of increasingly technologically sophisticated weapons and related systems whose research, development and production required military industrial firms to hire large quantities of technologists.

According to National Science Foundation (NSF) data, over the entire decade of the 1970's, the fraction of yearly Federal budget obligations for research and development going to the military and space programs averaged more than two-thirds of the total. More than half of this money was channeled to the military alone.[8] Looked at from another angle, as of the mid-1970's, 77% of the nation's research and development engineers and scientists (excluding social scientists) who received Federal support, received it from the Department of Defense (DoD), National Aeronautics and Space Administration (NASA) and the Atomic Energy Commission (AEC)—again more than 50% from the DoD alone.[9] Nearly three-quarters of the engineers and scientists employed by business and industry who received federal support in that year received it from the same three agencies.[10]

Estimation of the fraction of the nation's total engineering and scientific talent engaged in military-related research is quite a bit more tortuous a task than it should be, primarily because publicly available data are not categorized in such a manner as to expedite this effort. For instance, published NSF data on characteristics of the nation's engineering and scientific employment for 1974 contains a table entitled, "Number of Scientists and Engineers by Field, Highest Degree and Critical National Interest."[11]

Though some ten categories of "critical national interest" are listed, ranging from "health," "food," "housing," etc. to "space," military work or its standard euphemism "national defense" is *not* one of them. Apparently, the NSF does not consider national defense a "critical national interest." Not surprisingly, the two miscellaneous categories in the table, labelled "does not apply" and "no report," which must therefore contain the bulk of the military-related engineers and scientists, constitute more than 57% of the total.

While the making of an accurate, up-to-date estimate of the military sector pre-emption of scientific and engineering talent, given this obfuscation, would be an involved and arduous task without access to primary data, it is possible to produce reasonable and fairly conservative rough estimates by manipulating some of the published data for the mid-1970's (most recent, at this writing). For example, if one assumes that only half of the engineers and scientists falling into the two miscellaneous categories of the NSF's "critical national interest" table just discussed are engaged in military work (n.b. ten major categories of national interest have already been explicitly subtracted), an estimate just under 30% of the total national pool of engineers and scientists results, whether the calculation is done with or without social scientists, and whether or not personnel with less than a bachelor's degree are included. Adding in the numbers explicitly listed for "space" research, raises the fraction to just above 33%.

The estimate can be approached from another angle by extracting the numbers of full-time equivalent R&D scientists and engineers for three major military-oriented industry categories "electrical equipment and communication," "aircraft and missiles" and "machinery" from NSF data for 1967.[12] Assuming that roughly two-thirds of the R&D engineers and scientists in the first two industries and only one-quarter of those in the third industry are engaged in military-related work, and *ignoring all* other industries completely (industries *ignored* would include tank production, ordinance, nuclear submarines, etc.) results in an estimate of just under 33% for military-oriented engineering and scientific industrial R&D employment.

Though it is inappropriate to rely heavily on the accuracy of estimates so crudely developed, it would appear likely that an important fraction of the engineering and scientific personnel in the U.S. have been devoting their talents to the development of military-oriented technology, and unlikely that the fraction would be substantially less than one-third. In all probability, it is far higher. And in any case, it is important to remember that this magnitude of pre-emption of technological resources has been maintained for two to three decades or more.

Impact on civilian-oriented technological development. The kind of new technological knowledge that will ultimately emerge from any given research or development project will, of course, not be wholly predictable in advance. By definition, the researchers are engaged in a quest for new knowledge, and such explorations of the unknown and untried must always involve uncertainty and a degree of unpredictability. However, even while not wholly determinate, the kind of new technical knowledge developed is very strongly conditioned by the nature of the problems being studied and the type of solutions being sought. Since one-third or more of the nation's engineers and scientists have been seeking military-oriented solutions to military-oriented problems for the past several decades, it should be no surprise that the development of military technology has proceeded at a rapid pace in the U.S.—or that the development of civilian-oriented technology has become severely retarded here. How could it have been otherwise?

The much vaunted "spinoff" or "spillover" argument that military-oriented technological development produces massive improvements in areas of civilian application and thus does not retard civilian technological progress, makes very little conceptual sense, and more to the point, is massively contradicted by straightforward empirical observation. Of course, some transferability of technical knowledge between military and civilian application would be expected (in both directions), but conceptually it is difficult to see how directing attention to one area of technical research would routinely produce an *efficient* generation of knowledge pertaining to a completely different area.

On the empirical side, a 1974 report of a committee of the National Academy of Engineering stated:

"With a few exceptions the vast technology developed by Federally
funded programs since World War II has not resulted in widespread
'spinoffs' of secondary or additional applications of practical products,
processes and services that have made an impact on the nation's economic growth, industrial productivity, employment gains and foreign
trade."[13]

The seventh annual report of the National Science Board, governing
body of the National Science Foundation (*Science Indicators*-1974) expressed concern over the serious erosion of the U.S. predominance in science and technology. In several international comparisons the empirical
indicators behind this concern were detailed:

"The 'patent balance' of the United States fell by about 30% between
1966 and 1973. . . . the decline was due to an increasing number of U.S.
patents awarded to foreign countries and a decline (in 1973) in the number of foreign patents awarded to U.S. citizens. Overall, foreign patenting increased in the United States during the period by over 65%,
and by 1973 represented more than 30% of all U.S. patents granted.
This suggests that the number of patentable ideas of international merit
has been growing at a greater rate in other countries than in the United
States."[14]

Further, the report describes the relative production of a total of 492
major innovations by the U.S., the U.K., Japan, West Germany and
France over the twenty year period from 1953–1973:

"The U.S. lead . . . declined steadily from the late 1950's to the mid-
1960's, falling from 82 to 55% of the innovations. The slight upturn in
later years represents a relative rather than an absolute gain, and results
primarily from a decline in the proportion of innovations produced in
the United Kingdom, rather than an increase in the number of U.S. innovations."[15]

More recently, the NSF's *Science Indicators: 1978* (National Science
Board, 1979) points to a continuation of these downtrends, the foreign origin share of total U.S. patents having increased further from 30% in 1973
to 36% in 1977.[16] Furthermore, this high total share of foreign origin patents is clearly not the result of growing foreign success in only one or two
areas. "Foreign patents account for between one-third and one-half of all
U.S. patents across a wide spectrum of fields."[17] The NSF goes on to point
out:

"U.S. patenting has decreased abroad as well as at home . . . From 1966 to 1976, U.S. patenting activity abroad declined almost 30% in ten industrialized countries . . . The decline in U.S. patenting abroad could be attributable to a number of factors, including . . . a relative decline in the U.S. inventive activity . . ."[18]

The relatively poor showing of the U.S. is even more remarkable considering that these data do not specifically exclude military-related technology and hence are biased in favor of the U.S. It is interesting to note that in these comparisons, Japan and West Germany did quite well.

"Since 1963, inventors from West Germany have received the largest number of foreign origin U.S. patents (83,220). In fact, among U.S. foreign-origin patents, West Germany was first in 11 of the 15 major product fields and second in the remaining 4 . . .

"Japan ranks second in the number of total U.S. patents granted to foreign investors between 1963 and 1977 (61,510). Japan has the largest number of foreign patents in three product groups . . . and is second in an additional five categories . . . Since 1970, Japan has dramatically increased its patent activity by over 100% in every product field except the two areas in which it already had a large concentration of patents. This finding is significant in that it seems to dispute the widespread belief that Japanese R&D efforts are narrowly focused on specific technologies . . ."[19]

Not so coincidentally, these two countries averaged about 4.0% (Japan, 1961–1975) and 20.0% (West Germany, 1961–1967) of government R&D expenditures on defense and space, as opposed to a U.S. average of about 70% (1961–1977).[20]

In a conceptually related comparison Michael Boretsky of the U.S. Department of Commerce presents data bearing on the relative civilian equivalent R&D effort (allowing for 10% spinoff from defense and space R&D) of the U.S., six European countries, Canada and Japan in the 1960's.[21] In terms of R&D employment, Japan shows a civilian R&D effort nearly three times as intense as that for the U.S., West Germany ranks some 60% higher than the U.S.; in fact, only Italy and Canada rank lower.

Furthermore, again using absolute numbers of patents granted as a measure of technological progress, and looking at the U.S. industrial technological progress, and looking at the U.S. industrial technology situation overall, the NSF finds:

"The total number of patents granted annually to U.S. inventors generally increased from 1960 to the early 1970's but showed a steady decline from 1971 to 1977 . . . Complex influences on the level of

> patenting make analysis of patent data difficult . . . In the present case,
> since patenting has dropped in almost all product fields, the trends seem
> to indicate a real decline in the rate of production of inventions by U.S.
> industry from 1971 to 1977 . . . "[22]

Recognition of the serious retardation of civilian technological progress is also widespread in the nation's business community. In 1976 (February 26), *Business Week* ran an article entitled "The Breakdown of U.S. Innovation," the introduction of which included the phrase " . . . from boardroom to research lab there is a growing sense that something has happened to U.S. innovation. . . . " Apparently that "sense" continued to grow, because by July 3, 1978 the story had made the cover of that journal. The article, entitled "Vanishing Innovation" began, "A grim mood prevails today among industrial research managers. America's vaunted technological superiority of the 1950's and 1960's is vanishing. . . . " The government also clearly recognized that a severe problem existed, as the Carter Administration ordered a massive, 18 month long, 28-agency domestic policy review of the influence of the government on industrial innovation.

Given the huge amounts of money and technical personnel which have indisputably been poured into military-related research over the past several decades in the U.S., the severity of the slowdown in civilian technological progress would not have occurred if the 'spinoff' or 'spillover' effects had been anything more than marginal. But if the transferability of invention and innovation was and is actually low, then the decades long diversion of at least a third of the engineers and scientists in the U.S. to military related work would predictably have produced precisely the sort of civilian technological deterioration we have, in fact, experienced. Under conditions of low transferability it could not have failed to produce such a result.

Civilian technological progress and productivity growth. It is widely recognized that civilian technological progress is the keystone of productivity improvement and economic growth. As the National Science Board put it in their 1977 annual report (*Science Indicators: 1976*),

> " . . . the contribution of R&D to economic growth and productivity is
> positive, significant and high, and that such innovation is an important
> factor—perhaps the most important factor—in the economic growth of
> the United States in this century."

According to Boretsky of the Commerce Department,

> "The most relevant historical evidence suggests that American technol-
> ogy reached parity with Europe by 1870 or thereabout . . . and by the
> end of World War II it had become a literal 'wonder' to the rest of the

world . . . The present concern is not with the country's technology relevant to defense and the conquest of space which occupied the last two decades, but with technology relevant to the quality of life in society at large as well as more specifically, productivity and commercial markets at home and abroad."[23]

Civilian technological progress is that which is oriented to the development of knowledge leading to improved consumer and producer products and to more efficient ways of producing. These two aspects, new and better products and improved production methods are not so distinct as it might seem, since a major source of increase in productive efficiency is the employment of new machinery and equipment embodying superior technology.

Civilian technological progress contributes to the growth of labor productivity by encouraging increases in the quantity of capital per worker and to the growth of both labor and capital productivity through the development of production techniques enabling the more efficient use of productive resources in general. Accordingly, as the development of civilian technology became increasingly retarded in the U.S., productivity growth began to collapse.

From 1947 to 1975, output per hour grew at an average annual rate of 3.3% in the nonfarm business sector of the U.S., according to the Council of Economic Advisors. From 1965 to 1978, that rate of labor productivity growth was cut in half, averaging 1.6% per year. In recent years the United States has had the lowest rate of productivity growth of any major noncommunist economy. Furthermore, the productivity growth collapse is accelerating. While the annual growth rate for 1965–73 averaged 2.1%, from 1973–78 it was 0.8%. In the first six months of 1979, output per labor-hour in the private business sector actually *fell* at an annual rate of 3.3%. During the second quarter of 1979, "productivity fell at an annual rate of 5.7%, the largest quarterly decline ever recorded in this series of statistics, which began in 1947."[24]

Boretsky presents an international comparison bearing on both capital and labor productivity growth among major industrial countries in two periods, 1955–65 and 1965–71. The results of his calculations are presented in Table 2. The performance of the U.S. is abysmal, both relative to its own historical performance, and relative to other nations. In the latter period, its labor productivity growth is the lowest of any nation compared, and only the United Kingdom shows a lower capital productivity growth ratio. Note particularly that the West German and Japanese performance is once again strong relative to the U.S. and other nations in the latter period, particularly in terms of labor productivity.

Table 2. International comparison relevant to labor and capital productivity performance, selected countries.

Country	Labor Productivity (% average annual growth in GNP per civilian employed)		Capital Productivity Ratio* (% average annual growth in GNP/year ÷ % average annual growth in in fixed nonresidential investment)	
	1955–65	1965–71	1955–65 to 1953–63	1965–71 to 1963–69
United States	2.2	1.3	1.13	0.50
France	5.1	4.8	0.51	0.75
West Germany	4.5	4.3	0.56	0.80
Belgium-Luxembourg	2.7	3.7	0.59	0.85
Netherlands	3.1	4.3	0.62	0.63
Italy	5.6	5.5	0.63	4.42
United Kingdom	2.1	2.8	0.46	0.44
Canada	1.9	1.8	1.43	0.80
Japan	8.0	9.6	0.65	0.79
USSR	3.5	3.6	0.67	0.70

Source: Boretsky, M., "Trends in U.S. Technology: A Political Economist's View," *American Scientist* (January/February 1975), p. 72.

*Note: A two-year lag for the effects of new investment is assumed.

The fact of the productivity collapse is so overwhelming as to no longer be a matter of dispute. But its cause is still the source of much confusion and consternation. An article in the 19 October 1979 issue of *Science* by John Walsh bore witness to this situation. Its title and subtitle were: "Productivity Problems Trouble Economy—Everybody talks about the lag in the growth of productivity but nobody seems to know enough to do much about it." In the course of the article a number of candidates for cause of the productivity problem are cited: "Some economists assign major blame. . . . to a shift to a 'service' economy"; " . . . the recent rise in energy costs"; " . . . the increase in government regulation"; "changing attitudes among workers . . . a new devotion to leisure and relaxation" (a euphemistic way of stating the lazy worker hypothesis); even sexist " . . . the labor force has become increasingly inexperienced because of an influx of women . . . " and racist " . . . the transformation of the U.S. economy is proceeding in the direction taken by the British rather than the Japanese. Anglo Saxon attitudes may produce a less pressured, less competitive way of life. . . . " All these explanations have been given some credence.

The service sector argument is easily dismissed by the fact that productivity growth in U.S. manufacturing (i.e., excluding services) has been undergoing a similar pattern of deterioration. From 1947 to 1964, the average annual rate of productivity increase in U.S. manufacturing was 4.1%; from 1965 to 1975 the average annual rate had dropped by more than half to under 1.7% per year. As cited in the Walsh article referred to above, Victor Fuchs of the National Bureau of Economic Research has estimated that the growth of the service sector contributed only about 0.1% to the decline in productivity from the 1960's to the 1970's. Fuchs further estimates a similar extremely small contribution to the influx of women.

Edward F. Denison, a senior fellow at the Brookings Institution and a noted authority on productivity and economic growth has examined in detail and rejected a whole series of commonly offered explanations for the productivity problems as being responsible for too small a fraction of the decline to have real significance. These include stiffer environmental regulations, increased government paperwork, lazy workers, declining Yankee ingenuity, etc.[25]

On the matter of research and development, Walsh points out, "in the past, a belief that spending on R&D led to innovation was widely, rather uncritically held in the U.S. and used as blanket justification for government support of R&D. The view came to be considered as oversimplified both outside and inside government, and spending on R&D by government declined."[26] Denison argues that cuts in research and development spending are incapable of explaining the productivity drop.

On the other hand, Edwin Mansfield of the University of Pennsylvania, another noted authority on productivity and in particular its relation to R&D has stated, reflecting on 20 years of economic studies, "Research and development seems to have had a very significant effect on the rate of productivity growth in the industries and time periods that have been studied."[27]

The fact is technological development does have an extremely important effect on productivity growth, *if* it is civilian technological development oriented to such a purpose. One cannot hope to see, and therefore cannot hope to understand, the fundamental role of failing technological progress in producing this present and ongoing productivity deterioration in the U.S. until a clear and precise distinction is made between civilian and military related technological development. For it is most assuredly not the failure of technology as a whole that has produced our present productivity problems—the U.S. scientific and engineering community is not becoming less ingenious or less productive. Rather the collapse is a direct, inevitable though long-term result of the decades long diversion of a large fraction of the nation's critical scientific and engineering effort from productive civilian oriented technological development.

Productivity growth, inflation and unemployment. The improvement in productivity plays a crucial role in the countering of inflationary pressures, for it is sustained productivity growth that offsets the effects of rising input costs. It is not the separate cost of labor, fuels, materials, and capital that is relevant to the determination of product price, but rather the combined cost of these productive resources *per unit* of product. Thus, the rise in labor costs, for example, might be at least partially offset by substituting cheaper capital for increasingly expensive labor, or by organizing production to use labor more efficiently or both. As long as the net result is to produce more output per unit of input, rises in input costs need not be fully translated into rises in the cost per unit of product. Correspondingly, the upward "cost-push" pressures on price will be mitigated. But productivity is nothing more than a measure of output per unit input. Hence rising productivity permits absorption of rising prices of labor, fuels, etc. without full reflection of these resource cost increases in unit cost and thus in price.

It is therefore clear that the deterioration of productivity growth will substantially compromise this cost offsetting capability. In the absence of strong productivity improvement, rising costs of labor, fuels, etc. will be translated into rising product prices. As this occurs over a whole series of industries, a self-reinforcing rise in the general level of prices or "inflation" occurs.

The mid 1960's was the breakpoint for the growth of manufacturing productivity in the U.S. It should therefore also have been the point of shift for cost behavior in U.S. manufacturing industry from traditional "cost offsetting" or "cost minimizing" behavior to the sort of "cost passalong" or "cost indifferent" behavior just described—behavior in which input cost increases are simply translated or "passed along" into product price increases. A first empirical investigation of the possibility of this shift in modal cost behavior was performed by Byung Hong, in doctoral research at Columbia University.[28] Hong developed a simple multiple regression model consisting of one price equation and one wage equation which he fit to quarterly data for U.S. manufacturing for two periods: 1948 (second quarter) to 1964 (fourth quarter) and 1965 (first quarter) to 1975 (second quarter).

In the price equation, the percentage change in wholesale prices was said to depend upon the percentage changes in wages and raw materials costs moderated by changes in productivity, the level of capacity utilization (as a measure of demand pressure) and profit rates. Under conditions of cost offsetting behavior, the change in productivity would be expected to have a strong negative effect, as pressure was applied to improve productive efficiency in response to rising input costs, whereas under cost pass-along productivity growth would not be expected to have any significant impact on price increase. On the other hand, profit rate would have little effect on price under cost offsetting as compared to a clear positive effect under cost indifference, since profits are maintained or increased to a much greater extent by expansion of productivity in the former and by increase in price in the latter case. Furthermore, high capacity utilization would tend to lead to higher prices under cost offsetting ("demand pull") but *lower* prices under cost indifference because of lowered fixed cost per unit. Essentially all of the cost offset expectations are statistically supported in the earlier time period, and nearly all the expectations for cost indifference in the later time span.

In the wage equation, productivity change represents wage demand justification, past profits are wage demand targets, past consumer price inflation rates represent pressure for higher wages, and the unemployment rate is a kind of bargaining power variable. Under traditional cost offsetting behavior, the unemployment rate would be expected to have a significantly negative effect on wages, reflecting the Phillips curve type tradeoff, while no particular effect on wage increase would be expected under cost pass-along (since the source of inflation has nothing to do with demand pull pressures reflected in the unemployment rate). The consumer price variable would be stronger under cost pass-along than under cost offset as both rates of inflation and the price change expectations they generate are high and rising. All else held constant, a given increment in productivity growth might well have a larger effect on wage increase in a cost indifferent than in a cost offsetting environment because productivity growth would be so much weaker in such a period (a sort of decreasing marginal returns to productivity growth in terms of generating wage increases?). In any case, again nearly all of the expectations for cost offsetting behavior are statistically observed in the earlier period, and nearly all of the expectations for cost pass-along behavior are observed in the latter period, thus reinforcing the price equation results.

As the managements of U.S. industrial firms learned that cost indifference or passalong was a viable behavior, the incentives for the kind of internal vigilance necessary for cutting edge cost minimization were mitigated. And so, the decline of productivity growth was further exacerbated, reinforcing the shift to cost pass-along.

The implications of the productivity induced shift of modal cost behavior for stagflation are straightforward. As cost indifference became the order of the day, input cost increases were more and more rapidly and strongly translated into output price increases. And of course, via the usual wage price spiral augmented by external input cost increases (e.g. OPEC oil price actions) themselves perhaps partly engendered by output inflation, the process was made more severe. This has been a powerful inflationary engine. But the same mechanism has also generated unemployment.

As the prices of U.S. produced goods rose higher and higher, the nation's industry became less and less competitive *vis-à-vis* foreign competition. Overseas markets were lost and the U.S. export position weakened. Domestic markets were lost to foreign production and the U.S. import position worsened. The progressive loss of markets induced cutbacks in U.S.-based production with high unemployment rates the result. And this problem was exacerbated by the flight of U.S. owned production facilities to cheap labor havens abroad, as one logical response to the inability to offset higher costs in the U.S. because of the productivity failure. It is thus preeminently the declining competitiveness of U.S. industry resulting from decreasing productivity growth that has generated unemployment even in the face of high product demand.

Productivity growth thus is "the economic linchpin of the 1980's," as the Joint Economic Committee of the Congress described it in its mid-1979 analysis of prospects for the economy. Its warning that, as the *New York Times* put it, "The average American is likely to see his standard of living drastically reduced in the 1980's unless productivity growth is accelerated"[29] is precisely correct.

During the entire decade of the 1970's the dynamic process of deterioration which has been described here has produced the unprecedented simultaneous high inflation/high unemployment that has become a fact of our economic life. For an entire decade, the inflation rate has averaged near 7% at the same time the unemployment rate has averaged more than 6%.

The current military buildup being proposed by the Reagan Administration is, as Lester Thurow has pointed out, three times as large as that which took place during the Vietnam War. And it is taking place in a context of a much weaker domestic economy than that of the 1960's, counterposed against the economic strength of our chief economic adversaries (who are at the same time our military allies). In Thurow's words,

> "When a nation such as the U.S. sharply increases its military forces, it generally does so at a time when its industrial competitors are also attempting to increase their own military establishments, and are experiencing comparable economic strains. But the Reagan buildup is to take place in a time when our allies are not raising their military expenditures at anything like our pace. . . . This difference poses the problem of how the U.S. can maintain the industrial strength to compete with other countries in civilian production and sales."[30]

The economic prognosis for the coming decade is not good. If the arms race continues unabated, and we somehow manage to survive, these rates of inflation and unemployment—rates that were viewed as horrific at the beginning of the 1970's—may well look like economic good times compared to what will be commonplace by the end of the 1980's.

As damaging as the persistence of high levels of military spending has been to the domestic economy, and as dependent economic revitalization might be on a reversal of this situation, it is nevertheless true that the process of transition to a more fully civilian-oriented economy must be handled carefully. Producing a smooth economic conversion requires a clear understanding of the nature of the multifaceted transition problem. The solution to that problem lies at the core of the political economic strategy that is a key prerequisite to the linked process of reversing the present economic decay, particularly in the U.S. and USSR, and achieving real, meaningful arms reduction. It is to that problem that attention is now turned.

References

1. Dumas, Lloyd J., "National Insecurity in the Nuclear Age," *Bulletin of the Atomic Scientists* (May, 1976) and "Human Fallibility and Weapons," *Bulletin of the Atomic Scientists* (November, 1980).
2. Dumas, Lloyd J., "Armament, Disarmament and National Security: A Theo-

retical Duopoly Model of the Arms Race," *Journal of Economic Studies* (May, 1979).

3. York, Herbert F., *Race to Oblivion: A Participant's View of the Arms Race*, Simon & Shuster, 1970 (see especially Chapter 12).

4. Bureau of Economic Analysis, U.S. Department of Commerce, *Business Statistics* (1973) p. 69.

5. Ibid., p. 40.

6. For example, the Air Force's C5A transport plane, which experienced a $2 billion cost overrun (i.e. excess of actual cost over original cost estimates) was produced under a firm "fixed price" contract. Payment was simply adjusted upward to cover the overrun. Thus, the fixed price was fixed in name only. A number of fascinating "insiders" accounts of the operation of military procurement are available that document in detail these practices. Two such accounts are: *The High Priests of Waste* (New York: W. W. Norton, 1972) by A. Ernest Fitzgerald, former Air Force Deputy for Management Systems in the Pentagon (this includes much detail on the C5A); and *Arming America: How the U.S. Buys Weapons* (Boston: Harvard University Press, 1974) by J. Ronald Fox, former Assistant Secretary of the Army (for procurement).

7. Dumas, Lloyd J. "Payment Functions and the Productive Efficiency of Military Industrial Firms," *Journal of Economic Issues* (June, 1976)

8. National Science Board, National Science Foundation, *Science Indicators: 1978* (Washington: U.S. Government Printing Office, 1979), p. 182.

9. National Science Foundation, Surveys of Science Resources Series, *Characteristics of the National Sample of Scientists and Engineers: 1974, Part 2: Employment*, Table B-16 (pp. 128–142).

10. Ibid., Table B-15 (pp. 113–127).

11. Ibid., Table B-10 (pp. 85–89).

12. National Science Foundation, "Full-Time Equivalent Number of R&D Scientists and Engineers, by Industry and Source of Funds for R&D Projects: January, 1975 and January, 1976" (Table 93).

13. National Academy of Engineering Committee on Technology Transfer and Utilization "Technology Transfer and Utilization, Recommendations for Reducing the Emphasis and Correcting the Imbalance" (Washington, D.C.: National Academy, 1974), p. i.

14. National Science Board, National Science Foundation, *Science Indicators: 1974* (Washington: U.S. Government Printing Office, 1976) p. 17.

15. Ibid., p. 19.

16. Op. cit., NSF *Science Indicators: 1978*, p. 2.

17. Ibid., p. 18.

18. Ibid., pp. 20–21.

19. Ibid., pp. 19–20.

20. Ibid., pp. 146–147.

21. Boretsky, Michael, "Trends in U.S. Technology: A Political Economist's View," *American Scientist* (January/February, 1975) p. 76.

22. Op. cit., NSF, *Science Indicators: 1978*, pp. 78–79.

23. Op. cit., Boretsky, p. 70.
24. Farnsworth, Clyde H., "Lag in Productivity Called Major Peril to Living Standard," *New York Times* (August 13, 1979).
25. Denison, Edward F., *Accounting for Slower Economic Growth: The U.S. in the 1970's* (Washington, D.C.: The Brookings Institution, 1979).
26. Walsh, John, "Productivity Problems Trouble Economy," *Science* (19 October, 1979) p. 311.
27. Ibid.
28. Hong, Byung, *Inflation Under Cost Pass-Along Management* (New York: Praeger, 1979).
29. Op. cit., Farnsworth.
30. Thurow, Lester, "How to Wreck the Economy," *New York Review of Books* (May 14, 1981)

Questions

1. Can you think of any reasons besides defense spending that might help account for the deterioration of heavy industry in the U.S.?

2. If the Soviets can control unemployment and inflation, why can't they produce enough consumer goods?

3. What would you say to the argument that, if the U.S. had no defense establishment, there would be no prosperity or political freedom in this country?

4. What other sectors of American society besides the Pentagon must share the blame for inefficient weapons procurement procedures?

5. Has the author's prediction for the late 1980s come true? Explain. If not, why not?

5

Militarism in America

Staff of The Defense Monitor, #3, 1986

The following essay turns away from superpower confrontation and argues that a permanent war psychology may be threatening the very freedoms the United States seeks to defend. It was written by the staff of a newsletter published by the Center for Defense Information, a Washington-based "think tank" which has been a voice of moderation in military spending since 1972. In this article, the authors point to the growing influence of the military establishment on U.S. domestic and foreign policy since World War II. Under the label of "national security," policy-making has shifted from civilian agencies and has been entrusted to the military. Besides reordering domestic priorities from civilian needs and adding significantly to the national debt, the Pentagon budget, in this view, has damaged America's high-tech industry and scientific endeavor.

The authors view with alarm the glorification of the military in American society, citing popular films and toys, advertising campaigns for military recruitment and a general loss of sensitivity to the dangers of using force to achieve national goals.

The article cites with concern the pervasiveness of the "military-industrial complex," about which President Eisenhower warned in 1961. With so many companies doing business with the military establishment, the authors envision a nation on a permanent war economy. Congressional representatives, eager to preserve their local military installation or factory, appear unresponsive to the need to limit the defense budget. Besides making allies in Congress, the Pentagon is depicted as a major force in hiding legitimate scientific achievements under the label of secrecy. According to this article, the efforts of too many engineers, scientists and university researchers have been harnessed to the nation's war machine. The authors also take aim at Reserve Officer Training Programs (ROTC) on campus and even in high schools as other instances of the "militarization of America."

The increasing sales of war toys in the past few years are another con-

cern of the authors, as is the tremendous growth of pistols and automatic weapons in the hands of civilians.

The authors decry the impoverishment of civilian programs as a result of a bloated military budget. They call for what they consider more constructive methods to promote national interests through diplomatic, scientific, economic and cultural means.

Most Americans do not think of the United States as being particularly militaristic. We are not at war. Gun-toting soldiers do not patrol our streets. Young men are no longer drafted. In many ways, however, militarism pervades America.

Since 1945 the role of the military in American government and society has changed dramatically. Military issues have been given high priority in shaping American foreign and domestic policies. The militarization of our domestic political economy and everyday American society is an increasingly dangerous phenomenon that demands careful examination if we are to keep it in check.

In his Farewell Address to the American People in 1961, President Dwight D. Eisenhower warned Americans of the far-reaching effects of militarism when he said: "[The] conjunction of an immense military establishment and a large arms industry is new in the American experience.

"The total influence—economic, political, even spiritual—is felt in every city, every State house, every office of the Federal government. We recognize the imperative need for this development. Yet we must not fail to comprehend its grave implications. Our toil, resources and livelihood are all involved; so is the very structure of our society."

The Pentagon greatly influences America's foreign policy, domestic priorities, economy, and the nature of our government. The long established tradition of civilian control over the military is eroding as an increasing number of military men fill government positions previously held by civilians and our civilian leaders permit the military to play a greater role in policy-making.

Military concerns affect economic priorities nationwide. Hundreds of Billions of tax dollars are spent to support the largest peacetime military buildup in American history while social programs are cut, the debt becomes unmanageable and the probability of nuclear war increases.

In the post-WWII period military priorities have shaped American law and contributed to sweeping reorganization of the government. Defined almost exclusively in military terms, the abstraction of "*national security*" has been used to justify a broadening of the military's authority. More recently, *executive orders* and directives have been passed down from the White House taking policy-making power away from civilian agencies and entrusting it to the military.

America's lead in *high-tech* industry and the international scientific community is fading because of the reordering of national priorities to accommodate military requirements and rising levels of secrecy. Scholars and scientists are discouraged by far-reaching restrictions imposed in the interest of national security that prevent them from discussing their research with other scientists. Civilian resources—both intellectual and monetary—are being redirected to support programs like the Strategic Defense Initiative (Star Wars) that will yield few civilian benefits and commit the U.S. to even greater military spending.

America's increasing emphasis on the military as a means of maintaining and determining our position within today's complex world has many consequences for American society. Films like Rambo, Rocky IV, and Invasion U.S.A. urge the U.S. to impose America's will and establish world order through force. From Rambo to G.I. Joe, we are presented with the idea that Americans have the right to pursue military solutions so long as their convictions are strong and their arsenals well-stocked. Similarly, on the home front, aggressiveness and violence in society are more easily accepted as a normal means by which to achieve individual goals.

As paramilitary weapons, dress, jargon, and values are assimilated into everyday American life, we become desensitized to the dangers of employing force as a means of achieving our goals. Instead of viewing the growing influence of the military with a cautious and critical eye, we myopically see it as simply a sign of rekindled strength.

In subtle and provocative ways modern advertising calls to America's youth, portraying the Armed Services as a sort of large vocational institute offering opportunity and excitement, while calls for military reform and a definition of how U.S. forces fit in with overall national objectives remain unanswered. With new-found enthusiasm, universities and high schools across the country teach military values through the Senior and Junior Reserve Officer Training Corps. War toys and television initiate junior high and elementary school age children to state-of-the-art weaponry and military jargon.

The glorification of the military within American society has become a general trend in the United States—a trend which distorts our view of both foreign and domestic policy and raises serious concerns for the future of the democratic process in a stable, productive society.

The effects of militarism on foreign policy will be examined in a future *Defense Monitor*. This *Defense Monitor* details the rising trend of militarism in American society today and warns of the potentially dangerous consequences facing America if this trend remains unchecked.

NATIONAL SECURITY STATE

• Following World War II, the U.S. carved the world up into military regions for purposes of military planning, putting a four star general or admiral in charge of each. No other country has divided the world up in quite this way.

• The National Security Act of 1947 created the National Military Establishment (now the Department of Defense), the Central Intelligence Agency (CIA), and the main national security decision-making body, the National Security Council (NSC). The Act officially introduced the catchall abstraction "national security" that has since served to justify everything from the procurement of questionable weapons systems to the invasion of Grenada.

• NSC-68, a document drafted by the NSC in 1950, identified the "Soviet threat" as the foundation upon which to build U.S. foreign and domestic policy. NSC-68 assured Americans that, "The integrity of our system will not be jeopardized by any measures, covert or overt, violent or non-violent, which serve the purposes of frustrating the Kremlin design. . . . " Unfortunately, American society *is* being challenged and its integrity threatened. Preoccupation with military responses to the Soviet Union and rhetoric that conjures images of the "enemy" and an "evil empire" promote militarism by overstating the need for more military power. The frustration Americans feel with regard to combatting terrorism further aggravates growing militarism and promotes vigilantism within the United States.

• The military services, DoD, and the defense industries presently employ some 6.5 million people in the United States, generating well over $146 Billion in business between the Pentagon and private companies each year.

• The U.S. now has nearly half a million military personnel abroad at more than 333 military installations in 21 different countries. The U.S. also has plans to come to the defense of over 50 nations.

National security concerns are firmly entrenched and articulated in our foreign and domestic policies. Strong emphasis on "national security" is used over and over to justify unnecessary growth of the defense establishment.

PERMANENT WAR ECONOMY

• Preparing for war in peacetime has become big business in the U.S. In the 1940's, U.S. military production was carried out in an estimated 1,600 federally-owned plants. After WW II, the government relinquished direct power over production by contracting out to private firms. The government now owns only 72 defense production plants, 14 of which are on standby status.

• Over 30,000 companies are engaged in military production. Each day military agencies sign 52,000 contracts—more than 15 million a year.

• In FY85, America spent over 27% of all federal government expenditures on the military: nearly $1100 for each of its 234 million inhabitants. In contrast, the European NATO countries combined spent less than 10% of their government expenditures on the military, about $250 per person in a population of over 332 million.

• Companies not normally associated with defense have redirected their production in order to get a share of defense contracting dollars. Singer, IBM, Goodyear Tire, Motorola, AT&T, and Westinghouse are just a few companies which have crossed the line from civilian to military contracting. Some 80% of the Singer Company's revenues came from the firm's aerospace electronics business in 1985, compared to 15% ten years ago. Singer's nuclear-related contracts have included work on Trident and Pershing missiles, and simulators for the B-52 bomber.

• Today, close to 70% of every federal dollar allotted for Research and Development (R&D) goes to the military establishment. Since 1981 overall military research spending has increased by 62% above inflation, while funding for civilian research has decreased by 10%. Military R&D will rise to over $44 Billion in FY87.

• According to President Reagan's Commission on Industrial Competitiveness, over the past twenty years the U.S. has been losing ground in seven out of ten technology-oriented industries.

Ever-expanding military spending weakens the ability of the U.S. to compete in world markets by concentrating our resources on military production instead of the development of civilian technology.

UNWARRANTED INFLUENCE

"In the councils of government, we must guard against the acquisition of unwarranted influence, whether sought or unsought, by the military-industrial complex." Dwight D. Eisenhower, 1961

• Out of 3,041 counties in the U.S., only nine received less than $1,000 in DoD funds in 1984. Hundreds of military bases and facilities are spread across the U.S. Because people focus on short-term economic benefits resulting from weapons production, the military is often invited into communities without careful examination and questioning of the real costs involved.

• Political Action Committee (PAC) contributions from the twenty largest defense contractors have increased by 225% since the early eighties, totaling $3.6 million during the 1984 campaign. Some $440,000 went to members of the Senate Armed Services Committee, which authorizes funds for military spending.

• The Pentagon influences Congress through a process called legislative liaison which allows the Pentagon to maintain a permanent, active, and costly military lobby on Capitol Hill at the taxpayer's expense. The Pentagon circumvents direct lobbying restrictions by such questionable practices as offering to pay for entertainment and trips to the Paris Air Show.

• Representatives and Senators often vote in favor of weapons built within their districts regardless of whether or not those weapons fit in with national objectives. In FY83, Defense Secretary Weinberger accused Congress of tacking nearly $3 Billion worth of unnecessary items onto the Pentagon budget in deference to constituent demands for jobs.

Members of Congress often support DoD spending on weapons systems and military bases that provide their constituents with short-term economic benefits—benefits which are often incongruent with long-term national interests. PAC monies and legislative liaison push members of Congress to vote in support of weapons more for the number of jobs they will provide than for their effectiveness in defending the nation.

RISING SECRECY

• The Reagan Administration has made many attempts to restrict the flow of information from both the executive branch and the Pentagon to the public. Executive orders have been introduced which take away oversight powers from Congress, authorize the collection of "foreign intelligence" in the U.S., and challenge the integrity of academic freedom within the international scientific community.

• The Pentagon spends massive amounts of money each year on secret or "black" projects. The Department of Defense's FY87 budget request includes more than $22 Billion in secret funds, constituting a 300% increase in black funding since 1981. Huge secret projects include the Advanced Technology Bomber, a program whose total cost will be between $50 and $75 Billion, and the Advanced Cruise Missile program estimated to cost some $7 Billion.

• To date, two space shuttle missions have been classified in order "to deny our adversaries" information about satellite launches. No information was publicly disclosed on payloads, mission objectives, exact launching times or flight duration. Networks and newspapers were personally asked by Secretary of Defense Caspar Weinberger to suppress stories on secret space shuttle missions in the interest of national security. The National Aeronautics and Space Administration (NASA) estimates that military missions will make up 25-30% of all shuttle flights over the next decade.

• The Reagan Administration is classifying more documents in a misguided attempt to improve U.S. security. The "Preliminary Joint Staff Study on the Protection of National Secrets" reveals that in FY84 "the government classified 19,607,736 documents, a 9% increase over the previous year and a 60% increase from 1973." Nearly 4 million military, civilian and contractor personnel have security clearances, 164,000 of whom have been required to sign life-long legal contracts forbidding them to publish their views or "any information" relating to "intelligence." Instead of redefining the classification system, the Administration is weakening it by classifying more documents, censoring the work of government employees, and overemphasizing the importance of polygraph tests.

• Increased secrecy has greatly affected the press' ability to inform the public. In October 1983, the press was barred from reporting on military operations in Grenada. "It seems as though the reporters are always against us," Secretary of State George Shultz has said. "They're always seeking to report something that's going to screw things up." When asked, Shultz defined "us" as "Our side militarily—in other words, all of America." New practices requiring senior officials to obtain top-level approval before giving interviews indicate broader efforts to limit press coverage. All too often the information which the Administration seeks to suppress is already known to the Soviets through their intelligence system and satellites. Muzzling the press only leaves U.S. citizens in the dark.

To ensure that exorbitant amounts of money are not misspent it is crucial that the public and Congress be kept well informed about military projects and that security concerns be weighed thoughtfully against the values of an open and democratic society.

EVER-EXPANDING PENTAGON POWERS

• Administration officials have overstated national security concerns and emphasized the need for broader Pentagon powers.

• In March 1984, President Reagan signed a directive extending DoD's powers to matters previously handled by the Department of Commerce. The Pentagon gained new authority to block the export of high-tech products (microelectronics, computers, and sophisticated instruments that could have military application) to 15 non-communist countries. The Commerce Department and many U.S. companies fear that Pentagon interference may delay "harmless" or non-controversial trade and thus needlessly handicap U.S. exports.

• DoD Directive 5525.5 establishes new ties between DoD, civilian law enforcement agencies, and the U.S. Customs Service. The Directive sets a dangerous precedent by directing the use of military equipment and personnel for the gathering of intelligence, and the apprehension of drug transporters and illegal aliens. Not since 1878 when the militia was separated from the Armed Forces by law has the military been so closely involved with the enforcement of civilian law.

• A National Security Decision Directive (NSDD-145) signed in September 1984 allows a steering committee—composed mainly of military officers, with National Security Agency Director Lieutenant General William Odom as committee head—access to computer data banks in over 1,000 federal departments, agencies, boards, and commissions. The Directive orders a complete restructuring of government computer systems, giving NSA and DoD broad powers to classify information that is security "sensitive" and to "encourage, advise, and where appropriate, assist the private sector" in identifying "sensitive non-government information, the loss of which could adversely affect the national security."

• A recent report issued by the National Academy of Sciences reveals that the Pentagon is more frequently citing national security concerns to determine which papers will be presented at scientific conferences and the direction of studies to be pursued in American universities. "The Defense Department has embarked on a course that—as patriotic and well-intentioned as it may seem—may threaten the technological supremacy of the U.S.," says Richard J. Gowan, ex-President of the Institute of Electrical and Electronic Engineers. The unnecessarily broad application of security measures discourages scientific research.

• The Pentagon has now been given broad statutory powers to withhold unclassified technical data when responding to Freedom of Information Act requests. Seven new classification categories have been established, making it harder to obtain information on military tests and contractor performance.

In an effort to control espionage and leaks to the press, the Administration is giving DoD the power to restrict information to a degree which limits informed public debate on important military policies and programs. The Pentagon is gaining new authority in matters previously handled by civilian agencies, allowing the military to play an increasingly important role in determining foreign and domestic policy.

DoD ON CAMPUS

• Since WW II, approximately 42% of the U.S. scientific workforce has been employed in military-related projects. Today almost one-third of America's scientists and engineers are employed by the defense establishment.

• The Pentagon is pushing hard to expand its presence on campuses by calling for improved laboratory facilities and graduate and professor training programs designed to encourage scientists and engineers to undertake DoD research. In FY84, over 4,000 graduate students received Pentagon funding through university research programs. DoD has also devised a wide variety of new programs to interest undergraduate and high school students in working for the military.

• Universities are becoming more dependent on DoD as a source of funding and a provider of laboratory equipment that is not easily adaptable to non-military research. In 1983, DoD established a five-year, $150 million program to supply equipment for research of primary concern to the military. Under this program, over 650 grants have been awarded to 152 institutions located in 47 states, DC, Guam, and Puerto Rico.

• Universities now do about half of the Pentagon's basic research. Pentagon spending for basic research has grown by 217% over the past ten years, with an estimated $987 million going for basic research in FY87.

• Contracts involving Strategic Defense Initiative (SDI) research will add substantially to the growing military presence on campus. Universities pulled in some $206 million for SDI contracts in 1985, for a total of $254 million since 1983.

• "We're shaping research at the nation's universities in a line directed by the military," asserts physicist Vera Kistiakowsky from the Massachusetts Institute of Technology.

Military research conducted through universities saps available resources for more widely applicable civilian research and allows military funding and objectives to determine academic priorities. Imposed levels of secrecy reduce the efficiency of scientific development and threaten academic integrity.

STUDENT SOLDIERS

• Recruiters are targeting high school and college students with new-found zeal. Packaging the military as a leadership training program, DoD is pushing hard to increase the number of students recruited.

• In the Junior Reserve Officer Training Corps (JROTC) students as young as 14-years-old are instructed in military theory, the use of firearms, and military history. Students are taught to follow orders and unquestion-ingly accept a military curriculum which does not adequately prepare them for careers outside of the military. JROTC units may also participate in war simulations or undergo forms of basic training.

• At present 227,448 students participate in JROTC in over 1,375 high school units across the nation, up from 287 twenty years ago. In FY86 DoD's $52.1 million budget for JROTC bought texts, arms, and uniforms while schools were expected to provide a portion of the instructors' sala-ries, drill areas and classroom facilities with ample storage space for arms.

• With increasing college tuition and a decreasing number of non-DoD scholarships available, more students—especially women and mi-norities—are joining the Senior Reserve Officer Training Corps (ROTC). Senior ROTC is active in 530 college detachments and involves 110,872 students, up 50% from 1975.

• Skills learned in the Armed Services are difficult to market outside of the military due to differences between military and civilian applica-tions. A study conducted at Ohio State University in 1985 concluded that only 12% of men and 6% of women in a sample study could easily transfer their skills from the military to the civilian work force.

• Although recruiting quotas have been met with great success since 1981, the Pentagon is waging an aggressive recruiting campaign which will cost the taxpayer $1.8 Billion in FY86, with advertising budgets alone to-taling over $216 million. In 1985 the Army paid roughly $4,000 in recruit-ing costs for each new recruit.

• Recruiters promise students the opportunity to pick up valuable ca-reer skills but statistics compiled by the Defense Department's Manpower Data Center state otherwise. In 1983 only 17% of Army jobs required high-tech skills while less technical jobs, such as general infantry duties, accounted for close to 50%.

• Recruiters make use of referrals, phone books, and high school yearbooks to fill quotas. Schools are legally required to supply lists of grad-uates in 18 states. The distribution of literature and visits by recruiters are largely unregulated with over 15,000 military personnel working to re-cruit—roughly one for every 185 high school seniors in the public school system.

• The Armed Services Vocational Aptitude Battery Test (ASVAB) has been administered in at least 14,000 schools nationwide. The test provides recruiters with information on student qualifications and aptitude for mil-itary service. Students are frequently led to believe that the test is man-datory and are often uninformed as to how test results are used in the recruiting process.

• The services have gone to slick Madison Avenue-type advertising techniques to make the military an alluring and sexy career option. For example the Pentagon spent $60,000 to make a rock video featuring breakdancing to encourage registration for the Selective Service. The Army's Recruiting Support Command has another new gimmick in mobile units that have visited over 2,000 schools in 1984. Students are shown films about the Army and pressed to sign up for more information.

• Currently, 66 Civilian Aides to the Secretary of the Army act as recruiters and "good will ambassadors" for the military. Civilian Aides are influential members in communities who use their positions and contacts with the press to convince communities of the need for a larger military.

After being presented with a glamorous picture of the military, high school students are persuaded to make the military a career before being made aware of other career options available to them. School officials and parents have little or no control over course content yet are expected to help fund ROTC and JROTC programs at a time when other extracurricular funding is being cut.

RAMBOMANIA

• A spate of violent, militaristic films are developing cult followings, bringing military language, gear, and dress into vogue. Anti-Soviet films, commercials, and advertisements contribute to the perception that the Russians are a dehumanized enemy and that we are superior to them in every way.

• In its first 23 days "Rambo: First Blood Part II" grossed $75.8 million at the box office—a success topped only by two other films in history.

• Rambo spin-offs have flooded the market with some 25 companies negotiating distribution rights to Rambo-related merchandise. Rambo trivia games are broadcast on the radio and Sylvester Stallone lookalikes have made a business of delivering "Rambograms." The U.S. Army displays Rambo posters outside recruitment stations to encourage young people to sign up. The President is even caught up in Rambomania. "Boy, I saw Rambo last night," he commented, "Now I know what to do the next time this [terrorist seizure of hostages] happens."

• The Coleco Company, best known for its Cabbage Patch dolls, is marketing a new Rambo doll, claiming that "the character is emerging as a new American hero, a hero that has a high degree of excitement and patriotism and a thirst for justice associated with him."

• Militaristic films like Red Dawn, Commando, Missing In Action, Iron Eagle, and Invasion U.S.A. fuse chauvinism with righteousness to promote vigilantism.

American films and fads promote a sort of war hysteria that desen-

sitizes Americans to the gravity of military action as a means of foreign policy. Such films trivialize the use of force and promote the false idea that American might is always right.

TV AND TOYS-*ARE*-US

• Sales of war toys in the U.S. have increased 600% since 1982, making the war toys industry worth over $1 Billion in 1985. More than 218 million war toys and accessories were sold in 1985, roughly five for every child in the U.S.

• The major toy companies have joined forces with television producers to air cartoons featuring war toys. The number of cartoon series publicizing such toys jumped from zero in 1983 to ten in 1985.

• According to the National Coalition on Television Violence, the average American child is now exposed to 250 cartoons with war themes, and 800 television advertisements for war toys a year.

• While G.I. Joe and his team battle "jungle-dwelling guerrillas dedicated to totalitarian world takeover" on TV, Joe is muscling his way onto the breakfast table with his new cereal, G.I. Joe Action Stars.

• Other action figures like "HeMan" and "SheRa, the Princess of Power" promote victory through force. "Transformers," robots, and dolls with names like Ripsaw, Flashfists, Twinblade, Slice, and Clawgut come equipped with multiple machine guns, particle-beam cannons, and nuclear-powered laser guns.

• By the age of sixteen, the average child will have watched some 20,000 hours of TV, taking in 200,000 acts of violence and 50,000 attempted murders—33,000 of which will involve guns.

• A report from The Center for Media and Public Affairs, in which 500 television programs were monitored over the past thirty years, documents a noticeable shift towards the use of military-style assault weaponry. Popular television series like the "A-Team" and "Miami Vice" promote the use of guns as necessary for survival.

Television programs and war toys introduce Americans to military jargon, tactics, and weaponry from a very early age, teaching war in the spirit of play.

UNDER THE GUN

• America is the largest producer of firearms in the world and has the weakest gun control laws of any western democracy. Americans now own 35–40 million pistols and revolvers and over 100,000 registered machine guns. The number of people licensed to sell machine guns has tripled since 1980.

• There are an estimated 500,000 unregistered military-style assault guns owned in the United States.

• The sale of semi-automatic machine guns, which require a separate trigger pull for each shot fired, remains completely unregulated by federal law despite an increasing number of criminal incidents involving this type of gun. Semi-automatics can be easily converted into automatic weapons capable of firing up to 1,200 rounds per minute. Such conversions are on the rise, making illegal, unregistered machine guns accessible to the public and more difficult for police to trace.

Due to increased firepower, easier concealment, and greater availability, military-style assault weapons may soon replace the handgun as the weapon of choice on American streets. Gun control laws have not been revised to effectively regulate the flood of military weapons into the civilian market.

WAR GAMES PEOPLE PLAY

• In 1981, National Survival Inc. came out with a game that allows Americans to translate their fascination with guns into action. With approximately 600 playing fields, air gun games with names like Skirmish, Combat Zone, and the Ultimate Game are sweeping the United States. The game lasts approximately two hours, costs $20–$25, and provides the thrill of a man-hunt for over 50,000 Americans each week. Players capture the other team's flag then retreat to their camp, gunning down members of the opposing team with air guns that shoot paint pellets.

• Shooting galleries, once limited to penny arcades, are now in vogue in the U.S. But instead of using fake rifles to shoot plastic ducks, Americans today are using high-powered automatic machine guns to blast away at "commie pins" (bowling pins painted red) and posters of the Ayatollah Khomeini. These shooting galleries, largely unregulated by federal law, introduce people to the sense of power achieved by blazing away with Uzis, MAC-10s, and other paramilitary weapons.

• A new category of guns is capturing the market. Pistols, shotguns, and an impressive line of paramilitary guns can now be purchased in the form of "soft airguns." The guns look like the "real McCoy" but shoot plastic munitions and eject fake shells.

• According to the Federal Bureau of Investigation (FBI) 16 American survivalist camps now provide "differing types of programs to include firearms, martial arts, survivalist techniques and paramilitary training."

Paramilitary, survivalist and mercenary camps are presently operating in at least eleven states.

• Two schools in Michigan and Alabama have been described by the FBI as legal paramilitary schools. Known as the Mercenary Association, the schools train students in the use of firearms, guerrilla and counter-guerrilla operations, planning, tactics, logistics, armed and unarmed combat, land navigation, and other military instruction, and provide "information to their graduates regarding foreign employment in security and mercenary positions abroad."

• Frank Camper's Alabama mercenary school received a great deal of attention when a Sikh graduate of the course put his skills to test in a plan to assassinate Indian Prime Minister Rajiv Gandhi. Camper says his goal is "to train mercenary soldiers in international weapons and combat techniques and do it far better than the US Army Ranger School did. We lost the war in Vietnam. Maybe I keep fighting these wars because we lost our war there. Maybe if we had won, I could have stopped."

• Magazines like *Soldier of Fortune*, *SWAT*, *International Combat Arms*, and *Firepower* publicize mercenary camps as the place to learn or perfect survival skills before traveling to actual "hot spots" of armed conflict such as Central America or Angola. Over 500,000 people subscribe to magazines put out by the Omega Corporation, the company that publishes *Soldier of Fortune*.

• *Soldier of Fortune*'s founder and current editor, Robert K. Brown, asserts: "We have been the innovators in private-sector aid to resistance groups. We were the initiators. It goes back to sending a training team to Afghanistan in the fall of 1980. Then we got involved down in Salvador in early 1983 . . . For the immediate future we'll focus on El Salvador and assisting the Nicaraguan insurgents."

War simulations, machine gun ranges, and paramilitary magazines and camps introduce the average citizen to high-tech weapons and war tactics. War is associated with fun and sport, a connection which oversimplifies and desensitizes Americans to the grave consequences of using military force as a tool of diplomacy.

CONCLUSIONS

• Militarism is on the rise in the United States. While a strong military posture is essential, overemphasis on military power within the government and American society undermines our strength as a nation and jeopardizes the democratic process in the United States.

• Huge and increasing amounts of money support military programs while civilian programs are under-funded or eliminated altogether. This diversion of resources to the military threatens the American values our military is supposed to defend.

• Military concerns dominate America's foreign and domestic policies and its economy. Americans are persuaded to accept and support military actions instead of pursuing more constructive methods to promote U.S. interests through diplomatic, economic, scientific, and cultural means.

Questions

1. Do you think that America is pervaded by militarism? Give your reasons. Can you think of any opposing facts or arguments?

2. Is the government's emphasis on "national security" a legitimate response to espionage or an excuse to keep vital information from the people? What relationship do you see between the military (defense) budget and the funding available for domestic needs? Do you think the government's present policies are justified? Why, or why not?

3. Is the Pentagon too deeply involved on college campuses, through research projects and ROTC programs? Is there anything inherently wrong with the military services using advertising techniques ("Madison Avenue") to spur recruitment?

4. How closely related are Pentagon policies to the increase in automatic weapons, war toys and the growth of paramilitary schools?

5. What can the average citizen or student do to make sure that the U.S. does not become a highly militarized society? Give examples.

6
Deep Roots of the Arms Race

Sidney Lens

This article originally appeared in *Christianity & Crisis*, May 13, 1985.

Behind the seemingly interminable negotiations in Geneva to "freeze" or reduce nuclear stockpiles, Sidney Lens, editor of The Progressive, *Madison, Wis., draws a lesson from history. Since the technology exists both in the U.S. and the U.S.S.R. for verification, why should a nuclear freeze or reduction take months or years to negotiate? The answer lies in a mutual lack of trust, and the roots are imbedded in the origins of the Cold War.*

After the Second World War, the Marshall Plan was conceived to put Europe back on its feet. The author sees this massive relief program as Washington's way to enhance American power and to ensure markets for American goods. The alternative was worldwide depression, as no nation would have the money to buy American goods. The Western democracies readily agreed, but Lens sees Russia's refusal to cooperate as a (largely justified) fear that it would become another American satellite. The U.S. plan worked for the U.S. and its allies, but at the price of superpower conflict. The ensuing Cold War, in the author's view, was the natural result of two conflicting plans on how to organize the world.

Lens believes that both superpowers must now "change their way of life drastically or accept decline." In the face of a declining industrial base and massive debts in third world countries held by U.S. banks, he calls on this country to make peace with the rising expectations of the less developed countries and to change over to a planned economy at home. Otherwise, he says, the long-feared depression will begin.

Moscow too must undertake radical change—to decentralize its economy and to rely less on cheap labor, which is becoming scarce. General technological advance in the Soviet countries would require more managerial freedom and, ultimately, political freedom. Whether either government will undertake such reforms is a question he does not answer. Without such changes in Washington and Moscow, Lens concedes that "the best the negotiators in Geneva can do is regulate the arms race, not end it."

The second underlying reason for negotiations difficulties on nuclear weapons, in the author's view, is the lack of a truly effective world government. He considers the nation-state outmoded but declares that the lack of trust between the superpowers prevents establishment of a supranational authority. Negotiating an end to the arms race, he concludes, would be a relatively easy technical question, were it not for the psychological, political and economic roots found in the history of the arms race.

For most Americans the nuclear arms negotiations in Geneva must seem like a puzzle in ancient hieroglyphics. Since the two superpowers now have a combined arsenal equal in firepower to about 625,000 bombs like the one that destroyed Hiroshima 40 years ago (and killed 205,000 people), it would seem rather simple to cut back from that vast overkill capability. We alone have enough warheads to destroy every Soviet city of 100,000 or more (218 of them) at least 45 times over. Why can't we at least offer to freeze our stockpiles—and theirs—at present levels? That shouldn't take more than a day of negotiations since verification is no problem. Both they and we have the seismographs and satellites to monitor nuclear tests and deployments with at least 95 percent accuracy.

It isn't as if a freeze is something new that no one has ever discussed seriously; as a matter of fact the idea was first broached to Lyndon Johnson by neutral arms negotiators at the United Nations 21 years ago, in 1964. Johnson agreed to the proposal and ordered the negotiations which eventually evolved into three sets of strategic arms limitation talks, including the present one in Geneva. After 21 years one would think that both sides have had enough time to work out the details. Why then don't they enter into a quick agreement and be done with it?

After 39 years of proposals and counter-proposals on disarmament, "arms control," and "arms limitation," why should it take months or years to negotiate an agreement, as some in the Reagan administration have said it must? Early in the Cold War the Pentagon informed President Truman that 400 atomic bombs would be enough to restrain the Soviets. Some years later, in May 1956, General Earle Partridge told a congressional subcommittee that 50 nuclear devices would destroy or bring under fire 40 percent of the Soviet population and 60 percent of its industry. The National Planning Association, in a 1958 study, concluded that 200 warheads would be adequate to demolish "a large nation-state." During the Kennedy and Johnson years Defense Secretary Robert S. McNamara put the figure somewhat higher—400 big bombs, he said, would pulverize 76 percent of the Soviet industrial plant and kill 74 million of its people. We now have 12,000 strategic warheads—30 times the McNamara figure. Obviously we can give up quite a few and still have a strong deterrent position.

Why don't we? Militarists claim that our land-based Minutemen missiles are now vulnerable to land-based Soviet SS-18s. We need, it is said, some kind of nuclear mix that will always assure enough warheads for retaliation, even if the Russians strike first and destroy our land-based missiles. But that argument too is lame: We have more than 5,000 warheads on nuclear submarines that are invulnerable. The Russians do not have the technology, and won't have for a couple of decades, to track those submarines and destroy them. There are also the low-flying cruise missiles that are similarly difficult to track, as well as the Pershing II's and the missiles on aircraft carriers that can hit Russian soil so quickly (six to eight minutes) there can be no hope of immobilizing them.

DEEPER SOURCES OF DISAGREEMENT

There are other reasons why the arms negotiations are so complex and long-winded, specifically two basic subjects that never come up in the talks. One is the conflict on how the world should be organized—something that creates tensions even more formidable than those over armaments. In fact the latter is a coefficient of the former.

The problem traces back to the end of World War II. The U.S. had just won the greatest victory in its history, its gross national product had doubled, its economic plant now had twice the capacity of just a few years back—but no one knew where America would find buyers for its wares. The major nations of the world, including "winners" such as Britain, were prostrate, virtually broke. In this state of affairs Washington's leaders feared they would soon confront a depression like that of the 1930s, and unemployment of 20 or 25 percent—unless they refashioned the world in such a way that it would be able to buy U.S. products. The trick was turned by giving U.S. allies and would-be allies many billions in economic and military aid—in return for acceptance of the principle of free trade and acceptance of the dollar as the international medium of exchange. Since the U.S. plant was so much more efficient than any other it could undersell the rest of the world, if its customers did not construct barriers against trade such as high tariffs and quotas. The military aid was meant to keep in power those governments favorable to the American plan, even if they were dictatorships, as was very often the case, especially in the third world.

The U.S. plan worked, not only for the U.S. but for its allies. Worldwide recovery ensued. U.S. exports jumped from $3 billion a year before the war to $220 billion by 1980, investments from $11 billion in 1950 to $226 billion by 1983.

The Soviet Union was offered $6 to $9 billion in recovery loans to become part of the free-trade system, but it could not accept without giving up its socialist system or becoming a second-class power again. If Moscow were to remove restrictions on imports, American steel and other basic products would easily swamp the Soviet market and put Russian government industries out of business. Moscow rejected the U.S. offer and thus began the so-called Cold War. The U.S. initiated a big military buildup and took steps to isolate the Soviet Union economically—by imposing embargoes on vital goods, for instance. From 1945 to 1950 serious consideration was given not only to "containing" the Soviet Union but to a preventive war against it. The idea was dropped only because the U.S. did not have enough warheads to destroy the Soviet Union (as it conceded in a National Security Council document, NSC-68, written by Paul Nitze in 1950), whereas a Soviet Union under attack would overrun almost all of Western Europe in a few days with conventional arms. The Russians defended themselves in part by also producing atomic stockpiles, in part by supporting national and social revolutions in Europe and the third world. Though the Soviet Union had not been a revolutionary nation for decades, it operated on the age-old political thesis that "the enemy of my enemy is my friend."

It is this political reality of two superpowers with two divergent plans for organizing world affairs that inhibits the quest for disarmament. The U.S. fears that if it disarms, Moscow will give support to revolutions here, there, and everywhere, until American power crumbles and the American economy becomes a shambles of depression and unemployment. Moscow is afraid that if its military power weakens to the point where it cannot deter the U.S., it will be "Finlandized"—it will become a virtual satellite of Washington's, in the same way that Finland is a satellite of Moscow.

The irony is that both the U.S. and the Soviet Union are at a juncture in history where they must change their ways of life drastically or accept decline. The U.S. economy, though seemingly buoyant, is sick with massive national, corporate, and consumer debts, with a banking system weighted with hundreds of billions in third world debts that will never be paid, with smokestack industries that are rapidly dying, and a steady decline in living standards. To survive and prosper the U.S. will ultimately have to make peace with the revolution of rising expectations in the third world, and change over to a planned economy at home in order to avoid another disastrous depression.

Moscow too must make major changes in the near future—in the direction of a decentralized socialist system, like that of Yugoslavia, China, Hungary. Until the 1950s and 1960s the Soviets had a vast supply of redundant labor in the villages which they could bring to the cities to work in the factories and boost the gross national product. Now that supply is used up. Moscow must change from extensive use of labor to intensive use, from adding more workers to increasing technological efficiency, if it is to proceed further along the road of economic development. And to make this historical jump it must call on the initiative of its managers and workers, allow them more freedom both at the job site and in politics.

The obstacle to a quick reduction in arms, clearly, goes beyond the point of which weapons to scratch. It relates to the unwillingness of either side to make the social and economic changes dictated by history. Under the circumstances the best the negotiators in Geneva can do is regulate the arms race, not end it.

THE ROLE OF FORCE

The second big obstacle is a lack of machinery for resolving unresolved international disputes without violence. For 6,000 years the nation-state has operated in external relations in a manner exactly opposed to the way it operates in internal relations. Internal disputes are settled in an orderly manner. There is a system of law we must all abide by. There are courts to interpret those laws and resolve disputes. There are police to enforce the laws and judicial decisions. But in international relations there are no such mechanisms. The United Nations, it is true, listens to disputes, but has no police agency or courts with the power to resolve them. In the final analysis, when diplomacy fails, each nation-state must either retreat or go to war to enforce its will. There have been 140 such wars, with 20 to 50 million casualties, since the end of World War II.

Foreseeing the threat of future wars and the danger that they might escalate into a nuclear holocaust, men like Albert Einstein, Walter Lippmann, Bertrand Russell, Robert Maynard Hutchins proposed in the 1940s that the great powers establish a world government. The idea had considerable support but it did not take hold. Today it would be impossible to establish a world government in the quick-fix fashion that Einstein, for instance, proposed in 1945–46. It would take a long period—decades— and would have to begin with something like the "four Ps" program proposed by the late UN Secretary-General U Thant. U Thant suggested that the world establish four international agencies to prevent proliferation of nuclear weapons, eliminate pollution, reduce poverty, control population growth. Those agencies would have police powers to monitor and take action within any country in the world. Had the plan been accepted it would have been a major step toward inter-nationhood, and would have laid the groundwork for international agencies and police to interpose themselves between feuding nations to prevent their conflicts from erupting into war.

The negotiators at Geneva concern themselves with weapons systems; they do not dare come to grips with the nation-state system that undergirds the weapons race. They do not do so because neither of the superpowers has enough trust in the other to agree to a world court with the power to enforce its decisions through an international police force.

Clearly, disarmament is a more complex problem than imposing a freeze (welcome as that would be) or getting rid of a certain number of warheads. It calls, in addition, for solidarity with the revolution of rising expectations, for terminating all intervention such as is now taking place by indirect means in Nicaragua, for unqualified recognition of the right of self-determination—in Afghanistan as well as Nicaragua and El Salvador. It also requires that the nations and peoples of the world take the first steps to establish rudimentary machinery for resolving international disputes without resort to military force.

Questions

1. Why, in the author's view, have nuclear arms negotiations proven so difficult to complete? Do you agree or disagree? Why?
2. Which subjects cited by the author have never come up in arms control talks? How important do you consider them to be? Give your reasons.
3. Why does Lens think the two superpowers fear to disarm? Do you think the reasons given are valid? Why, or why not?
4. What major readjustments are the U.S. and the U.S.S.R. called upon to make in order to meet the needs of a changing world? Which country do you consider the more likely to change? Why?
5. Cite the arguments the author uses to call for world government? How persuasive do you find them?

7

Nuclear Terror: Moral Paradox

James Finn

This article originally appeared in *America*, February 19, 1983.

Another journalistic contribution to the debate on how best to achieve world peace comes from James Finn, editor of Freedom at Issue, *a publication of Freedom House in New York City. Approaching his subject from a philosophical point of view, Finn upholds the "just war" doctrine, which has its roots in the thought of Plato, Aristotle and Cicero, and in the writings of Augustine (430 A. D.) and Thomas Aquinas (1274). In brief, this teaching allows warfare only when such conditions as these have been met: (1) it must be waged by a public authority for the common good; (2) a just cause is required; (3) it must be fought with right intentions; (4) the harm done by war must not exceed the good that comes of it (proportionality).*

The author acknowledges that the war/peace question today is without precedent, with nuclear weapons capable of destroying entire nations. No country can reliably protect its citizens from external attack. Nuclear weapons serve a purpose, says Finn, only if they are not used. But, in the absence of a credible international authority capable of resolving disputes among nations, he argues that each nation-state must rely on its own intelligence and resources to prevent war.

While respectful of the other great Christian tradition—that of pacifism—Finn finds modern-day pacifists well-intentioned but supremely unhelpful in addressing the nuclear dilemma. After disposing of the pacifist approach, the author comes to grips with the paradox of deterrence. Traditional moral teaching insists that if it is immoral to perform an action (e.g., to use nuclear weapons), it is immoral to threaten to do so. In the nuclear age, states Finn, this reasoning is turned on its head. Nuclear deterrence, he points out, has so far prevented major conflicts between the superpowers. "We threaten to do what it would be immoral to execute," he says, "in order to deter the execution."

Finn has difficulties with unilateral nuclear disarmament, with a declared policy of "no first use" of nuclear weapons, and with an immediate and verifiable freeze. He rejects the first option on the grounds that unilateral disarmament would bring about the very holocaust that everyone fears. His problem with "no first use" rests on the frequently overlooked corollary that it would necessitate a massive buildup of NATO's conventional forces, an expensive and politically unpopular step. While he does not give his reasons for opposing a nuclear "freeze," it is clear from other comments that James Finn is convinced that the Soviet leaders, although neither irrational nor insane, simply cannot be trusted to honor international agreements. "With all their faults," he writes, "the democracies of NATO are morally superior to the Soviet Union, which is a tyranny and behaves as one."

A nuclear terror haunts our time. The phrase is that of John Paul II, but the perception is general. That perception lies behind many proposals about nuclear weapons that are being pressed upon us in the name of peace by various advocates. The awareness that nuclear weapons are capable of destroying much of the life on this earth is necessary if we are to respond adequately to the threat, but it is not sufficient.

Mere fear can paralyze or lead to spasmodic reactions. What we need is a steady, constant passion for peace, a passion that must pervade all our approaches to nuclear weapons. But as our Catholic tradition teaches, even this passion is not enough. We must bring our full intellectual resources to bear if we are even to begin to cope with the political and moral issues that are intertwined with nuclear weapons.

There is within Catholicism a tradition of uncompromising pacifism, a witness to transcendent values, a determination to "do right though the heavens fall." I am prepared to believe that in the fullness of time this may prove to have been the better position. It is not, however, my position. It provides no practical assistance to those whose task it is to guard the security of the United States and its allies. It is not the prevailing tradition within the Catholic Church. That tradition is the philosophical realism associated with Augustine, Aquinas, the scholastics and recent papal and conciliar teaching. In common with pacifism, its presumption is always against the taking of life. In contrast to pacifism, it states that under certain conditions, which are defined in terms of responsibility and consequences, that presumption can be overridden where war is justifiable and may be a moral requirement.

This tradition of Catholic realism insists that reason and intelligence must inform our moral judgments. Furthermore, it is a mark of Catholic realism to start our deliberations from where we are, not from some fanciful present we would have preferred or from a future goal we wish to attain. Among the pertinent characteristics of our present nuclear situation the following are central:

1. Our present situation is unprecedented. There are nuclear weapons that can destroy us, other countries, much of the world.

2. Unlike other weapons, these best serve their purpose by not being used in war-fighting. They are intended to serve, and for over three decades have served, as deterrents. A large-scale use of these weapons in war would destroy what they are intended to protect.

3. The development of these weapons has deprived even the most powerful of the nation-states of one of the purposes for which they are established. They can no longer guarantee the protection of their citizens from external attack.

4. We can never revert to a nonnuclear situation. The world will never again be free of nuclear weapons or the knowledge of how to construct them. The nuclear genie cannot be forced or enticed back into its jar.

5. Since there is no international authority capable of resolving conflicts between the great powers, the outcome of such conflicts is left to those powers. Today these powers threaten each other with nuclear weapons.

6. There is no completely satisfactory resolution to this situation, in political, military or moral terms. One must currently choose between the unsatisfactory and the still more unsatisfactory. Anyone who thinks otherwise has not grasped the strange and desperate quality of our situation.

Those of us who participate in the current debate should acknowledge that, in spite of changing military technology and shifting United States-Soviet relations, we have lived under these conditions for more than three decades. And for three decades individuals and groups have reacted with varying degrees of fear, sensible concern, idealism, anger, despair and willed blindness. For example, even before the Soviets had developed their atomic weapons, Bertrand Russell was repelled by the vision of an atomic exchange between the two superpowers. He therefore advocated a pre-emptive strike at Soviet atomic facilities. Moved by the same vision after the Soviets developed atomic weapons, he advocated unilateral nuclear disarmament by the United States. Thus one thinker's apolitical, immoral and ineffective "solution."

In the 1950's, Robert Hutchins and a number of his followers concluded that all future wars—certainly those in which a superpower was involved—would be morally unjustified. Typically, the complex reasoning was encapsulated in a syllogism: All future wars will be atomic wars; all atomic wars will be total (unjustifiable) wars; therefore, all future wars will be unjustifiable.

Since then the world has seen about 40 conflicts that deserve to be labeled wars, in which approximately 10 million people have been killed.

Some have involved the United States and/or the Soviet Union; in none have nuclear weapons been used in the fighting.

Some time later the novelist C. P. Snow, invoking his expertise as a scientist, said that unless we managed to limit and reduce the world's nuclear forces there would be, by a date which he gave, a nuclear conflict. He stressed that he did not offer this prediction as an opinion or a matter of high probability but as a fact subject to scientific proof. The date he offered has come and gone.

The most recent addition to this distinguished list—to which other notables could be added—is Jonathan Schell. His work, so admirable in its intentions, so deleterious in its consequences, has the same magnificent sweep. After conscientiously and meticulously laying out the ghastly results of nuclear war, he retreats from the scene with the sibylline admonition that if we wish to avoid those results we must change our politics. About the first step to take he does not presume to tell us.

I recall these different positions not to mock the people who took them nor to marvel that highly intelligent people can be misguided and unhelpful, but to note that the Catholic tradition of realism leads to none of these positions. That tradition would reject the pre-emptive strike recommended by Mr. Russell, the abstract rationalism of Mr. Hutchins, the predictive certainty of Mr. Snow, the apolitical and apocalyptic admonitions of Mr. Schell. These and equally unhelpful approaches to modern weapons still flourish in our society, some within the Catholic community. Nevertheless, moderate realism dictates another path.

To see where that path leads we must first grasp fully the paradox of our deterrent system under which we have lived for three decades. We have built weapons of vast destructive power in order not to use them. Their utility lies in the threat they convey. They will have successfully served their purpose when they are dismantled. Any large-scale use of these weapons would be a massive failure in military, political and moral terms. It would be an unprecedented disaster.

The paradox inherent in these weapons extends to other aspects of military strategy, civilian defense and our ways of thinking about them. For example, the A.B.M. (anti-ballistic missile), which is purely defensive and ought therefore to be an attractive and safe measure to employ, is frequently rejected as destabilizing and dangerous because it could be read as preparation for actual war-fighting. Weapons aimed at cities are judged to be stabilizing since they reduce the incentive of an adversary to strike first.

This paradox invades the moral realm as well. Traditional teaching advised us that what it would be immoral to do, it is also immoral to threaten to do. The security of that reasoning crumbles when it is applied to nuclear weapons. We threaten to do what it would be immoral to execute—in order to deter the execution. In terms of proportionality—a traditional moral criterion—we must ask whether the threat is disproportionate to the evil it deters. High among actions it is intended to deter, and so far has, is war between the superpowers and political capitulation by the United States and its allies.

We can apprehend this paradox by reflecting on this question: Would you rather reduce the levels of nuclear arms or reduce the chance of nuclear war? Of course, we would rather do both. But those of us who immediately moved to that answer should realize that we have already asserted that what we want is stability and safety, not simply the reduction of weapons. To make this clearer we can break this question down further. For example, if a particular reduction of nuclear weapons was destabilizing and increased the chances of war, would you favor it? If a particular increase or development in nuclear weapons enhanced that stability and reduced the chances of war would you oppose it? And with what moral justification?

We should ask such questions when we consider the principal options that are now being presented for our consideration: 1) unilateral nuclear disarmament, 2) a declared policy of no first use of nuclear weapons and 3) an immediate and verifiable freeze.

An explicit policy of unilateral nuclear disarmament would not compel much attention among Catholics if a number of Catholic bishops had not publicly espoused it. One bishop has said that one obvious meaning of the cross is unilateral disarmament; another that unilateral disarmament is not wrong simply because other nations would not follow our example; a third prayed that we could look in each other's faces and see that there are no enemies. The faith that leads to such positions must be formidable since these positions are unsupported by reason and contradicted by history. Unilateral nuclear disarmament would radically change the balance, upset the stability of the deterrent system. It would engender greater fear and increase the risk of conflict in both the long and the short run. The moderate realism of traditional Catholicism would reject it on both political and moral grounds. Pope John Paul II reiterated this in his New Year's homily of 1983. It is difficult, he said, "to imagine how the problem of peace in the world can be resolved in a unilateral manner, without the participation and concrete commitment of all."

The other two options merit extended reflection and analysis. I will, however, focus on the no-first-use proposal to illustrate the way in which a moderate realism would address each of these issues. The no-first-use proposal is practically self-defining: The nuclear powers pledge not to be the first to use nuclear weapons. The simplicity of this proposal is its strength. If every nuclear power made this pledge and lived up to it, they would never engage in nuclear war. This long-standing proposal received renewed attention when a quartet of influential Americans (McGeorge Bundy, George F. Kennan, Robert McNamara and Gerard Smith) raised it in Foreign Affairs. The goal that powers the proposal is wholly admirable. The questions, however, are whether a declared no-first-use policy would enhance or diminish the overall prospects for peace, and whether it would establish a barrier, a firebreak, between conventional war and nuclear war.

Since the Eisenhower Presidency, NATO policy has been the deterrence of Soviet military aggression by a combination of conventional and nuclear defense, partly because nuclear weapons are both more destructive and much less expensive than conventional weapons. For over 35 years, Eastern Europe has been dominated by the Soviets through the threat and actual use of military force. The Soviets have recently reinforced and modernized not only their nuclear but their conventional forces. We have no reason to trust that NATO's present conventional forces—without nuclear backing—are sufficient to deter Soviet forces. In a passage generally overlooked, the American quartet said that while they believed "it is time to move decisively toward a policy of no-first-use, it is obvious that any such policy would require a strengthened confidence in the adequacy of the conventional forces of the Alliance. . . . "

To bring about "the adequacy" of conventional forces, NATO powers would have to increase present military expenditures by 4 percent or more per year, or approximately $10.64 billion a year. Are NATO powers prepared to make these expenditures? After stating the need to strengthen confidence in conventional forces if a no-first-use policy were to be adopted, the American quartet assumed an agnostic position on whether the Western powers had "the necessary political will" to do so. Are those who favor a no-first-use policy prepared to scuttle the present NATO strategy of flexible response and then to summon up the necessary political will to support more expenditures as the best political and moral alternatives?

But perhaps the danger of initiating nuclear warfare is so great that we should adopt the no-first use policy in any case. After all, other countries including the Soviet Union have done so. While no one can predict with certitude what the reactions of the Soviets or our allies would be if the United States unilaterally adopted that policy, a real possibility is that allied confidence in collective defense would be weakened, Western Europe would be more exposed to Soviet pressure, and the Soviets could be tempted to push and probe and test the Western willingness to resist from a position of conventional military inferiority. The danger and possibility of conventional warfare would certainly increase. And, no matter what they had previously declared, would NATO forces—or the Soviets—refrain from using tactical nuclear weapons if they seemed to be facing defeat?

The conclusion should be clear. The initiation of conventional war between the superpowers is as much to be feared as the initiation of nuclear war, not only because it would itself be so destructive but because it could so readily escalate to nuclear levels. A policy of no-use of either conventional or nuclear weapons by either side based on credible deterrence and self-interest is preferable to a policy of no-first-use of nuclear weapons based on unwarranted trust. Not surprisingly, early criticisms of the American quartet came from West German leaders, some of whose expressed reservations I have borrowed.

A complete examination of the no-first-use proposal would have to address questions of weapons and troop deployment, comparative advantages and disadvantages of geography, anticipated loyalties of troops and a number of other questions. However, the results would probably not modify significantly the responses people now give to the question of whether a no-first-use would weaken our deterrence and, therefore, lower the barriers to military conflict.

Even if this examination were dutifully carried out, there would be another major issue to which common sense and moderate realism would direct us. We are not, after all, discussing weapons in isolation from political reality. The major military threat to the United States, Western democracies and other countries comes from the Soviet Union, which also possesses immense military forces. It is a profound mistake—but not uncommon—to discuss nuclear weapons as if the rough military symmetry between the superpowers were matched by a moral symmetry. Such is not the case. With all their faults, the democracies of NATO are morally superior to the Soviet Union, which is a tyranny and behaves as one. This does not mean that Soviet policy is directed by irrational leaders striving insanely for world conquest at any cost. The present events in Eastern Europe and Afghanistan confirm that the Soviet Union is brutal and expansionist. But Soviet leaders have been prudent in dealing with events that might lead to military conflict with NATO forces. It should be the purpose of U.S. strategy to reinforce, not weaken, prudential decisions of the Soviets based on respect for the retaliatory might of the United States. It is not evident that a no-first-use policy would do so; there are sound reasons to judge otherwise.

I recognize that the general principles I have followed do not lead inevitably to my particular conclusions. Between the general principles and the specific conclusions one makes on these grave issues, there are a large number of contingent judgments to be made. Different people will, we may be sure, make different judgments. There is no single person or group of persons—in the Catholic Church or in Government—who can assert that they have arrived at political and moral conclusions to which all other people must defer. On these issues we live, and will continue to live, in a condition of pluralism. That is, on these issues American Catholics like other Americans can and do arrive at differing military, political and moral positions. Furthermore, they do so with differing degrees of authority and responsibility for these judgments.

But those of us who reject as faulty, under present conditions, proposals for unilateral disarmament, no-first-use and an immediate freeze cannot rest satisfied with present conditions. Advances in military technology make the future appear more, not less dangerous. Every rational person must have no-use of nuclear weapons as a high and constant goal. The problem is how to inch back off the nuclear branch. Every proposal must meet severe tests.

In the long run, we know what we need. It has been a theme running through papal statements for decades. Phrased in a different way, it is a world community, freely formed, with the authority and structures capable of keeping the world free, not of conflict, but of war. We are not close to such a community now. Until we are, we must work for what is possible, foregoing the heady pleasure of calling loudly for what is ultimately desirable while dismissing small gains. The results of the strategic arms limitations talks (SALT), to which the present Administration has given support, represent such an achievement. These gains can be built on through continuing negotiations. They will not be if, overlooking the paradoxical nature of nuclear deterrence, we condemn as immoral the threat which is necessary to its credibility and substitute good intentions for likely consequences.

But I would end my statement as I began it, with the words of John Paul II: "War is the most barbarous and least effective way of resolving conflict. More than ever before, human society is forced to provide itself with the means of consultation and dialogue which it needs in order to survive, and therefore with the institutions necessary for building up justice and peace."

Questions

1. Does Finn do justice to the pacifist tradition? What other arguments could be used to bolster the pacifist position?

2. What is the "paradox of deterrence"? Do you accept the author's contention that there is a proportional relationship between the deployment of nuclear weapons and the evil they seek to deter? State your reasons.

3. Do you find Finn's critique of unilateral nuclear disarmament convincing? What if one of the superpowers took a unilateral first step toward reduction? Would this be likely to make a difference in your response? Why, or why not?

4. Does the reliance on conventional weapons implicit in the "no first use" proposal make it impractical, as the author asserts? Apart from tactical questions, do you think that "no first use" might have a psychological effect on one's adversary?

5. The author warns against dismissing small gains toward disarmament as unimportant. Can you think of any small gains that have been taken recently? Can you suggest others that might be taken?

8

Are You a Conscientious Objector?

Pamphlet, Central Committee for Conscientious Objection, April 1986

With brevity and directness, the authors of this pamphlet ask the young of draft age the question: "Could you kill another person?" Even an uncertain answer, in their view, leaves the door open. Following the prescriptions of draft law and military law, conscientious objection is defined as opposition to "participation in war in any form." Such an attitude does not preclude acceptance of some forms of force, such as that used in law enforcement.

The article describes the two types of conscientious objectors (C.O.'s) recognized by the U.S. government: those whose conscience forbids them from serving in any way, and those who "can be part of the military as long as they're not required to kill." Those in the first category are obliged to do civilian work for the duration of a war. Everyone of draft age, C.O. or not, is bound by law to register for the draft.

Selective conscientious objection—opposition to some wars but not to all—is not recognized by law. Nevertheless, the authors urge selective objectors to apply for C.O. status. They reason that the law may change and state that it helps to have one's reasons on record.

In regard to religious affiliation, say the authors, "The law makes no distinction among religious, moral, and ethical beliefs."

This article provides a helpful summary for those liable to draft registration. It spells out the conditions for C.O. status, the penalties for noncompliance and the importance of getting one's convictions on record at the earliest possible date.

Do you think you'd be willing to fight in a war? Could you kill another person? If you aren't certain, you may be a conscientious objector (CO). A conscientious objector is a man or woman who believes war is wrong and can't be part of it.

To qualify for CO status under draft or military law, you must object to "participation in war in any form" because of your religious or moral beliefs. You don't have to be a member of any special religion—or any religion at all. You don't need to be against all force or violence. The law doesn't even require you to be against all killing. You only need to object to war.

TWO TYPES OF CONSCIENTIOUS OBJECTORS

Many people cannot serve in the military in any way because for them all military jobs support war. Others find that they can be part of the military as long as they're not required to kill.

The law recognizes both kinds of COs. If you're against all military duty but are willing to do civilian work instead, you can be classified 1-O. If you object to war but are willing to serve as a soldier without using weapons (noncombatant duty), you can be classified 1-A-O.

There's no provision for those who oppose both military and civilian duty. And it's against the law to refuse to register for the draft.

SELECTIVE OBJECTION

To be a CO under current law, you must be against "war in any form"—meaning all wars which you might be asked to face. If you think you might fight in some wars but not in others, try to be clear about just when you would fight. What makes some wars right and others wrong? Do you think any modern war can meet your standards?

If you find it hard to believe that any war in today's world could be right, you may be opposed to "war in any form," because you are opposed to every war that could really happen. Some COs, for example, base their claims on the Christian "just war theory," which says a war must meet certain moral standards in order to be right. They believe no modern war can meet the just war standards—even though past wars might have met them—because today's weapons would kill too many innocent people.

Some COs would fight in a spiritual war between the powers of good and evil. This is not a "war" under the law. As long as you wouldn't fight in a "flesh and blood war," you can qualify as a CO.

After you've thought about it, you may find that you're opposed to some wars but not to others. This means you probably don't qualify for CO status. You are a "selective conscientious objector." "Selective objectors" believe that sometimes it is necessary and right to take part in war, although they may be strongly opposed to a particular war.

A selective objector can still apply for CO status—and you should do so. Draft or military authorities may decide that you qualify even though you thought you didn't. The law may change. And if you're prosecuted—

for refusing to register, refusing orders, or other offenses—having your views on record can show that there was a moral reason for your actions.

CONSCIENTIOUS OBJECTION AND RELIGIOUS BELIEF

If you're not a member of a church or synagogue, or if you don't think your beliefs are religious, you can still be a CO. According to the Supreme Court, you need to have a sincere and meaningful belief that occupies a place in your life like that of a more traditional religion. The law makes no distinctions among religious, moral, and ethical beliefs.

COs came from over 230 denominations during World War II. The law has long recognized COs who belong to no religious body. Practically all religious groups—including Protestant, Catholic, Jewish, and many others—recognize and support conscientious objectors.

CONSCIENTIOUS OBJECTION IN THE MILITARY

If you join the military, the recruiter won't tell you anything about conscientious objection. You'll only hear promises of travel, education, skills training, and interesting jobs. But once you're in you will find that you're being trained to kill. And you may start wondering whether you should really be a soldier.

If your conscience won't let you stay in the military, it's still not too late. You can be honorably discharged or transferred to noncombatant duty as a conscientious objector. Many people have. CCCO can send you more information about applying for CO status. And we can put you in touch with a civilian counselor who can help you with your application.

DRAFT REGISTRATION

In July, 1980, President Carter ordered men to register for the draft for the first time since 1975. Today the law requires you to register within thirty days before or twenty-nine days after your 18th birthday.

Some men believe that draft registration is wrong. For them, registering for the draft means supporting a system that is part of war. They can't do this. They are conscientious objectors to registration. If you agree and can't register, the law makes no provision for you.

You can't make a formal CO claim when you register for the draft. But you can get your stand on record. If you decide to register, you can write a brief claim on the registration card, make a copy of the card, and keep the copy for your records. Selective Service won't acknowledge your claim or do anything with it, but the fact that you tried to make it may help if you are called under a future draft.

You can also register with CCCO using our Conscientious Objector Card. This isn't an official CO claim, but in a future draft, it will show that your beliefs aren't something new. Filling out a CO card is also a good idea if you decide not to register for the draft. When you register with CCCO, you will receive information on changes in draft law and other issues which you might find helpful.

If you decide not to register, you could face legal charges. The punishment for breaking the draft law is up to five years in prison and up to $250,000 fine. But few non-registrants receive these maximum penalties. From 1980 through 1985, out of over one million men who failed to register, only 20 were charged. As of February, 1986, fourteen had been convicted. None of these received the maximum punishment.

Before you decide whether to register for the draft, try to get counseling so you can be sure you know your choices and what they might lead to. CCCO can help you find a draft counselor. And we can send you information on draft resistance.

CONSCIENTIOUS OBJECTION UNDER THE DRAFT

Draft calls can't begin again without an act of Congress. But the rest of the draft law remains on the books. So do Selective Service regulations which tell how the draft system might process your CO claim or other claim for deferment or exemption.

As the draft now stands, you can't make any claims until you've been sent an induction order. You'd then have ten days from the issue date of the order to file your claims. In practice, this would mean you might have as few as five or six days to act.

That isn't much time. So it's best for you to decide now what you're going to do. CCCO can give you more information on the draft, conscientious objector status, draft resistance, and other deferments and exemptions. Write for our literature list. And we can refer you to a draft counselor near you so you can talk about your choices and your beliefs.

Questions

1. How does the present law distinguish the types of C.O.'s? Do you fit into either category? Briefly explain your reasons.

2. Does the fact that you do not belong to a church or synagogue disqualify you from C.O. status? What is the basis for your reply?

3. Does a person already in the military have any recourse regarding C.O. status? Explain the possible consequences.

4. What advice do the authors have for those whose consciences do not permit them to register for the draft?

5. What are the chances of prosecution for those who do not register? Does this strike you as a sufficient reason for avoiding registration? Explain.

9

Military Service:
A Moral Obligation

Donald Kagan

This article originally appeared in *The New York Times*, December 4, 1983.

Do those who refuse military service answer the call of conscience against the overwhelming power of the state? Or are they deficient in their moral obligations as citizens? Donald Kagan, professor of history at Yale University, argues that—whatever their high motives—conscientious objectors and pacifists hold views that threaten all governments, especially democracies.

New Haven, Conn.—The killing of 239 servicemen in Lebanon and the invasion of Grenada have reminded Americans of the military's role in pursuit of the nation's purposes and once again have raised the question of the citizen's obligation to do military service when called upon. This question still is before us because of continuing controversy over a law requiring students seeking Federal aid to register for the draft.

It would seem obvious that in a world of independent and sovereign states that come into conflict and threaten one another's vital interests— sometimes even existence itself—citizens who choose to remain in a particular country are morally obliged to serve in its armed forces when the need arises.

Critics of this view appeal to a higher morality in which an individual may refuse to serve if such service violates his conscience. Some assert the right, even the duty, to refuse service when they do not approve of the national policy that leads to the need for military action, even though they do not oppose serving when they approve the cause. To accept such a claim would be to destroy all governments but especially democracies, which rely on the willingness of their citizens to accept the decisions that duly elected and appointed bodies and officials arrive at, even if they are wrong.

That is not to say that citizens are morally obliged to accept the decisions of any country in which they live, no matter how wicked and despotic—only in legitimate ones. My definition of a legitimate state is one that permits the open advocacy of different opinions, the possibility of changing the laws by peaceful means and, most important, emigration without penalty. A regime that fails to meet these criteria imposes its will by force alone and has no moral claim on the obedience of its subjects.

On the other hand, a nation that meets them has every claim to its citizens' allegiance and especially to the service most vital to its existence. When a citizen has become an adult and has not chosen to leave the country, he tacitly approves of its legitimacy and consents to its laws. He benefits from their protection and has the moral obligation to obey them if he wants to stay. To enjoy the enormous advantages provided by a free society while claiming the right to ignore or disobey the laws selectively, especially those essential to its survival and most demanding of its citizens, is plainly immoral.

Some recusants are pacifists who refuse to fight regardless of the occasion. Their position, though it lacks the absurdity of claiming the right of each citizen to conduct his own foreign policy, is also deficient. Leaving the country would not solve their problem, since wherever they go they will find a state that will be prepared to use force in the national interest when necessary and will ask its citizens to do military service. One solution has been to refuse to serve and accept the legal penalty without complaint. Another has been to accept auxiliary service, such as in the medical corps, which, though dangerous, does not require killing. These responses prove sincerity and courage but they do not satisfy the moral demands of citizenship. Pacifists in this imperfect world can pursue their beliefs only in free societies and only because their fellow citizens are willing to fight and protect them. There were no protected pacifists in Hitler's Germany and Stalin's Russia; there are none in Yuri V. Andropov's.

Pacifists are not alone in hating the need to kill. Most American soldiers find it impossible to pull the trigger in their first combat experience and find it profoundly painful even later. Yet they do their duty, though there is no way to know if they dislike killing any less than those refusing to fight. A decent, free society is right to allow concern for personal conscience a place in its considerations and to afford special treatment to those who refuse to fight on plausible grounds of conscience. But those who accept such treatment must realize that they are getting a free ride and failing in their moral responsibility as citizens.

Questions

1. How does Kagan justify the government's practice of the draft and draft registration?
2. What is his definition of a legitimate state?

3. Do you agree that selective obedience to law is immoral? Why, or why not?

4. What are the alternatives to military service in this country?

5. Do you agree that conscientious objectors are getting a "free ride"? Why, or why not?

10
ROTC Today and Tomorrow

Col. Robert F. Collins

This article originally appeared in *Military Review*, May 1986.

A spirited defense of the Reserve Officer Training Corps (ROTC) is offered by an Army colonel involved in campus recruitment. He decries the low priority given to these programs by senior army leadership, especially in view of the fact that three-quarters of all officers enter the Army by this route.

Far from contributing to the "militarization of America," Collins regards ROTC programs as the best guarantee that the services will not be run by "a highly specialized, rigid, elitist group of mercenaries." He sees ROTC officers, drawn from a representative portion of American society, as a contribution to the ideal of "citizen soldiers."

The author argues for more funding for ROTC and for promotion of its graduates on an equal level with those who graduate from the military academies. His concluding argument draws on the experience of Vietnam, when the American people did not support what the military was doing. To ensure popular support for future conflicts, he feels that ROTC, as a civilian-based program, will play a critical role. The program, as Col. Collins pictures it, is "the presence of the university in the military," rather than vice versa.

The Reserve Officers' Training Corps (ROTC) is the lifeblood of the Army officer corps. It is critical to the nation's security, but the senior Army leadership today does not appear to properly value the contribution ROTC makes to the Army's mission.

Currently, ROTC commissions approximately 75 percent of all officers entering the Army—an incredible statistic. Three out of every four new lieutenants entering the Army are products of this program. Last year, approximately 8,300 college graduates were commissioned from ROTC programs offered at more than 1,400 colleges and universities throughout the nation.

But, public support of ROTC is not a given, nor is continued high enrollment in the program guaranteed. ROTC has received increased interest by the news media. Most of the articles are factual, objective and balanced, but there are also opinions questioning the presence of ROTC in civilian universities.

For various reasons, the authors challenge the need for a strong military, the "militarization" of American society, the military-industrial complex, the nuclear arms race, terrorism, Department of Defense contracting abuses, mounting deficits, and so forth. They somehow relate these issues to ROTC or, more generally, to the Army or the current administration. In my view, not only is the US military one of the brighter components of our democratic success story, but ROTC is one of the strengths of our democratic form of government.

Laying aside arguments on the size of the military, percentage of the gross national product for defense, minimalist versus maximalist theories of deterrence, and so forth, the bottom line is—whom do we want to lead our Army? Do we prefer a highly specialized, rigid, elitist group of mercenaries schooled only in military tactics who will react unquestioningly and unthinkingly to all orders no matter what they might be? Or do we prefer to entrust the leadership of our young men and women to well-educated, idealistic, questioning and responsible college graduates representative of all sectors of society?

Do we not prefer a citizen-soldier-led Army with a small professional career group of officers providing guidance and direction to those citizen-soldiers? Do we not want our military to be strengthened by the constant infusion of bright young men and women who serve a limited time on active duty and then return to the civilian community with a better understanding of this nation's security needs? Both common sense and history tell us that the larger interests of a free society are best served by military officers who are drawn from the society they serve, share its values, are broadly representative of the best that is in us, reflect the richness of our diverse origins and are committed to the great and common purposes of our nation.*

The vast majority of the people commissioned by ROTC will not make the Army a career, but they will serve their country honorably on active duty for a short period and then return to civilian life. They bring new ideas, new perspectives and a productive vitality to our Armed Forces. They return to civilian life, perhaps to continue to serve in the Reserve

---

*Dewitt C. Smith Jr., "To Protect a Free Society: Maintaining Excellence in the Military." *Educational Record*, Winter 1985. Lieutenant General Smith is rightly regarded as one of the nation's leading soldier-statesmen. He has been a most eloquent military spokesman on the importance of the Reserve Officers' Training Corps (ROTC). My views on ROTC have been strongly influenced by Smith's writings and conversations with him about ROTC.

components, having gained leadership experience, managerial skills, a sense of responsibility and service, and tremendous self-confidence. This pool of leadership will serve our country well in the event of a national emergency. Who else can better defend the country?

ROTC is vital to our security in another way. Effective military leaders, supported by both the troops and the public, are absolutely essential if the United States is to prevail in any future conflict. For a variety of reasons, the American public, historically and today, views the military with skepticism, mistrust and sometimes open hostility. Officers operating in this environment are called upon to understand and support the liberal values and traditions of society while nurturing and safeguarding the controls established in the US Constitution.

US officers undeniably must be different from those in other societies in outlook, commitment, perspective, responsibility, obligation and approach. Here is the main strength of ROTC—it prepares officers who are varied in perspective and representative of our entire society. No other system for selecting the majority of our military leaders can work as well as ROTC. Actions associated with the Total Army concept—Active Army, Army National Guard and US Army Reserve—strengthen the importance of ROTC's role in promoting our national security. ROTC is providing the officers to fill the previously unmanned spaces in the total force structure.

In spite of its importance to national security, the contributions of ROTC are largely unappreciated by the senior Army leadership and, consequently, the Army at large. Admittedly, my perceptions may be biased because of my close association with ROTC as a professor of military science. However, I spent 23 years in the Army listening to disparaging remarks about ROTC before becoming involved in the program. The senior Army leadership provides neither requisite funding for the contributions provided by the program nor the necessary leadership emphasis to the program to attract qualified officers to seek ROTC assignments. Regardless, the Army has received excellent returns from the ROTC program, and it seems that it will try to obtain these returns "on the cheap" in the future. What job in the Army in peacetime is more important than training its future leaders?

The prevailing perception in the Army today is that an ROTC assignment is a necessary evil that is to be avoided if one wants to advance one's career. This perception is not going to change until two events occur—the senior Army leadership provides more support to the program through increased funding and active promotion of the importance of ROTC, and promotions, assignments, schooling, and so forth show that ROTC assignments make those officers competitive with their peers.

Indications are that ROTC assignments are not highly regarded by promotion boards, nor are the Army's best officers encouraged to seek ROTC jobs. Current policies that do not portray these assignments in a positive manner are extremely shortsighted. The relative "good times" that the program now enjoys will not last as both public opinion and demographics will work against sustaining ROTC enrollments in the future. Unfortunately, the wide appeal of the glitz and glitter of technology has obscured once again the basic truth that the real strength of the US Army is its people. We have to put forth our best efforts to identify, motivate and mold the future leaders of the Army—that is what ROTC does.

ROTC has been a successful program, and it represents something uniquely American. We should encourage our bright, dedicated young men and women to participate in the program. We bear the responsibility of providing the best possible preparation for our future leaders. The strength of our nation and our democratic system is due, in large measure, to our differing origins and perspectives that promote individual worth and dignity ahead of subservience to the government. ROTC serves as a guarantor that our form of government will endure.

We should have learned many lessons from Vietnam, but perhaps the most important lesson is the fact that the US Army is a people's Army. If the American people do not support what the Army is doing, then the effort is futile and invariably will result in failure. It is arguable as to how best to obtain the people's support over the long term, but it is certain that support will not be given if the people cannot identify with their soldiers. That is why ROTC is critical. It provides leaders from the society the Army serves—that is, ROTC creates a people's Army.

In an oft-quoted remark, "ROTC is not the presence of the military in the university, but rather the presence of the university in the military." All of us in the military, particularly the senior Army leadership, have a vital stake in promoting ROTC. ROTC provides the balance and perspective needed in the US military. It helps prepare us for the future. Our world is not so much inherited from our ancestors as on loan from our children.

Questions

1. What are some of the reasons for questioning the presence of the ROTC on college campuses? Some people associate the ROTC with their concerns about government defense policies, Pentagon cost overruns and other complaints against the current administration. Do you think this is fair? Why, or why not?

2. Do you think the ROTC represents the presence of the military in the university or the presence of citizens in the military? How do they affect each other?

3. Besides making up for "unmanned spaces" in the officer corps, what other benefits does the author attribute to the ROTC? Do you agree?

4. What changes does Collins call for in the army's attitude toward the ROTC?

5. After reading this article, do you consider the ROTC a bulwark against U.S. militarism or an adjunct to it? Why?

11
Investigating New Options in Conflict and Defense

Gene Sharp

This article originally appeared in *Teachers College Record*, Fall 1982.

Gene Sharp of Southeastern Massachusetts University and the Center for International Affairs, Harvard University, is a man of one idea. This implies no criticism, inasmuch as his idea is a very good one. For more than fifteen years, he has publicized the crucial role that civilian populations can play in resisting organized tyranny. His 1970 book, Exploring Nonviolent Alternatives, *was a ground-breaking venture. In this article, the author gives some indication of how much needs to be learned on a subject in which he is an expert.*

Sharp designates four realities as the major signs of political violence in our times: dictatorship, genocide, war and systematic oppression of peoples. Though differing, what they have in common, he says, is (1) the large scale use of political violence by a small group of people, and (2) a sense of powerlessness felt by the majority of the population. He criticizes as ineffective the use of counter-violence in the face of these evils, but admits the need for some kind of sanctions. (By sanctions, the author means the application of punishment or reprisals for failure to behave in a desired manner.)

In the international arena, he says, such non-violent sanctions already exist, in the form of diplomatic and economic boycotts and similar activities. He finds the same to be true on the domestic scene, where activist groups have waged successful campaigns for redress of grievances through strikes, boycotts and various forms of non-cooperation.

Although non-violent sanctions are nothing new, Sharp seeks to expand their scope to gradually replace the resort to force, which has so often failed. A pragmatist, he also wants to know why non-violent actions have not succeeded. For answers to these questions he calls for greater research and education. In regard to research and policy studies on non-violent resistance (which he distinguishes from most current curricula on peace studies), Sharp warns against accepting either military or pacifist assumptions. Until more is known about what makes non-violent resistance "tick," the author feels that most people will not embrace them as alternatives to violent sanctions; i.e., war.

Turning to education, Sharp states the need for more widespread public awareness of "civilian struggle and non-violent forms of action so that people come to understand what it really is, instead of the misconceptions which are common." He faults many contemporary forms of "peace studies" for focusing almost exclusively on "the evils of war and the merits of conciliation, arbitration, compromise, and social change, while largely neglecting nonviolent struggle." Under the rubric of education, the author includes all forms of mass media, every level of formal education and informal study groups. He urges that such educational efforts should be unbiased, aiming to provide knowledge and to promote fair evaluation, and not to indoctrinate people to accept a particular view of policy.

Sharp foresees great opportunities in the study and practice of popular non-violent resistance as a means of overcoming the effects of dictatorship, genocide, war and social oppression. Expensive as such research and education might be, it should be borne in mind that in the first forty years of the universally acclaimed Fulbright Exchange Program, 156,000 people have been educated, in the words of Sen. Fulbright, "at a cost that wouldn't buy half a submarine."

UNSOLVED PROBLEMS

Severe dangers still face humanity. Efforts to improve the human condition have often failed. Specifically, we must face the fact that we have failed to solve the four problems of dictatorship, genocide, war, and systems of social oppression. Strong forces work to create a world very different from that which most people want.

In our century we have seen the development of the most extreme forms of dictatorship, including the Nazi and Stalinist varieties. We have seen the rise of modern war with the most destructive forms of weaponry yet to be developed. We have experienced a widespread sense of personal and political powerlessness. We have seen the efforts of social reformers to achieve justice produce very limited results, or even disaster, as they created societies which were (as in Russia) more tyrannical than the old ones. We have seen genocide, which had happened before, conducted massively by a supposedly civilized country. We have seen terror used both to maintain systems and to change them. We have observed and experienced increasing attacks and restrictions on anything that approximates freedom.

Many attempts based upon established political assumptions and policies to solve these problems have been made. Nevertheless, we have not moved significantly toward their resolution. The future prospects in these areas can give us little comfort. The dangers are likely to continue to increase in the coming years. What is happening to the technological capacity of modern weaponry is scarcely imaginable. Future dictators will have far greater means at their disposal for controlling human societies and individuals than did Hitler and Stalin, for example. The technical capacity to kill off people en masse is even now much more developed than the means that Hitler's henchmen had.[1]

These problems have become even more serious as the institutionalized and technical capacities for such violence and controls have increased. Yet the means at the disposal of governments to wield violence and to dominate continue to be developed to an extreme degree. As the perception that improvements are possible recedes, individuals and whole societies increasingly see such problems as insoluble and perceive themselves as powerless to shape their futures. Their resulting inaction passes as apathy.

These problems are, however, human problems, created and continued by human beings. Therefore it is within our capacities to reverse direction and to solve them. New thought, greater knowledge, and increased understanding about such problems are needed to help us develop policies and chart a course of action to change this situation.

SEEKING SOLUTIONS

Our task is at least two-fold: first, to find out what is the nature of those problems and what may be required to face all of them collectively (because they may mutually reinforce each other), and then, to learn what are the steps to chart a strategy for change in the face of these four problems. The development of strategies for change for the coming decades will be determined by our view of the basic causes of those problems and therefore what is required to correct them. There are, of course, other grave problems—including those of environment, water, food, population, and destruction of nonliterate cultures—which lie outside this discussion but require attention and action as well, and whose solution would be aided by resolution of the four problems on which attention is focused here.

Those four problems can be viewed as possessing two broad characteristics. One is the capacity for the large-scale use of political violence by relatively small groups of people in command of political machines of internal and international violence. The other characteristic is that much of the population in these countries, and most clearly the victims of this violence and domination, have experienced a widespread and deep sense of powerlessness. Two key parts of the problem are therefore how to remove that violence, or keep it controlled, and how to empower people so that they will be able to gain and maintain control of their own lives and destinies, despite severe threats.

These four problems—dictatorship, genocide, war, and systems of social oppression—are perhaps not separate problems for which separate solutions are required, or even possible, as we have usually assumed. It may be that they are tied together, that they are four expressions of a single problem: the use of organized violence for political purposes.

Political violence here means physical violence used or threatened for political purposes. That includes imprisonment, war, torture, assassinations, coups d'etat, terrorism, guerrilla war, beatings, riots, and other forms. The capacity for such violence becomes institutionalized in such forms as prison systems, concentration camps, military forces, militia, political police, and assassination squads.

Without institutionalized political violence, dictatorship, genocide, war, and systems of social oppression could not exist. How could one maintain an oppressive social system without the capacity to arrest the discontented, without facilities to imprison them, or ability to send in troops to put down unrest? How could one have a dictatorship without capacity for internal violence to hold down the enslaved population? Without political violence, major international conflicts would take other forms than modern war. One could not commit genocide without the capacity to kill large numbers of people.

As institutionalized political violence, this violence is not the spontaneous outburst of "aggression" or "frustration." It is the systematic, deliberate organized use of violence by institutions which have been established deliberately to be able to apply that violence. That creates a severe danger which has gone largely unrecognized: when an institution is set up to use political violence for one purpose—even a good one—that same institution can be used for a different purpose. For example, an army organized to defend a country from foreign attack can attack its own government and replace it by a coup d'etat, or be shifted to suppress movements for greater internal freedoms or social justice. The institutions of political violence are not tied to a particular purpose, even to their original designated task. Their capacity may be shifted to other uncontemplated or unwanted purposes, sometimes under orders and sometimes autonomously.[2]

Violent sanctions for political objectives are, therefore, integral to some of the most serious problems of our time. At the same time, however, they are intrinsic to modern governments and the State apparatus as requirements for enforcing rule and law internally and for maintaining sovereignty and interests internationally. Violent sanctions are believed to be needed because of the perception that they are the most powerful means of action available.

At the same time, however, grounds for dissatisfaction with violence as the ultimate sanction exist: (1) the destructive capacity of violence has reached unacceptable levels; (2) satisfactory ways to deal with certain types of political violence—such as terrorism, genocide, and nuclear weapons—have not been found; (3) reliance on violence to struggle against an opponent with continued superior capacity for violence tends to force submission, self-destruction, or defeat by attrition; and (4) there are undesirable long-term structural consequences of political violence as the society's ultimate sanction, related in part to the interchangeability of the purposes for which it may be used but rooted also in other factors.[3]

SANCTIONS AND POLITICAL VIOLENCE

If modern political systems depend on political violence to maintain themselves, is it not then impossible to lift this reliance on political violence, and hence impossible to eliminate those four problems?

Clearly, sanctions cannot simply be abolished or renounced. Any society requires some kind of final sanctions. (Sanctions are understood here as means of applying punishment or reprisals for failure to behave in the desired manner.) Within a society people, groups, and the society as a whole require some final sanction to deal with acute conflicts, to enforce certain minimal standards of human behavior, some means of dealing with very destructive and violent acts within a society, and to prevent internal usurpations and suppression. Internationally, a society faces conflicts in which important issues are at stake. The dangers are often very real. Countries do get invaded, even small "innocent" ones striving to be neutral in a wider conflict, and people who were no provocation to anybody have been oppressed, enslaved, and exterminated by foreign attackers.

Sanctions are relied upon either to hold in reserve to facilitate the successful operation of more routine procedures, or to wield directly in face of opposition when regular procedures have failed, are closed, or are inappropriate. Sanctions are used by States to help enforce the obedience of the populace, by the citizenry against the State, by certain nongovernmental groups against others, and by States against each other. Sanctions in domestic and international politics are usually a key element in political power. Most violent sanctions are applied basically as punishments for disobedience or violation of expectations and not primarily to achieve the aim of the original command or wish. But some violent sanctions and more often nonviolent sanctions may be used with the primary intent of achieving the original objective which has been withheld or refused. In many situations simply the capacity to wield, or the threat to apply, sanctions may induce the desired behavior.

Serious issues are often involved in acute domestic and international conflicts. Failures to wage conflicts, or failures to do so successfully, are often of lasting and fundamental significance, as much of the history of the twentieth century demonstrates. When large groups of people and whole countries lack adequate sanctions, they are unable to resist domination by foreign aggressors, internal dictators, or economic oppressors.

There is, then, a legitimate need for some kind of sanctions, some means of protecting against external dangers and of meeting certain internal needs. This need is widely recognized and underlies the support for institutionalized political violence including war. The need for sanctions for at least certain minimal purposes—on which opinions may differ—is such a basic societal need that it cannot be simply removed or renounced. This applies irrespective of the type of social, economic, or political system.[4]

Most people and regimes are confident that in extreme situations in domestic and international politics, political violence—threatened or applied—provides the only available realistic sanction, the ultimate sanction offering reasonable chances of effectiveness. This does not mean that political violence has always been welcomed as a positive good. Mostly it has been accepted only as a necessary evil. Recognition of its dangers has led in liberal democracies to legal and constitutional restrictions or prohibitions on the use of political violence. That has not, however, solved the problem since the institutions of political violence can always ignore or defy the restrictions or prohibitions. We have assumed that we had to rely on violence as the only available ultimate sanction, although we did not always like it, although we tried to modify it and make it just, although we tried to restrict it in various ways. People and societies have thus placed their confidence in the very phenomenon which has contributed to such tragic and fundamental consequences.

But is it true that political violence is the only available set of sanctions capable of effectiveness in crises?

ALTERNATIVE NONVIOLENT SANCTIONS

Contrary to the common assumption, a very different type of sanctions also exists which has been widely applied instead of violent sanctions, both domestically and internationally by individuals, groups, social movements, whole societies, and governments in diverse conflict situations. Internationally, nonviolent sanctions have included noncooperation, economic embargoes, diplomatic boycotts, and even nonviolent invasions.

Domestically, they have included civilian insurrections, civil disobedience campaigns, strikes, economic boycotts, civil liberties struggles, minority rights campaigns, mutinies, and even nonviolent sanctions for law enforcement. These nonviolent sanctions have been used in widely differing periods of history, cultures, and political conditions, and also for a wide variety of purposes.[5]

This group of sanctions is called the technique of nonviolent action. It includes many types of nonviolent "weapons," or penalties and other pressures, used to oppose or to achieve given objectives. At least 198 specific methods of action have been identified. Actions included in the technique range from methods of mild symbolic protest, through the potentially paralytic forms of social, economic, and political noncooperation, to the large group of diverse disruptive forms of nonviolent physical, psychological, social, economic, and political intervention.[6]

The methods of nonviolent noncooperation include diverse forms of economic boycotts, strikes, and political noncooperation which, when applied with other methods under appropriate circumstances, can produce paralysis of the institutions against which they are directed. These methods can make it impossible for a hostile regime to achieve its objectives. This type of struggle does not, and must not, use violence, for a major part of its working is produced by political jiu-jitsu in which violent repression operates to undermine support for the opponent and to increase that for the nonviolent side.

This type of action is based on the view that political power derives from cooperation and assistance of people and institutions. This help may be provided, restricted, or refused to any given institution, policy, or regime. Contrary to popular assumptions, people using the nonviolent technique can operate successfully against a violent, repressive regime without needing to shift to violence. The technique has defeated and even destroyed dictatorial systems. Nonviolent action can at times not only alter people's beliefs and opinions, but also gain objectives by the mechanisms of accommodation and nonviolent coercion.[7]

Nonviolent sanctions using noncooperation operate by directly cutting off the sources of power of the opponent. This is possible because all regimes, including the most dictatorial ones, are dependent for the sources of their power upon the people they rule; when obedience and cooperation are withheld or withdrawn, those sources of power are restricted or severed, and in time the regime is thereby disintegrated. Change by accommodation and nonviolent coercion can be achieved because with this technique the population is able to mobilize its own sources of social, economic, and political power and also to undermine the availability of the sources of power of hostile regimes and oppressive rulers.

These means, when developed and applied skillfully, can be more effective for social and political goals compatible with popular participation and freedom than is political violence.

These nonviolent means have in particular instances, defeated Nazis, frustrated Communist rulers, undermined dictators, disintegrated empires, battled foreign invaders, and dissolved coups d'etat. These nonviolent sanctions and forms of struggle have been applied in many cultures and parts of the world by people who never were, and never became, believers in "nonviolence." Yet, these "common" people were capable not only of great courage but also great power to determine their own present and future.

Therefore, despite the violence of our age, we are not without resources for developing alternatives to political violence. There is a vast history of people and institutions applying nonviolent sanctions on which we can draw as our heritage. This we ought not simply to imitate. We can regard past nonviolent struggles as primitive prototypes of what could be. These have been cases of actions carried out by people drawing upon inspiration, intuition, and improvisation. With the benefit of what they have accomplished, we can if we want apply ourselves to learn how to multiply the effectiveness of this type of struggle. We would then have revealed before us a power capacity which is not merely equal to political violence but far greater.

Nonviolent sanctions have the potential to be applied as substitute sanctions in place of political violence. This could enable us simultaneously to oppose major political oppression and international aggression, and in the long run reduce the total quantum of institutionalized political violence. That could have highly beneficial consequences.

In order to develop and evaluate the potential of nonviolent sanctions, two important tasks are required: (1) research and policy studies and (2) educational work. These will differ in significant ways from established "peace research" and "peace studies." The focus in these would be primarily (1) on the nature and potential of nonviolent sanctions, as compared to violent ones, and (2) on the four problems which require institutionalized political violence for their existence and which nonviolent sanctions would be intended to remove.

RESEARCH AND POLICY STUDIES

In the past, the concern that research should be used to help prevent war and other violence has been expressed in peace research programs and institutes and even national peace research institutes or academies. Whether such research efforts are highly useful, only moderately so, a waste of resources, or actually harmful is to a large degree determined by their orientation and the tasks which they are given. The choice of orientation and tasks is therefore crucial and will require careful thought.[8]

Such programs ought to avoid two dangers: (1) acceptance of military assumptions, and (2) acceptance of the assumptions of a variety of peace groups. If military assumptions are accepted, not only would one be duplicating much existing work but also would be building on assumptions that have failed to bring world peace and contributed to the present extreme dangers. If peace group assumptions are accepted, one would also be building on approaches which have failed to abolish war, at least in part because of failure to face fully the need for effective means to wage acute conflicts and resist hostile forces.

Research and policy studies are urgently needed which do not fall into the trap of accepting either set of assumptions but which do face fully the reality of conflict, the need for sanctions, and the gravity of domestic and international dangers of aggression, usurpations, dictatorships, genocide, systems of social oppression, terrorism, and political violence in general.

Various other approaches to peaceful resolution of conflicts—such as negotiation, arbitration, conciliation, mediation, and similar means involving compromise—have certain merits and utility; these comments are not intended to belittle them. Many of these can make important future contributions to resolving those conflicts in which the issues are not fundamental to the direction of the society or to its moral principles, and in which one is not facing an opponent ready to apply organized violence to achieve an objective. Issues exist, however, on which compromise is properly morally and politically unacceptable. In such cases those approaches to conflict resolution which rely on willingness to compromise (such as arbitration and conciliation) are inappropriate. Resort has commonly been had to violence in these situations. Almost without exception, the traditional approaches to peace have failed to address the need for sanctions by which to struggle on issues which are not suitable for compromise. Peace proposals which ignore the need for sanctions suffer from a fatal flaw. Similarly, researchers who accept the assumption that violent sanctions are required without rigorous investigation of alternatives irresponsibly help to perpetuate the grave problems, including war, which follow inextricably from that assumption.

Therefore, a responsible approach to research and education on the problems of conflict and peace needs to face the most important and difficult issue blocking the way to the abolition of war: the need for sanctions in conflicts in which compromise is unacceptable or impossible. Prime attention is then needed to alternative nonviolent means of waging conflict.[9]

We do not know enough about these alternative nonviolent sanctions, including their problems and potentials in extreme conflicts—such as defending against foreign invasion or internal usurpation. Such knowledge is vital in order to wage such struggles most effectively, and confidence in the potential for effectiveness is essential for widespread, permanent, adoption of nonviolent sanctions. Such limitations on knowledge, effectiveness, and confidence have a predictable result: few people are willing to give up reliance on political violence (including war) for facing attacks on the society's constitutional system and independence. The consequent resort to political violence threatens in such internal conflicts widespread civil disorder and even civil war, while in international conflicts it brings the danger of massive war and annihilation.

Other conflicts, in which lesser issues are at stake on which compromise is possible and acceptable, are also important; efforts to resolve them peacefully are also needed. However, the acute conflicts are by far more serious. Therefore, it is crucial that financial, institutional, and intellectual resources be primarily concentrated on those acute conflicts, rather than on the lesser ones which can be resolved by better skills in negotiation and similar means involving compromise. It is in the acute conflicts in which people and governments believe military action and other political violence are required that we lack sufficient knowledge of nonviolent sanctions and adequate alternative policies based upon them to enable skeptics to accept alternative nonviolent sanctions. Therefore, the primary task of studies aimed to prevent war and ensure peace and to remove political violence should be on research and policy studies about nonviolent sanctions.

As in other fields, we can gain greater knowledge of nonviolent sanctions by basic research into their practice and workings. We can help make them more effective than in the past by applying the results of problem-solving research, policy studies, and by preparations and training. We can expand their future utility in place of military means by policy studies designed to adapt deliberate and prepared nonviolent struggle to destroy dictatorships, defeat coups d'etat, and defend against international aggressors. This advance development of viable nonviolent alternatives would make possible a choice to use them instead of war and other political violence.

The broad areas for basic research include:

- the nature and dynamics of nonviolent struggle;
- its requirements for effectiveness;
- its mechanisms of change;
- principles of strategy and tactics;
- case studies of past nonviolent struggles;

- weaknesses of dictatorships; and
- requirements for establishing and preventing control by usurpers.

Problem-solving research is required into these and other areas:

- how best to mobilize, prepare, and train a population for using non-violent sanctions rather than military ones;
- how to increase the effectiveness of nonviolent sanctions;
- how people can better persist in their nonviolent resistance despite violent repression;
- how the problems of leadership and diffusion of responsibility among all participants can be solved;
- how weaknesses in the usurper's regime and society may best be utilized to help bring success to the nonviolent defenders;
- how temporary defeats can be prevented from producing demoralization; and
- how a series of successes can be transformed into full victory against the attack.

Policy studies need to deal with such tasks as these:

- the degree of adequacy or inadequacy of policies relying upon nonviolent sanctions in place of violent ones for national defense against foreign invaders and internal usurpers;
- the potential of such civilian means of defense to meet the defense needs of present U.S. allies so that they would become more self-reliant without contributing to dangerous military arms races and nuclear proliferation;
- how these nonmilitary means can best be used to liberalize or disintegrate established dictatorships by actions of their own populations;
- how people living under extreme social oppression can use nonviolent sanctions to establish a more just social system instead of using guerrilla warfare and single-party dictatorship;
- how a society can structure its institutions in order best to be able to use civilian-based defense against hostile attacks while maximizing the humane qualities of its own society;[10]
- how attempts to commit genocide can best be prevented and if launched defeated;
- how the general population and the independent institutions of the society can best become willing and able to apply these alternative means of national defense in place of military means; and

- how such a program of transarmament—the transition to the new policy—can be carried out with maximum economic benefit to the society.

These examples illustrate a wider range of topics which need investigation.[11] Institutions established to conduct such studies ought to communicate relevant results of research and policy studies on alternatives to military preparations and action to both nongovernmental bodies and to governmental ones—legislative, executive, military, and others—which will make decisions whether in crises to resort to military action or to nonviolent sanctions. Research centers with this orientation and these projects could make major contributions to the resolution of the great problems of our time.

EDUCATIONAL OPPORTUNITIES

In addition to research and policy studies, deliberate educational efforts are urgently required on alternative nonviolent sanctions and the four identified problems. This focus differs from "peace studies." "Peace studies" or "nonviolent studies" seem generally to be far more diffuse. They often give major attention to the evils of war and the merits of conciliation, arbitration, compromise, and social change, while largely neglecting nonviolent struggle. They almost always exclude or give minimal attention to dictatorships, genocide, internal usurpations, and international aggression. Instead, a focus on nonviolent sanctions in the context of the four identified problems is more directly relevant to major crises and to the decision how to wage struggle in acute conflicts.

A widespread interest now exists in alternatives to violence generally, and a much greater interest than ever before in learning specifically about nonviolent sanctions and their potential for defense and other purposes. Yet there are grossly inadequate educational opportunities and resources available to meet this need. Development of new educational opportunities and resources and improvements in existing ones, are therefore urgently needed in this field throughout the whole range from popularized forms to rigorous academic approaches. These will include efforts within formal educational institutions from grade school through universities, adult education programs, and informal study groups. Additional efforts are needed by the media of public communication.

It is highly important that such educational efforts be as unbiased and as high in quality as is achievable; the purpose is to provide knowledge and understanding to assist thought and fair evaluation, not to indoctrinate people to accept a particular view or policy.

We need a general public education program on the nature of civilian struggle and nonviolent forms of action so that people come to understand what it really is, instead of all the misconceptions which are common. This program could include such means as books, newspaper articles, fiction, historical novels, adult education courses, television drama series, radio programs, videotapes, magazine features, and the like.

Study groups on nonviolent sanctions and their potential can be a very useful educational format. They can be used by small numbers of people, or the groups can multiply so that very large numbers of people partici-pate. There is flexibility in their scheduling and timing, and, with ade-quate literature, videotapes, and the like, "experts" are not required as leaders. Study groups can be completely independent, or can be associ-ated with other such groups, or with an organization with broader or dif-ferent interests. There are now indications that a remarkable number of people are ready to join study groups on nonviolent sanctions. Develop-ment and dissemination of good educational resources and knowledge of how to organize and conduct such groups are therefore highly important.

In schools and colleges, we need curriculum changes to introduce into regular courses and disciplines specific information of a suitable academic type about nonviolent forms of struggle. For example, this information may include the role it has played in various historical situations, how it operates, its psychological dynamics, and other dimensions. In colleges, on the high school level, and perhaps even earlier, we need specific courses on nonviolent struggle. This means developing curriculum ma-terials, textbooks, videotapes, films, and other resources.[12]

Where courses on nonviolent sanctions are already offered, there is usually room for improvement. For example, efforts might be made to im-prove the variety and quality of such courses, to increase their academic rigor, to add new resources, to deepen the understanding and knowledge offered and sought, to improve the balance and fairness of presentations, and to expand the offerings of those and related courses.

In colleges and universities special programs of study may be launched. Normally a specific phenomenon such as nonviolent sanctions would not be the focus of a special department or program. It would in-stead be examined repeatedly in the context of the studies of the regular departments and programs. We face here, however, an unusual situation: a vast and highly significant field of human experience, in many countries, societies, and historical periods, has usually been left out of our historical studies and our research and teaching in social psychology, sociology, po-litical science, and the like. With unusual exceptions, nonviolent struggle is not among the phenomena studied in those fields, and their faculties are inadequately familiar with this specific subject matter. The problem is compounded by a whole series of gross misunderstandings and erroneous assumptions which are part of the popular perceptions of "nonviolence."

Therefore, special attention is required which can only be provided by special programs with trained faculty. Such special programs, however, must collaborate closely with existing departments and disciplines, and students will need to undertake major studies in them.

Such steps as the following can be taken to improve education about nonviolent alternatives in schools and colleges:

- preparation for grade schools and high schools of courses and curriculum materials on alternative sanctions and the problems of dictatorship, genocide, war, and systems of social oppression;
- preparation of guides and suggestions for instructors in courses in this field at various educational levels, including both recommendations which could be implemented directly, and also encouragement to modify them, or to create new courses and approaches;
- selection and development of historical studies which provide corrective treatment to the past relative neglect of nonviolent struggle;
- preparation of new texts, study guides, and other printed curriculum materials focusing on alternative sanctions and the four selected problems, and their opposite positive conditions, providing sound informational backgrounds and balanced presentations, and raising new questions about all of these;
- development of table games for home and classroom use as learning and problem-solving tools in the evaluation and use of nonviolent sanctions in acute conflicts;
- preparation of new films, dramatized and documentary television programs, videotapes, and the like about these phenomena and problems;
- exploration of participatory educational methods for possible use in courses on nonviolent alternatives designed to stimulate and facilitate the learners' active involvement in their own educations;
- establishment of grants to provide (1) aid to educational institutions to develop and expand undergraduate and graduate programs in these fields; (2) scholarships and grants to graduate students wishing to specialize in this field including support for writing their doctoral dissertations; and (3) support for researchers and educators to prepare educational resources—textbooks, syllabi, films, video programs, and others—and to make educators aware of their availability;
- development of interdisciplinary programs of undergraduate studies on nonviolent sanctions and the four identified problems;

- offering of individual graduate courses, seminars, and dissertation supervision, and the like, on nonviolent sanctions and the four problems within established departments and programs;
- development of interdisciplinary graduate studies, courses, seminars, dissertation supervision, and the like in this area in cooperation with established departments and programs;
- offering special summer courses on alternative sanctions and the identified problems for (1) visiting students from other universities, (2) high school teachers leading courses in this field, and (3) college and university faculty from other institutions leading courses on these phenomena and problems (courses (2) and (3) may focus both on substance and on educational methods and approaches);
- assistance in the establishment of quality M.A. and Ph.D. programs to train future researchers, policy analysts, and educators in the study of alternative sanctions and the four related problems;
- encouragement of the expansion or development of small and large libraries focused on the whole area or on specific phenomena and problems; and
- development of formal and informal networks through which educators, students, and researchers working in this field in various institutions may consult with each other and share their problems, experiences, and insights.

CONCLUSION

A great variety of opportunities and tasks lie before us in learning more about the nature and potential of nonviolent sanctions for resolving some of our most serious problems. These tasks require the assistance of a great variety of people and institutions. This work will help provide the knowledge and understanding needed to evaluate the potential contribution of alternative nonviolent sanctions. These studies may help us better to understand our world, our problems, and our options, and may also help us to deal with and resolve some of our most serious problems. The effort is needed.

Notes

1. These four problems are examined in much greater detail in Gene Sharp, *Social Power and Political Freedom* (Boston: Porter Sargent, 1980). Other relevant

material on strategy for liberation from oppression and related ethical questions can be found in idem, *Gandhi as a Political Strategist, with Essays on Ethics and Politics* (Boston: Porter Sargent, 1979), especially chap. 12, "Morality, Politics, and Political Technique."

2. This analysis of the role of institutionalized political violence draws on "The Societal Imperative," chap. 11 in Sharp, *Social Power and Political Freedom,* pp. 285–308.

3. On the structural consequences of violent and nonviolent sanctions, see "Popular Empowerment," in ibid., pp. 325–56.

4. See also "The Societal Imperative," in ibid., pp. 291–93.

5. See Gene Sharp, *The Politics of Nonviolent Action* (Boston: Porter Sargent, 1973), especially "The Nature and Control of Political Power," chap. 1, pp. 7–62; and "Nonviolent Action: An Active Technique of Struggle," chap. 2, pp. 63–105. Many additional historical examples are cited and described in the remainder of the book.

6. On these methods, see "The Methods of Nonviolent Action," part 2, in ibid., pp. 107–445.

7. On these mechanisms, see "Three Ways Success May Be Achieved," ibid., chap. 13, pp. 705–76.

8. This discussion draws heavily on my written testimony "Recommendations on a 'National Peace Academy' " presented to the U.S. Commission on Proposals for the National Academy of Peace and Conflict Resolution, meeting in Boston, Massachusetts, June 2, 1980. A passage from my oral testimony is included in *To Establish the United States Academy of Peace: Report of the Commission for the National Academy of Peace and Conflict Resolution to the President of the United States and the Senate and House of Representatives of the United States Congress* (Washington, D.C.: U.S. Government Printing Office, 1981), p. 133.

9. For a list of the major components of a multifaceted program for research, education, and consideration of nonviolent sanctions see, "Twenty Steps in Development and Evaluation of Nonviolent Sanctions," Appendix B in Sharp, *Social Power and Political Freedom,* pp. 383–90.

10. For some studies on this policy, see "For Further Reading" at the end of this article.

11. For listings and brief descriptions of areas for research and policy studies on alternative nonviolent sanctions, see Gene Sharp, *Exploring Nonviolent Alternatives* (Boston: Porter Sargent, 1970), "Research Areas on Nonviolent Alternatives," chap. 4, pp. 73–113; and idem, "Research Areas on the Nature, Problems and Potentialities of Civilian Defense" in *Gandhi: Theory and Practice, Social Impact and Contemporary Relevance: Proceedings of a Conference,* ed. S. C. Biswas (Simla: India Institute of Advanced Studies, 1969), pp. 393–413.

12. The first such videotapes for educational use are now available: *Alternatives to Violence: A Video Series,* funded by the Fund for the Improvement of Postsecondary Education, U.S. Department of Education, through the University City Science Center, Philadelphia. Enquiries to: W.T.L. (Distribution), Box 351, Primos, Pa. 19018.

Questions

1. By describing war and other social evils as human problems, what does the author imply about their solutions? Do you agree or disagree with his assumptions—and why?

2. What effect is the use of widespread non-violent resistance likely to have on the popular sense of powerlessness?

3. Why does the author exclude from his discussion other grave problems such as the shortage of water and food, threats to the environment and population growth?

4. Do you think Sharp's observations on peace studies programs are on target? Why, or why not?

5. What sources of funding might be available for an extensive research and education program such as the author envisages? How realistic would it be to expect such funds to be forthcoming?

12
Inheritance, Extinction and Personal Honesty

Donovan Russell

This article originally appeared in *The Social Studies*, May/June 1984.

Viewed by someone from another planet, our earthly preoccupation with warfare might seem bizarre and irrational. In a sense, this "outsider's" perspective is taken by Russell, who is coordinator of a U.S. Agency for International Development project in Lesotho, Africa. He reflects on the origins of human life on our planet, calling it "a fantastic miracle." Unlike the other articles in this section, the following is a "cry from the heart" based on the precariousness and uniqueness of human life in the vast universe. This article does not espouse any particular ideology, political program or technical solution for the elimination of the arms race. It simply records the thoughts and feelings of someone in mid-life who has become personally and painfully aware of the treasure that is ours and of the imminent danger that it may all be blown away.

It is estimated that the sun is one of the 100,000 million stars in our galaxy alone.

The number of planets which attend these stars is beyond imagination. Comprehending the tremendous scale of the universe is perhaps impossible for the human mind. Galaxies are, in many cases, thousands of millions of light years away. For example, the gulf that separates us from the neighboring star island in Andromeda is more than 2 million light years. The most distant galaxy photographed is approximately 5,000 million light years away. It would take a spaceship travelling at a speed of a million miles an hour almost 3,000 years to reach the nearest star. If there is life in space, it is not nearby.

Life on earth can only be described as a miraculous thing. For life to develop, a highly fortuitous series of events had to occur. The earth had to be just the right distance from the sun. The sun had to have the right temperature. The earth had to possess the right chemical compounds at the right time and they had to be in proximity to each other. Certain elements of the earth had to be worn down into a mixture of organic compounds. The seas had to be appropriate hosts and the atmosphere had to be modified by sunlight. Life could have been easily extinguished by any number of events or natural forces. It was a complicated and unlikely process. The odds against it happening were unbelievably high. And it didn't happen over night. Some six billion years ago matter came into existence in our neighborhood with the advent of our galaxy. Four to five billion years ago our sun began to provide radiation to this matter. Some four billion years ago our solar system came into being. Five hundred thousand to a billion years after that the very simplest form of life appeared on earth. Life evolved slowly through amphibia, reptiles, mammals and birds over thousands and thousands of years. Finally, only one million years ago man-like apes appeared. Only 50,000 years ago the Neanderthal man appeared. And civilization as we think of it is only about 10,000 years old.

Life, as it appears on earth, is tremendously isolated. Life, as it appears on earth, is a fantastic miracle. Life is precious beyond comprehension. The miraculous process that gave life makes it precious.

Some thirty-eight years ago a sign was given in the detonation of the first atomic bomb. It happened at Alamogordo, New Mexico. There were people at the time who referred to this as the birth of a baby. The baby has grown rapidly into a monster. In fact it has been projected that if a full scale nuclear war were to erupt, all life, everyplace on the planet, would cease to exist and conditions on earth would be altered such that no life could ever again come into being. It is acknowledged by credible scientists that the concept of winning a nuclear war is a dream. Those who hold such an idea are living in a past that has been forever swept away. Since 1945 mankind has built nuclear weapons so effectively and so fast that the release of them now would eradicate human life several times over and indeed would eradicate all animal and plant life. The great effort which nature has made over the last six billion years would be sacrificed to nothingness forever. Man has finally succeeded in a mastery of nature so extensive that he can make mother earth into a lifeless moon.

In 1977 the United States Department of Defense spent 95.6 billion dollars for war preparation. Present spending plans call for the Department of Defense to be spending 356 billion dollars on annual war preparations by 1987. The USSR has a similar record and a similar intent. Lesser nations fall into the same picture proportionately.

I am now forty-three years of age. Given the annihilation potential that mankind has held for several years, I am grateful that I have been able to reach this age. I am also grateful that my children have been able to reach the ages of twenty-one, seventeen and fourteen.

But what sort of a person would talk this way? In your mind, am I some sort of a fanatic? Am I a lunatic? Am I, in some strange way, unpatriotic? Do I have an unrealistic view of the way things really are? Am I an alarmist?

In actual fact I suspect that nearly everyone has had the same passing thought, i.e., they are grateful to have had the years thus allowed in the nuclear age. Why then are people quiet? Why is not everyone out to turn back the madness, insanity, and evil which is increasingly enveloping the world of our ancestors, the world of our children, and the world of all future life? Is life not precious to us anymore? Have we somehow lost appreciation for the great creativity of our forebears? Are all other things, in which we are engaged, more important than the survival of life on earth? Does it take lowest priority? How much time from each twenty-four hour day do individuals give this issue?

There are other questions which are in the back of our minds—questions that we do not ask publicly for fear of being though weird. Through some kind of twisted logic we have come to label people who publicly speak these questions. They are labelled immature or crackpot or unbalanced or troublemaking. They unsettle us. And yet when we allow ourselves to listen, our own conscience speaks these questions. Really now, how does the existence of nuclear weapons make my life more secure? If the U.S. and USSR can destroy each other several times over, why is each continuing to develop more weapons?

In fact why are the U.S. and USSR enemies? What is it really, that we have to be enemies about? If we were to destroy each other (along with the rest of the world) what would it be for? What have the Russians done to us that makes us want to build bomb after bomb for them? And what have we done to the Russians that they want to build bomb after bomb for us? Really now, what is this madness all about? Why can't we stop it? Do we actually want to stop it? Is it all that complicated? Are we the victim of a giant lie that we keep telling ourselves? Can we bear to ask ourselves these questions? Can we bear to think hard about them? Do we have it in us to take on any responsibility in this matter at all? Whose responsibility is it to prevent the extinction of ourselves, our offspring, and all future life? Is it utopian to think that the course of events toward extinction can be changed? If life on earth is to be saved from extinction, will it have to be done by people who are living now?

Some six billion years ago matter came into existence in our neighborhood. Natural forces carefully edged it along toward life, as we know it, over billions of years. Thirty-eight years ago a baby was born at Alamogordo, New Mexico. For thirty-eight years we have been feeding, nurturing and helping this baby to grow as fast as possible. In thirty-eight years we have made the baby so big that tomorrow it could swallow all the wonderful miracles that nature has painstakingly created over the past six billion years. And in some strange way we have allowed the baby to twist our minds. We say with perfectly straight faces that our baby of death is an instrument of life. We say that we must be willing, without reservation, to annihilate life (present and future) to keep from annihilating all life. The baby's presence has numbed our heads and caused us to lie to ourselves. It has cast a spell on us—somehow making us think that we are rightly destined to sacrifice ourselves to it. This same spell has caused us to be suspicious, disdainful, and even threatened by anyone who dares to describe it as it is. Somehow the baby's presence has caused us to confuse falsehood with truth and death with life. God help us!

Questions

1. What does the author mean by stating that life on earth is "miraculous"?

2. Do you find his reference to the atomic bomb as a "baby" appropriate. Why, or why not?

3. How would you explain the fact that most people accept life in the nuclear age as a matter of course? What could change this perception?

4. Could you explain why the U.S. and the U.S.S.R. are enemies? Can you think of ways in which a convergence—or at least mutual tolerance—could take place?

5. How does the author regard the question of nuclear deterrence? Does this article affect your thinking and feeling on the matters of war and peace? In what ways?

SECTION TWO

Justice for All

1

Pacem in Terris

Pope John XXIII, #130–145

Pope John XXIII's encyclical letter "Pacem in Terris" ("Peace on Earth") has been called the Pontiff's "last will and testament." He died less than two months after it was issued "to all men of good will" (a new departure) on April 11, 1963. Written in the heat of the Cuban missile crisis in the fall of 1962, the Pope's letter declared, among other things, that "it is hardly possible to imagine that in the atomic era war could be used as an instrument of justice." John builds on the teachings of his predecessors but he goes beyond them in enumerating the rights of all persons to profess their religion publicly and the rights of newly independent nations to determine their own destinies. Striking a positive note throughout, Pope John lists three characteristics of the modern age: the economic and political gains of the working class, the advances made by women in public life and the passing of colonialism.

The selections cited from "Pacem in Terris" (#130–145) call attention to the growing interdependence among the countries of the world. As parts of "one world economy," nation-states' social progress, order, security and peace are "necessarily connected" with those of all other countries. The corollary of this insight is that nations can no longer pursue their own interests "in isolation." By positing a "universal common good," the Pontiff calls on nations to seek this goal in concert, by freely entering into a "public authority of the world community." Nations in isolation or in complete autonomy "are no longer capable of facing the tasks of finding a solution to . . . problems." What this supranational authority will be, the Pope leaves to others to work out.

The point of reference of these global efforts is not the nation-state, the Church itself or even God. It is the dignity of the human person. John's view, filled with faith, is clearly anthropocentric. Ignoring those "prophets of doom" who condemn the shortcomings of the United Nations, John emphasizes its achievements and expresses the hope that it "may become ever more equal to the magnitude and nobility of its tasks." In like manner, he praises the U.N. for its Universal Declaration of Human Rights, calling

*it "an important step on the path toward the juridical-political organization
of the world community."*

In the tradition of papal teaching, Pope John stresses the principle of
subsidiarity, which states that higher authorities should not take over functions equally well performed by smaller groups. But he applies this principle in the other direction by stating that a supranational authority is
needed because "individual states are not in a position to tackle them
(problems) with any hope of resolving them satisfactorily."

INTERDEPENDENCE BETWEEN POLITICAL COMMUNITIES

130.   Recent progress of science and technology has profoundly
affected human beings and influenced men to work together and live as
one family. There has been a great increase in the circulation of goods, of
ideas and of persons from one country to another, so that relations have
become closer between individuals, families and intermediate associations
belonging to different political communities, and between the public authorities of those communities. At the same time the interdependence of
national economies has grown deeper, one becoming progressively more
closely related to the other, so that they become, as it were, integral parts
of the one world economy. Likewise the social progress, order, security
and peace of each country are necessarily connected with the social progress, order, security and peace of all other countries.

131.   At the present day no political community is able to pursue
its own interests and develop itself in isolation, because the degree of its
prosperity and development is a reflection and a component part of the
degree of prosperity and development of all the other political communities.

EXISTING PUBLIC AUTHORITY NOT EQUAL
TO REQUIREMENTS OF THE UNIVERSAL COMMON GOOD

132.   The unity of the human family has always existed, because
its members were human beings all equal by virtue of their natural dignity.
Hence there will always exist the objective need to promote, in sufficient
measure, the universal common good, that is, the common good of the
entire human family.

133.   In times past, one would be justified in feeling that the public authorities of the different political communities might be in a position
to provide for the universal common good, either through normal diplomatic channels or through top-level meetings, by making use of juridical
instruments such as conventions and treaties, for example: juridical in-

struments suggested by the natural law and regulated by the law of nations and international law.

134.   As a result of the far-reaching changes which have taken place in the relations within the human community, the universal common good gives rise to problems that are very grave, complex and extremely urgent, especially as regards security and world peace. On the other hand, the public authorities of the individual nations—being placed as they are on a footing of equality one with the other—no matter how much they multiply their meetings or sharpen their wits in efforts to draw up new juridical instruments, they are no longer capable of facing the task of finding an adequate solution to the problems mentioned above. And this is not due to a lack of good will or of a spirit of enterprise, but because their authority lacks suitable force.

135.   It can be said, therefore, that at this historical moment the present system of organization and the way its principle of authority operates on a world basis no longer correspond to the objective requirements of the universal common good.

RELATIONS BETWEEN THE COMMON GOOD AND PUBLIC AUTHORITY IN HISTORICAL CONTEXT

136.   There exists an intrinsic connection between the common good on the one hand and the structure and function of public authority on the other. The moral order, which needs public authority in order to promote the common good in civil society, requires also that the authority be effective in attaining that end. This demands that the organs through which the authority is formed, becomes operative and pursues its ends, must be composed and act in such a manner as to be capable of furthering the common good by ways and means which correspond to the developing situation.

137.   Today the universal common good poses problems of worldwide dimensions, which cannot be adequately tackled or solved except by the efforts of public authorities endowed with a wideness of powers, structure and means of the same proportions: that is, of public authorities which are in a position to operate in an effective manner on a world-wide basis. The moral order itself, therefore, demands that such a form of public authority be established.

PUBLIC AUTHORITY INSTITUTED BY COMMON CONSENT AND NOT IMPOSED BY FORCE

138.   A public authority, having world-wide power and endowed with the proper means for the efficacious pursuit of its objective, which is

the universal common good in concrete form, must be set up by common accord and not imposed by force. The reason is that such an authority must be in a position to operate effectively; yet, at the same time, its action must be inspired by sincere and real impartiality: in other words, it must be an action aimed at satisfying the objective requirements of the universal common good. The difficulty is that there would be reason to fear that a supranational or world-wide public authority, imposed by force by the more powerful political communities, might be or might become an instrument of one-sided interests; and even should this not happen, it would be difficult for it to avoid all suspicion of partiality in its actions, and this would take from the efficaciousness of its activity. Even though there may be pronounced differences between political communities as regards the degree of their economic development and their military power, they are all very sensitive as regards their juridical equality and their moral dignity. For that reason, they are right in not easily yielding in obedience to an authority imposed by force, or to an authority in whose creation they had no part, or to which they themselves did not decide to submit by conscious and free choice.

THE UNIVERSAL COMMON GOOD AND PERSONAL RIGHTS

139. Like the common good of individual political communities, so too the universal common good cannot be determined except by having regard to the human person. Therefore, the public authority of the world community, too, must have as its fundamental objective the recognition, respect, safeguarding and promotion of the rights of the human person; this can be done by direct action when required, or by creating on a world scale an environment in which the public authorities of the individual political communities can more easily carry out their specific functions.

THE PRINCIPLE OF SUBSIDIARITY

140. Just as within each political community the relations between individuals, families, intermediate associations and public authority are governed by the principle of subsidiarity, so too the relations between the public authority of each political community and the public authority of the world community must be regulated by the light of the same principle. This means that the public authority of the world community must tackle and solve problems of an economic, social, political or cultural character which are posed by the universal common good. For, because of the vastness, complexity and urgency of those problems, the public authorities of the individual States are not in a position to tackle them with any hope of resolving them satisfactorily.

141.   The public authority of the world community is not intended to limit the sphere of action of the public authority of the individual political community, much less to take its place. On the contrary, its purpose is to create, on a world basis, an environment in which the public authorities of each political community, its citizens and intermediate associations, can carry out their tasks, fulfill their duties and exercise their rights with greater security.[1]

MODERN DEVELOPMENTS

142.   As is known, the United Nations Organization (UN) was established on June 26, 1945, and to it there were subsequently added Intergovernmental Agencies with extensive international tasks in the economic, social, cultural, educational and health fields. The United Nations Organization had as its essential purpose the maintenance and consolidation of peace between peoples, fostering between them friendly relations, based on the principles of equality, mutual respect, and varied forms of co-operation in every sector of human society.

143.   An act of the highest importance performed by the United Nations Organization was the Universal Declaration of Human Rights, approved in the General Assembly of December 10, 1948. In the preamble of that Declaration, the recognition of and respect for those rights and respective liberties is proclaimed as an ideal to be pursued by all peoples and all countries.

144.   Some objections and reservations were raised regarding certain points in the Declaration. There is no doubt, however, that the document represents an important step on the path towards the juridical-political organization of the world community. For in it, in most solemn form, the dignity of a person is acknowledged to all human beings; and as a consequence there is proclaimed, as a fundamental right, the right of free movement in the search for truth and in the attainment of moral good and of justice, and also the right to a dignified life, while other rights connected with those mentioned are likewise proclaimed.

145.   It is Our earnest wish that the United Nations Organization—in its structure and in its means—may become ever more equal to the magnitude and nobility of its tasks. May the day soon come when every

---

1. Cf. Pius XII's *Allocution* to youth of Catholic Action from the dioceses of Italy gathered in Rome, September 12, 1948, A.A.S. XL, p. 412.

human being will find therein an effective safeguard for the rights which derive directly from his dignity as a person, and which are therefore universal, inviolate and inalienable rights. This is all the more to be hoped for since all human beings, as they take an ever more active part in the public life of their own political communities, are showing an increasing interest in the affairs of all peoples, and are becoming more consciously aware that they are living members of a universal family of mankind.

Questions

1. The world has changed since 1963. Give examples of recent developments in science and technology. Do these developments strengthen or weaken the Pope's assertion that a "one world economy" is emerging? Why?

2. Do you agree with John that no political community can pursue its own interests and develop itself in isolation? Name two nations that developed in isolation in the past. How have conditions changed today?

3. What is one outstanding factor in evaluating the adequacy of a public authority (nation)? Give current examples of the limitations of nation-states in the world today.

4. Which nations was the Pope likely to have had in mind when he warned against imposing a worldwide public authority by force? Give examples.

5. Though issued by a Roman Pontiff, "Pacem in Terris" is addressed to "all men of good will." In what ways is his reasoning apt to be acceptable to persons of different religious and cultural traditions?

2
Universal Declaration of Human Rights

United Nations General Assembly, Dec. 10, 1948

The Universal Declaration of Human Rights, adopted by the United Nations General Assembly in 1948, is a remarkable document. Assuming the sincerity of its signatory states, it represents a level of agreement on fundamental issues that few would have predicted in the years preceding its adoption. From one perspective, it is a compilation of the political wisdom of the Western world. But the U.N. also included states from the officially atheistic Soviet bloc and non-Western nations. While disputes could arise on the origin of the rights of the human person (whether from the Creator or from natural evolutionary processes, for example), the declaration provided a platform from which has been proclaimed the fact that such rights do exist without distinction. In a divided world, that in itself is no small achievement.

Based loosely on such documents as the Magna Carta (1215) in England, the U.S. Declaration of Independence (1776) and Constitution (1787) and the French Declaration of the Rights of Man (1789), the Universal Declaration reaches back to the "common sense" of all humanity, which thinkers such as Pope John XXIII would equate with the natural moral law. The declaration goes beyond these previous documents in specifying the rights which belong to every member of humanity.

Cynics may affirm that, in most countries, these rights are ignored when reasons of state find them inconvenient. To be sure, laws were not made to be broken, but their very existence holds individuals and nations to a higher standard that would otherwise be possible.

The declaration itself is relatively short and unambiguous. It deserves to be read slowly and thoughtfully. Many of its thirty short articles point an accusing finger at present-day abuses—slavery and torture, detention and exile, deprivation of nationality, to mention a few. Quite a few have legal overtones, because it is in the administration of justice—or of its opposite—that dedication to human rights is tested. Nor are the rights of the family—especially mothers and children—neglected. Primary education is affirmed as a natural human right, as is participation in government. Economic rights, such as the right to a job, to decent compensation and other social benefits, are up-held.

Even though the Universal Declaration's noble aims have been ig-nored or abused—and the Helsinki Accords of 1976 have not fared any better—nevertheless this document forms the proximate basis for most of the human rights organizations and activities in today's world.

PREAMBLE

Whereas recognition of the inherent dignity and of the equal and in-alienable rights of all members of the human family is the foundation of freedom, justice and peace in the world,

Whereas disregard and contempt for human rights have resulted in barbarous acts which have outraged the conscience of mankind, and the advent of a world in which human beings shall enjoy freedom of speech and belief and freedom from fear and want has been proclaimed as the highest aspiration of the common people,

Whereas it is essential, if man is not to be compelled to have recourse, as a last resort, to rebellion against tyranny and oppression, that human rights should be protected by the rule of law,

Whereas it is essential to promote the development of friendly rela-tions between nations,

Whereas the peoples of the United Nations have in the Charter re-affirmed their faith in fundamental human rights, in the dignity and worth of the human person and in the equal rights of men and women and have determined to promote social progress and better standards of life in larger freedom,

Whereas Member States have pledged themselves to achieve, in co-operation with the United Nations, the promotion of universal respect for and observance of human rights and fundamental freedoms,

Whereas a common understanding of these rights and freedoms is of the greatest importance for the full realization of this pledge,

Now, Therefore,

THE GENERAL ASSEMBLY
proclaims

THIS UNIVERSAL DECLARATION OF HUMAN RIGHTS as a common standard of achievement for all peoples and all nations, to the end that every individual and every organ of society, keeping this Declaration constantly in mind, shall strive by teaching and education to promote respect for these rights and freedoms and by progressive measures, national and international, to secure their universal and effective recognition and observance, both among the peoples of Member States themselves and among the peoples of territories under their jurisdiction.

Article 1. All human beings are born free and equal in dignity and rights. They are endowed with reason and conscience and should act towards one another in a spirit of brotherhood.

Article 2. Everyone is entitled to all the rights and freedoms set forth in this Declaration, without distinction of any kind, such as race, colour, sex, language, religion, political or other opinion, national or social origin, property, birth or other status.

Furthermore, no distinction shall be made on the basis of the political, jurisdictional or international status of the country or territory to which a person belongs, whether it be independent, trust, non-self-governing or under any other limitation of sovereignty.

Article 3. Everyone has the right to life, liberty and security of person.

Article 4. No one shall be held in slavery or servitude; slavery and the slave trade shall be prohibited in all their forms.

Article 5. No one shall be subjected to torture or to cruel, inhuman or degrading treatment or punishment.

Article 6. Everyone has the right to recognition everywhere as a person before the law.

Article 7. All are equal before the law and are entitled without any discrimination to equal protection of the law. All are entitled to equal protection against any discrimination in violation of this Declaration and against any incitement to such discrimination.

Article 8. Everyone has the right to an effective remedy by the competent national tribunals for acts violating the fundamental rights granted him by the constitution or by law.

Article 9. No one shall be subjected to arbitrary arrest, detention or exile.

Article 10. Everyone is entitled in full equality to a fair and public hearing by an independent and impartial tribunal, in the determination of his rights and obligations and of any criminal charge against him.

Article 11. (1) Everyone charged with a penal offence has the right to be presumed innocent until proved guilty according to law in a public trial at which he has had all the guarantees necessary for his defence.

(2) No one shall be held guilty of any penal offence on account of any act or omission which did not constitute a penal offence, under national or

international law, at the time when it was committed. Nor shall a heavier penalty be imposed than the one that was applicable at the time the penal offence was committed.

Article 12. No one shall be subjected to arbitrary interference with his privacy, family, home or correspondence, nor to attacks upon his honour and reputation. Everyone has the right to the protection of the law against such interference or attacks.

Article 13. (1) Everyone has the right to freedom of movement and residence within the borders of each state.

(2) Everyone has the right to leave any country, including his own, and to return to his country.

Article 14. (1) Everyone has the right to seek and to enjoy in other countries asylum from persecution.

(2) This right may not be invoked in the case of prosecutions genuinely arising from non-political crimes or from acts contrary to the purposes and principles of the United Nations.

Article 15. (1) Everyone has the right to a nationality.

(2) No one shall be arbitrarily deprived of his nationality nor denied the right to change his nationality.

Article 16. (1) Men and women of full age, without any limitation due to race, nationality or religion, have the right to marry and to found a family. They are entitled to equal rights as to marriage, during marriage and at its dissolution.

(2) Marriage shall be entered into only with the free and full consent of the intending spouses.

(3) The family is the natural and fundamental group unit of society and is entitled to protection by society and the State.

Article 17. (1) Everyone has the right to own property alone as well as in association with others.

(2) No one shall be arbitrarily deprived of his property.

Article 18. Everyone has the right to freedom of thought, conscience and religion; this right includes freedom to change his religion or belief, and freedom, either alone or in community with others and in public or private, to manifest his religion or belief in teaching, practice, worship and observance.

Article 19. Everyone has the right to freedom of opinion and expression; this right includes freedom to hold opinions without interference and to seek, receive and impart information and ideas through any media and regardless of frontiers.

Article 20. (1) Everyone has the right to freedom of peaceful assembly and association.

(2) No one may be compelled to belong to an association.

Article 21. (1) Everyone has the right to take part in the government of his country, directly or through freely chosen representatives.

(2) Everyone has the right of equal access to public service in his country.

(3) The will of the people shall be the basis of the authority of government; this will shall be expressed in periodic and genuine elections which shall be by universal and equal suffrage and shall be held by secret vote or by equivalent free voting procedures.

Article 22. Everyone, as a member of society, has the right to social security and is entitled to realization, through national effort and international co-operation and in accordance with the organization and resources of each State, of the economic, social and cultural rights indispensable for his dignity and the free development of his personality.

Article 23. (1) Everyone has the right to work, to free choice of employment, to just and favourable conditions of work and to protection against unemployment.

(2) Everyone, without any discrimination, has the right to equal pay for equal work.

(3) Everyone who works has the right to just and favourable remuneration ensuring for himself and his family an existence worthy of human dignity, and supplemented, if necessary, by other means of social protection.

(4) Everyone has the right to form and to join trade unions for the protection of his interests.

Article 24. Everyone has the right to rest and leisure, including reasonable limitation of working hours and periodic holidays with pay.

Article 25. (1) Everyone has the right to a standard of living adequate for the health and well-being of himself and of his family, including food, clothing, housing and medical care and necessary social services, and the right to security in the event of unemployment, sickness, disability, widowhood, old age or other lack of livelihood in circumstances beyond his control.

(2) Motherhood and childhood are entitled to special care and assistance. All children, whether born in or out of wedlock, shall enjoy the same social protection.

Article 26. (1) Everyone has the right to education. Education shall be free, at least in the elementary and fundamental stages. Elementary education shall be compulsory. Technical and professional education shall be made generally available and higher education shall be equally accessible to all on the basis of merit.

(2) Education shall be directed to the full development of the human personality and to the strengthening of respect for human rights and fundamental freedoms. It shall promote understanding, tolerance and friend-

ship among all nations, racial or religious groups, and shall further the activities of the United Nations for the maintenance of peace.

(3) Parents have a prior right to choose the kind of education that shall be given to their children.

Article 27. (1) Everyone has the right freely to participate in the cultural life of the community, to enjoy the arts and to share in scientific advancement and its benefits.

(2) Everyone has the right to the protection of the moral and material interests resulting from any scientific, literary or artistic production of which he is the author.

Article 28. Everyone is entitled to a social and international order in which the rights and freedoms set forth in this Declaration can be fully realized.

Article 29. (1) Everyone has duties to the community in which alone the free and full development of his personality is possible.

(2) In the exercise of his rights and freedoms, everyone shall be subject only to such limitations as are determined by law solely for the purpose of securing due recognition and respect for the rights and freedoms of others and of meeting the just requirements of morality, public order and the general welfare in a democratic society.

(3) These rights and freedoms may in no case be exercised contrary to the purposes and principles of the United Nations.

Article 30. Nothing in this Declaration may be interpreted as implying for any State, group or person any right to engage in any activity or to perform any act aimed at the destruction of any of the rights and freedoms set forth herein.

Questions

1. What is the underlying assumption of the declaration regarding the relation of the individual to the nation-state? Does it favor any particular form of government? Explain.
2. Enumerate the benefits noted in the preamble that flow from respect for personal rights.
3. List some of the rights that the declaration upholds in common with the U.S. Constitution. Name some that are not mentioned in the American document.
4. Why does the declaration single out marriage and the family unit for special mention?
5. Why does the declaration urge "teaching and education" as means of promulgating knowledge of human rights? Think of some of the implications of your answer.

3

The Arms Race and Its
Consequences for Developing Countries

Georgy Kim

This article originally appeared in *Asian Survey*, November 1984.

A Soviet viewpoint, as put forth by a member of the Academy of Sciences of the U.S.S.R., shows that serious commentators, whatever their ideology, agree on the basic facts of our nuclear-threatened world. Georgy Kim recognizes that arms buildups have a particularly severe effect on social progress in third world countries. Using Western sources (e.g., SIPRI—Stockholm International Peace Research Institute), Kim documents a rapid increase of weaponry that is drawing the newly independent nations into the vortex of superpower tensions.

The author deplores the weakening of detente ("relaxation of tensions") that took place in the 1970's and describes U.S. global strategy in terms that mirror Western perceptions of Soviet actions. Local conflicts in Asia, Africa and Latin America are exacerbated, in Kim's opinion, by arms from the West given to support "open confrontation" with the Soviet Union. In fact, he asserts, the more "potentially explosive regions are receiving larger consignments of arms than the less troublesome regions." Such infusions of armaments from East and West are having a destabilizing effect on a fragile global peace.

The author dismisses the arguments that such arms transfers are non-nuclear since "the gap between conventional and tactical arms is narrowing all the time." Indeed, the "conventional" weapons of today are far more powerful than their counterparts in World War II. Nor does the danger of nuclear proliferation to at least fifteen developing countries escape his attention.

In social and economic terms, Georgy Kim shows the deleterious effect of arms expenditures on the payments deficit of developing countries, with serious consequences on their health and education budgets. He has little patience with arguments that the establishment of war industries introduces needed technological advances into the poorer countries, thus stimulating the growth of employment. This Soviet spokesman, by declaring that "the present-day world is indivisible" and that the arms race

145

is "senseless and wasteful," sounds very much like critics of the arms race in the West. Citing "United Nations experts," he proposes a twenty percent reduction in world military spending as a necessary step toward third world economic development.

The author concludes, not surprisingly, with recommendations that the West give serious consideration to various Eastern bloc proposals "for ensuring security and peace on earth." Although such proposals gloss over the complicated nature of arms reduction talks and the absence of mutual trust, they show that the Soviet Union is sensitive to the high cost in human terms (not least to itself) of the spiraling arms race.

The sharp aggravation of the anti-relaxation of tensions and confrontation processes accompanied by the impetuous arms buildup at a global level is turning into the most dangerous reality of present-day developments in the world. Regretful as it may be, developing countries are being drawn more and more intensively into the arms race.

Needless to say, mounting confrontation and the arms race at global and regional levels lead to a destabilization of the world situation and enhance the threat of thermonuclear conflict. The current prominent trend in world relations of showing military strength and escalating militarism and the arms buildup not only increases the probability of a global thermonuclear catastrophe but also slows down social progress as a whole and exerts a particularly negative influence on the social and economic development of the newly free countries.

Now that the developing countries of Asia, Africa, and Latin America face the tremendous task of carrying through social and economic reforms designed to help them do away with backwardness, poverty, starvation, and disease, the general climate of international relations that would allow them to concentrate their efforts on solving the above-mentioned problems acquires primary importance.

The involvement of the developing countries in the system of contemporary international relations with all its negative consequences caused by confrontation and anti-relaxation factors leaves open to doubt their ability to put into effect national development programs. According to the Stockholm International Peace Research Institute (SIPRI), in 1982 spending on arms around the world reached the astronomic sum of 750 billion dollars.[1] This is approximately a 23-fold increase over the 1930s. Since 1978 military spending in the world has risen at an average annual rate of 4%, surpassing the annual growth rate of the world capitalist economy (1.5%).[2] The purpose of this essay is not to deal with the main aspects of the arms race in today's world but to concentrate instead on how the arms buildup affects developing countries. Events of the past few years show that as the global arms race accelerates, it tends to involve developing countries more and more in the general militarization process, promotes mini arms races, and creates dangerous hotbeds of confrontation between those countries, thus aggravating the already complicated international situation. In this context the anti-relaxation process that began developing in the mid-1970s has in our opinion considerably multiplied the negative influence of the global arms race on the arms buildup in developing countries.

It was in those years that the United States, after making the strategy of "open confrontation" with the Soviet Union at global and regional levels a cornerstone of its foreign policy course, began qualifying any social or political developments in the newly liberated countries as the result of the Soviet Union's "underhanded scheming" that infringed upon the vital interests of the United States. Interpreting freely the notion of the "defense of national or vital interests," the U.S. government, in fact, takes advantage of the situation in developing countries to meet its geopolitical ends and to tip the balance of forces in the world in its favor. As is known, the United States officially based its departure from the policy of relaxation of tension and its move toward greater confrontation on the unfavorable changes in developing countries that allegedly occurred there through the fault of the Soviet Union, who ostensibly used the relaxation process of the 1970s to achieve its own purposes. There is no need to dwell at length on this one-sided and tendentious approach of the U.S. government to the processes taking place in the so-called third world. Much more important here is the awareness that the implementation of the U.S. strategy of "open confrontation" in Asia, Africa, and Latin America, and also on the high seas, led and still leads to the drastic expansion of a conflict zone. It adds a global nature to conflicts and increases the level of tension. This in turn stimulates the general militarization trend and worsens the international situation by speeding up the arms race and drawing more and more countries and regions of the developing world into it.

All these factors taken together have created a situation in the Asian, African, and Latin American countries in which the relationship between the general strategy of the West and the global arms race, on the one hand, and local conflicts and mini arms races, on the other, has become more distinct and tangible, causing an ever greater instability in international relations and intensifying the negative effect of that instability on the developing countries.

Whenever there is talk about conflict areas on this planet, our eyes turn to developing countries, first and foremost. From the end of World War II up to 1982, a total of almost 150 local armed conflicts in which more than 10 million people died were registered in the world. Some 50 conflicts counted in the world today are all concentrated in the zone of the national liberation movement. There is no need to prove that the developing countries have sustained tremendous losses because of all these conflicts. The still continuing Iran-Iraq war alone has already taken, according to modest estimates, many thousands of human lives.

The anti-relaxation process has not only extended the developing countries' participation in conflicts but, first of all, has brought about a sharp rise in their military spending—from 27.8 billion dollars in 1970 to more than 125 billion dollars in 1982.[3] By 1982 the share of the developing countries in the world's total military spending amounted to 16% (as against 7.2% in 1970). The developing world leaves behind the industrially advanced countries in the ratio of this spending to GNP (5.9%). There are 15 million men in the armies of the newly liberated countries—60% of all the servicemen in the world. The developing countries account today for about 75% of the world's arms imports.[4]

The potentially explosive regions are receiving larger consignments of arms than other less troublesome spots. As SIPRI reported in 1983, in the years between 1978 and 1982, spending for military purposes increased by 18 billion dollars in the Middle East, by 12 billion dollars in East Asia (excluding China), by 8 billion dollars in Southern Africa, and by 7.5 billion dollars in Latin America; in other words, over this short period of time, military spending in the most conflict-prone regions rose by a total sum of 50 billion dollars.[5]

The mechanism escalating the arms race in developing countries is identical to the one escalating the global race—the purchases of new consignments and systems of arms by one group of countries automatically elicits similar moves in neighboring countries. This is a kind of chain reaction resulting in permanent expansion, an uninterrupted replenishment of military arsenals, a kind of race in the quantitative and qualitative accumulation of arms. Concerned with their security, many peace-loving genuinely nonaligned countries often have to seek help from alternative sources, redirecting their already scanty resources to military spending. For example, large deliveries of U.S. arms to Pakistan have proved to be, as Indian leaders point out, a destabilizing factor in the South Asian region. Former Indian President Reddi warned that these deliveries could upset the existing balance and set the stage for an arms race.[6] As a counterstep India had to sign an agreement with France on the delivery of 150 Mirage-2000 aircraft[7] and lately has been employing measures to further strengthen its security.

The relationship between the arms race and the social and economic development of the countries in Asia, Africa, and Latin America, requires a more detailed examination, especially since there are different opinions on that matter. Some researchers in the West tend to belittle the importance of mini arms races in the newly free countries, emphasizing the relatively small overall share of developing countries in the world's spending on military purposes. It's obvious, however, that for the developing world, with its backwardness, poverty, and starvation, even a one percent share in the world's spending on arms is not the same as it is for the industrially advanced countries. If this 1% share, which amounts to 7 billion dollars, were used for peaceful purposes, it could give the peoples of the developing countries additional opportunities to solve their most pressing economic and social problems.

One argument often advanced is that these countries are building up conventional and not nuclear arms and that therefore this does not deserve the serious attention of the world public. Naturally, nothing is said about the fact that the gap between conventional and tactical nuclear arms is narrowing all the time. During the Middle East war in 1973, it took only a few days to destroy by "conventional arms" the same amount of equipment it took weeks to destroy during major operations in World War II. Aviation in 1973 used concrete piercing and pellet bombs to demolish protected targets and increase casualties, and it used anti-air radar missiles and the latest in reconnaissance. In 1982 American-made "implosion" or "vacuum" bombs and also phosphorous and pellet bombs and shells were used in Lebanon for the first time. Consequently, as experience shows, so-called conventional arms have actually turned into "near-nuclear weapons"—that is, weapons whose destructive capacity can be equated with that of tactical warheads.

The escalation of the arms race in the developing world and the growing confrontation between individual countries has become the source of a perilous new danger—the possibility that some newly liberated countries may be given access to nuclear arms. The Brookings Institution in the United States claims that about 15 developing countries will be able to begin producing nuclear weapons in the near future.[8] Moreover, close to nuclear possession are several countries that nurture aggressive plans in relation to their neighbors. If these countries ever obtain nuclear arms it would have catastrophic consequences for all nations and would shatter the system of nuclear arms nonproliferation. The risk of a war with the use of nuclear arms would be enhanced many times. Consequently, the international community cannot afford complacency regarding "mini" arms races in developing countries.

Let's now look at the social and economic consequences of the arms race. It is a common view that arms purchases are a heavy burden on state budgets in many newly free countries and that they cause a growing deficit in balance of payments. Already in 1978 spending on arms accounted for half of all the developing countries' deficits of current accounts. Since then, as is known, this spending has been continuously and rapidly increasing. This tendency looks particularly alarming in light of the recent prediction issued by the International Bank for Reconstruction and Development. It says that the payments deficit of the developing countries is expected to exceed 276 billion dollars by 1995. Mention should be made at this point of the growing debt of the developing countries, which in 1983 reached the enormous sum of almost 700 billion dollars.

Some researchers claim that military spending exerts no serious negative influence on the economic growth rate and on the social infrastructure in developing countries. Dealing only with total sums of military expenditures, they often overlook deep economic and social consequences of military preparations that greatly upset the order of development priorities.

It is common knowledge that military spending in developing countries results in more "lost opportunities" than in the advanced countries. The weaker the economic and industrial foundation and the heavier the burden of formally equal (in terms of GNP) military expenditures, the stronger is their detrimental impact on the national economies since military expenditures in this case represent a straight deduction from the already low accumulation share. The developing countries' own military buildup in this case enlarges even further the imbalances in their economies and deforms their so far inadequate social and economic structures.

The case is not rare when the world's poorest countries, whose social and economic problems require urgent solution, become buyers of arms. It has been estimated, for example, that each dollar spent by these countries on military purposes cuts investments to the national economy by 25 cents. While channeling some 6% of their GNPs into military buildup, the poorest nations spend at the same time only 1% on health services and 2.8% on education.[9]

Being drawn more and more into general militarization processes, some developing countries have embarked on the creation of their own war industries. According to SIPRI experts, such industries already exist in at least 30 developing countries. At present 16 developing countries are producers of aircraft, 20 of military vessels, 8 of missiles, 5 of armored personnel vehicles, and so on.[10]

Some Western experts and researchers claim that the building of war industries in developing countries introduces advanced technology into their economies. In other words, they say the building of the war industry and scientific and technological progress are two inseparable processes. This opinion, however, is far removed from reality. Experience in the establishment of war industries in some developing countries proves that against the background of the generally backward industrial foundation, war industries demand a concentration of capital, high technology enterprises, and a skilled labor force—all ensured at the expense of civil production. What we are dealing with in this case are two peculiar industrial layers: the top military layer and the low civilian. As a result, war industries assume a closed, enclave nature. They function autonomously within the national economic system as an independent organism inside the economies of newly free countries, as a parasite on other industries. Arguments that war industries stimulate economic growth by acting as catalysts of scientific and technological advance cannot hold water. In any case, the negative influence is immeasurably greater than the positive contribution that war industries in developing countries make to the scientific and technological revolution.

By spending about 6% of their GNPs for military purposes, the developing countries cut their rate of economic growth by 1.6% to 2.1%.[11] This widens further the economic gap between the West and the developing countries. By the beginning of the 1980s, the gap between the advanced capitalist and the developing (non-oil-producing) countries in the rate of per capita income growth stood at a 22 to 1 ratio and exerted an increasingly unfavorable influence on the general climate of international relations. Furthermore, arms buildups in developing countries entail a huge nonproductive waste of labor resources of their most valued category—technical personnel. The technological level of the arms and military hardware manufacturing industries surpasses many times over that of the civilian branches of industry. The army and munitions industry makes it impossible to use for productive purposes the most able and well-trained workers, technicians, and engineers, who are always in short supply.

Some Western experts still believe that military spending and investments in the war industry, above all, are an effective means of maintaining and boosting employment, or at least relieving unemployment. In reality the effect is just the opposite: instead of bringing the unemployment level down, military investments send it up. It has been estimated that the investment of one billion dollars in the war industry creates jobs for approximately 75 thousand people, while the same sum invested in civilian production would create 92 thousand jobs in transport, 100 thousand in the building industry, 139 thousand in the health services, or 187 thousand in education. According to some estimates, a 30% cut in military spending and the use of the money thus released for civilian purposes would reduce unemployment in the United States by 2.1%.[12]

The unfavorable consequences of military buildups for advanced economies prove to be even more detrimental to the economies of developing countries. Maintained at the current rate, the military buildup in developing countries results in their economic stagnation, making it extremely difficult or even impossible for them to enter the road to social and economic progress.

There is one more, extremely important aspect to that problem. As a continuation and component part of the global arms race, the arms race in developing countries is turning more and more into a booster of international tension. This connection between two sides of one process preordains the concrete economic losses of developing countries caused by international tension and precludes the economic benefits that these countries might derive from the relaxation of tension and the halt of the arms race on both a global and regional scale. Through this relationship between the relaxation of tension and development one can see clearly that the present-day world is indivisible and that all the peoples of this planet are equally interested in preventing a new world war and in ending the senseless and wasteful arms race.

This demand of the times reaches more and more people in developing countries, where some have felt until recently that questions of war and peace were not of primary importance for those countries but the prerogative of the advanced countries and even the exclusive concern of the great powers. Experience, however, has refuted that theory. It has proved that at the current level of military technology increased tension affects all countries and peoples. Positive shifts in the developing countries' approach to war and peace were displayed at the 7th conference of nonaligned countries in Delhi in early 1983. The conference outlined as key tasks of the developing countries' foreign policy the need to work to defend peace, promote the relaxation of tension, and slow down the arms race. At the 6th session of the United Nations Conference for Trade and Development (UNCTAD), envoys of many developing countries pointed in their speeches to the relationship between international trade and economic cooperation. As Indian Prime Minister Indira Gandhi has declared, the progress of all countries, both advanced and developing, fully depends on world peace.[13]

Naturally, disarmament alone can hardly be a key to the solution of all the problems of social and economic development in the newly liberated countries, but to a great extent it would help improve the world economic order in which many problems experienced by developing countries are deeply rooted. United Nations experts believe that even a 20% reduction in the world's total military spending would not only satisfy the most pressing economic needs but also narrow considerably the gap in economic development between advanced and developing countries.[14] It would create additional opportunities for essentially increasing help to developing countries, as well as open new opportunities that would arise from a reduction in the military spending by developing countries themselves and from a possible rechanneling of their resources to the economic and social sphere with the aim of combating poverty, starvation, disease, and illiteracy.

Along with bringing obvious social and economic benefits, disarmament would also exert a favorable psychological effect on relations between people by helping them realize their common interests and their interdependence on this planet. Then the calls for a joint solution of global problems would have a considerably more active response from all the peoples on earth.

We are most certain that the proposals of the Soviet Union, the rest of the socialist community, and a number of developing countries contain concrete and realistic measures for ensuring security and peace on earth. They include the pledge not to be the first to use nuclear arms and the call for freezing American and Soviet nuclear arms and for signing an agreement between the Warsaw Treaty and NATO countries on the non-use of military force. There is also the pledge not to use nuclear arms against the nonnuclear countries, the call for creating peace and nuclear-free zones. In addition, these proposals provide for the nonproliferation of nuclear arms in any form, for a reduction of nuclear arms and their subsequent elimination in keeping with the principle of equality and equal security, for a cut in military budgets, and for many other measures designed not only to curb the arms race at a global level but also to weaken militarist trends in the developing world.

> Taking into account that growing military expenditures are closely linked to the escalation of the arms race, the political declaration adopted by the Warsaw Treaty countries in 1983 states that the participants in the meeting appeal to NATO countries to agree not to increase military spending and to subsequently reduce spending on a percentage basis or in absolute terms. . . . The money saved as a result of cuts in military spending would be used for economic and social development and in particular for helping developing countries progress along those lines.[15]

Similar ideas are contained in the proposal made by the Warsaw Treaty countries to NATO members on March 5, 1984.

Equally constructive could be joint initiatives aimed at promoting security, say, in the Indian Ocean, where there are genuine opportunities to establish a peace zone—an idea toward which India is working so persistently. Also important could be confidence-building measures in East Asia or an all-embracing settlement in the Middle East. Humanity is now confronted with a dilemma: either to find ways to ease international ten-

sions through the joint efforts of nations or to let the world slide down at
an increasing speed toward the abyss of a nuclear conflict. A third alternative simply does not exist.

Notes

1. SIPRI, *Yearbook 1983*, p. XL.

2. Ibid., OCED, May 1981; May, November 1982; May 1983.

3. See SIPRI, *Yearbook 1983*, p. 161 (the Chinese People's Republic,
Egypt, South Africa, and Israel are not included).

4. F. Castro, *The World Economic and Social Crisis* (Havana, 1983), pp.
204, 207. UNCTAD, *Trade and Development Report, 1982*, p. 123.

5. SIPRI, *Yearbook 1983*, p. 157.

6. *Time*, October 26, 1981.

7. Ibid.

8. E. Lefever, *Nuclear Arms in the Third World: U.S. Policy Dilemma*
(Washington, D.C.: Brookings Institution, 1979), p. 23.

9. *The Economist*, February 19, 1983, p. 54; IBRD, *World Development Report*, 1982, p. 110.

10. *Jeune Afrique* (Paris), Juillet 15, 1981, p. 62.

11. The estimates are made on the basis of UN Doc. A/8469/Rev. 1, 1978, p.
56.

12. *Der Spiegel*, No. 36, 1981, p. 42.

13. *FCIB*, No. 69, 1983, p. 1.

14. *Peace and Disarmament. Scientific Studies* (Moscow, 1980), p. 55.

15. *Pravda*, January 7, 1983.

Questions

1. Were you surprised by the relative lack of polemics in this article?
What reasons would you give for this?

2. Why did the author cite almost exclusively Western and United Nations sources for his data? What implications, if any, do you see in this
for the future of the social sciences?

3. What was the author's purpose in writing this article? Do you think he
succeeded? Give reasons.

4. Would Kim's points have been more persuasive if he had been more
specific in the sources he cites? Give three examples.

5. Identify the largest single element omitted in this article. How would
its inclusion have affected his conclusion?

4
The Perils of Intervention

Nicholas O. Berry

This article originally appeared in *Worldview*, March 1985.

There is a saying in the world of art that "less is more." Nicholas Berry, head of the department of political science at Ursinus College in Pennsylvania, applies this axiom to the world stage. Just as Georgy Kim warned that the arms race was hurting developing countries, Berry contends that superpower interference in the third world brings about results exactly opposite to what is intended.

Citing the American experience in such countries as Vietnam and Iran, the author judges intervention to be more trouble than it is worth. Berry generalizes that involvement in third world countries makes the local rulers less dependent on their own people, imposes an alien culture, misjudges the sources of unrest, excludes major sectors of the client nation from economic progress and encourages repression.

Berry distinguishes between external threats, where U.S. help can be productive, and internal ones, where it cannot. He does not in so many words propose "benign neglect," but his arguments tend in that direction. Alternatives suggested include multilateral foreign aid, partial debt forgiveness, the training of local civil servants (using the U.N.) and greatly increased educational exchanges.

The old ways of promoting peace, democracy and economic progress have largely failed. Berry feels that some fresh approaches are worth a try.

It is a truth, if not universally acknowledged at least widely accepted, that the United States Government would like its Third World allies and client states to be stable, progressive, democratic, and domestically popular. While the U.S. feels it must protect these allies and clients from direct Soviet aggression, ideally they would manage their internal problems themselves.

Unfortunately, the ideal is the exception in the Third World. Many of America's allies and clients face a disloyal opposition at home, and often one that seeks or attracts assistance from the Soviet Union or its surrogates. With few exceptions, these governments are neither democratic nor want to be: For every Costa Rica there is an El Salvador or a Guatemala; for every Singapore there is a South Korea or a Philippines.

Washington, therefore, confronts a dilemma. If it contemplates a hands-off policy, the U.S. is perceived as delivering the ally to the disloyal opposition and its Soviet or Cuban patrons. Yet when the U.S. does intervene to build the foundation of a stable democracy by recruiting leaders, helping with policy formulation, developing the country's infrastructure, and training the military, it is even more likely to aid the disloyal opposition. As recent administrations of both political stripes have shown, the United States has still to learn the lesson that massive intervention in the affairs of friendly governments actually puts those governments at considerable risk. Post mortems on Cuba, Vietnam, Ethiopia, Iran, Lebanon, and Nicaragua reveal five dangers of intervention.

First, U.S. intervention loosened the political elite's dependence upon the people. Before the significant U.S. presence, one became a member of the indigenous political elite by attracting a local following through patronage and protection. Once the U.S. with its largesse intervened, the political elite had a much more lucrative source of support. Government did not need the people. If the U.S. went so far as to send in troops, as in Vietnam, this effectively relieved the people of their duty to defend their society and government. U.S. aid also had the effect of strengthening government bureaucracies, which the elites then used to protect their interests in the cities and in the countryside, often by force. Finally, U.S. intervention linked the underdeveloped economy to the international economy, usually through a cash crop (Cuba's sugar) or a mineral resource (Iran's oil). This made the economy that served the people less important, less able to attract government attention—a process that Benedict J. Kerkvliet, in his perceptive study of the Huk rebellion in the Philippines, called "the ravages of progress." At base, democracy rests upon a government's relationship with its people, and U.S. intervention unwittingly breaks that relationship. In serving Washington's goals, governments come to depend upon the U.S., fail to serve their people, and give the opposition a motive for disloyalty.

Second, U.S. intervention in the affairs of friendly Third World states, involving as it does quantities of U.S. personnel, injects—even imposes—an alien culture. Americans abroad are always willing to pay for—and there are always those who are ready to sell—whatever is marketable, whether alcohol, food, music, or women. And the native government, closely associated with the U.S., becomes a partner in the corruption of the culture. A massive sector of the society gradually becomes disaffected, and the role of defending the indigenous culture is delivered to the rebel group. The Viet Cong and the Ayatollah Khomeini were quick to seize the mantle of nationalism, as is the FMLN in El Salvador today.

Third, U.S. intervention brings with it an outpouring of policy advice from Washington officials about how to deal with the problems of ignorance, poverty, and disease that is inevitably a reflection of Washington's priorities. Americans take it as an article of faith that these are the sources of social unrest. They are not sources of unrest—injustice alone is—but the advice flows anyway.

The U.S. has plans for increasing crop yields, advancing education, providing sanitation and health care, establishing voting procedures, improving counterinsurgency techniques, and much more. Local elites may attempt to resist adopting American-made plans to avoid looking to their people like American puppets. Some, notably Ngo Dinh Diem in South Vietnam, resisted too much. But the U.S. is willing to pay for cooperation, asking only that standards of human rights set by Congress or other government agencies be observed, and the deal is finally too good to pass up. Opposition forces, rightly perceiving that policy made in Washington better serves the interests of Washington than the interests of the indigenous people, have a motive for crying "imperialism."

Fourth, as U.S. policy, dollars, and experts are helping to ameliorate ignorance, poverty, and disease, and as new ties to the world economy are bringing wealth to the modern sector of the local economy, new social groups are born. Naturally these groups—unionized agricultural and industrial workers, small-scale entrepreneurs, teachers, writers, managers, and middle-class professionals—expect to join in the political process. The old elites, using a spectrum of techniques from death squads to manipulated election results, thwart the entrance of the new groups' leaders into the political establishment. With national resources often meager at best, they are unwilling to share power and wealth in order to gain the support of the new groups. And why should they? They have U.S. support. Democracy and its hopes are seen to be as frauds.

Fifth, although U.S. intervention brings calls by American officials for democracy and human rights (since this is how governments attract popular support), to the elite these demands appear to threaten its political status and to protect the disloyal opposition. Democracy lets "irresponsible" elements into government and eventually into complete political control. The opposition, always labeled Marxist, is viewed as making "demogogic" appeals to gullible masses. If it ever gains power, it will deliver on its promises by taking the wealth, land, and prestige of the old elite. There must be repression if the social order is to be saved—or so Batista believed in Cuba, Diem in Vietnam, Haile Selassie in Ethiopia, the shah in Iran, Somoza in Nicaragua, and so the military believe today in El Salvador. Meanwhile the opposition is confirmed in disloyalty. The political system has failed them: They have been excluded from power, their interests are neglected, they suffer repression. Extralegal action remains their only option. No matter how the U.S. intervenes, it appears, friendly governments are weakened and the disloyal opposition is strengthened.

SENSE AND NONSENSE

This was not always so. During the period 1947 to 1961 the world was dangerously bipolar and U.S. intervention did not appear to corrupt friendly regimes, no matter how weak or undemocratic, because intervention could be and was explained in terms of combatting external subversion. In his speech to Congress declaring the cold war on March 12, 1947, President Truman stated: "I believe that it must be the policy of the United States to support free peoples who are resisting attempted subjugation by armed minorities or by outside pressure." It made sense. U.S. assistance to Greece and Turkey and a host of other countries was not seen as American imperialism but as the selfless protection of vulnerable free world friends. The U.S., in John Lewis Gaddis's words, gained an empire by invitation.

By the early 1960s—when Charles de Gaulle began to assail the United States, the Chinese relationship with the USSR was deteriorating, and Europe and Japan had recovered economically from World War II— the world was no longer bipolar. To treat it as such, as the U.S. and USSR do today, is to create an artificial cold war, one that is intended to legitimize massive intervention by the two major powers. Undoubtedly, both states believe in their explanations. Armed to the teeth, what other status can they seek but leader of the socialist camp or leader of the free world? And when major powers act as if they believe in the cold war, they lend it a certain credibility. So both the U.S. and the USSR try to subvert the allies and clients of the other by supporting the disloyal opposition or countering the opposition's subversion, and both powers succeed in corrupting the very governments they intended to aid and preserve.

Meanwhile, within the client countries the conflict continues between old elites in power and new groups seeking political entry. The governing elites friendly to the U.S. label the new groups Marxist and repress them, and the U.S. finds itself aiding and abetting this process; indeed, the governing elites often reach the point of using the U.S. in their strategy of repression. But this strategy, which the U.S. makes both possible and likely, fails in the end. From Cuba to Iran, the forces of nationalism have ultimately rallied to the side of the opposition.

U.S. intervention, then, though it tends to weaken the opportunity for rebellion, greatly increases the motivation for it; and so we witness periodic upheavals that result in the establishment of yet other regimes hostile to the United States. The problem for Washington is how to get the old elites to open their political systems and accept democratic reforms, reversing their current counterproductive policies. How can revolution by authoritarian extremists with Soviet, Cuban, or Vietnamese sponsorship be avoided? How, ultimately, can the balance of power be preserved?

THE MAILED FIST

Historically, one overriding, pervasive political condition has spawned democracy: the threat of revolution and violence. Perhaps Americans ignore this condition because its contradicts the conventional idea of U.S. history and sullies the myth of democracy's enlightened and rational basis.

Liberals, conservatives, and Marxists alike fail to understand the power of a revolutionary threat for effecting political change. Liberals and conservatives see it as an aberration; Marxists as insufficient. But see what it has done! The American experience is illustrative. In the nineteenth century, workers resorted to sporadic violence to win economic and political rights, a phenomenon that carries with it the threat of permanent violence against the established order if just grievances are not redressed. At the turn of the century there were massive demonstrations for women's suffrage; after the Second World War there were demonstrations to demand civil rights for black citizens. Both movements, it is true, were largely nonviolent. However, the charm of nonviolent strategy, as Mohandas Gandhi and Martin Luther King, Jr., well knew, is the threat of ultimate violence. For if the government does not satisfy the just demands expressed in nonviolent protest, the government is rejecting not just the demands but nonviolence as well, stating in effect that it prefers violent protest. Such a government begs for attacks upon itself. It condemns itself as unjust, unreasonable, and self-destructive.

Governments without patrons to prop them up will concede much to avoid domestic violence. Violence implies that the government has so failed a segment of its people that they must rebel, leaving the government in the absurd position of protecting itself from its own citizens. Violence is expensive for the government in money and blood. It is also contagious, attracting others with grievances, feeding upon itself, drawing in the friends and relatives of those incarcerated, injured, or killed. Violence always threatens to get out of control. And the government might lose everything. Better to open the franchise and accept gradual change; better to preserve the legitimacy of the political system. The experiences of Britain, France, Spain, and even of the Federal Republic of Germany and of Japan (where the threat of violence emanated from the occupying authorities) are all examples of such change.

The development of stable, popular, friendly governments requires that nothing be done by the U.S. to lessen the opportunity for revolution in Third World client states. If the opportunity for revolution is wide open, governments will have to avoid creating the motives for revolution. It appears to go against common sense to say that the weaker the government in a Third World client state, the more the U.S. must restrain itself. Yet that is the case if the United States wants to avoid converting a threat of revolution into the act of revolution.

This is not a call for benign neglect but, rather, for the end of massive, clumsy, often arrogant intervention. Alternative policies exist, both active and sophisticated. The encouragement of regional international organizations, an increase in multilateral foreign aid (especially to diversify Third World economies), the use of bilateral aid to satisfy the demands of new groups brought into the political system, the negotiation of measures for partial debt-forgiveness, the training (especially through the U.N.) of civil servants, the diffusion of knowledge through greatly expanded educational exchanges, agreements to stabilize the terms of trade—these are but a few of the directions U.S. Third World diplomacy might take.

Questions

1. The author names six countries in which U.S. intervention has backfired. In what ways is this true? How did the internal situations of these countries differ?

2. How does the author understand the meaning of "intervention"? Is it only military? How else does a large country intervene in the affairs of a smaller one?

3. Does the threat of "imposition of an alien culture" constitute a sufficient reason not to intervene in another country? What would be other reasons?

4. What factors would have to be present for you to support a major intervention in another country? List the pros and cons.

5. Do the author's warnings on global intervention apply to the Soviet Union as well? Give examples.

5

The Costly Business of Arming Africa

Patrick Fitzgerald and Jonathan Bloch

This article originally appeared in *African Business*, February 1985.

Of all the continents, today's Africa appears to be the most politically chaotic and economically underdeveloped. Most of the continent's divisions are internal, with nascent rebellions fomented by outside forces. The authors contend that large subsidies from the industrial powers make arms exports possible. These powers could, if they wanted, impose what the authors call "rational controls."

It may come as a surprise to learn that the U.S.S.R. is the leading arms supplier to sub-Saharan Africa, followed by France, Great Britain, West Germany and the U.S. The United States faces heavy competition in its effort to secure a larger share of the African weapons market and so has turned to other methods to secure a greater foothold. Other advanced countries trying to expand their share include South Africa and Israel, which maintain close collaboration in research, development and production of weapons systems.

The authors confine themselves to the basic facts of arms sales. Their article should be read against the background of widespread starvation, soil erosion, massive population increase and weak government infrastructure. Given these conditions, the marketing of lethal weapons takes on a horrendous dimension.

Although official secrecy shrouds the full dimensions of military sales to African countries, the authors paint an ominous picture of rich countries dragging their poorer cousins into a geopolitical confrontation they may not desire and they certainly cannot afford.

Although the rate of growth has recently declined slightly, sub-Saharan Africa's arms bill between 1980 and 1983 was a staggering $7.5bn. And unlike many other purchases abroad, these funds do not help create any extra wealth in society.

Selling arms is as controversial as using them, but large export subsidies by the main suppliers mean that it is from the industrialised world that the main impetus to improve rational controls must come. The latest

161

voice to be added to this is that of senior US Senator Mark Hatfield, a Republican from Oregon, who has just presented a new report to President Reagan on the world arms trade with the plea, "I implore you to reject the sad and seemingly universal notion that arms sales are uncontrollable and that there is little use in trying to negotiate restraints among the world's major suppliers."

MAJOR CUSTOMERS

The major importers are Ethiopia, Nigeria, Angola and Sudan, all of which spent over $100m each in 1982 (the last year for which figures are available), followed by Somalia, Kenya and Zimbabwe.

The patterns are well established. Angola, for instance, imports so much because it is fighting a war, and oil revenues make the imports easier than otherwise. Oil income applies to Nigeria too, but the size of the military establishment is more a natural result not just of civil war but also of a long succession of military governments. Last year's budget allocation for defence rose higher than that for any other sector of the economy.

Ethiopia and Sudan, however, although ruled by regimes with very important military components, are much poorer than Angola and Nigeria. Their massive arms build-up has been amassed largely on outright grants or credit from their major suppliers, which both have political objectives of their own expressed in the arms traffic which outweigh financial considerations. And alliances tend to be stronger when one of the parties is heavily in debt to the other.

However, several countries without the major superpower interest and under severe foreign-exchange problems—like Zambia and Tanzania—have been obliged to leave the big-spender league.

MAJOR SUPPLIERS

The largest single exporter to sub-Saharan Africa is the USSR, which supplies around half the market, with a virtual monopoly in Ethiopia and Angola. After the Soviets come the French, who hold a strong position in Nigeria and a 10% share overall. Britain, which also supplies Nigeria's as well as most of Zimbabwe's arms requirements, and West Germany have around 6% each. The US, despite being the largest single supplier to the Third World as a whole, has cornered only 4.5% of the sub-Saharan African market.

WHO SELLS WHAT

Beyond this simple hierarchy of suppliers are relative strengths and weaknesses in the provision of different types of weapons systems. In recent years, the Soviet Union has dominated the supply of tanks, artillery, supersonic combat aircraft and missiles, while Western European companies have led in deliveries of ships, armoured cars and subsonic aircraft.

In the long term the Soviet market position is under greater threat from the Reagan administration's more aggressive policy towards Africa and from the entry into the market of new suppliers like Israel and Brazil. This presents a political as well as an economic problem, since recipient countries usually continue to rely on the original supplier for repairs and maintenance, thus providing the supplier with a valuable political lever. Both Eastern and Western influence is maintained by the "spare parts dependency" factor, of which they make routine use. This factor also significantly raises defence costs beyond the expectations at the time of purchase.

SATURATED MARKET

The US government, which has set a high political value on African arms sales, faces difficulties in entering an already saturated market. They have concentrated, therefore, on the growing demand for military training and ancillary services, covering internal security forces as well as the orthodox military. During 1985, 18 African countries will get direct US funding, which includes five "major country programs" in Botswana, Cameroon, Liberia, Senegal and Zaire. The US has only recently introduced these grants, although they have long been standard Soviet practice. In 1982 the Reagan administration also created the Special Defence Acquisition Fund, which stockpiles arms and equipment to allow quicker transfers abroad, and in each succeeding year has sought to increase the size of the fund.

AID LESS TIED

The unique feature of the US grants is that for the first time, the recipient will not be obliged to make its purchases from donor-country manufacturers—a condition normally attached to military aid. Under the terms of the 1981 strategic co-operation agreement between the US and Israel, US military aid can be used to purchase Israeli-made weapons. Since 1983,

Israel has sold arms to Zaire, Liberia and the anti-government National Resistance Movement (MNR) in Mozambique.

Israel is not the only newcomer to the African arms market. According to the Stockholm International Peace Research Institute (Sipri), Brazil is now the foremost Third World producer of complete weapons systems and has built up a sizeable export industry for them. Most sales have gone to the Middle East (Libya and Egypt) and to Central America, but at least two African countries—Zimbabwe and Gabon—have bought Brazilian armoured cars.

SA EXPORTS

Another keen exports-seeker is the South African government-owned arms manufacturing company Armscor, which has launched an intensive search for overseas markets to compensate for the slackening of domestic demand while at the same time using it as a vehicle to reduce its own political isolation. Armscor has so far secured orders in Latin America, Morocco and possibly Oman (only these have become public knowledge) but has had no success reported in sub-Saharan Africa for obvious reasons. But the South Africans have benefitted indirectly from Israeli sales, since both countries have collaborated closely in research, development and production of a wide range of weapons systems. They benefit also from the continuing Israeli diplomatic offensive in Africa, in which arms sales play a vital role.

STRONG DEMAND

Whoever the supplier is, the reasons for the acquisition of large quantities of arms are often as much to do with prestige as with potential security threats, even though conflict shows no sign of diminishing in Africa. And if export subsidies and bribes to pliant ministers are considered, it is easy to see how African countries can accumulate weapons they cannot reasonably afford. Certainly, there is no chance that the coming years will see reductions in the arms trade on the continent so long as the most powerful nations in the world continue to see a large inventory of their own weapons as the most reliable index of a country's political support.

Questions

1. What would account for the fact that the U.S. has lagged behind Europe as an arms supplier to Africa?

2. In which military items does the U.S.S.R. lead in exports to Africa? In which items is Europe predominant?

3. What is meant by "spare parts dependency"? How does it work?

4. How does U.S. aid to Africa differ from its policy toward other third world nations? What reasons can you think of to explain this policy change?

5. Give at least two reasons that Israel has for arms sales to Africa.

6
Whose Development?:
Women Strategize

Laurien Alexandre

This article originally appeared in *Christianity & Crisis*, September 16, 1985.

At the conclusion of the United Nations Decade for Women in 1985, two conferences—one official and the other non-governmental—were held in Nairobi, Kenya, a nation in which women's exploitation is visible on all sides. The author, who teaches journalism at the University of California in Northridge, attended Forum '85, the non-governmental gathering.

Ms. Alexandre's summary of Forum '85 is a condensation of hundreds of meetings and workshops in which world peace was repeatedly linked to development, and development to the liberation of women from oppressive social structures. The targets of the feminist critiques were many: poor development planning, economic crises, militarization and traditional patriarchal attitudes.

Drawing on U.N. documents, the participants discussed the fact that most of the productive work in Africa—and in other developing areas—is done by women, but that they have benefited little from economic development projects. In some cases, women ended the decade worse off than when they began. The work of non-governmental organizations (NGOs) was decisive in collecting and evaluating the worldwide data on the condition of women.

Going beyond male-dominated programs and sexist ideology, the seminar leaders found fault with the colonial heritage which still kept land in the hands of the few and resulted in environmental damage, the growth of urban slums, the rise in prostitution and other social ills.

After independence, most countries did little or nothing to change practices inherited from the colonial powers. Even the entry of women into technologically advanced industries, such as electronics, has left them vulnerable to economic and personal exploitation. The motto of the Forum '85 conference was: "Women do two-thirds of the world's work, earn ten percent of the world's income and own one percent of the world's property." Women's domestic roles of wife and mother, which are not even

166

calculated in official studies of labor, must be added to all the other work they do.

Various solutions were offered to the massive problems facing the world's poor women, many of them focusing on locally based cooperatives and grass-roots organizations. Given the link between peace, justice and women's development, the world's future has much to gain by acting on the insights of a concerned feminist perspective.

In 1975, the International Women's Year Conference announced to the world the opening of a decade dedicated to women's progress. Since that time, women's role in the economic, social, and political development process has been a major component of national and international forums. The World Conference for the Review and Appraisal of the UN Decade for Women, and the simultaneously held nongovernmental gathering known as FORUM '85, both of which were convened in Nairobi, Kenya, in July, were the latest steps in this international women's campaign.

One of the most important lessons learned from the decade was the realization that the entire issue of development planning must be re-thought. It must be reconceptualized from an inherently feminist per-spective if women, and society as a whole, are to truly reap its rewards. As a participant in FORUM '85, I was overwhelmed by the complexity of the development theme, impressed by the sophistication of the analysis and by the collective ingenuity of women under the worst of social, polit-ical, and economic conditions. I was also struck by the incredible urgency of this feminist reconceptualization. Many thousands of lives are indeed at stake.

The tremendous concern devoted to this issue stems from the very real fact that over the last two United Nations Development Decades (1960–1980) the situation of women in developing countries deteriorated, and that trend is continuing. This is not simply because of faulty devel-opment planning, but also because of the world economic crisis, militari-zation, and traditional patriarchal attitudes.

The main themes of the UN Decade for Women were development, peace, and equality. Literally hundreds of workshops at the Nairobi forum repeatedly stressed that peace is not separate from development (eco-nomic, social, political) and that development is unattainable without full equality. The feminist critique assumes that without full social political, and economic equality, neither a nation nor its people can progress. And if nations suffer under the weight of famine, poverty, and social inequities, there can be no peace within or between countries. This conceptual lin-kage was stated in a publication from DAWN (Development Alternatives with Women for a New Era) prepared for Nairobi. In the booklet's synthesis of feminism and development the writers note, "Equality for women is impossible within the existing economic, political, and cultural processes that reserve resources, power, and control for small sections of people. But neither is development possible without greater equity for and participation by women. Our vision of feminism has at its very core a process of economic and social development geared to human needs through wider access to economic and political power."

The United Nations conducted the first comprehensive, interdisciplinary and multisectoral world survey on the role of women in overall development as a major project of the decade. The conclusions, and accompanying charts, graphs, and data were presented at the World Conference as a key document entitled World Survey on the Role of Women in Development. The publication discusses women in rural and urban development, as well as women's participation in social and political life, focusing on an overview of development, women in agriculture, industry, finance, science and technology, trade, conservation and energy, the concept of self-reliance and the integration of women in development. It is not only dry but disheartening to read. The document concludes that women are a very significant part of development but that they benefit far less from it than men. In fact, what it conclusively illustrates is that women have been left out of the development process, deflating widely accepted assumptions about the universal distribution of development benefits. In many cases, women's lives have actually deteriorated as a result of programs which many thought were beneficial, or at least, benign.

Much of the decade's research on development was also conducted by nongovernmental organizations (NGOs) working on national, regional, and global levels. This list of active NGOs would include groups ranging from Planned Parenthood and Save the Children Federation, to the SWAPO Women's Council, Church Women United, and the National Federation of Indian Women. In recent years, NGOs have exercised an increasingly important role in the work of the UN agencies. While they lack official decision-making powers, their impact as a force which investigates conditions, educates the uninformed, activates the concerned, and lobbies government machineries has changed the human environment and pushed forward the goals of women's advancement. There are literally hundreds of NGOs worldwide—from rural-oriented to professional, from reformist to revolutionary, from religious to secular—that have participated in the collection and evaluation of data on, about, and for women during this past decade. Their findings and experiences provided the central foundation of FORUM '85.

While the spirit of the gathered women was empowering and uplifting, what was quantitatively and qualitatively shown is that the consequences of many development programs have resulted in interlinked crises of growing impoverishment, inequality, food insecurity, financial and monetary disarray, and environmental degradation. The ideological and economic climate for genuine human development is gloomier today than it was at the start of the decade. Society's acceptance of male domination and female subordination has pervaded development work, adding insult to injury already existing because of drought, hunger, militarization, and the like.

But the feminists' critiques of development policies go far beyond the identification of male-dominated programming and sexist ideology. As accurate as the critiques may be, they are insufficient. The existing inequities, not only between men and women, but also between classes, ethnic groups, and nations, need to be understood within the context of the third world's colonial heritage. The colonial era laid the basis for many of these incquities by its particular positioning of third world countries in the world economy. For example, primary exports became the most important development pole in most of these countries because that is what served the needs and desires of the colonizers. Large segments of the native population were limited in their access to land, or were alienated from it under highly exploitative conditions which fostered degradation of soils, forests, and people, the rapid growth of urban slums, the rise of prostitution, and other by now well-known social ills.

Female poverty increased significantly under colonial rule as did the absolute and relative economic gap between the sexes. This process set the landscape upon which development policies and modernization were to evolve in future generations. It was simply not true that Western rule brought with it egalitarian relations. In fact, according to many, the reverse is far more accurate. In one publication prepared for the Nairobi forum, *Women: Protagonists of Change*, an article entitled "Losing the Land" notes that "Egalitarian relations or at least mutually respectful relations were a living reality in much of the world in precolonial times, which was far from the case in Western culture."

Postcolonial development processes and strategies have often exacerbated gender-based subordinations. For many countries, there has been little structural realignment since the 1960s independence movements. Many have retained their dominant feature from the colonial era as primary export enclaves within the world economic order. Development strategies during the first two development decades were often designed to satisfy the requirements of an economy open to the flows of foreign trade rather than the needs of national populations.

The development debates over the last three decades have generally

DIVISION OF LABOUR

Women in Africa do up to three quarters of all agricultural work in addition to their domestic responsibilities.

Ploughing 30%

Planting 50%

Livestock 50%

Harvesting 60%

Weeding 70%

Processing and storing crops 85%

Domestic work 95%

WOMEN   MEN

Source: UN Economic Commission for Africa.

focused on competing positions concerning growth versus people-centered development, export-led growth versus inward-oriented production, the problems of international money and finance, the proper role and functioning of multinational corporations, and on technological modernization and appropriateness. Today, with the pressures of world recession, slowdowns in trade, and the burden of the economic debt, third world countries are under greater pressure than ever to open their economies to foreign capital, to divert resources for exports, and to use scarce capital to repay interest on debts rather than subsidize much needed social services.

As a result, the survival of large sections of the population in third world countries has become increasingly uncertain and vulnerable. For women, this vulnerability is further reinforced by traditional male domination which, on the one hand, denies or limits their access to economic resources, political participation, and social equality, and on the other hand, imposes sexual divisions of labor that allocate to them the longest hours of work, and the most onerous, labor-intensive, poorly rewarded tasks both inside and outside the home.

THROUGH WOMEN'S EYES

The vantage point of women in the development debate is unique and crucial. First, if the goals of development include removal of poverty, access to dignified employment, and reduction in societal inequality, then it is essential to start with women. Secondly, women's work, as undervalued as it is, is vital to the survival and ongoing reproduction of human beings in all societies. Thirdly, in many societies women's work in trade, services, and traditional industries is widespread. Finally, it is now recognized that women workers are often predominant in the most technologically advanced industries such as electronics and export production, as well as primary producers in the more agriculturally-based economies. Suffice to say, women are everywhere, doing everything, and being undervalued and underpaid for their efforts. A slogan sums it up: Women do two-thirds of the world's work, earn ten percent of the world's income, and own just one percent of the world's property.

The feminists' critiques of development have questioned its orientation and its ramifications through a thorough examination of development strategies and a rigorous analysis focusing on the multinationals; rural development and food production (including appropriate technologies and income generation); health, migration, and tourism; education; and communication. Each one of these areas, and many more, received attention at Nairobi through films, dialogues, encounters, panels, and workshops, as thousands of participants searched for an enriched feminist understanding of development.

Labor is a case in point. Researchers during the women's decade raised a fundamentally important question about the data collection and assessment of women's work. What has become strikingly apparent is that women's work is underestimated in official statistics largely because such work tends to be confined to sectors that "escape" registration: work in the informal and agricultural sectors, and most especially, domestic work. Being unpaid labor, it lowers the cost of reproducing the labor force (and of sustaining it) and therefore is a powerful factor in the accumulation of capital in many countries at all levels of development. "One of the major underlying causes of women's inequality," says the UN-prepared State of the World's Women 1985, is that "a woman's domestic role as wife and mother—which is vital to the well-being of the whole of society, which consumes around half of her time and her energy—is unpaid and under-valued." Not only have development programs not taken this into account, but often male development planners have neglected to even consider this labor as "work." One of the strongest grassroots efforts witnessed at the NGO forum and lobbied for at the UN Conference was the demand of Wages for Housework, a British-based group which has given birth to an international campaign to get governments to count the contributions of unpaid work that women do in the home, farm, and other fields. The Wages for Housework campaign wants women's work to be valued and reflected in every Gross National Product.

What about agricultural labor? Have rural women's lives been bettered by development programs? The answer, while not absolute in all cases, is unfortunately no. Women's work is especially under-enumerated in agriculture, despite the fact that in many developing countries, notably in Africa, women constitute the predominant labor force in this sector. According to the previously discussed UN survey, in some countries women constitute as much as 80 percent of agricultural labor, although they receive a much smaller proportion of the income and of the benefits from national development. Rural women's access to land, labor, new technology, extension services, and credit appears to have worsened in most parts of the third world. When land reforms have been undertaken, they have often reduced women's control over land by ignoring their traditional use-rights and giving titles solely to male heads of households. When agricultural mechanization has occurred, it has worsened or at best not improved women's absolute and relative economic positions. Mechanization of food-processing technologies often drastically reduces women's employment and income. Even the general premise that women and men will be affected in the same direction by processes of commercialization cannot be upheld. In parts of West Africa, for example, the introduction of cash crops has improved the economic position of some men but worsened the income and work status of women from the same households. Women's workloads in tasks such as fuel gathering and water collection have in fact tended to increase with development in many instances, as waste and common lands have been privatized. Again, according to the UN report on the women's decade, agricultural modernization has not only failed to increase the living standard of rural women but "It has failed to affect women's productivity because it bypassed them, or even pushed women out of work by mechanizing the work traditionally done by them."

The effects of industrial development on women are mixed and contradictory. In the industrialized economies, the increase in employment opportunities for women during the decade was apparent, but they filled most of the low-paying and less skilled jobs in this sector. The employment of third world women in certain export-based industrialized jobs—often called the global assembly lines—has also increased. And while there is no doubt that for many third world women with no skills and few other options for wages, such employment is viewed as an opportunity, the benefits to women of this primarily multinational factory work is questionable. Within these industries, women tend to be segregated into a relatively narrow range of occupations. Employment tends to be short term, with high turnover and low wages.

Of special concern to the forum's workshops on development was this whole issue of third world women and multinationals. Hundreds of workshops examined transnational corporations (TNCs), to use the UN's term, and the effect they have on the lives of women in both developing and developed countries. Discussion after discussion focused on the gender structure of employment in the world economy, with third world women providing cheap labor for transnational corporations headquartered in the developed nations, primarily the United States. A virtually unlimited supply of young women who will accept the lowest wages and unbearable working conditions is one of the primary attractions for these corporations. Women are often the best selling points for the industrializing world. As a Malaysian government brochure says, "The manual dexterity of the Oriental female is famous the world over. Her hands are small and she works fast and with extreme care." If this is development, we must ask for whom?

WHO DETERMINES WHAT DEVELOPMENT?

It was noted by many Nairobi participants that the World Bank and the U.S. Agency for International Development have pressured many developing countries to accept development projects which foster conditions favorable to investment and multinational outposts. The feminists' critique of this aspect of development policy seems self-evident. The health and safety of women workers must come before the desirability of free trade zones which entice TNCs with lax work codes and by banning union activity. The solution offered in The Effects of Racism and Militarization on Women's Equality, prepared by the U.S.-based Women's Coalition was "to remove the incentive to shift production to the third world by building strong trade unions and raising wages to a comparable level around the world." The document suggests controls which should be imposed on TNCs and the necessary unity of action by women workers in both the developed and developing world. It asserts, "We must be every bit as conscious of the need for coordinated international actions as are the corporations who now determine the quality of all our lives."

Another aspect of economic development which received significant attention in Nairobi is that of the impact of emerging technologies on women. In many ways, technological change is at the heart of development. The critical concern voiced at the gathering by numerous participants is that the introduction of new technology often undermines traditional forms of production, tends to displace women and households, and wreaks havoc with the environment. Consistent with the male-dominated orientation of development planning, women have seldom participated in designing the new technologies nor in being consulted before one is introduced. Women's organizations around the world and as a result of the decade's research are attempting to stop this neglect because the results of it are proving fatal.

The campus of the university in Nairobi hosted an ongoing exhibition known as Tech and Tools. Here, workshops, demonstrations, videos, and encounters examined the use of technology by and for women. The poster hanging outside the site's entrance proclaimed, "If it is not appropriate for women, it is not appropriate." Tech and Tools provided participants with a visual reminder of the ingenious creativity of many women in developing countries, as well as the misapplication by donor organizations and nations of technologies which failed to take the female user into consideration. The introduction of new technologies may be inevitable, but it is important that women participate in the planning, designing, manufacturing, managing, and utilizing of these emerging products.

During the past decade, concerned researchers and involved organizations have rethought the women and development issue. Workshops at the forum in Nairobi presented the results of the intellectual and experiential process. Many participants developed sophisticated analyses of the errors and faults of traditional development planning. Grassroots initiative, rural women's projects, locally-based cooperatives and other types of community organizations have developed in opposition to the top-down approach of many development agencies. Hundreds of successful rural women's projects in Asia, Africa, and Latin America have evolved during the decade. But many hundreds more have failed, because of underfunding, lack of expertise or managerial support, and tremendous external obstacles imposed by tradition, politics, and economics. Far beyond the small but significant gains resulting from any one particular project, many Nairobi participants pointed to the increased self-confidence of the women involved in even the smallest of income-generating projects. By reinforcing, for example, women's expertise in food gathering and food production, their skills and experience became valued. The key word was "empowering." It is the goal of feminist development projects to empower women (and have women empower themselves) so they can alter their personal lives and build movements for social change.

In the long run, many involved in this feminist critique of development planning see that not only must patriarchy be challenged, but that all the structures which create and perpetuate inequities—be they social, political, or economic—must be opposed and transformed. There is no one strategy to insure equitable development for all in every country and region. Whether they be reformist strategies which help alleviate problems without attention to primary causes, or whether they be radical strategies which propose alternatives to existing structures believed to be the root of inequities, the feminist development approaches assert that at the very core, economic and social development must be geared toward human needs. The hope is that the worldwide formal and informal women's networks forged during the decade and solidified at the African gathering will ensure that women—as individuals and as groups—will continue to push forward for development, peace, and equality. Feminism was not an abstract principle in Nairobi. Nor was development a distant bureaucratic practice. Both were, and are, concrete goals to be achieved through a continuing process of open debate and global networking toward united action.

Questions

1. Why does the author assert that the entire issue of development planning must be rethought? Give examples.
2. What does "full equality" mean in the context of the problems of poor women?
3. Why did the participants at Nairobi link peace, development and liberation? In what ways does this linkage apply to the poor in this country?
4. What role has colonialism played in the status of women in Africa? Why have such attitudes and practices continued to the present?
5. How has the entry of transnational (multinational) corporations affected women's employment in the third world? How can citizens of this country affect corporate activities overseas?

7
Seedlings of Survival

Barbara Howell

This article originally appeared in *Christianity & Crisis*, September 16, 1985.

Not all the news coming out of Africa is bad. Barbara Howell of Bread for the World, a Christian citizens' lobby concerned with world hunger, reports on the Nairobi women's conference from the ground up. Through the life of Nonkera, a woman of Kenya, she describes how a reforestation project in Njemps Flats offers hope to the women of the third world. With the help of overseas development organizations, women like Nonkera have been given equal access with men to loans, seeds, fertilizer and good advice. "The result," writes Howell, "was that women made more efficient use of the land and produced bigger harvests than the men." Though such projects for women are few and far between, the author concludes that they provide a key to the process by which peace and justice can be achieved in a world which has fared badly under male domination.

In the hot, dusty Njemps Flats near Lake Baringo, on the floor of the Great Rift Valley, a geophysical marvel which splits Kenya from north to south, a woman paused in her weeding to speak with a group of foreigners who had come from the United Nations Women's Conference in Nairobi to observe the work of a development project.

"My name is Nonkera," she told us through an interpreter. "I am happy that my family now has maize to eat."

Nonkera, a member of the small Njemps tribe who are mostly herders and subsistence farmers, comes to the forestry and soil conservation demonstration project five days a week, for five hours a day. She prepares the soil, plants and weeds drought-resistant tree seedlings and sorghum as part of a joint "food-for-work" development project of the UN World Food Program, the Food and Agriculture Organization, and the Kenyan government. She is paid with weekly rations of corn (called "maize" in Kenya) and cooking oil.

Although Kenya escaped the worst ravages suffered in neighboring Ethiopia, the most severe drought in many years struck in 1983 and 1984.

Cattle, sheep, and goats, the tribe's main source of income and food, died and vegetation in the overgrazed area was further decimated. The semiarid conditions prevailing in a large part of the country make it especially vulnerable to bad environmental practices such as overgrazing, and to drought.

Even before the drought, the need for major replanting of trees in the area was apparent. Nonkera must walk two miles a day to find wood, carrying it home on her back to cook her food. The fast-growing varieties of trees she is planting will make this time-consuming task easier in years to come. In the meantime, she and her six children need the donated food for which she works, and she is learning new skills.

About 200 miles south of the Njemps Flats is Nairobi, the capital of Kenya, where delegates from 159 nations to the UN Women's Conference were plowing through a document called "Forward-Looking Strategies to the year 2000" recommending actions to achieve the goals of the UN's just-ended Decade for Women. The majority of the recommendations under the Decade's themes—equality, development, and peace—focus on women's important role in development.

Appropriately, this final conference of the Decade was held in Africa, where the importance of development is urgently apparent. Its location not only enabled women from other parts of the world to see first hand development projects their countries had helped fund (members of the U.S. delegation took time out from the UN sessions to visit some projects), but it provided the opportunity to expose African women and men to the goals of the Decade.

Unlike the 1980 mid-Decade gathering in Copenhagen, where two-thirds of the women in attendance were from developed countries, more than half of the 12,000 (mostly) women who poured into Nairobi to attend the nongovernmental FORUM '85—an exuberant gathering that overlapped the more staid official UN conference—were Africans. Kenyan women were especially prominent, coming from every part of the country as a result of well-promoted preparatory meetings.

The African women's majority presence in Nairobi colored (both literally and figuratively) the proceedings and raised the problems faced by third world women to a much higher place on the women's agenda. In turn, their exposure to the issues of women's rights and challenges to the culturally accepted role of women's subordination to men strengthened African women's groups' determination to press for equal rights.

Most Kenyans, as well as other Africans, had not even known there was a Women's Decade before the preparations for this conference began. By the end, many more African women and men had discussed and debated issues important to women and to national development.

After the conference, the leader of the Kenyan delegation (a woman) proclaimed—perhaps a bit too optimistically—"Kenyan women will never be the same!"

Despite the upbeat feeling of empowerment and sisterhood which permeated FORUM '85 and the final jubilation of the UN conference delegates when the "Forward-Looking Strategies" document was signed by all the countries there, the majority of women in the world, like Nonkera, subsisting in rural poverty, are unaware of the hopes and plans for their future expressed in July at Nairobi.

WOMEN FEEDING AFRICA

In Africa three-quarters of the agricultural production is done by women, more than anywhere else in the world. The current food crisis should force governments and private development agencies to focus much more of their development efforts on enabling women to produce more food. But if the past is any guide, they will be slow to learn.

African participants at a FORUM '85 workshop on agriculture and food, organized by Kenyan women, expressed their frustration at the constraints faced by women farmers. "The Kenyan government does not recognize women as economic producers but only as subsistence farmers. It is hard for women to become more than subsistence farmers because they have little access to credit needed to purchase seeds, fertilizers, or tools. (Land and property which could be used as collateral for loans are mostly owned by men.) And agriculture training programs are planned for and available mainly to men; only 0.4 percent of trained agricultural personnel in Kenya are women."

In a special experiment Kenyan women were given the same access as men to loans, hybrid seeds, fertilizer, and advice on how and what to plant. The result was that women made more efficient use of the land and produced bigger harvests than the men. Nevertheless, according to the UN Food and Agriculture Organization (FAO), neither Kenya nor any other country in the world has implemented national agriculture projects aimed specifically at women.

One of the reasons women do not get agriculture training is that they do not have time to go to training classes or to put to effective use what they learn. An African woman at the workshop commented, "An 18-hour day is not uncommon for the rural woman in my country. She must bear and raise (often many) children, wash and mend the family's clothes, and usually spend several hours a day searching for firewood and water and preparing the food."

The UN development project at the Njemps Flats attempts to alleviate one of these domestic burdens on the local women by providing a source of firewood close to home. It will also help prevent further deterioration of the soil which could eventually prevent the land from being of any use.

This project is one of 40 demonstration plots in 26 communities in Kenya's Baringo district employing 540 local laborers, 80 percent of whom are women. The workers, with the technical advice of FAO staff and Kenyan agricultural personnel, have prepared the soil, contouring it so that any rain that falls will be trapped and used by the seedlings (a process called "water harvesting"). They have planted different varieties of drought-resistant trees, such as parkinsonia aculeata, which is good for fodder, and a fast-growing eucalyptus providing excellent firewood. The cereal sorghum, one of the few crops that can be relied on to survive dry climate conditions, is intercropped with the tree plants to make maximum use of the land. Workers also maintain a large nursery at the nearby town of Marigat and provide thousands of tree seedlings to local people.

"Training is a continuous task," according to FAO associate expert at the site J. B. Haansen, "not only in preparing the plot but in managing it now and in the future when I am gone." Agriculture extension agents are trained at each demonstration site to encourage local farmers to plant the trees and to teach them the water harvesting techniques. A woman extension agent from Marigat has contacted many of the ubiquitous women's groups in the district and involved them in planting trees at their homes and encouraging their friends to plant trees.

Area schools have also been brought into the act. I visited N'gambo Primary School to observe another use of food aid in the daily free lunch of corn and beans provided since the drought by the World Food Program. Pupils had recently planted trees (and protected them from wandering goats with branches of the prickly thorn tree) in the otherwise barren ground surrounding their school. The small plants were the only touch of green on the flat, ocher plain.

A final piece of the Barinto district "food-for-work" project is soil conservation demonstration plots in the nearby lower Tugen Hills. Bad planting practices on the steep slopes have severely eroded the soil. It will soon be completely unproductive unless soil conservation measures are adopted.

Well-planned and executed small-scale development projects such as this one appear to be a good use of food aid (so often badly misused in creating dependency and undermining local farm economies). They are improving the lives of a relative handful of the millions of poor people struggling against great odds to survive.

The emphasis in Nairobi on small-scale development projects directed at improving women's ability to live healthy and productive lives was part of the consciousness raising that many participants experienced. The important strategies for development, equality, and peace outlined at the conference could lead to a better life for women—and men.

As I looked at the young trees struggling to survive in the harsh equatorial sun on the Njemps Flats, I hoped that they would make it in spite of the odds against them. And I recalled the words of hope for women everywhere expressed by Dr. Eddah Gachukia, chairwoman of the Kenya NGO Organizing Committee, at the close of FORUM '85: "Women of the world have planted a seed here in Nairobi which will germinate and grow with the years into a forest. The achievements of FORUM '85 will become apparent and grow increasingly stronger as the years go by."

Questions

1. Describe the "food for work" program run by the United Nations for people like Nonkera. What are the advantages of small projects over large-scale development efforts?
2. Why was it decided to hold the two conferences in Africa instead of Europe or America? How did the results bear out the wisdom of this choice?
3. What problems do women encounter with governments like that of Kenya? What are some of the other obstacles women face in getting agricultural training?
4. Why is tree-planting such an important factor in developing countries?
5. What does consciousness-raising in Africa have in common with the process in this country? In what ways does it differ?

8

The Case against Helping the Poor

Garrett Hardin

This article originally appeared in *Psychology Today*, 1980.

Garrett Hardin, professor of biology at the University of California, Santa Barbara, plays the "devil's advocate" role in opposing an open-handed food and immigration policy on the part of the world's rich nations. By turning the "spaceship earth" metaphor of environmentalists into a "lifeboat ethic," he poses hard questions.

The first question is one of capacity. How many "swimmers in the sea" can each lifeboat (rich nation) take in? By following either the Christian or Marxist ethic, he says, the lifeboats will be swamped. If only some are let in, on what basis are the others excluded? The continuing growth of earth's population—principally in the poor nations—only compounds the problem, he says. "The philanthropic load created by the sharing ethic can only increase," he concludes.

Switching metaphors, Professor Hardin calls attention to "the tragedy of the commons," in which those who are less responsible will spoil things for everybody else. He enlarges on the perceived shortcomings of Public Law 480, in which "though all U.S. taxpayers were forced to contribute to the cost . . . certain special interests gained handsomely under the program." A World Food Bank, he predicts, would lead to the same problems created by this "combination of silent selfish interests and highly vocal humanitarian apologists." Granting such a bank would be used only for emergencies, what will be the attitude, he asks, of rich nations to those poor ones that did not take prudent steps in normal times?

Hardin turns the tables on the "environmentalists" by emphasizing the "draft on all aspects of the environment: food, air, water, forest, beaches, wildlife, scenery and solitude" that every new human being represents. In effect, he makes a strong plea for strict population control. He then moves to the "immigration vs. food supply" dilemma, which makes the same point.

In his criticism of the food and immigration solutions for the problems of the world's poor, Hardin is forced to state the need for "a true world government to control reproduction and the use of available resources."

Until such time that this becomes a reality, he says, "our survival demands that we (the rich nations) govern our actions by the ethics of a lifeboat, harsh though that may be."

Environmentalists use the metaphor of the earth as a "spaceship" in trying to persuade countries, industries, and people to stop wasting and polluting our natural resources. Since we all share life on this planet, they argue, no single person or institution has the right to destroy, waste, or use more than a fair share of its resources.

But does everyone on earth have an equal right to an equal share of its resources? The spaceship metaphor can be dangerous when used by misguided idealists to justify suicidal policies for sharing our resources through uncontrolled immigration and foreign aid. In their enthusiastic but unrealistic generosity, they confuse the ethics of a spaceship with those of a lifeboat.

A true spaceship would have to be under the control of a captain, since no ship could possibly survive if its course were determined by committee. Spaceship Earth certainly has no captain; the United Nations is merely a toothless tiger, with little power to enforce any policy upon its bickering members.

If we divide the world crudely into rich nations and poor nations, two-thirds of them are desperately poor, and only one-third comparatively rich, with the United States the wealthiest of all. Metaphorically each rich nation can be seen as a lifeboat full of comparatively rich people. In the ocean outside each lifeboat swim the poor of the world, who would like to get in, or at least to share some of the wealth. What should the lifeboat passengers do?

First, we must recognize the limited capacity of any lifeboat. For example, a nation's land has a limited capacity to support a population and as the current energy crisis has shown us, in some ways we have already exceeded the carrying capacity of our land.

Adrift in a Moral Sea. So here we sit, say, 50 people in our lifeboat. To be generous, let us assume it has room for 10 more, making a total capacity of 60. Suppose the 50 of us in the lifeboat see 100 others swimming in the water outside, begging for admission to our boat or for handouts. We have several options: we may be tempted to try to live by the Christian ideal of being "our brother's keeper," or by the Marxist ideal of "to each according to his needs." Since the needs of all in the water are the same, and since they can all be seen as "our brothers," we could take them all into our boat, making a total of 150 in a boat designed for 60. The boat swamps, everyone drowns. Complete justice, complete catastrophe.

Since the boat has an unused excess capacity of 10 more passengers, we could admit just 10 more to it. But which 10 do we let in? How do we choose? Do we pick the best 10, the neediest 10, "first come, first served"? And what do we say to the 90 we exclude? If we do let an extra 10 into our lifeboat, we will have lost our "safety factor," an engineering principle of critical importance. For example, if we don't leave room for excess capacity as a safety factor in our country's agriculture, a new plant disease or a bad change in the weather could have disastrous consequences.

Suppose we decide to preserve our small safety factor and admit no more to the lifeboat. Our survival is then possible, although we shall have to be constantly on guard against boarding parties.

While this last solution clearly offers the only means of our survival, it is morally abhorrent to many people. Some say they feel guilty about their good luck. My reply is simple. "Get out and yield your place to others." This may solve the problem of the guilt-ridden person's conscience, but it does not change the ethics of the lifeboat. The needy person to whom the guilt-ridden person yields his place will not himself feel guilty about his good luck. If he did, he would not climb aboard. The net result of conscience-stricken people giving up their unjustly held seats is the elimination of that sort of conscience from the lifeboat.

This is the basic metaphor within which we must work out our solutions. Let us now enrich the image, step by step, with substantive additions from the real world, a world that must solve real and pressing problems of overpopulation and hunger.

The harsh ethics of the lifeboat become even harsher when we consider the reproductive differences between the rich nations and the poor nations. The people inside the lifeboat are doubling in numbers every 87 years; those swimming around outside are doubling, on the average, every 35 years, more than twice as fast as the rich. And since the world's resources are dwindling, the difference in prosperity between the rich and the poor can only increase.

As of 1973, the U.S. had a population of 210 million people, who were increasing by 0.8 percent per year. Outside our lifeboat, let us imagine another 210 million people (say the combined populations of Colombia, Ecuador, Venezuela, Morocco, Pakistan, Thailand and the Philippines), who are increasing at a rate of 3.3 percent per year. Put differently, the doubling time for this aggregate population is 21 years, compared to 87 years for the U.S.

Multiplying the Rich and the Poor. Now suppose the U.S. agreed to pool its resources with those seven countries, with everyone receiving an equal share. Initially the ratio of Americans to non-Americans in this model would be one-to-one. But consider what the ratio would be after 87 years, by which time the Americans would have doubled to a population of 420 million. By then, doubling every 21 years, the other group would have swollen to 354 billion. Each American would have to share the available resources with more than eight people.

But, one could argue, this discussion assumes that current population trends will continue, and they may not. Quite so. Most likely the rate of population increase will decline much faster in the U.S. than it will in the other countries, and there does not seem to be much we can do about it. In sharing with "each according to his needs," we must recognize that needs are determined by population size, which is determined by the rate of reproduction, which at present is regarded as a sovereign right of every nation, poor or not. This being so, the philanthropic load created by the sharing ethic of the spaceship can only increase.

The Tragedy of the Commons. The fundamental error of spaceship ethics, and the sharing it requires, is that it leads to what I call "the tragedy of the commons." Under a system of private property, the men who own property recognize their responsibility to care for it, for if they don't they will eventually suffer. A farmer, for instance, will allow no more cattle in a pasture than its carrying capacity justifies. If he overloads it, erosion sets in, weeds take over, and he loses the use of the pasture.

If a pasture becomes a commons open to all, the right of each to use it may not be matched by a corresponding responsibility to protect it. Asking everyone to use it with discretion will hardly do, for the considerate herdsman who refrains from overloading the commons suffers more than a selfish one who says his needs are greater. If everyone would restrain himself, all would be well; but it takes only one less than everyone to ruin a system of voluntary restraint. In a crowded world of less than perfect human beings, mutual ruin is inevitable if there are no controls. This is the tragedy of the commons.

One of the major tasks of education today should be the creation of such an acute awareness of the dangers of the commons that people will recognize its many varieties. For example, the air and water have become polluted because they are treated as commons. Further growth in the population or per-capita conversion of natural resources into pollutants will only make the problem worse. The same holds true for the fish of the oceans. Fishing fleets have nearly disappeared in many parts of the world, technological improvements in the art of fishing are hastening the day of complete ruin. Only the replacement of the system of the commons with a responsible system of control will save the land, air, water, and oceanic fisheries.

The World Food Bank. In recent years there has been a push to create a new commons called a World Food Bank, an international depository of food reserves to which nations would contribute according to their abilities and from which they would draw according to their needs. This humanitarian proposal has received support from many liberal international groups, and from such prominent citizens as Margaret Mead, U.N. Secretary General Kurt Waldheim, and Senators Edward Kennedy and George McGovern.

A world food bank appeals powerfully to our humanitarian impulses. But before we rush ahead with such a plan, let us recognize where the greatest political push comes from, lest we be disillusioned later. Our experience with the "Food for Peace Program," or Public Law 480, gives us the answer. This program moved billions of dollars worth of U.S. surplus grain to food-short, population-long countries during the past two decades. But when P.L. 480 first became law, a headline in the business magazine *Forbes* revealed the real power behind it. "Feeding the World's Hungry Millions: How It Will Mean Billions for U.S. Business."

And indeed it did. In the years 1960 to 1970, U.S. taxpayers spent a total of $7.9 billion on the Food for Peace program. Between 1948 and 1970, they also paid an additional $50 billion for other economic-aid programs, some of which went for food and food-producing machinery and technology. Though all U.S. taxpayers were forced to contribute to the cost of P.L. 480, certain special interest groups gained handsomely under the program. Farmers did not have to contribute the grain; the government, or rather the taxpayers, bought it from them at full market prices. The increased demand raised prices of farm products generally. The manufacturers of farm machinery, fertilizers and pesticides benefited by the farmers' extra efforts to grow more food. Grain elevators profited from storing the surplus until it could be shipped. Railroads made money hauling it to ports, and shipping lines profited from carrying it overseas. The implementation of P.L. 480 required the creation of a vast government bureaucracy, which then acquired its own vested interest in continuing the program regardless of its merits.

Extracting Dollars. Those who proposed and defended the Food for Peace program in public rarely mentioned its importance to any of these special interests. The public emphasis was always on its humanitarian effects. The combination of silent selfish interests and highly vocal humanitarian apologists made a powerful and successful lobby for extracting money from taxpayers. We can expect the same lobby to push now for the creation of a World Food Bank.

However great the potential benefit to selfish interests, it should not be a decisive argument against a truly humanitarian program. We must ask if such a program would actually do more good than harm, not only momentarily but also in the long run. Those who propose the food bank usually refer to a current "emergency" or "crisis" in terms of world food supply. But what is an emergency? Although they may be infrequent and sudden, everyone knows that emergencies will occur from time to time. A well-run family, company, organization or country prepares for the likelihood of accidents and emergencies. It expects them, it budgets for them, it saves for them.

Learning the Hard Way. What happens if some organizations or countries budget for accidents and others do not? If each country is solely responsible for its own well-being, poorly managed ones will suffer. But they can learn from experience. They may mend their ways, and learn to budget for infrequent but certain emergencies. For example, the weather varies from year to year, and periodic crop failures are certain. A wise and competent government saves out of the production of the good years in anticipation of bad years to come. Joseph taught this policy to Pharaoh in Egypt more than 2,000 years ago. Yet the great majority of the governments in the world today do not follow such a policy. They lack either the wisdom or the competence, or both. Should those nations that do manage to put something aside be forced to come to the rescue each time an emergency occurs among the poor nations?

"But it isn't their fault!" some kindhearted liberals argue. "How can we blame the poor people who are caught in an emergency? Why must they suffer for the sins of their governments?" The concept of blame is simply not relevant here. The real question is, what are the operational consequences of establishing a food bank? If it is open to every country every time a need develops, slovenly rulers will not be motivated to take Joseph's advice. Someone will always come to their aid. Some countries will deposit food in the world food bank, and others will withdraw it. There will be almost no overlap. As a result of such solutions to food shortage emergencies, the poor countries will not learn to mend their ways, and will suffer progressively greater emergencies as their populations grow.

Population Control the Crude Way. On the average, poor countries undergo a 2.5 percent increase in population each year; rich countries, about 0.8 percent. Only rich countries have anything in the way of food reserves set aside, and even they do not have as much as they should. Poor countries have none. If poor countries received no food from the outside, the rate of their population growth would be periodically checked by crop failures and famines. But if they can always draw on a world food bank in time of need, their population can continue to grow unchecked, and so will their "need" for aid. In the short run, a world food bank may diminish that need, but in the long run it actually increases the need without limit.

Without some system of worldwide food sharing, the proportion of people in the rich and poor nations might eventually stabilize. The overpopulated poor countries would decrease in numbers, while the rich countries that had room for more people would increase. But with a well-meaning system of sharing, such as a world food bank, the growth differential between the rich and the poor countries will not only persist, it will increase. Because of the higher rate of population growth in the poor countries of the world, 88 percent of today's children are born poor, and only 12 percent rich. Year by year the ratio becomes worse, as the fast-reproducing poor outnumber the slow-reproducing rich.

A world food bank is thus a commons in disguise. People will have more motivation to draw from it than to add to any common store. The less provident and less able will multiply at the expense of the abler and more provident, bringing eventual ruin upon all who share in the commons. Besides, any system of "sharing" that amounts to foreign aid from the rich nations to the poor nations will carry the taint of charity, which will contribute little to the world peace so devoutly desired by those who support the idea of a world food bank.

As past U. S. foreign-aid programs have amply and depressingly demonstrated, international charity frequently inspires mistrust and antagonism rather than gratitude on the part of the recipient nation.

Chinese Fish and Miracle Rice. The modern approach to foreign aid stresses the export of technology and advice, rather than money and food. As an ancient Chinese proverb goes: "Give a man a fish and he will eat for a day; teach him how to fish and he will eat for the rest of his days." Acting on this advice, the Rockefeller and Ford Foundations have financed a number of programs for improving agriculture in the hungry nations. Known as the "Green Revolution," these programs have led to the development of "miracle rice" and "miracle wheat," new strains that offer bigger harvests and greater resistance to crop damage. Norman Borlaug, the Nobel Prize-winning agronomist who, supported by the Rockefeller Foundation, developed "miracle wheat," is one of the most prominent advocates of a world food bank.

Whether or not the Green Revolution can increase food production as much as its champions claim is a debatable but possibly irrelevant point. Those who support this well-intended humanitarian effort should first consider some of the fundamentals of human ecology. Ironically, one man who did was the late Alan Gregg, a vice-president of the Rockefeller Foundation. Two decades ago he expressed strong doubts about the wisdom of such attempts to increase food production. He likened the growth and spread of humanity over the surface of the earth to the spread of cancer in the human body, remarking that "cancerous growths demand food; but, as far as I know, they have never been cured by getting it."

Overloading the Environment. Every human born constitutes a draft on all aspects of the environment: food, air, water, forest, beaches, wildlife, scenery and solitude. Food can, perhaps, be significantly increased to meet a growing demand. But what about clean beaches, unspoiled forests, and solitude? If we satisfy a growing population's need for food, we necessarily decrease its per capita supply of the other resources needed by men.

India, for example, now has a population of 600 million, which increases by 15 million each year. This population already puts a huge load on a relatively impoverished environment. The country's forests are now only a small fraction of what they were three centuries ago, and floods and erosion continually destroy the insufficient farmland that remains. Every one of the 15 million new lives added to India's population puts an additional burden on the environment and increases the economic and social costs of crowding. However humanitarian our intent, every Indian life saved through medical or nutritional assistance from abroad diminishes the quality of life for those who remain, and for subsequent generations. If rich countries make it possible, through foreign aid, for 600 million Indians to swell to 1.2 billion in a mere 28 years, as their current growth rate threatens, will future generations of Indians thank us for hastening the destruction of their environment? Will our good intentions be sufficient excuse for the consequences of our actions?

My final example of a commons in action is one for which the public has the least desire for rational discussion—immigration. Anyone who publicly questions the wisdom of current U.S. immigration policy is promptly charged with bigotry, prejudice, ethnocentrism, chauvinism, isolationism or selfishness. Rather than encounter such accusations, one would rather talk about other matters, leaving immigration policy to wallow in the crosscurrents of special interests that take no account of the good of the whole, or the interests of posterity.

Perhaps we still feel guilty about things we said in the past. Two generations ago the popular press frequently referred to Dagos, Wops, Polacks, Chinks and Krauts, in articles about how America was being "overrun" by foreigners of supposedly inferior genetic stock. But because the implied inferiority of foreigners was used then as justification for keeping them out, people now assume that restrictive policies could only be based on such misguided notions. There are other grounds.

A Nation of Immigrants. Just consider the numbers involved. Our government acknowledges a net inflow of 400,000 immigrants a year. While we have no hard data on the extent of illegal entries, educated guesses put the figure at about 600,000 a year. Since the natural increase (excess of births over deaths) of the resident population now runs about 1.7 million per year, the yearly gain from immigration amounts to at least 19 percent of the total annual increase, and may be as much as 37 percent if we include the estimate for illegal immigrants. Considering the growing use of birth control devices, the potential effect of educational campaigns by such organizations as Planned Parenthood Federation of America and Zero Population Growth, and the influence of inflation and the housing shortage, the fertility rate of American women may decline so much that immigration could account for all the yearly increase in population. Should we not at least ask if that is what we want?

For the sake of those who worry about whether the "quality" of the average immigrant compares favorably with the quality of the average resident, let us assume that immigrants and native born citizens are of exactly equal quality, however one defines that term. We will focus here only on quantity; and since our conclusions will depend on nothing else, all charges of bigotry and chauvinism become irrelevant.

Immigration vs. Food Supply. World food banks move food to the people, hastening the exhaustion of the environment of the poor countries. Unrestricted immigration, on the other hand, moves people to the food, thus speeding up the destruction of the environment of rich countries. We can easily understand why poor people should want to make this latter transfer, but why should rich hosts encourage it?

As in the case of foreign-aid programs immigration receives support from selfish interests and humanitarian impulses. The primary selfish interest in unimpeded immigration is the desire of employers for cheap labor, particularly in industries and trades that offer degrading work. In the past, one wave of foreigners after another was brought into the U.S. to work at wretched jobs for wretched wages. In recent years the Cubans, Puerto Ricans, and Mexicans have had this dubious honor. The interests of the employers of cheap labor mesh well with the guilty silence of the country's liberal intelligentsia. White Anglo-Saxon Protestants are particularly reluctant to call for a closing of the doors to immigration for fear of being called bigots.

But not all countries have such reluctant leadership. Most educated Hawaiians, for example, are keenly aware of the limits of their environment, particularly in terms of population growth. There is only so much room on the islands, and the islanders know it. To Hawaiians, immigrants from the other 49 states present as great a threat as those from other nations. At a recent meeting of Hawaiian government officials in Honolulu, I had the ironic delight of hearing a speaker, who like most of his audience countered: "How can we shut the doors now? We have many friends and relatives in Japan that we'd like to bring here some day so that they can enjoy Hawaii too." The Japanese-American speaker smiled sympathetically and answered: "Yes, but we have children now, and someday we'll have grandchildren too. We can bring more people from Japan only by giving away some of the land that we hope to pass on to our grandchildren some day. What right do we have to do that?"

At this point, I can hear U.S. liberals asking: "How can you justify slamming the door once you're inside? You say that immigrants should be kept out. But aren't we all immigrants, or the descendants of immigrants? If we insist on staying, must we not admit all others?" Our craving for intellectual order leads us to seek and prefer symmetrical rules and morals: a single rule for me and everybody else; the same rule yesterday, today, and tomorrow. Justice, we feel, should not change with time and place.

We Americans of non-Indian ancestry can look upon ourselves as the descendants of thieves who are guilty morally, if not legally, of stealing this land from its Indian owners. Should we then give back the land to the now living American descendants of those Indians? However morally or logically sound this proposal may be, I, for one, am unwilling to live by it and I know no one else who is. Besides, the logical consequence would be absurd. Suppose that, intoxicated with a sense of pure justice, we should decide to turn our land over to the Indians. Since all our other wealth has also been derived from the land, wouldn't we be morally obliged to give that back to the Indians too?

Pure Justice vs. Reality. Clearly, the concept of pure justice produces an infinite regression to absurdity. Centuries ago, wise men invented statutes of limitations to justify the rejection of such pure justice, in the interest of preventing continual disorder. The law zealously defends property rights, but only relatively recent property rights. Drawing a line after an arbitrary time has elapsed may be unjust, but the alternatives are worse.

We are all the descendants of thieves, and the world's resources are inequitably distributed. But we must begin the journey to tomorrow from the point where we are today. We cannot remake the past. We cannot safely divide the wealth equitably among all peoples so long as people reproduce at different rates. To do so would guarantee that our grandchildren, and everyone else's grandchildren, would have only a ruined world to inhabit.

To be generous with one's own possessions is quite different from being generous with those of posterity. We should call this point to the attention of those who, from a commendable love of justice and equality, would institute a system of the commons, either in the form of a world food bank, or of unrestricted immigration. We must convince them if we wish to save at least some parts of the world from environmental ruin.

Without a true world government to control reproduction and the use of available resources, the sharing ethic of the spaceship is impossible. For the foreseeable future, our survival demands that we govern our actions by the ethics of a lifeboat, harsh though they may be. Posterity will be satisfied with nothing less.

Questions

1. What are the advantages and disadvantages of using figures of speech like "spaceship" and "lifeboat" in argumentation?
2. Is Hardin correct in stating there are those who favor "uncontrolled immigration and foreign aid"? What reasons might he have had for making this statement?
3. What are the underlying assumptions of the author?
4. How would you respond to Hardin's charge that "international charity frequently inspires mistrust"?
5. Do you think that a "true world government" would solve many of the problems posed by the author? Explain.

9
Chief Seattle's Message

Addressed to President Pierce, 1854

As his tribe, the Coastal Salish of the northwest, was being forced by the U.S. Army to abandon its ancestral lands, Chief Seattle addresses a prophetic message to the American President. He shows a fine sense of irony and a realistic appreciation of the military weakness of his position. Instead of railing at the injustice of being forced to transfer his people's ancestral lands to the powerful U.S. government, the chief takes a higher moral ground. He raises the interesting question of whether any human can really be said to "own" the earth. In contrast to the white man who uses up the land, the animals and natural resources in a wasteful manner, Seattle reminds "the great chief in Washington" that "every part of the earth is sacred to my people."

In proud dignity, Chief Seattle responds that he will consider the government's offer, even though he has little choice. A keen psychologist, he reflects on the cultural differences between the two races, leaving no doubt which culture he considers superior. He contrasts the two ways of life and comments with irony that "I am a savage and do not understand any other way."

But just as the chief sees the divine hand in the power given the whites to dominate his people, Seattle prophesies that the whites too will pass away, "perhaps sooner than all other tribes." Although the native American leader's words seem not to have had much impact on his intended audience, he has left a legacy to us who can still ponder his insights and try to learn from him that humanity is part of the cycle of nature and that in despoiling the earth we hasten our own destruction.

Nonviolence did not appear in this land with the arrival of European immigrants. Native Americans had a reverence for life, respected human dignity, and understood the interconnection of all things to an extent that has yet to be surpassed. The genocide perpetrated by the United States on the Indian tribes and cultures—a pattern which still continues today—remains one of the most thorough indictments of white civilization. In 1854, Chief Seattle, leader of the Suquamish tribe in the Washington territory, delivered this prophetic speech to mark the transferral of ancestral Indian lands to the federal government.

The Great Chief in Washington sends word that he wishes to buy our land.

The Great Chief also sends us words of friendship and good will. This is kind of him, since we know he has little need of our friendship in return. But we will consider your offer. For we know that if we do not sell, the white man may come with guns and take our land.

How can you buy or sell the sky, the warmth of the land? The idea is strange to us.

If we do not own the freshness of the air and the sparkle of the water, how can you buy them?

Every part of this earth is sacred to my people. Every shining pine needle, every sandy shore, every mist in the dark woods, every clearing and humming insect is holy in the memory and experience of my people. The sap which courses through the trees carries the memories of the red man.

The white man's dead forget the country of their birth when they go to walk among the stars. Our dead never forget this beautiful earth, for it is the mother of the red man. We are part of the earth and it is part of us. The perfumed flowers are our sisters; the deer, the horse, the great eagle, these are our brothers. The rocky crests, the juices in the meadows, the body heat of the pony, and man—all belong to the same family.

So, when the Great Chief in Washington sends word that he wishes to buy our land, he asks much of us.

So, the Great Chief sends word he will reserve us a place so that we can live comfortably to ourselves. He will be our father and we will be his children.

So we will consider your offer to buy our land. But it will not be easy. For this land is sacred to us.

This shining water that moves in the streams and rivers is not just water but the blood of our ancestors. If we sell you land, you must remember that it is sacred, and you must teach your children that it is sacred, and that each ghostly reflection in the clear water of the lake tells of events and memories in the life of my people. The water's murmur is the voice of my father's father.

The rivers are our brothers, they quench our thirst. The rivers carry our canoes, and feed our children. If we sell you our land, you must remember, and teach your children, that the rivers are our brothers, and yours, and you must henceforth give the rivers the kindness you would give any brother.

The red man has always retreated before the advancing white man, as the mist of the mountain runs before the morning sun. But the ashes of our fathers are sacred. Their graves are holy ground, and so these hills, these trees, this portion of earth is consecrated to us. We know that the white man does not understand our ways. One portion of land is the same to him as the next, for he is a stranger who comes in the night and takes from the land whatever he needs. The earth is not his brother, but his enemy, and when he has conquered it, he moves on. He leaves his fathers' graves behind, and he does not care. He kidnaps the earth from his children. He does not care. His fathers' graves and his children's birthright are forgotten. He treats his mother, the earth, and his brother, the sky, as things to be bought, plundered, sold like sheep or bright beads. His appetite will devour the earth and leave behind only a desert.

I do not know. Our ways are different from your ways. The sight of your cities pains the eyes of the red man. But perhaps it is because the red man is a savage and does not understand.

There is no quiet place in the white man's cities. No place to hear the unfurling of leaves in spring or the rustle of insects' wings. But perhaps it is because I am a savage and do not understand. The clatter only seems to insult the ears. And what is there to life if a man cannot hear the lonely cry of the whippoorwill or the arguments of the frogs around a pond at night? I am a red man and do not understand. The Indian prefers the soft sound of the wind darting over the face of a pond, and the smell of the wind itself, cleansed by a midday rain, or scented with the pinon pine.

The air is precious to the red man, for all things share the same breath—the beast, the tree, the man, they all share the same breath. The white man does not seem to notice the air he breathes. Like a man dying for many days, he is numb to the stench. But if we sell you our land, you must remember that the air is precious to us, that the air shares its spirit with all the life it supports. The wind that gave our grandfather his first breath also receives his last sigh. And the wind must also give our children the spirit of life. And if we sell you our land, you must keep it apart and sacred, as a place where even the white man can go to taste the wind that is sweetened by the meadow's flowers.

So we will consider your offer to buy our land. If we decide to accept, I will make one condition: The white man must treat the beasts of this land as his brothers.

I am a savage and do not understand any other way. I have seen a thousand rotting buffaloes on the prairie, left by the white man who shot them from a passing train. I am a savage and I do not understand how the smoking iron horse can be more important than the buffalo that we kill only to stay alive.

What is man without the beasts? If all the beasts were gone, men would die from a great loneliness of spirit. For whatever happens to the beasts, soon happens to man. All things are connected.

You must teach your children that the ground beneath their feet is the ashes of our grandfathers. So that they will respect the land, tell your children that the earth is rich with the lives of our kin. Teach your children what we have taught our children, that the earth is our mother. Whatever befalls the earth, befalls the sons of the earth. If men spit upon the ground they spit upon themselves.

This we know. The earth does not belong to man; man belongs to the earth. This we know. All things are connected like the blood which unites one family. All things are connected.

Whatever befalls the earth befalls the sons of the earth. Man did not weave the web of life; he is merely a strand in it. Whatever he does to the web, he does to himself.

But we will consider your offer to go to the reservation you have for my people. We will live apart, and in peace. It matters little where we spend the rest of our days. Our children have seen their fathers humbled in defeat. Our warriors have felt shame, and after defeat they turn their days in idleness and contaminate their bodies with sweet foods and strong drink. It matters little where we pass the rest of our days. They are not many. A few more hours, a few more winters, and none of the children of the great tribes that once lived on this earth or that roam now in small bands in the woods will be left to mourn the graves of a people once as powerful and hopeful as yours. But why should I mourn the passing of my people? Tribes are made of men, nothing more. Men come and go like the waves of the sea.

Even the white man, whose God walks and talks with him as friend to friend, cannot be exempt from the common destiny. We may be brothers after all; we shall see. One thing we know, which the white man may one day discover—our God is the same God. You may think now that you own him as you wish to own our land; but you cannot. He is the God of man, and his compassion is equal for the red man and the white. This earth is precious to him, and to harm the earth is to heap contempt on its Creator. The white too shall pass; perhaps sooner than all other tribes. Continue to contaminate your bed, and you will one night suffocate in your own waste.

But in your perishing you will shine brightly, fired by the strength of the God who brought you to this land and for some special purpose gave you dominion over this land and over the red man. That destiny is a mystery to us, for we do not understand when the buffalo are all slaughtered, the wild horses are tamed, the secret corners of the forest heavy with the scent of many men, and the view of the ripe hills blotted by talking wires. Where is the thicket? Gone. Where is the eagle? Gone. And what is it to say goodbye to the swift pony and the hunt? The end of living and the beginning of survival.

So we will consider your offer to buy our land. If we agree, it will be to secure the reservation you have promised. There, perhaps, we may live out our brief days as we wish. When the last red man has vanished from this earth, and his memory is only the shadow of a cloud moving across the prairie, these shores and forests will still hold the spirits of my people. For they love this earth as the newborn loves its mother's heartbeat. So if we sell you our land, love it as we've loved it. Care for it as we've cared for it. Hold in your mind the memory of the land as it is when you take it. And with all your strength, with all your mind, with all your heart, preserve it for your children, and love it . . . as God loves us all.

One thing we know. Our God is the same God. This earth is precious to him. Even the white man cannot be exempt from the common destiny. We may be brothers after all. We shall see.

Questions

1. What similarities can you see between Chief Seattle's people and the peoples of the third world?
2. In which passages does Seattle show his dignity and leadership qualities?
3. Describe briefly the worldview of the native American peoples and that of the industrialized West?
4. Which aspects of Seattle's speech are particularly relevant today?
5. Where does Seattle show a profound sense of history?

10
Amnesty International

A pamphlet

To many people, their first knowledge of Amnesty International came through a series of "Conspiracy of Hope" rock concerts held in the United States in the summer of 1986. These events, held in San Francisco, Los Angeles, Denver, Atlanta, Chicago and the New York area, were celebrations of the organization's twenty-fifth anniversary.

The objects of Amnesty International's (AI) concern are men and women in any country imprisoned because of their beliefs, specifically those who have never used or advocated violence. Aware that any nation shrinks from the glare of unfavorable publicity, AI turns the spotlight on government misconduct wherever it may be found and documented. The organization claims 150,000 members and supporters in 150 countries. Meeting in small groups, they "write letters, publicize and organize actions in behalf of prisoners of conscience and work on special campaigns." The effect of such letters and campaigns may be gauged from the following statements made by prisoners who were released through AI's efforts:

"When the first two hundred letters came, the guards gave me back my clothes. Then the next two hundred letters came, and the prison director came to see me. When the next pile of letters arrived, the director got in touch with his superior. The letters kept coming and coming, three thousand of them. The President was informed. The letters still kept arriving, and the President called the prison and told them to let me go." (A released prisoner of conscience from the Dominican Republic)

"We could always tell when international protests were taking place . . . the food rations increased and the beatings were fewer. Letters from abroad were translated and passed around from cell to cell, but when the letters stopped, the dirty food and repression started again." (A released prisoner of conscience from Vietnam)

"For years I was held in a tiny cell. My only human contact was with my torturers. . . . My only company were the cockroaches and mice. . . . On Christmas Eve the door to my cell opened and the guard tossed in a crumpled piece of paper. It said, 'Take heart. The world knows you're

197

alive. We're with you. Regards, Monica, Amnesty International.' That let-
ter saved my life." (A released prisoner of conscience from Paraguay)

In 1977, the Nobel Peace Prize was awarded to AI for its work on
behalf of 25,000 prisoners around the world.

The following article is taken from a pamphlet describing Amnesty
International's history, purposes and activities.

Thousands of people are in prison because of their beliefs. Many are
held without charge or trial. Torture and the death penalty are widespread. In many countries men, women, and children have "disappeared"
after being taken into official custody. Still others have been killed without
any pretense of legality. These human rights abuses occur in countries of
widely differing ideologies.

Amnesty International is a worldwide movement of people acting on
the conviction that governments must not deny individuals their basic human rights. The organization was awarded the 1977 Nobel Peace Prize for
its efforts to promote global observance of the United Nations' Universal
Declaration of Human Rights.

Amnesty International works specifically for:

- the release of prisoners of conscience—men, women, and children imprisoned for their beliefs, color, sex, ethnic origin, language, or religion; provided they have neither used nor
  advocated violence;
- fair and prompt trials for all political prisoners;
- an end to torture and executions in all cases.

Amnesty International's effectiveness depends on its impartial application of a single standard of human rights to every country in the world.
The organization is independent of all governments, political factions,
ideologies, economic interests, and religious creeds. It accepts no financial
contribution from any government and is funded entirely by donations
from its supporters. To safeguard impartiality, groups do no work for prisoners of conscience held within their own countries.

Amnesty International seeks the most effective means of helping individuals whose rights have been violated. Techniques include long-term
adoption of prisoners of conscience; publicizing patterns of human rights
abuses; meetings with government representatives; and, in cases where
torture or death are feared, a network of volunteers who send urgent telegrams indicating international concern.

Amnesty International members send letters, cards, and telegrams
on behalf of individual prisoners to government officials. Constant action generates effective pressure. One well-written letter to a minister
of justice is not pressure; ten letters are. Hundreds of letters were sent

on behalf of an adopted prisoner detained for many years in Soviet psychiatric hospitals. Later he said that his release had been a direct result of the letters from Amnesty. He believes they were also the key to better treatment during imprisonment.

Amnesty International members also organize public meetings, collect signatures for petitions, and arrange publicity events, such as vigils at appropriate government embassies. They work on special projects, such as the Campaign to Abolish Torture. At its launching Amnesty members met with more than half of the United States' congressional representatives to voice their concern and outline Amnesty International's program to eradicate torture. Members also raise money to send medicine, food, and clothing to prisoners and their families.

Amnesty International sends missions to countries to appeal in person for the protection of human rights. A medical delegation to Bolivia successfully convinced the government to allow a prisoner to be flown abroad for a lifesaving operation. Another group went to Gambia in response to reports that prisoners were held in leg irons and denied access to friends and relatives. Within months Gambia's President had taken steps to improve conditions.

When Amnesty International hears of political arrests or people facing torture or execution, it concentrates first on getting the facts. At the organization's headquarters in London, the Research Department (with a staff of 150 recruited from over 20 countries) collects and analyzes information from a wide variety of sources. These include hundreds of newspapers and journals, government bulletins, transcripts of radio broadcasts, reports from lawyers and humanitarian organizations, along with letters from and interviews with prisoners and their families. Amnesty International representatives frequently go on missions to collect on-the-spot information. Amnesty legal observers often attend trials where accepted international standards are at issue.

Since it was founded in 1961, Amnesty International has worked on behalf of more than 25,000 prisoners around the world. Last year 150 of the prisoners of conscience adopted by groups in the United States were released. These aren't just numbers. Amnesty members give direct and effective assistance to people who become more than a number and more than a name. A released prisoner from Malaysia wrote to a group member, "Today I took out all the letters and cards you sent me in the past, reread them, looked at them again, and it is hard to describe the feelings in my heart . . . these things I regard as precious jewels."

A released prisoner from Pakistan wrote, "A woman in San Antonio had written some kind and comforting words that proved to be a bombshell for the prison authorities and significantly changed the prisoners' conditions for the better . . . Suddenly I felt as if the sweat drops all over my body were drops from a cool, comforting shower."

Questions

1. Why does Amnesty International limit its efforts to governments rather than include revolutionary or terrorist groups?
2. How does AI seek to preserve its reputation for impartiality?
3. How does AI describe "pressure"? Why is it sometimes effective?
4. Besides letters and publicity campaigns, how does AI assist prisoners and their families?
5. What are the two goals of AI's health professionals' group?

11
Aims and Means of the Catholic Worker

This article originally appeared in the *Catholic Worker*, May 1986.

The Catholic Worker movement was founded in New York City in 1933 by Dorothy Day, a newspaper reporter and former communist, and Peter Maurin, a self-taught French peasant with a gift for reducing theological principles to understandable terms. Both embraced Catholicism, pacifism, poverty and a distaste for current economic and political systems. Together they started a movement, a newspaper (The Catholic Worker) and a series of houses of hospitality throughout the country. Though they were devout believers in their Church's teachings, the practical implications they drew from their faith were radical.

By condemning both capitalism and communism for neglecting the concerns of the human person, they disturbed the peace of both Church and state. Over the years, hundreds of dedicated people, most of them Catholic and many of them young, were attracted by the lives and writings of these two unusual people. Though most adherents remained at Catholic Worker houses for relatively short periods—studying Gandhi and Catholic social thought, feeding the hungry, befriending the poor and exploited, and occasionally participating in civil disobedience—they remained "Catholic Workers" in their hearts for the rest of their lives.

The following article is a distillation of the group's philosophy and goals. The fact that the Catholic Worker outlived its founders (Day died in 1981 and Maurin in 1949), testifies to the power of religious convictions, wedded to poverty and non-violence, to capture the imagination of successive generations of people even in our consumer-oriented society.

The aim of the Catholic Worker movement is to live in accordance with the justice and charity of Jesus Christ. Our sources are the Hebrew and Greek Scriptures as handed down in the teachings of the Roman Catholic Church, with our inspiration coming from the lives of the saints, "men and women outstanding in holiness, living witnesses to Your unchanging love." (Eucharistic Prayer)

This aim requires us to begin living in a different way. We recall the words of our founders, Dorothy Day who said, "God meant things to be much easier than we have made them," and Peter Maurin who wanted to build a society "where it is easier for people to be good."

When we examine our society, which is generally called capitalist (because of its methods of producing and controlling wealth) and is bourgeois (because of a prevailing concern for acquisition and material interests, and its emphasis on respectability and mediocrity), we find it far from God's justice.

In economics, private and state capitalism bring about an unjust distribution of wealth, for the profit motive guides decisions. Those in power live off the sweat of another's brow, while those without power are robbed of a just return for their work. Usury (the charging of interest above administrative costs) is a major contributor to the wrong-doing intrinsic to this system. We note especially how the world debt crisis leads poor countries into great deprivation and a dependency from which there is no foreseeable escape. Here at home, the number of hungry and homeless and unemployed people rises in the midst of increasing affluence.

In labor, human need is no longer the reason for human work. Instead, the unbridled expansion of technology, necessary to capitalism and viewed as "progress," holds sway. Jobs are concentrated in productivity and administration for a "high-tech," war-related, consumer society of disposable goods, so that laborers are trapped in work that does not contribute to human welfare. Furthermore, as jobs become more specialized, many people are excluded from meaningful work or are alienated from the products of their labor. Even in farming, agribusiness has replaced agriculture, and, in all areas, moral restraints are run over roughshod, and a disregard for the laws of nature now threatens the very planet.

In politics, the state functions to control and regulate life. Its power has burgeoned hand in hand with growth in technology, so that military, scientific and corporate interests get the highest priority when concrete political policies are formulated. Because of the sheer size of institutions, we tend towards government by bureaucracy; that is, government by nobody. Bureaucracy, in all areas of life, is not only impersonal, but also makes accountability, and, therefore, an effective political forum for redressing grievances, next to impossible.

In morals, relations between people are corrupted by distorted images of the human person. Class, race and sex often determine personal worth and position within society, leading to structures that foster oppression. Capitalism further divides society by pitting owners against workers in perpetual conflict over wealth and its control. Those who do not "produce" are abandoned, and left, at best, to be "processed" through institutions. Spiritual destitution is rampant, manifested in isolation, madness, promiscuity and violence.

The arms race stands as a clear sign of the direction and spirit of our age. It has extended the domain of destruction and the fear of annihilation, and denies the basic right to life. There is a direct connection between the arms race and destitution. "The arms race is an utterly treacherous trap for humanity, and one which injures the poor to an intolerable degree." (Vatican II)

*   *   *

In contrast to what we see around us, as well as within ourselves, stands St. Thomas Aquinas' doctrine of the Common Good, a vision of a society where the good of each member is bound to the good of the whole in the service of God. To this end, we advocate:

—**Personalism,** a philosophy which regards the freedom and dignity of each person as the basis, focus and goal of all metaphysics and morals. In following such wisdom, we move away from a self-centered individualism toward the good of the other. This is to be done by taking personal responsibility for changing conditions, rather than looking to the state or other institutions to provide impersonal "charity." We pray for a Church renewed by this philosophy and for a time when all those who feel excluded from participation are welcomed with love, drawn by the gentle personalism Peter Maurin taught.

—**A Decentralized Society** in contrast to the present bigness of government, industry, education, health care and agriculture. We encourage efforts such as family farms, rural and urban land trusts, worker ownership and management of small factories, homesteading projects, food, housing and other cooperatives—any effort in which money can once more become merely a medium of exchange, and human beings are no longer commodities.

—**A "Green Revolution,"** so that it is possible to re-discover the proper meaning of our labor and our true bonds with the land; a Distributist communitarianism, self-sufficient through farming, crafting and appropriate technology; a radically new society where people will rely on the fruits of their own soil and labor; associations of mutuality, and a sense of fairness to resolve conflicts.

We believe this needed personal and social transformation should be pursued by the means Jesus revealed in His sacrificial love. With Christ as our Exemplar, by prayer and communion with His Body and Blood, we strive for the practices of:

—**Nonviolence.** "Blessed are the peacemakers, for they shall be called children of God." (Matt. 5:9) Only through nonviolent action can a personalist revolution come about, one in which one evil will not be replaced simply by another. Thus, we oppose the deliberate taking of life for any reason, and see every oppression as blasphemy. Jesus taught us to take suffering upon ourselves rather than inflict it upon others and He calls us to fight against violence with the spiritual weapons of prayer, fasting and non-cooperation with evil. Refusal to pay taxes for war, to register for conscription, to comply with any unjust legislation; participation in nonviolent strikes and boycotts, protests or vigils; withdrawal of support for dominant systems, corporate funding or usurious practices are all excellent means to establish peace.

—**The works of mercy** (as found in Matt. 25:31-46) are at the heart of the Gospel and they are clear mandates for our response to "the least of our brothers and sisters." Houses of hospitality are centers for learning to do these acts of love, so that the poor can receive what is, in justice, theirs: the second coat in our closet, the spare room in our home, a place at our table. Anything beyond what we immediately need belongs to those who go without.

—**Manual labor** in a society that rejects it as undignified and inferior. "Besides inducing cooperation, besides overcoming barriers and establishing the spirit of brotherhood (besides just getting things done), manual labor enables us to use our body as well as our hands, our minds." (Dorothy Day) The Benedictine motto "Ora et Labora" reminds us that the work of human hands is a gift for the edification of the world and the glory of God.

—**Voluntary Poverty.** "The mystery of poverty is that by sharing in it, making ourselves poor in giving to others, we increase our knowledge and belief in love." (Dorothy Day) By embracing voluntary poverty, that is, by casting our lot freely with those whose impoverishment is not a choice, we would ask for the grace to abandon ourselves to the love of God. It would put us on the path to incarnate the Church's "preferential option for the poor."

We must be prepared to accept seeming failure with these aims, for sacrifice and suffering are part of the Christian life. Success, as the world determines it, is not the final criterion for judgment. The most important thing is the love of Jesus Christ and how to live His truth.

Questions

1. What does the Catholic Worker mean by private and state capitalism? Why does the movement find these two economic systems repugnant?

2. What is the Catholic Worker's central criticism of bureaucracy?

3. What is unusual about the emphasis on "social relationships" in its statement on morality? Contrast this with the understanding of "morality" that one usually associates with the Christian churches.

4. How do the Houses of Hospitality tie in with the Catholic Worker's dedication to voluntary poverty and social justice?

5. What is the chief source of the Catholic Worker's adherence to nonviolence, or pacifism? How does this position differ from the traditional "just war" doctrine of most Christian churches?

SECTION THREE

Non-Violence: Philosophy and Strategy

1
Ahimsa, or the
Way of Nonviolence

Mohandas K. Gandhi

This article originally appeared in *All Men Are Brothers*, UNESCO, 1958.

*In these excerpts from Gandhi's writings over many years, the un-
wavering consistency of his beliefs comes to the surface. It is well to recall
that, at the time of writing these thoughts, Gandhi had no assurance—
apart from his own conviction—that "soul force" would eventually lead to
a British withdrawal from the subcontinent of India. He wrote in the dark-
est days of a forty-year struggle, without the benefit of hindsight.*

*As a product of Eastern thought, Gandhi does not argue with the lin-
ear logic of the West. His reasoning, which is more in tune with the approach of the Hebrew and Christian Scriptures, tends to repeat itself in
widening circles of insight. One could find many parallels to Jesus' thought
in such phrases as "readiness to die" (cf. Jn 10:11), "to love those that hate
us" (cf. Mt 5:44), "the impossible ever becoming possible" (cf. Mt 19:20),
and others too numerous to mention.*

*From Gandhi's Autobiography, we read: "Man and his deed are two
distinct things (11), a concept that was taken up by Pope John XXIII in his
encyclical "Peace on Earth" (#159), which has been widely interpreted as
a reference to communism and its adherents. Ever a realist, Gandhi had
little regard for a non-violence that has not been tested in a hostile environment (12). Somewhat surprisingly, the Indian holy man discounts
ahimsa as a "means of personal salvation" (14). Rather, he envisions it as a
heartfelt response to "social injustice." (15) One is reminded of the apostle
John who wrote: "Anyone who loves God must also love his brother" (1 Jn
4:23).*

*Gandhi distinguishes ahimsa from the utilitarianism made popular by
the British philosopher Jeremy Bentham (1748–1832), who sought the
"greatest good for the greatest number." Gandhi, on the contrary, says
that the followers of ahimsa "will strive for the greatest good of all and die
in the attempt to realize the ideal" (17).*

*In a passage that will challenge an age given to hedonism and the
avoidance of pain, Gandhi upholds suffering as "the law of human beings"*

(20). It is suffering that "opens up the inner understanding in man"—this applies to oneself and to one's opponents. We could apply to the current arms race Gandhi's final statement in this section about fear and even cowardice being linked with the possession of arms. The non-violent cannot be true to their calling without "unadulterated fearlessness."

Critics have dismissed Gandhi as a dreamer. They argue that successful non-violent action is overly dependent on a charismatic leader. On the other hand, not all critics have studied his philosophy and methods with any seriousness or tried to put them into practice in seemingly hopeless situations.

Nonviolence is the greatest force at the disposal of mankind. It is mightier than the mightiest weapon of destruction devised by the ingenuity of man. Destruction is not the law of the humans. Man lives freely by his readiness to die, if need be, at the hands of his brother, never by killing him. Every murder or other injury, no matter for what cause, committed or inflicted on another is a crime against humanity.   *1*

Harijan, July 20, 1931

I claim that even now, though the social structure is not based on a conscious acceptance of nonviolence, all the world over mankind lives and men retain their possessions on the sufferance of one another. If they had not done so, only the fewest and the most ferocious would have survived. But such is not the case. Families are bound together by ties of love, and so are groups in the so-called civilized society called nations. Only they do not recognize the supremacy of the law of nonviolence. It follows, therefore, that they have not investigated its vast possibilities. Hitherto, out of sheer inertia, shall I say, we have taken it for granted that complete nonviolence is possible only for the few who take the vow of non-possession and the allied abstinences. Whilst it is true that the votaries alone can carry on research work and declare from time to time the new possibilities of the great eternal law governing man, if it is a law, it must hold good for all. The many failures we see are not of the law but of the followers, many of whom do not even know that they are under that law willy-nilly. When a mother dies for her child she unknowingly obeys the law. I have been pleading for the past fifty years for a conscious acceptance of the law and its zealous practice even in the face of failures. Fifty years' work has shown marvellous results and strengthened my faith. I do claim that by constant practice we shall come to a state of things when lawful possession will commend universal and voluntary respect. No doubt such possession will not be tainted. It will not be an insolent demonstration of the inequalities that surround us everywhere. Nor need the problem of unjust and unlawful possession appal the votary of nonviolence. He has at his disposal the non-violent weapon of Satyāgraha and non-cooperation which hitherto has been found to be a complete substitute of violence whenever it has been applied honestly in sufficient measure. I have never claimed to present the complete science of nonviolence. It does not lend itself to such treatment. So far as I know, no single physical science does, not even the very exact science of mathematics. I am but a seeker. 8

Harijan, February 22, 1942

In the application of Satyāgraha, I discovered in the earliest stages that pursuit of truth did not admit of violence being inflicted on one's opponent but that he must be weaned from error by patience and sympathy. For, what appears to be truth to the one may appear to be error to another. And patience means self-suffering. So the doctrine came to mean vindication of truth, not by infliction of suffering on the opponent, but on one's self. 9

Young India, November, 1919

In this age of wonders no one will say that a thing or idea is worthless because it is new. To say it is impossible because it is difficult, is again not in consonance with the spirit of the age. Things undreamt of are daily being seen, the impossible is ever becoming possible. We are constantly being astonished these days at the amazing discoveries in the field of violence. But I maintain that far more undreamt of and seemingly impossible discoveries will be made in the field of nonviolence. 10

Harijan, August 25, 1940

Man and his deed are two distinct things. It is quite proper to resist and attack a system, but to resist and attack its author is tantamount to resisting and attacking oneself. For we are all tarred with the same brush, and are children of one and the same Creator, and as such the divine powers within us are infinite. To slight a single human being is to slight those divine powers, and thus to harm not only that being but with him the whole world. 11   *An Autobiography*

Nonviolence is a universal principle and its operation is not limited by a hostile environment. Indeed, its efficacy can be tested only when it acts in the midst of and in spite of opposition. Our nonviolence would be a hollow thing and worth nothing, if it depended for its success on the good-will of the authorities. 12   *Harijan, November 12, 1938*

Some friends have told me that truth and nonviolence have no place in politics and worldly affairs. I do not agree. I have no use for them as a means of individual salvation. Their introduction and application in every-day life has been my experiment all along.   *14*

Harijan, November 12, 1938

No man could be actively nonviolent and not rise against social injustice no matter where it occurred.   *15*   *Harijan, April 20, 1940*

A votary of ahimsā cannot subscribe to the utilitarian formula (of the greatest good of the greatest number). He will strive for the greatest good of all and die in the attempt to realize the ideal. He will therefore be willing to die, so that the others may live. He will serve himself with the rest, by himself dying. The greatest good of all inevitably includes the good of the greatest number, and, therefore, he and the utilitarian will converge in many points in their career but there does come a time when they must part company, and even work in opposite directions. The utilitarian to be logical will never sacrifice himself. The absolutist will even sacrifice himself.   *17*   *Young India, December 9, 1926*

Suffering is the law of human beings; war is the law of the jungle. But suffering is infinitely more powerful than the law of the jungle for converting the opponent and opening his ears, which are otherwise shut, to the voice of reason. Nobody has probably drawn up more petitions or espoused more forlorn causes than I and I have come to this fundamental conclusion that if you want something really important to be done you must not merely satisfy the reason, you must move the heart also. The appeal of reason is more to the head but the penetration of the heart comes from suffering. It opens up the inner understanding in man. Suffering is the badge of the human race, not the sword.   *20*

Young India, November 4, 1931

Nonviolence is a power which can be wielded equally by all—children, young men and women or grown up people—provided they have a living faith in the God of Love and have therefore equal love for all mankind. When nonviolence is accepted as the law of life it must pervade the whole being and not be applied to isolated acts.   *21*

Harijan, September 5, 1936

Nonviolence and cowardice go ill together. I can imagine a fully armed man to be at heart a coward. Possession of arms implies an element of fear, if not cowardice. But true nonviolence is an impossibility without the possession of unadulterated fearlessness.   *68*   *Harijan, July 15, 1939*

Questions

1. Do you think that every injury, for whatever cause, is a crime against humanity? How should this statement be interpreted in regard to the death penalty imposed by the state? Give your reasons.

2. Can you think of an instance in which your willingness to accept suffering might have changed the attitude of an adversary?

3. Do you agree with Gandhi that *ahimsa* is for everybody and not just for the few? Give your reasons.

4. What consequences do you see in Gandhi's insistence that non-violence is not for individual salvation but rather for "worldly affairs" and "against injustice"? Do you find this viewpoint reflected in your own religious experience? Explain.

5. Do you think that reason alone is sufficient for the resolution of disputes? Give examples where the appeal to the heart is more efficacious.

2
Gandhi's Nonviolence

Haridas T. Muzumdar

This article originally appeared in *Friends Journal*, November 1, 1983.

Millions around the world got their first glimpse of Mohandas K. Gandhi through the moving picture based on his life. To serious students of ahimsa (non-violence), the film treatment may have seemed superficial but no viewer could fail to be impressed by this frail man who inspired his followers to accept pain and punishment in the pursuit of justice.

In this article, which appeared in a Quaker publication, Haridas T. Muzumdar, a friend and early biographer of the Mahatma, seeks to answer the question of how Gandhi would have confronted a more ruthless foe than the British Empire. Would a Hitler or a Stalin have reacted as the English did to the persistent, non-violent tactics of this Indian holy man who abandoned the practice of law to answer a higher call? No one really knows, but the author gives his opinion that ahimsa would have worked even in the very different conditions of Nazi Germany or Stalinist Eastern Europe.

Muzumdar cites Gandhi's dedication to Hindu spirituality and to the teachings of Jesus of Nazareth, especially in his Sermon on the Mount (Matthew 5—7). As a Quaker, the author embraces the Society of Friends' understanding of non-violence as a method of non-cooperation and as a constructive program that leads to healing and reconciliation. The reader can verify these claims in the following article, which quotes Gandhi's own words.

The author emphasizes Gandhi's distinction between an evil system and the evildoer as a person. The system must be resisted, but in such a way that one seeks to change the opponent into a friend. This was something, as the barrister Gandhi knew, beyond the scope of human law. The author asks us to consider what must have gone through the mind of a Roman officer whose Jewish subject walked the "extra mile" freely and without compulsion (Mt 5:41). Some nineteen hundred years later, Gandhi himself presented an English judge with much the same opportunity for conversion.

Returning to his original question, Muzumdar hazards the guess that

214

Gandhi *"implicitly believed that his philosophy of non-violence would work against a Hitler or a Stalin." The world, to its great loss, will never know.*

On a more modest scale, such methods did succeed in Western Europe, according to the testimony of Trygve Lie and a young Quaker in Nazi-occupied France. The reader is left to ponder whether non-violence has a chance to resolve the superpower confrontation of the U.S. and the U.S.S.R. The facts of history tell us that the philosophy of force and counter-force has not brought to the world a real peace but, at best, an uneasy and distrustful avoidance of nuclear holocaust.

The movie Gandhi vividly portrays the triumph of nonviolence over violence, of Gandhi's ahimsa (nonviolence: love) or soul force against the British Raj. The question has been raised time and again: Would Gandhi's technique have worked against Hitler or Stalin? The question must be faced squarely and answered logically. To answer the question, however, we must fully understand the man Gandhi and his philosophy of life.

To understand Gandhi the man properly, we must take into account two factors: the all-pervasive influence of his Hindu heritage and the profound impact during his student days in London of the life of Jesus, especially the Sermon on the Mount.

The Sermon on the Mount fails to make a striking impression on people born and reared in a society which professes the name of Jesus without fully understanding his life or the meaning of his core teachings embodied in the Beatitudes. But Jesus and his core teachings do make a never-to-be-forgotten impact on one who comes fresh to the Sermon on the Mount from another cultural milieu.

I have called the Sermon on the Mount "The Technique for Converting the Wrong-Doer." There are legitimate differences of opinion in regard to the interpretation of the phrase: "Resist not evil." Some translate it to mean "nonviolent nonresistance." And they would be in good company. The Mennonites to this day fashion their lifestyle according to this interpretation. And if I am not mistaken, the other two Historic Peace Churches, Quakers and Brethren, also accepted that interpretation at one time.

Gradually the Quakers broadened their concept of nonviolence to embrace works of healing and reconciliation ("the constructive program" of Gandhi's nonviolence) as well as noncooperation with violence and warfare. The broader concept of Gandhi's ahimsa implies that in addition to what is manifest in warfare, violence may be built into an unjust social structure or into certain interpersonal and intergroup relations, such as discrimination, segregation, and exploitation. This broader concept gives the follower of ahimsa a wider scope for inventing and utilizing new and creative nonviolent strategies for fighting existing evils and injustices in society.

I submit that every generation must interpret and reinterpret the sacred Scriptures and their precepts. I interpret "Resist not evil" to mean "Resist not evil violently." Such an interpretation leaves open to the votary of ahimsa the scope for resisting evil—of course nonviolently, without malice or hatred.

One of Gandhi's eternal contributions to the new type of thinking necessitated by the horrendous death-dealing armaments, by the balance of terror, is the distinction he made between the system of wrongdoing and the operators of the system of wrongdoing. The system we have every right to quarrel with and strive to alter or abolish. But human beings, the human agents who operate the system, we have no right to quarrel with, much less to destroy. Judgment and punishment rests with God; ours is the humbler task of converting wrongdoers, not of judging and destroying them. It is precisely in this respect that Jesus' Sermon on the Mount makes its supreme contribution. In Gandhi, the young Hindu barrister makes the selfsame statement: Jesus "understood" the full implications of nonviolence.

Jesus' injunction about walking the second mile illustrates his conception of nonviolence. Under imperial Roman law, it was perfectly permissible and legal for a Roman officer to commandeer the services of a Jew to carry a load for one mile. Under the circumstances, Jesus exhorted his compatriots: By all means, carry the load one mile, since that is the law of the land (unjust though it be). Then at the end of the one mile, offer freely to carry the load the second mile.

At this unrehearsed and unexpected response, the Roman officer would be compelled to raise questions about the sanity of the Jew or his own sanity or the validity and justice of the system of which he was an integral part. When the officer is forced to raise such questions posed by the nonviolent behavior, half the battle is won by the victim of the system. Two thousand years later, similarly, at the famous trial in Ahmadabad (1922), Gandhi called upon the judge to resign his post if the system he was helping to administer was not good for India; otherwise, to impose upon him (Gandhi) the severest penalty the law permits. It was the Mahatma's nonviolence in thought, word, and deed that led the honorable English judge and the entire court to rise in respect when Gandhi the prisoner was being brought to the dock.

Would Gandhi's technique of nonviolence have worked against Hitler or Stalin? My answer has always been that Gandhi implicitly believed that his philosophy of nonviolence would work against a Hitler or a Stalin successfully as it did against the British Raj in southern Africa and in India, albeit with perhaps greater sacrifices on the part of the votaries of non-violence.

His broad concept of the scope and meaning of ahimsa would give Gandhi plenty of latitude for evolving creative, constructive programs of action to mobilize the whole nation in the fight against the injustices of a Hitler or a Stalin. Nor would he give up on a Hitler and a Stalin as hope-less, irredeemable devils. They, too, maintained the Mahatma, possessed though they might have been by satanic impulses, had a divine spark un-derneath the veneer of their ideology. Likewise the ideologically oriented followers had in them the divine spark. And it is this divine spark that Gan-dhi would kindle, as Jesus and Buddha, Mahavira and Lao-tse, had taught us long ago.

Instances abound of the triumph of the divine spark over ideological myopia. Trygve Lie, the first secretary general of the United Nations (1946–1953), told us the story of a little-noticed episode during World War II at an Institute of International Relations held under the auspices of the American Friends Service Committee.

At the end of World War I, because of the Allied blockade of Ger-many, no foodstuff could reach the German people. Sensing the danger to the children, the people of Norway invited a number of German young-sters as their guests and treated them as members of their own families—an act of "constructive" nonviolence. These German youngsters learned the Norwegian language and became familiar with the Norwegian coun-tryside with its fiords and mountains.

During World War II the German High Command was delighted to have hundreds of well-trained, indoctrinated Nazi soldiers who knew Nor-wegian and the countryside and the people of Norway. They selected these Nazi youths, briefed them about the "impending" invasion of Nor-way by the British, and asked them if they would volunteer to go to Nor-way's defense. All those young men in Nazi military uniform, reared by Norwegian families, enthusiastically agreed to go to the aid of Norway. Two battleships carried these youths, along with a large expeditionary force of other German soldiers, supposedly to help Norwegians repel Brit-ish aggression. Upon landing, these German youths discovered that they were called upon to fight the Norwegians, not the British. Whereupon these young soldiers went back to their ships, told their superiors that they would not fight the Norwegians, and risked being shot. The German High Command, eager to have the services of well-trained soldiers, shipped them off to other battlefronts.

The nonviolence or soul force of Norwegians in the form of "construc-tive" activity of goodwill was repaid handsomely by the beneficiaries of

Norwegian hospitality—despite their Nazi ideology and military drilling. Justifiably the Mahatma could declaim (1909): "Soul Force is a two-edged sword. It blesses him who uses it and him against whom it is used."

A young American Quaker relief worker in occupied France wanted to pass through a checkpoint; he had no military pass with him. But when the young Nazi soldier standing guard learned that the American represented Quaker relief work in Europe, he let the worker enter without a hitch and volunteered the information that, as a youngster in Germany at the end of World War I, he had been fed by the American Quakers.

In terms of the concrete situation of the present relations between the two superpowers, the United States and the USSR, the adversary relationship is brought about because leaders of both powers have been captives of the traditional mode of thinking, namely, that to resolve mutual differences and fears they must resort to the arbitrament of war. Neither party chooses to trust the other's word. Lack of mutual trust, Gandhi would say, is at the bottom of each party's fear of suspected wrongdoing and first strike by the other.

It is strange that the superpowers should be bogged down in haggling over irrelevant details, while both genuinely profess belief in safeguarding peace for their own people and for the peoples of the world. Why don't the superpowers enter into an agreement not to resort to war for any cause whatsoever? Then, why don't they agree to put all their cards—their grievances against each other—on the table and find ways to resolve differences on the basis of trust and goodwill? Such a scenario would fit Gandhi's non-violence in the present context.

Questions

1. How does the impact on Gandhi of the Sermon on the Mount compare with its effect on most Christians? How can you account for this?

2. Can you give instances of non-violent resistance to an oppressive system not mentioned in this article?

3. If, as the author says, each generation must reinterpret its Scriptures for itself, how would you see the relevance of the Sermon on the Mount to today's violent struggles?

4. Do you agree with the author that Gandhi's philosophy would have worked against a Stalin or a Hitler? Why or why not?

5. Do you think that the author's suggestions for lessening superpower confrontation, as listed in his concluding paragraph, are practical and helpful for the attainment of genuine peace? Why or why not?

3

Letter from a Birmingham Jail

Martin Luther King, Jr.

This article originally appeared in *Why We Can't Wait*, Harper & Row, 1963.

Many of history's outstanding figures have spent time in jail—Socrates, the Jewish prophets, Jesus, St. Paul, Martin Luther, St. Ignatius Loyola, Gandhi, the Russian dissidents and Martin Luther King. Imprisonment usually strengthens the resolve of people of conscience and gives them time for reflection and expression.

Such was the case with Dr. King, the inspiration and tactical leader of America's black people in the mid-twentieth century. Imprisoned for leading a civil rights demonstration without a permit in April 1963, he sent a reply to eight Alabama clergymen who found his tactics too extreme. In a reply abounding in references to the Jewish and Christian Scriptures and to philosophers ancient and modern, Dr. King met his critics head-on and left a timeless written legacy of his non-violent approach to oppression.

The letter begins with praise for the good will of his detractors and a patient rebuttal of the charge that the writer is an "outside agitator." Not only was he invited by the local chapter of the Southern Christian Leadership Conference, he says, but as a minister of the Gospel he declares his obligation to carry the Christian message to every hamlet where injustice still exists.

With delicacy and tact, Dr. King reminds the ministers that the demonstration he led may be unfortunate, but that "the white power structure of this city left the Negro community with no other alternative." Reviewing the long record of police brutality and unsolved bombings of churches in Birmingham, the author instructs his critics in the four steps of any non-violent campaign: (1) collection of the facts; (2) negotiation; (3) self-purification; (4) direct action. With such arguments, he denies that he acted irresponsibly.

In the crisis created by direct action, Dr. King sees hope for "creative tension"—through the acceptance of beatings and other suffering—which can change an oppressor into an ally. In this, he echoes Gandhi's appeal to "self-suffering." He replies to the charge of being in too much of a hurry by recounting the long centuries of slavery and segregation and their ef-

fects on black people, especially little children. "I hope, sirs," he says with no little irony, "you can understand our legitimate and unavoidable impatience."

Quoting St. Thomas Aquinas, the medieval Catholic philosopher, King distinguishes between just laws and unjust ones, insisting all the while that his followers accept the penalties of even unjust legislation. He expresses his impatience with the "white moderate" who is "more devoted to 'order' than to justice."

As to the charge of extremism, King places his movement midway between black nationalist groups which have lost faith in America and segregationists who play into their hands. "If his (the Negro's) repressed emotions do not come out in these non-violent ways," he writes, "they will come out in ominous expressions of violence," a prophecy fulfilled after his own assassination in 1968.

By drawing out the implications of traditional Christianity in the turmoil of daily events, King forges a synthesis that challenges those who separate their faith from everyday life.

April 16, 1963
Birmingham, Alabama
MY DEAR FELLOW CLERGYMEN:

While confined here in the Birmingham city jail, I came across your recent statement calling my present activities "unwise and untimely." Seldom do I pause to answer criticism of my work and ideas. If I sought to answer all the criticisms that cross my desk, my secretaries would have little time for anything other than such correspondence in the course of the day, and I would have no time for constructive work. But since I feel that you are men of genuine good will and that your criticisms are sincerely set forth, I want to try to answer your statement in what I hope will be patient and reasonable terms.

I think I should indicate why I am here in Birmingham, since you have been influenced by the view which argues against "outsiders coming in." I have the honor of serving as president of the Southern Christian Leadership Conference, an organization operating in every southern state, with headquarters in Atlanta, Georgia. We have some eighty-five affiliated organizations across the South, and one of them is the Alabama Christian Movement for Human Rights. Frequently we share staff, educational, and financial resources with our affiliates. Several months ago the affiliate here in Birmingham asked us to be on call to engage in a nonviolent direct-action program if such were deemed necessary. We readily consented, and when the hour came we lived up to our promise. So I, along with several members of my staff, am here because I was invited here. I am here because I have organizational ties here.

But more basically, I am in Birmingham because injustice is here. Just as the prophets of the eighth century B.C. left their villages and carried their "thus saith the Lord" far beyond the boundaries of their home towns, and just as the Apostle Paul left his village of Tarsus and carried the gospel of Jesus Christ to the far corners of the Greco-Roman world, so am I compelled to carry the gospel of freedom beyond my own home town. Like Paul, I must constantly respond to the Macedonian call for aid.

Moreover, I am cognizant of the interrelatedness of all communities and states. I cannot sit idly by in Atlanta and not be concerned about what happens in Birmingham. Injustice anywhere is a threat to justice everywhere. We are caught in an inescapable network of mutuality, tied in a single garment of destiny. Whatever affects one directly, affects all indirectly. Never again can we afford to live with the narrow, provincial "outside agitator" idea. Anyone who lives inside the United States can never be considered an outsider anywhere within its bounds.

You deplore the demonstrations taking place in Birmingham. But your statement, I am sorry to say, fails to express a similar concern for the conditions that brought about the demonstrations. I am sure that none of you would want to rest content with the superficial kind of social analysis that deals merely with effects and does not grapple with underlying causes. It is unfortunate that demonstrations are taking place in Birmingham, but it is even more unfortunate that the city's white power structure left the Negro community with no alternative.

In any nonviolent campaign there are four basic steps: collection of the facts to determine whether injustices exist; negotiation; self-purification; and direct action. We have gone through all these steps in Birmingham. There can be no gainsaying the fact that racial injustice engulfs this community. Birmingham is probably the most thoroughly segregated city in the United States. Its ugly record of brutality is widely known. Negroes have experienced grossly unjust treatment in the courts. There have been more unsolved bombings of Negro homes and churches in Birmingham than in any other city in the nation. These are the hard, brutal facts of the case. On the basis of these conditions, Negro leaders sought to negotiate with the city fathers. But the latter consistently refused to engage in good-faith negotiation.

Then, last September, came the opportunity to talk with leaders of Birmingham's economic community. In the course of the negotiations, certain promises were made by the merchants—for example, to remove the stores' humiliating racial signs. On the basis of these promises, the Reverend Fred Shuttlesworth and the leaders of the Alabama Christian

Movement for Human Rights agreed to a moratorium on all demonstrations. As the weeks and months went by, we realized that we were the victims of a broken promise. A few signs, briefly removed, returned; the others remained.

As in so many past experiences, our hopes had been blasted, and the shadow of deep disappointment settled upon us. We had no alternative except to prepare for direct action, whereby we would present our very bodies as a means of laying our case before the conscience of the local and the national community. Mindful of the difficulties involved, we decided to undertake a process of self-purification. We began a series of workshops on nonviolence, and we repeatedly asked ourselves: "Are you able to accept blows without retaliation?" "Are you able to endure the ordeal of jail?" We decided to schedule our direct-action program for the Easter season, realizing that except for Christmas, this is the main shopping period of the year. Knowing that a strong economic-withdrawal program would be the by-product of direct action, we felt that this would be the best time to bring pressure to bear on the merchants for the needed change.

Then it occurred to us that Birmingham's mayoral election was coming up in March, and we speedily decided to postpone action until after election day. When we discovered that the Commissioner of Public Safety, Eugene "Bull" Connor, had piled up enough votes to be in the run-off, we decided again to postpone action until the day after the run-off so that the demonstrations could not be used to cloud the issues. Like many others, we waited to see Mr. Connor defeated, and to this end we endured postponement after postponement. Having aided in this community need, we felt that our direct-action program could be delayed no longer.

You may well ask, "Why direct action? Why sit-ins, marches, and so forth? Isn't negotiation a better path?" You are quite right in calling for negotiation. Indeed, this is the very purpose of direct action. Nonviolent direct action seeks to create such a crisis and foster such a tension that a community which has constantly refused to negotiate is forced to confront the issue. It seeks so to dramatize the issue that it can no longer be ignored. My citing the creation of tension as part of the work of the nonviolent-resister may sound rather shocking. But I must confess that I am not afraid of the word "tension." I have earnestly opposed violent tension, but there is a type of constructive, nonviolent tension which is necessary for growth. Just as Socrates felt that it was necessary to create a tension in the mind so that individuals could rise from the bondage of myths and half-truths to the unfettered realm of creative analysis and objective appraisal, so must we see the need for nonviolent gadflies to create the kind of tension in society that will help men rise from the dark depths of prejudice and racism to the majestic heights of understanding and brotherhood.

The purpose of our direct-action program is to create a situation so crisis-packed that it will inevitably open the door to negotiation. I therefore concur with you in your call for negotiation. Too long has our beloved Southland been bogged down in a tragic effort to live in monologue rather than dialogue.

One of the basic points in your statement is that the action that I and my associates have taken in Birmingham is untimely. Some have asked: "Why didn't you give the new city administration time to act?" The only answer that I can give to this query is that the new Birmingham administration must be prodded about as much as the outgoing one, before it will act. We are sadly mistaken if we feel that the election of Albert Boutwell as mayor will bring the millennium to Birmingham. While Mr. Boutwell is a much more gentle person than Mr. Connor, they are both segregationists, dedicated to maintenance of the status quo. I have hoped that Mr. Boutwell will be reasonable enough to see the futility of massive resistance to desegregation. But he will not see this without pressure from devotees of civil rights. My friends, I must say to you that we have not made a single gain in civil rights without determined legal and nonviolent pressure. Lamentably, it is an historical fact that privileged groups seldom give up their privileges voluntarily. Individuals may see the moral light and voluntarily give up their unjust posture; but, as Reinhold Niebuhr has reminded us, groups tend to be more immoral than individuals.

We know through painful experience that freedom is never voluntarily given by the oppressor; it must be demanded by the oppressed. Frankly, I have yet to engage in a direct-action campaign that was "well timed" in view of those who have not suffered unduly from the disease of segregation. For years now I have heard the word "Wait!" It rings in the ear of every Negro with piercing familiarity. This "Wait" has almost always meant "Never." We must come to see, with one of our distinguished jurists, that "justice too long delayed is justice denied."

We have waited for more than 340 years for our constitutional and God-given rights. The nations of Asia and Africa are moving with jetlike speed toward gaining political independence, but we still creep at horse-and-buggy pace toward gaining a cup of coffee at a lunch counter. Perhaps it is easy for those who have never felt the stinging darts of segregation to say, "Wait." But when you have seen vicious mobs lynch your mothers and fathers at will and drown your sisters and brothers at whim; when you have seen hate-filled policemen curse, kick, and even kill your black brothers and sisters; when you see the vast majority of your twenty million Negro brothers smothering in an airtight cage of poverty in the midst of an affluent society; when you suddenly find your tongue twisted and your speech stammering as you seek to explain to your six-year-old daughter why she can't go to the public amusement park that has just been advertised on television, and see tears welling up in her eyes when she is told that Funtown is closed to colored children, and see ominous clouds of inferiority beginning to form in her little mental sky, and see her beginning to distort her personality by developing an unconscious bitterness toward white people; when you have to concoct an answer for a five-year-old son who is asking, "Daddy, why do white people treat colored people so mean?"; when you take a cross-country drive and find it necessary to sleep night after night in the uncomfortable corners of your automobile because no motel will accept you; when you are humiliated day in and day out by nagging signs reading "white" and "colored;" when your first name becomes "nigger," your middle name becomes "boy" (however old you are) and your last name becomes "John," and your wife and mother are never given the respected title "Mrs."; when you are harried by day and haunted by night by the fact that you are a Negro, living constantly at tiptoe stance, never quite knowing what to expect next, and are plagued with inner fears and outer resentments; when you are forever fighting a degenerating sense of "nobodiness"—then you will understand why we find it difficult to wait. There comes a time when the cup of endurance runs over, and men are no longer willing to be plunged into the abyss of despair. I hope, sirs, you can understand our legitimate and unavoidable impatience.

You express a great deal of anxiety over our willingness to break laws. This is certainly a legitimate concern. Since we so diligently urge people to obey the Supreme Court's decision of 1954 outlawing segregation in the public schools, at first glance it may seem rather paradoxical for us consciously to break laws. One may well ask: "How can you advocate breaking some laws and obeying others?" The answer lies in the fact that there are two types of laws: just and unjust. I would be the first to advocate obeying just laws. One has not only a legal but a moral responsibility to obey just laws. Conversely, one has a moral responsibility to disobey unjust laws. I would agree with St. Augustine that "an unjust law is no law at all."

Now, what is the difference between the two? How does one determine whether a law is just or unjust? A just law is a man-made code that squares with the moral law or the law of God. An unjust law is a code that is out of harmony with the moral law. To put it in the terms of St. Thomas Aquinas: An unjust law is a human law that is not rooted in eternal law and natural law. Any law that uplifts human personality is just. Any law that degrades human personality is unjust. All segregation statutes are unjust because segregation distorts the soul and damages the personality. It gives the segregator a false sense of superiority and the segregated a false sense of inferiority. Segregation, to use the terminology of the Jewish philosopher Martin Buber, substitutes an "I-it" relationship for an "I-thou" relationship and ends up relegating persons to the status of things. Hence segregation is not only politically, economically, and sociologically unsound, it is morally wrong and sinful. Paul Tillich has said that sin is separation. Is not segregation an existential expression of man's tragic separation, his awful estrangement, his terrible sinfulness? Thus it is that I can urge men to obey the 1954 decision of the Supreme Court, for it is morally right; and I can urge them to disobey segregation ordinances, for they are morally wrong.

Let us consider a more concrete example of just and unjust laws. An unjust law is a code that a numerical or power majority group compels a minority group to obey but does not make binding on itself. This is difference made legal. By the same token, a just law is a code that a majority compels a minority to follow and that it is willing to follow itself. This is sameness made legal.

Let me give another explanation. A law is unjust if it is inflicted on a minority that, as a result of being denied the right to vote, had no part in enacting or devising the law. Who can say that the legislature of Alabama which set up that state's segregation laws was democratically elected? Throughout Alabama all sorts of devious methods are used to prevent Negroes from becoming registered voters, and there are some counties in which, even though Negroes constitute a majority of the population, not a single Negro is registered. Can any law enacted under such circumstances be considered democratically structured?

Sometimes a law is just on its face and unjust in its application. For instance, I have been arrested on a charge of parading without a permit. Now, there is nothing wrong in having an ordinance which requires a permit for a parade. But such an ordinance becomes unjust when it is used to maintain segregation and to deny citizens the First-Amendment privilege of peaceful assembly and protest.

I hope you are able to see the distinction I am trying to point out. In no sense do I advocate evading or defying the law, as would the rabid segregationist. That would lead to anarchy. One who breaks an unjust law must do so openly, lovingly, and with a willingness to accept the penalty. I submit that an individual who breaks a law that conscience tells him is unjust, and who willingly accepts the penalty of imprisonment in order to arouse the conscience of the community over its injustice, is in reality expressing the highest respect for law.

Of course, there is nothing new about this kind of civil disobedience. It was evidenced sublimely in the refusal of Shadrach, Meshach, and

Abednego to obey the laws of Nebuchadnezzar, on the ground that a higher moral law was at stake. It was practiced superbly by the early Christians, who were willing to face hungry lions and the excruciating pain of chopping blocks rather than submit to certain unjust laws of the Roman Empire. To a degree, academic freedom is a reality today because Socrates practiced civil disobedience. In our own nation, the Boston Tea Party represented a massive act of civil disobedience.

We should never forget that everything Adolf Hitler did in Germany was "legal" and everything the Hungarian freedom fighters did in Hungary was "illegal." It was "illegal" to aid and comfort a Jew in Hitler's Germany. Even so, I am sure that, had I lived in Germany at the time, I would have aided and comforted my Jewish brothers. If today I lived in a Communist country where certain principles dear to the Christian faith are suppressed, I would openly advocate disobeying that country's anti-religious laws.

I must make two honest confessions to you, my Christian and Jewish brothers. First, I must confess that over the past few years I have been gravely disappointed with the white moderate. I have almost reached the regrettable conclusion that the Negro's great stumbling block in his stride toward freedom is not the White Citizen's Counciler or the Ku Klux Klanner, but the white moderate, who is more devoted to "order" than to justice; who prefers a negative peace which is the absence of tension to a positive peace which is the presence of justice; who constantly says, "I agree with you in the goal you seek but I cannot agree with your methods of direct action"; who paternalistically believes he can set the timetable for another man's freedom; who lives by a mythical concept of time and who constantly advises the Negro to wait for a "more convenient season." Shallow understanding from people of good will is more frustrating than absolute misunderstanding from people of ill will. Lukewarm acceptance is much more bewildering than outright rejection.

I had hoped that the white moderate would understand that law and order exist for the purpose of establishing justice and that when they fail in this purpose they become the dangerously structured dams that block the flow of social progress. I had hoped that the white moderate would understand that the present tension in the South is a necessary phase of the transition from an obnoxious negative peace, in which the Negro passively accepted his unjust plight, to a substantive and positive peace, in which all men will respect the dignity and worth of human personality. Actually, we who engage in nonviolent direct action are not the creators of tension. We merely bring to the surface the hidden tension that is already alive. We bring it out in the open, where it can be seen and dealt with. Like a boil that can never be cured so long as it is covered up but must be opened with all its ugliness to the natural medicines of air and light, injustice must be exposed, with all the tension its exposure creates, to the light of human conscience and the air of national opinion, before it can be cured.

In your statement you assert that our actions, even though peaceful, must be condemned because they precipitate violence. But is this a logical assertion? Isn't this like condemning a robbed man because his possession of money precipitated the evil act of robbery? Isn't this like condemning Socrates because his unswerving commitment to truth and his philosophical inquiries precipitated the act by the misguided populace in which they made him drink hemlock? Isn't this like condemning Jesus because his unique God-consciousness and never-ceasing devotion to God's will precipitated the evil act of crucifixion? We must come to see that, as the federal courts have consistently affirmed, it is wrong to urge an individual to cease his efforts to gain his basic constitutional rights because the quest may precipitate violence. Society must protect the robbed and punish the robber.

I had also hoped that the white moderate would reject the myth concerning time in relation to the struggle for freedom. I have just received a letter from a white brother in Texas. He writes: "All Christians know that the colored people will receive equal rights eventually, but it is possible that you are in too great a religious hurry. It has taken Christianity almost two thousand years to accomplish what it has. The teachings of Christ take time to come to earth." Such an attitude stems from a tragic misconception of time, from the strangely irrational notion that there is something in the very flow of time that will inevitably cure all ills. Actually, time itself is neutral; it can be used either destructively or constructively. More and more I feel that the people of ill will have used time much more effectively than have the people of good will. We will have to repent in this generation not merely for the hateful words and actions of the bad people, but for the appalling silence of the good people. Human progress never rolls in on wheels of inevitability; it comes through the tireless efforts of men willing to be co-workers with God, and without this hard work, time itself becomes an ally of the forces of stagnation. We must use time creatively, in the knowledge that the time is always ripe to do right. Now is the time to make real the promise of democracy and transform our pending national elegy into a creative psalm of brotherhood. Now is the time to lift our national policy from the quicksand of racial injustice to the solid rock of human dignity.

You speak of our activity in Birmingham as extreme. At first I was rather disappointed that fellow clergymen would see my nonviolent efforts as those of an extremist. I began thinking about the fact that I stand in the middle of two opposing forces in the Negro community. One is a force of complacency, made up in part of Negroes who, as a result of long years of oppression, are so drained of self-respect and a sense of "somebodiness" that they have adjusted to segregation; and in part of a few middle-class Negroes who, because of a degree of academic and economic security and because in some ways they profit by segregation, have become insensitive to the problems of the masses. The other force is one of bitterness and hatred, and it comes perilously close to advocating violence. It is expressed in the various black nationalist groups that are springing up across the nation, the largest and best-known being Elijah Muhammad's Muslim movement. Nourished by the Negro's frustration over the continued existence of racial discrimination, this movement is made up of people who have lost faith in America, who have absolutely repudiated Christianity, and who have concluded that the white man is an incorrigible "devil."

I have tried to stand between these two forces, saying that we need emulate neither the "do-nothingism" of the complacent nor the hatred and despair of the black nationalist. For there is the more excellent way of love and nonviolent protest. I am grateful to God that, through the influence of the Negro church, the way of nonviolence became an integral part of our struggle.

If this philosophy had not emerged, by now many streets of the South would, I am convinced, be flowing with blood. And I am further convinced that if our white brothers dismiss as "rabble-rousers" and "outside agitators" those of us who employ nonviolent direct action, and if they refuse to support our nonviolent efforts, millions of Negroes will, out of frustration and despair, seek solace and security in black-nationalist ideologies—a development that would inevitably lead to a frightening racial nightmare.

Oppressed people cannot remain oppressed forever. The yearning for freedom eventually manifests itself, and that is what has happened to the American Negro. Something within has reminded him of his birthright of freedom, and something without has reminded him that it can be gained. Consciously or unconsciously, he has been caught up by the Zeitgeist, and with his black brothers of Africa and his brown and yellow brothers of Asia, South America, and the Caribbean, the United States Negro is moving with a sense of great urgency toward the promised land of racial justice. If one recognizes this vital urge that has engulfed the Negro community, one should readily understand why public demonstrations are taking place. The Negro has many pent-up resentments and latent frustrations, and he must release them. So let him march; let him make prayer pilgrimages to the city hall; let him go on freedom rides—and try to understand why he must do so. If his repressed emotions are not released in nonviolent ways, they will seek expression through violence; this is not a threat but a fact of history. So I have not said to my people, "Get rid of your discontent." Rather, I have tried to say that this normal and healthy discontent can be channeled into the creative outlet of nonviolent direct action. And now this approach is being termed extremist.

But though I was initially disappointed at being categorized as an extremist, as I continued to think about the matter I gradually gained a measure of satisfaction from the label. Was not Jesus an extremist for love: "Love your enemies, bless them that curse you, do good to them that hate you, and pray for them which despitefully use you, and persecute you." Was not Amos an extremist for justice: "Let justice roll down like waters and righteousness like an ever-flowing stream." Was not Paul an extremist for the Christian gospel: "I bear in my body the marks of the Lord Jesus." Was not Martin Luther an extremist: "Here I stand; I cannot do otherwise, so help me God." And John Bunyan: "I will stay in jail to the end of my days before I make a butchery of my conscience." And Abraham Lincoln: "This nation cannot survive half slave and half free." And Thomas Jefferson: "We hold these truths to be self-evident, that all men are created equal. . . . " So the question is not whether we will be extremists, but what kind of extremists we will be. Will we be extremists for hate or for love? Will we be extremists for the preservation of injustice or for the extension of justice? In that dramatic scene on Calvary's hill three men were crucified. We must never forget that all three were crucified for the same crime—the crime of extremism. Two were extremists for immorality, and thus fell below their environment. The other, Jesus Christ, was an extremist for love, truth, and goodness, and thereby rose above his environment. Perhaps the South, the nation, and the world are in dire need of creative extremists.

I had hoped that the white moderate would see this need. Perhaps I was too optimistic; perhaps I expected too much. I suppose I should have realized that few members of the oppressor race can understand the deep groans and passionate yearnings of the oppressed race, and still fewer have the vision to see that injustice must be rooted out by strong, persistent, and determined action. I am thankful, however, that some of our white brothers in the South have grasped the meaning of this social revolution and committed themselves to it. They are still all too few in quantity, but they are big in quality. Some—such as Ralph McGill, Lillian Smith, Harry Golden, James McBride Dabbs, Ann Braden, and Sarah Patton Boyle— have written about our struggle in eloquent and prophetic terms. Others have marched with us down nameless streets of the South. They have languished in filthy, roach-infested jails, suffering the abuse and brutality of policemen who view them as "dirty niggerlovers." Unlike so many of their moderate brothers and sisters, they have recognized the urgency of the moment and sensed the need for powerful "action" antidotes to combat the disease of segregation.

Let me take note of my other major disappointment. I have been so greatly disappointed with the white church and its leadership. Of course, there are some notable exceptions. I am not unmindful of the fact that each of you has taken some significant stands on this issue. I commend you, Reverend Stallings, for your Christian stand on this past Sunday, in welcoming Negroes to your worship service on a nonsegregated basis. I commend the Catholic leaders of this state for integrating Spring Hill College several years ago.

But despite these notable exceptions, I must honestly reiterate that I have been disappointed with the church. I do not say this as one of those negative critics who can always find something wrong with the church. I say this as a minister of the gospel, who loves the church; who was nurtured in its bosom; who has been sustained by its spiritual blessings and who will remain true to it as long as the cord of life shall lengthen.

When I was suddenly catapulted into the leadership of the bus protest in Montgomery, Alabama, a few years ago, I felt we would be supported by the white church. I felt that the white ministers, priests, and rabbis of the South would be among our strongest allies. Instead, some have been outright opponents, refusing to understand the freedom movement and misrepresenting its leaders; all too many others have been more cautious than courageous and have remained silent behind the anesthetizing security of stained-glass windows.

In spite of my shattered dreams, I came to Birmingham with the hope that the white religious leadership of this community would see the justice of our cause and, with deep moral concern, would serve as the channel through which our just grievances could reach the power structure. I had hoped that each of you would understand. But again I have been disappointed.

I have heard numerous southern religious leaders admonish their worshipers to comply with a desegregation decision because it is the law, but I have longed to hear white ministers declare: "Follow this decree because integration is morally right and because the Negro is your brother." In the midst of blatant injustices inflicted upon the Negro, I have watched white churchmen stand on the sideline and mouth pious irrelevancies and sanctimonious trivialities. In the midst of a mighty struggle to rid our nation of racial and economic injustice, I have heard many ministers say: "Those are social issues, with which the gospel has no real concern." And I have watched many churches commit themselves to a completely otherworldly religion which makes a strange, un-Biblical distinction between body and soul, between the sacred and the secular.

I have traveled the length and breadth of Alabama, Mississippi, and all the other southern states. On sweltering summer days and crisp autumn mornings I have looked at the South's beautiful churches with their lofty spires pointing heavenward. I have beheld the impressive outlines of her massive religious-education buildings. Over and over I have found myself asking: "What kind of people worship here? Who is their God? Where were their voices when the lips of Governor Barnett dripped with words of interposition and nullification? Where were they when Governor Wallace gave a clarion call for defiance and hatred? Where were their voices of support when bruised and weary Negro men and women decided to rise from the dark dungeons of complacency to the bright hills of creative protest?"

Yes, these questions are still in my mind. In deep disappointment I have wept over the laxity of the church. But be assured that my tears have been tears of love. Yes, I love the church. How could I do otherwise? I am in the rather unique position of being the son, the grandson, and the great-grandson of preachers. Yes, I see the church as the body of Christ. But, oh! How we have blemished and scarred that body through social neglect and through fear of being nonconformists.

There was a time when the church was very powerful—in the time when the early Christians rejoiced at being deemed worthy to suffer for what they believed. In those days the church was not merely a thermometer that recorded the ideas and principles of popular opinion; it was a thermostat that transformed the mores of society. Whenever the early Christians entered a town, the people in power became disturbed and immediately sought to convict the Christians for being "disturbers of the peace" and "outside agitators." But the Christians pressed on, in the conviction that they were "a colony of heaven," called to obey God rather than man. Small in number, they were big in commitment. They were too God-intoxicated to be "astronomically intimidated." By their effort and example they brought an end to such ancient evils as infanticide and gladiatorial contests.

Things are different now. So often the contemporary church is a weak, ineffectual voice with an uncertain sound. So often it is an archdefender of the status quo. Far from being disturbed by the presence of the church, the power structure of the average community is consoled by the church's silent—and often even vocal—sanction of things as they are.

But the judgment of God is upon the church as never before. If today's church does not recapture the sacrificial spirit of the early church, it will lose its authenticity, forfeit the loyalty of millions, and be dismissed as an irrelevant social club with no meaning for the twentieth century. Every day I meet young people whose disappointment with the church has turned into outright disgust.

Perhaps I have once again been too optimistic. Is organized religion too inextricably bound to the status quo to save our nation and the world? Perhaps I must turn my faith to the inner spiritual church, the church within the church, as the true ekklesia and the hope of the world. But again I am thankful to God that some noble souls from the ranks of organized religion have broken loose from the paralyzing chains of conformity and joined us as active partners in the struggle for freedom. They have left their secure congregations and walked the streets of Albany, Georgia, with us. They have gone down the highways of the South on tortuous rides for freedom. Yes, they have gone to jail with us. Some have been dismissed from their churches, have lost the support of their bishops and fellow ministers. But they have acted in the faith that right defeated is stronger than evil triumphant. Their witness has been the spiritual salt that has preserved the true meaning of the gospel in these troubled times. They have carved a tunnel of hope through the dark mountain of disappointment.

I hope the church as a whole will meet the challenge of this decisive hour. But even if the church does not come to the aid of justice, I have no despair about the future. I have no fear about the outcome of our struggle in Birmingham, even if our motives are at present misunderstood. We will reach the goal of freedom in Birmingham and all over the nation, because the goal of America is freedom. Abused and scorned though we may be, our destiny is tied up with America's destiny. Before the pilgrims landed at Plymouth, we were here. For more than two centuries our forebears labored in this country without wages; they made cotton king; they built the homes of their masters while suffering gross injustice and shameful humiliation—and yet out of a bottomless vitality they continued to thrive and develop. If the inexpressible cruelties of slavery could not stop us, the opposition we now face will surely fail. We will win our freedom because the sacred heritage of our nation and the eternal will of God are embodied in our echoing demands.

Before closing I feel impelled to mention one other point in your statement that has troubled me profoundly. You warmly commended the Birmingham police force for keeping "order" and "preventing violence." I doubt that you would have so warmly commended the police force if you had seen its dogs sinking their teeth into unarmed, nonviolent Negroes. I doubt that you would so quickly commend the policemen if you were to observe their ugly and inhumane treatment of Negroes here in the city jail; if you were to watch them push and curse old Negro women and young Negro girls; if you were to see them slap and kick old Negro men and young boys; if you were to observe them, as they did on two occasions, refuse to give us food because we wanted to sing our grace together. I cannot join you in your praise of the Birmingham police department.

It is true that the police have exercised a degree of discipline in handling the demonstrators. In this sense they have conducted themselves rather "nonviolently" in public. But for what purpose? To preserve the evil system of segregation. Over the past few years I have consistently preached that nonviolence demands that the means we use must be as pure as the ends we seek. I have tried to make clear that it is wrong to use immoral means to attain moral ends. But now I must affirm that it is just as wrong, or perhaps even more so, to use moral means to preserve immoral ends. Perhaps Mr. Connor and his policemen have been rather nonviolent in public, as was Chief Pritchett in Albany, Georgia, but they have used the moral means of nonviolence to maintain the immoral end of racial injustice. As T. S. Eliot has said, "The last temptation is the greatest treason: To do the right deed for the wrong reason."

I wish you had commended the Negro sit-inners and demonstrators of Birmingham for their sublime courage, their willingness to suffer, and their amazing discipline in the midst of great provocation. One day the South will recognize its real heroes. They will be the James Merediths, with the noble sense of purpose that enables them to face jeering and hostile mobs, and with the agonizing loneliness that characterizes the life of the pioneer. They will be old, oppressed, battered Negro women, symbolized in a seventy-two-year-old woman in Montgomery, Alabama, who rose up with a sense of dignity and with her people decided not to ride segregated buses, and who responded with ungrammatical profundity to one who inquired about her weariness: "My feets is tired, but my soul is at rest." They will be the young high school and college students, the young ministers of the gospel and a host of their elders, courageously and nonviolently sitting in at lunch counters and willingly going to jail for conscience' sake. One day the South will know that when these disinherited children of God sat down at lunch counters, they were in reality standing up for what is best in the American dream and for the most sacred values in our Judaeo-Christian heritage, thereby bringing our nation back to those great wells of democracy which were dug deep by the founding fathers in their formulation of the Constitution and the Declaration of Independence.

Never before have I written so long a letter. I'm afraid it is much too long to take your precious time. I can assure you that it would have been much shorter if I had been writing from a comfortable desk, but what else can one do when he is alone in a narrow jail cell, other than write long letters, think long thoughts, and pray long prayers?

If I have said anything in this letter that overstates the truth and indicates an unreasonable impatience, I beg you to forgive me. If I have said anything that understates the truth and indicates my having a patience that allows me to settle for anything less than brotherhood, I beg God to forgive me.

I hope this letter finds you strong in the faith. I also hope that circumstances will soon make it possible for me to meet each of you, not as an integrationist or a civil-rights leader but as a fellow clergyman and a Christian brother. Let us all hope that the dark clouds of racial prejudice will soon pass away and the deep fog of misunderstanding will be lifted from our fear-drenched communities, and in some not too distant tomorrow the radiant stars of love and brotherhood will shine over our great nation with all their scintillating beauty.

> Yours for the cause of Peace and Brotherhood,
> Martin Luther King, Jr.

Questions

1. Explain the importance of the four steps in non-violent action.

2. Critics of Martin Luther King, Jr. have denounced him as a communist. Do you find anything in this letter that supports or rebuts this charge?

3. Why does King sprinkle his letter with citations from so many authorities? Does this strengthen or weaken his case? Why?

4. Given the history of the civil rights movement in the United States since King's death in 1968, do his non-violent methods appear to have been more effective than other forms of protest? Explain.

5. Why do you think that no civil rights leader of comparable stature has come forward since Dr. King's death? What have been the consequences of this fact?

4
First Letter to the Delaware Indians

William Penn

This article originally appeared in *Nonviolence in America: A Documentary History* Staughton Lynd, ed., 1966.

William Penn (1644–1718) was that exception among European colonizers—a man of peace. An English Quaker who had been imprisoned for his beliefs, Penn never forgot the virtue of tolerance. When King Charles II granted him proprietorship of the colony that was to bear his name, he established it as a haven for those persecuted because of their religious and political beliefs.

This letter, written in 1681 to the Native American inhabitants of the new commonwealth, combines faith in a common God with the notion of accountability for human actions. The proposal he makes for rectifying disputes between Indians and colonists springs from his deep adherence to simple justice. Though Penn spent only two three-year periods in the New World, the Quaker settlers maintained peaceful relations with the original inhabitants.

My Friends—There is one great God and power that hath made the world and all things therein, to whom you and I, and all people owe their being and well-being, and to whom you and I must one day give an account for all that we do in the world; this great God hath written his law in our hearts, by which we are taught and commanded to love and help, and do good to one another, and not to do harm and mischief one to another. Now this great God hath been pleased to make me concerned in your parts of the world, and the king of the country where I live hath given unto me a great province, but I desire to enjoy it with your love and consent, that we may always live together as neighbors and friends; else what would the great God say to us, who hath made us not to devour and destroy one another, but live soberly and kindly together in the world? Now I would have you well observe, that I am very sensible of the unkindness and injustice that hath been too much exercised toward you by the people of these parts of the world, who sought themselves, and to make great advantages by you, rather than be examples of justice and goodness unto you, which I hear hath been a matter of trouble to you, and caused great grudgings and animosities, sometimes to the shedding of blood, which hath made the great God angry. But I am not such a man, as is well known in my own country; I have great love and regard toward you, and I desire to win and gain your love and friendship, by a kind, just and peaceable life, and the people I send are of the same mind, and shall in all things behave themselves accordingly; and if in anything any shall offend you or your people, you shall have a full and speedy satisfaction for the same, by an equal number of just men on both sides, that by no means you may have just occasion of being offended against them. I shall shortly come to you myself, at what time we may more largely and freely confer and discourse of these matters. In the meantime, I have sent my commissioners to treat with you about land, and a firm league of peace. Let me desire you to be kind to them and the people, and receive these presents and tokens which I have sent to you, as a testimony of my good will to you, and my resolution to live justly, peaceably, and friendly with you.

I am your loving friend,

William Penn

Questions

1. What might have been the course of American history had Penn's example been followed by other European settlers?

2. Could Penn's imprisonment in England for his beliefs have influenced him in a direction other than the one he took? Give instances from your knowledge of how imprisonment transformed people, for better or worse.

3. What was Penn's remedy for the injustice imposed on the original inhabitants of the territory?

4. Describe the connection between justice and peace as exemplified in Pennsylvania.

5. In what way do members of the Society of Friends (Quakers) reflect the attitudes of William Penn today?

5

The Challenge of Peace:
God's Promise and Our Response; A Pastoral Letter
on War and Peace

National Conference of Catholic Bishops, May 3, 1983

The National Council of Catholic Bishops of the United States, in the section of their pastoral titled "A New Moment," say "no" to nuclear war as a means of resolving international disputes. In hearings that involved the testimony of many experts over a three-year period, the drafting committee listened thoughtfully to a wide range of views, from those of pacifists to those of "just warriors." The result was a 101-page pamphlet which gave a nuanced and detailed but definitive decision against the use of nuclear arms.

By going beyond their own previous statements and those of the Holy See and other episcopal conferences on questions of peace and war, the bishops demonstrated courage and sophistication. The section quoted below (#126–138) notes the changed conditions of politics and morals brought about by the nuclear age. They label the nuclear weapons race as "an act of aggression against the poor and a folly which does not provide the security it promises." They praise the Vatican for pointing out the "folly and danger of the arms race," but they give special credit to scientists and physicians for alerting the public to the concrete consequences of nuclear war. They cite a statement by the Pontifical Academy of Sciences as being of particular relevance to the public debate in the United States. The statement, a description of the death and disease that would result from a nuclear exchange, concluded with the words: "Prevention is essential for control."

The bishops despair of the possibility of placing political or moral limits on a nuclear war once begun. Before it is too late, they plead not only for "new ideas and a new vision, but (for) what the gospel calls a conversion of the heart." They declare themselves sobered and perplexed by the testimony they have heard. Seeking to do more than restate general moral principles, they try to relate their judgment to the specific elements of the nuclear problem.

While showing an awareness of how the nuclear stalemate came about, the bishops express some puzzlement about how to connect their "no" to nuclear war with the "personal and public choices which can move us in a new direction." The very destructiveness of the atom has made it impossible for nation states to protect their own territory and populations, they state. "Threats are made," they say, "which it would be suicidal to implement." Like other human beings caught on the horns of the nuclear dilemma, the prelates ask whether a nation may threaten what it may never do, or possess what it may never use. In the end, the hierarchy shows a commendable willingness to enter into the public debate on the nuclear issue, not from the Olympian heights of moral superiority, but at the tortured level of every other citizen and organization in a threatened world.

A. THE NEW MOMENT

126.   At the center of the new evaluation of the nuclear arms race is a recognition of two elements: the destructive potential of nuclear weapons, and the stringent choices which the nuclear age poses for both politics and morals.

127.   The fateful passage into the nuclear age as a military reality began with the bombing of Nagasaki and Hiroshima, events described by Pope Paul VI as a "butchery of untold magnitude."[56] Since then, in spite of efforts at control and plans for disarmament (e.g., the Baruch Plan of 1946), the nuclear arsenals have escalated, particularly in the two superpowers. The qualitative superiority of these two states, however, should not overshadow the fact that four other countries possess nuclear capacity and a score of states are only steps away from becoming "nuclear nations."

128.   This nuclear escalation has been opposed sporadically and selectively but never effectively. The race has continued in spite of carefully expressed doubts by analysts and other citizens and in the face of forcefully expressed opposition by public rallies. Today the opposition to the arms race is no longer selective or sporadic, it is widespread and sustained. The danger and destructiveness of nuclear weapons are understood and resisted with new urgency and intensity. There is in the public debate today an endorsement of the position submitted by the Holy See at the United Nations in 1976: the arms race is to be condemned as a dan-

---

56. Paul VI, "World Day of Peace Message 1976," in *Documents*, p. 198.

ger, an act of aggression against the poor, and a folly which does not provide the security it promises.[57]

129.   Papal teaching has consistently addressed the folly and danger of the arms race; but the new perception of it which is now held by the general public is due in large measure to the work of scientists and physicians who have described for citizens the concrete human consequences of a nuclear war.[58]

130.   In a striking demonstration of his personal and pastoral concern for preventing nuclear war, Pope John Paul II commissioned a study by the Pontifical Academy of Sciences which reinforced the findings of other scientific bodies. The Holy Father had the study transmitted by personal representative to the leaders of the United States, the Soviet Union, the United Kingdom, and France, and to the president of the General Assembly of the United Nations. One of its conclusions is especially pertinent to the public debate in the United States:

> Recent talk about winning or even surviving a nuclear war must reflect a failure to appreciate a medical reality: Any nuclear war would inevitably cause death, disease and suffering of pandemonic proportions and without the possibility of effective medical intervention. That reality leads to the same conclusion physicians have reached for life-threatening epidemics throughout history. Prevention is essential for control.[59]

131.   This medical conclusion has a moral corollary. Traditionally, the Church's moral teaching sought first to prevent war and then to limit its consequences if it occurred. Today the possibilities for placing political and moral limits on nuclear war are so minimal that the moral task, like the medical, is prevention: as a people, we must refuse to legitimate the idea of nuclear war. Such a refusal will require not only new ideas and new vision, but what the gospel calls conversion of the heart.

132.   To say "no" to nuclear war is both a necessary and a complex task. We are moral teachers in a tradition which has always been prepared to relate moral principles to concrete problems. Particularly in this letter we could not be content with simply restating general moral principles or repeating well-known requirements about the ethics of war. We have had

---

57. "Statement of the Holy See to the United Nations" (1976), in *The Church and the Arms Race;* Pax Christi-USA (New York: 1976), pp. 23–24.

58. R. Adams and S. Cullen, *The Final Epidemic: Physicians and Scientists on Nuclear War* (Chicago: 1981).

59. Pontifical Academy of Sciences, "Statement on the Consequences of the Use of Nuclear Weapons," in *Documents*, p. 241.

to examine, with the assistance of a broad spectrum of advisors of varying persuasions, the nature of existing and proposed weapons systems, the doctrines which govern their use, and the consequences of using them. We have consulted people who engage their lives in protest against the existing nuclear strategy of the United States, and we have consulted others who have held or do hold responsibility for this strategy. It has been a sobering and perplexing experience. In light of the evidence which witnesses presented and in light of our study, reflection, and consultation, we must reject nuclear war. But we feel obliged to relate our judgment to the specific elements which comprise the nuclear problem.

133.   Though certain that the dangerous and delicate nuclear relationship the superpowers now maintain should not exist, we understand how it came to exist. In a world of sovereign states, devoid of central authority and possessing the knowledge to produce nuclear weapons, many choices were made, some clearly objectionable, others well-intended with mixed results, which brought the world to its present dangerous situation.

134.   We see with increasing clarity the political folly of a system which threatens mutual suicide, the psychological damage this does to ordinary people, especially the young, the economic distortion of priorities—billions readily spent for destructive instruments while pitched battles are waged daily in our legislatures over much smaller amounts for the homeless, the hungry, and the helpless here and abroad. But it is much less clear how we translate a "no" to nuclear war into the personal and public choices which can move us in a new direction, toward a national policy and an international system which more adequately reflect the values and vision of the kingdom of God.

135.   These tensions in our assessment of the politics and strategy of the nuclear age reflect the conflicting elements of the nuclear dilemma and the balance of terror which it has produced. We have said earlier in this letter that the fact of war reflects the existence of sin in the world. The nuclear threat and the danger it poses to human life and civilization exemplify in a qualitatively new way the perennial struggle of the political community to contain the use of force, particularly among states.

136.   Precisely because of the destructive nature of nuclear weapons, strategies have been developed which previous generations would have found unintelligible. Today military preparations are undertaken on a vast and sophisticated scale, but the declared purpose is not to use the weapons produced. Threats are made which would be suicidal to implement. The key to security is no longer only military secrets, for in some instances security may best be served by informing one's adversary publicly what weapons one has and what plans exist for their use. The presumption of the nation-state system, that sovereignty implies an ability to

protect a nation's territory and population, is precisely the presumption denied by the nuclear capacities of both superpowers. In a sense each is at the mercy of the other's perception of what strategy is "rational," what kind of damage is "unacceptable," how "convincing" one side's threat is to the other.

137. The political paradox of deterrence has also strained our moral conception. May a nation threaten what it may never do? May it possess what it may never use? Who is involved in the threat each superpower makes: government officials? or military personnel? or the citizenry in whose defense the threat is made?

138. In brief, the danger of the situation is clear; but how to prevent the use of nuclear weapons, how to assess deterrence, and how to delineate moral responsibility in the nuclear age are less clearly seen or stated. Reflecting the complexity of the nuclear problem, our arguments in this pastoral must be detailed and nuanced; but our "no" to nuclear war must, in the end, be definitive and decisive.

Questions

1. The bishops state that "nuclear escalation has been opposed sporadically and selectively but never effectively." Cite several instances of this opposition and give your reasons why they have not succeeded.

2. Describe several non-religious organizations, such as those of physicians and scientists, which have alerted the public to the effects of nuclear war on civilian populations.

3. Why do the bishops endorse the statement that "prevention is essential for control"?

4. Do you think that the bishops make a convincing case against nuclear war? Why, or why not?

5. Do you think the section on deterrence (#137) takes an unequivocal position on the question? Why, or why not?

6
Murderous Evil: Does Nonviolence Offer a Solution?

John Garvey

This article originally appeared in *Commonweal*, September 20, 1985.

Columnist John Garvey raises the question most frequently asked of those who espouse absolute non-violence—the question of whether it would have worked against Hitler. Staking out a middle course between the political right and left, he devotes most of his attention to the perceived blind spots of the (pacifist) left.

Garvey distinguishes between pacifism and "real morality," which to his mind involves using force to protect an elderly person from assault by a robber. In an adaptation of the scriptural story of the good Samaritan (Lk 10), he asks what this benefactor would have done had he come upon the highwaymen in the act of beating up the traveler from Jericho to Jerusalem. "Would he have stayed in the background while the robbers beat the stuffing out of the victim the Samaritan later tended?" he asks. Advocates of non-violence would perhaps come up with other alternatives.

The author concedes that "resistance does not always have to mean murder," though he seems to equate resistance with the use of physical force. Garvey dismisses as "perverse" the teaching of moral theologians who would completely exonerate those who use violence to protect the innocent. Referring to the story of Oedipus, who unknowingly slept with his mother and killed his father, he concludes: "Human beings can find themselves implicated in evil despite all of their best choices." He advises for those caught in hard cases: "Accept violence and then repent."

Given the complicated—and implicating—world of difficult moral choices, Garvey affirms the presence of evil in our world. In the case of Hitler, he calls it "murderous evil." He feels that those who would dismiss Hitler as pathological (so psychologically deformed that he could not be held responsible) run the risk of banishing the reality of moral evil.

Garvey's quarrel with pacifism is that "there are times when non-violence simply doesn't work." By stating his case against absolute non-violence, he compels its advocates to think more deeply about principles and methods and to make careful distinctions.

In his July 12 *Commonweal* article, "Appointment with Hitler," Peter Steinfels raises some difficult and necessary questions. The question of our response to Hitler is of supreme importance, and it has not been dealt with well by those of us who believe that Christianity demands nonviolence. Steinfels rightly points out that such statements as "War never solves anything" or the assertion that all wars are fought ultimately for reasons which are exploitative, racist, based on misunderstanding, or simple devices to benefit the military-industrial complex—all of these duck the question posed by Hitler: What are we to do when confronted by murderous evil? The fact that the Allies themselves were guilty of evil actions and that all motives were not pure does not change this central truth: Nazism was uniquely evil. At least some people who fought in that war did so, not because they did not understand the other side or the nature of the struggle being waged, but precisely because they did.

Much about World War II has become myth. Neville Chamberlain's attempt to appease Hitler, for example, is frequently cited by conservatives as similar to the attitude of liberals towards the Soviets: allow them a little leeway, and they'll settle down. Things aren't so simple as that, of course. Appeasement was, in fact, defended in part as an anti-Communist move. Hitler was a buffer against the Communists, the lesser of those two evils. Much about appeasement has more in common with the current conservative attitudes towards South Africa and the dictatorships of Latin America. According to this line of thinking, it makes sense to support, or at least not oppose, right-wing dictatorships, because the alternative is Communism. The right is correct to raise the question of liberal double standards: the assumption that left-wing tyranny is excusable while right-wing tyranny is reprehensible, so that Marcos, for example,—a terrible man, to be sure—gets a worse press than the leaders of China or the Soviet Union. (Poets in the Philippines, unlike China or the Soviet Union, are not in legal trouble for failing to write poems praising tractor production.) Still, the right has its own set of blind spots, which in some cases take over most of the field of vision.

Both right and left use the myths generated by a war which seems more justifiable than any in history. If the right waves appeasement around, the left does the same thing with fascism. Any oppression is compared to Nazism; any killing above the level of a fatal mugging is compared to the Holocaust. The problem with our use of the war and its myths is that it erodes our appreciation of the fact that there was, in Hitler, in Mengele, in the response to Hitler on the part of German people and on the part of many ugly Nazi-like groups in the countries Germany occupied, something uniquely evil.

Pacifists have argued that to respond to violence with violence makes us no better than those violent people we oppose. That looks neat on paper, but in fact what does it mean? I may choose to accept violence against myself rather than be violent—I mean this in theory, because I am not at all sure that confronted with such a choice I would be able to accept what I believe I should do—but would it be right for me to accept the violence done to another person? If someone mugs me and I hand over my wallet and allow him to slug me rather than resist him violently, that's one thing. I am hardly working from the same place, morally, if I allow him to rob and slug an old lady while I stand by. Abstract nonviolence could argue equally for both courses of action (or inaction), but real morality can't.

Violent action can indeed reduce the people who are directly or indirectly involved in it, and it always implicates us in evil. But the heroes of the Resistance are not morally equivalent to the Nazis, nor were they, compared to the signers of the Oxford Union motion, naive.

Christians who believe in nonviolence face a number of dilemmas. I believe that we must hold on to the belief in nonviolence, and confront the dilemmas honestly without reducing them for rhetorical purposes.

Here is one dilemma: we believe that all human beings—not just those within our borders—are equally loved by God, made in God's image, and are, for that reason, to be revered. To kill anyone for reasons of state, or to allow any government to define other human beings as those we may kill (and this is something which happens in every war), would violate something central to our faith.

At the same time, it is right to ask what the Good Samaritan would have done if he had arrived on the scene a little earlier. Would he have stayed in the background while the robbers beat the stuffing out of the victim the Samaritan later tended? The victim would in that case have been a victim as much of the Samaritan's nonintervention as he was of the robbers' violence.

One answer to this is that resistance does not always have to mean murder. One can resist, even forcefully, without killing. But what if this isn't always the case? If a Japanese pacifist were, by some odd chance, seated at the controls of an anti-aircraft weapon; and if he spotted the Enola Gay; and if, knowing somehow that it was about to drop the bomb, he refrained from shooting it down on the reasonable grounds that doing so might kill someone, would he have done the right thing?

What I want to suggest is that the way we have done moral theology is often perverse, and it is further complicated these days by the desire of religious people to make secular sense. The perversity is this: we have tried to find ways through moral dilemmas which ignore the mystery of evil by saying, more or less, that any necessity becomes good by virtue of the fact of necessity itself. If to kill the Nazis hidden in the basement I must bomb the orphanage, then I am not guilty of sin. If in order to save my family I must kill the madman with an ax because, given the situation I find myself in, there is no other real choice available, then I should not feel defiled. A good teacher once suggested that Oedipus was right to feel defiled for sleeping with his mother and murdering his father, even though he did not know that the man he killed was his father and the woman he slept with was his mother. Human beings can find themselves implicated in evil despite all of their best choices; they can find themselves confronted at times with only two paths, each of which leads to an evil end.

Any suggestion that evil is a presence in the world leads these days to the charge of Gnosticism or Manicheism. But it was Jesus, not Mani, who referred to "the Prince of this world." There is something present in the world, in the life of each of us, which does not love humanity and which distracts us from what has been revealed as our salvation. It is a vanishing, or at least a diminishing, of this understanding which allows us to think of a Hitler as sick, rather than evil. To suggest that evil is real is not to say that Hitler had nothing sick about him, or that he was so taken over by an evil and alien power that his own will was powerless, or his sickness irrelevant. The reality of evil means that a person—free, and at the same time perhaps blighted by sickness—can turn to the desire for power and manipulation rather than to compassion and, because this exposes us to the will of others, to weakness; in this turning, a choice is made which allows murder to be born. Something which affects us personally allows us to make this choice, and it is not wrong to call it satanic.

What about the dilemma facing the person who believes absolutely in the need for nonviolence, but who is confronted with occasions on which the only possible moral action seems to demand a violence which will lead to the evil of another's death? It may be that there are times when the only thing to do is accept violence and then repent. There were canons in the early church which demanded that those who had shed blood, even in self-defense, were required to refrain from the Eucharist for a period of years.

This makes sense to me, as does the possibility that someone might have to shed blood. On the one hand, it is important to bear witness to the fact that the life of any human being, even a bloodthirsty one, is sacred. On the other, there are occasions when there may be no alternative to killing another human being—unless the alternative of allowing yet another to be killed seems acceptable.

I am not, in saying this, defending the right of governments to conscript people into their wars, nor am I denying that not enough time has been spent in urging nonviolent alternatives to conflict at every level. The point is, rather, that there are times when nonviolence simply doesn't work. It isn't, I realize, always meant to. As Gandhi insisted, at its best nonviolence is not so much a strategy as a witness to truth—about yourself and about the life of the person who faces you as an enemy. But there may be circumstances when this does not seem morally possible, and at such times violence may seem—and may in fact be—the only moral alternative. Moral theology should not find ways to make these moments acceptable; they can be encountered only with fear, trembling, and profound repentance. The celebration of war, or of revolutionary violence, is obscene.

But another moral theology, one which simply denies the possibility that war and other forms of violence are ever anything other than exploitative or fearful responses to situations which could in every case be responded to nonviolently, is dangerously naive. I said above that the need felt by a lot of religious people to make secular sense complicates our view of this question. What I mean is that the pacifism of many people—the small fraction of French intellectuals to whom Steinfels refers, for example, and those who insist that only misunderstanding could cause the tensions between the West and the Soviets—is based less on the Gospel than on secular thinking. It is not Christian, but only silly, to think that Communism is not a repressive form of government in all of its historical incarnations. Christian nonviolence says that this is not reason enough to kill Communists. It does not say that all of our difficulties with Communism would disappear if only we better understood Communist nations. Christian nonviolence does not depend on solutions; its end is the cross. If a nonviolent response to evil works, that is nice, but it isn't the point. The point is that all human life has been revealed in Christ's incarnation as holy, even the lives of enemies and oppressors. This has nothing to do with the pacifism of those who think of Nazis or Communists as peace-loving sorts who would settle down and be good if only we didn't provoke them.

Questions

1. Do liberal and conservative thinkers use double standards in defending regimes they favor? Cite examples of each.
2. The author cites two possible responses to the situation of an elderly person attacked by a robber. Can you think of alternatives?
3. Do you think that Oedipus was guilty or not of the acts he committed unknowingly against his parents? What distinctions, if any, would you make in your reply? What does the story tell us of the nature of evil?

4. Does the existence of moral evil damage or invalidate the principle of *ahimsa* (non-violence) as enunciated by Gandhi? What if the advocates of non-violence are likely to fail?

5. Is the type of pacifism criticized by the author in his concluding paragraph the same as the non-violence espoused by a King or a Gandhi? Cite the differences, if any.

7

Identifying Alternatives to Political Violence: An Educational Imperative

Christopher Kruegler and Patricia Parkman

This article originally appeared in *Harvard Educational Review*, February 1985.

Somewhat like the weather, violence is something everybody complains about, but few do much to change. The authors, who teach at Harvard University, ask themselves—and the reader—why governments and movements still "cling to its use." They conclude that the efficacy of violence as a means of resolving disputes is overrated and they give their reasons why they believe this to be so.

Kruegler and Parkman cite the world's current trouble spots as instances of the stalemate and simmering revolts that remain even after the introduction of massive force—Vietnam and Afghanistan being two outstanding examples.

The authors develop their thesis for non-violent problem-solving from the history of successful political change through other than military means: the 1944 general strike in El Salvador, the 1905 "first" Russian revolution and the Danish resistance to Nazism during World War II. Though each of these movements had its mixture of success and failure, the authors issue this reminder: "When violent sanctions fall short of achieving their objectives, we do not usually conclude that violence has been tried and found wanting." They ask for equal treatment of non-violence.

Their final plea is for educators to do far more empirical research on the strategy and tactics of non-violence, with the goal of helping people to "envision credible alternatives to armed conflict."

Few would disagree that organized political violence has had disastrous consequences for human life and civilization in this century. War, dictatorship, terrorism, genocide, and systems of social oppression have conspired to take millions of lives, divert precious economic resources from other human enterprises, and place the continued existence of humanity in question.[1]

Yet, while we conclude rationally that we may not survive our collective dependence on violence, both nation-states and insurgent movements

248

cling to its use. In the absence of the international rule of law or a just world order, organized violence appears to be the ultimate recourse against intolerable conditions and grave threats to our lives, interests, and values. It persists, on the one hand, because of a widespread but largely unexamined belief that it "works" and, on the other, because there are no generally recognized alternative means of resolving those critical conflicts in which one or both parties perceive the stakes as too high to permit compromise.[2]

In this article, we argue that the efficacy of organized violence is overrated and, more important, that nonviolent sanctions offer a greatly underrated and underdeveloped source of political power which could replace armed force and free humanity from its heavy costs and incalculable dangers. We see a major role for educators in breaking down the cultural conditioning that perpetuates reliance on violence and in making nonviolent sanctions more effective, and therefore, more relevant to the critical conflicts of our time.

To say that the efficacy of organized violence is overrated is not to say that it never works, but merely that its recent history is not one of unqualified success. On a tactical level, superior armed force can control many, if not all, situations. Any act of resistance that is limited in time and place can be negated by sufficiently ruthless opponents. On the strategic and political levels, however, the probable effects of violence become less easy to calculate. Most armed struggles involve at least one clear loser. Moreover, victory is often achieved at terribly high or unanticipated costs. Finally, stalemate must be considered as a possible outcome. These less desirable outcomes for one or both protagonists waging violent struggle have been frequent enough to warrant a serious investigation of nonviolent alternatives.

Political scientist John Stoessinger has observed that "no nation that *began* a major war in this century emerged a winner."[3] Aside from possible disagreement over which wars should be classified as "major," it is correct that those powers which have struck first in the larger wars of this century have met military defeat, despite the range of possible outcomes described above. Stoessinger analyzes the moments of decision when statesmen chose either war or escalation and finds that these moments were almost always characterized by mutual misperception of each other's intentions and capabilities and the potential risks of armed conflict. Thus, he suggests, war functions as a sort of reality therapy in which expectations are most often adjusted in a context of defeat or stalemate.[4]

The complete failure of military power to secure policy objectives is perhaps best typified by the U.S. experience in Vietnam, and the same fate may well await the Soviet Union in Afghanistan. These are examples of asymmetrical conflicts: the vast preponderance of power, conventionally understood, appears to be on one side. In such conflicts, the ostensibly weaker parties are sometimes able to control the political aspects of the conflict and turn even military defeats to their own advantage. Thus the Tet offensive of 1968, technically a military victory for the United States, became a watershed for American antiwar sentiment simply because the opponent was still able to mount a major offensive at that point in the struggle. The My Lai massacre stands as another tactical "victory," whose counterproductive political effects far outweighed its military value.

If the Vietnam War demonstrates the limits of military methods for a superpower like the United States, does it not conversely support a case for successful use of unconventional warfare by Vietnam? Here, the question of costs becomes relevant. Although Vietnam can claim that it won, as many as two million of its people died. Its countryside is poisoned with chemical toxins and defaced by some twenty million bomb craters.[5] Independence of a sort was achieved, but for the foreseeable future Vietnam will probably be a military, economic, and political dependent of the Soviet Union. Vietnam's authoritarian regime, a product of thirty years of warfare, has alienated many of its citizens. Continuing regional conflict is another legacy of this war.

Hidden costs may also accrue to the winners of less significant conflicts. Both the British victory in the Falklands/Malvinas crisis and the recent invasion of Grenada by the United States were hailed by their architects as unequivocal triumphs. The former victory, however, obliged the Thatcher government to commit itself to an indefinite and expensive military presence in another hemisphere, while the latter reaped for the United States the dubious political prestige that results from defeating such a small opponent.

Stalemate is an outcome that appears to be occurring with increasing frequency. The Korean War is probably the clearest example of a large-scale, painful struggle that ended in the frustration of both sides' objectives. The interminable wars of the Middle East, in which the local participants draw encouragement and support from their big-power sponsors, have also been inconclusive. Fifteen years of paramilitary struggle in Northern Ireland have not significantly changed the balance of power in favor of the separatist forces in that country, while military occupation, special police powers, and other repressive measures on the part of the British government have failed either to restore the status quo ante or to remove the threat of terror.

Despite this record, news media, history books, and popular culture consistently focus on the results achieved by violence. Moreover, they give more attention to violent struggles that fail to achieve their objectives than to nonviolent struggles that succeed. Hence, few people are aware of the alternative ways to wage serious conflict that have been widely used for centuries.

THE HIDDEN HISTORY OF NONVIOLENT SANCTIONS

Nonviolent sanctions are those punishments and pressures which do not kill or threaten physical harm but which, nonetheless, thwart opponents' objectives and cause them to alter their behavior.[6] The power of nonviolent sanctions is essentially that of denying opponents the support or cooperation which they need to attain their objectives. Many people associate nonviolent action exclusively with the work of Mohandas Gandhi and Martin Luther King, Jr. While the contributions of these men and their followers are extremely important, they do not encompass or exhaust the potential of this form of power. Its use does not require a commitment to nonviolence as an ethical principle, although its most effective deployment does require an understanding of the special dynamics of nonviolent struggle.

There is, in fact, a vast hidden history of nonviolent sanctions.[7] Much of this history has simply been overlooked because of the selective perception noted above. Nonviolent sanctions have also gone unrecognized because they were not consciously chosen and identified as such. In many cases they have been used side by side with violent sanctions. Lacking a conceptual framework from which to do so, historians have often failed to ask questions or collect data that would enable us to assess the significance of the nonviolent facets of a conflict.

Of the hundreds of conflicts in which nonviolent action has played a significant role, only a few have been sufficiently researched to assess the strategic effect of nonviolent sanctions. The three cases that follow are among those which have received such study. They challenge common stereotypes about the conditions under which nonviolent sanctions can be effective. In none of the three were the nonviolent protagonists committed to nonviolence as an ethical principle, nor were their opponents liberal democratic governments. On the contrary, the opponent in each case was a dictatorship with a record of ruthlessness, and in two cases the opponent responded to the nonviolent action with violent repression.

Maximiliano Hernández Martínez was El Salvador's most notorious dictator, best known for the massacre of 1932 which followed a brief, easily suppressed peasant uprising. Estimates of the number of people executed in cold blood range from eight thousand to thirty thousand in a country that, at the time, had a total population of about one million. The Martínez regime then suppressed the fledgling labor movement and all political parties except its own.

Twelve years of one-man rule gradually alienated many people who initially supported Martínez, including the majority of the big landowners, businessmen, professionals, and junior military officers. On April 2, 1944, the small Salvadoran air force and two army regiments took up arms against the government. The revolt quickly became a tragicomedy of overconfidence, bungling, and division among the insurgent leaders. Troops loyal to the president crushed the revolt within forty-eight hours.

Two weeks later, with the surviving opposition leaders imprisoned, in exile, or in hiding, university students, women, and collaborators in various occupational groups began to organize a completely nonviolent general strike that escalated rapidly from May 5–8. At the height of the action, buses and taxis disappeared from the streets of the capital city. Market stalls, shops, banks, and professional offices were closed. Government employees abandoned their work. The nation's railroads stopped running, and the strike began to spread to other cities.

Taken by surprise, divided, and demoralized, the government took no effective action to counter the strike. When a frightened or trigger-happy policeman shot and killed a boy on May 7, angry, though peaceful, crowds filled the streets. Martínez' cabinet panicked and resigned. After hours of negotiations on May 8, Martínez announced his decision to give up the presidency. The next morning the National Assembly received the president's resignation and named his successor.[8]

How has the memory of these events been preserved in El Salvador? April 2—not May 9—was declared a national holiday. As late as 1976, ceremonies still commemorated a botched military coup. Salvadoran periodical literature abounds with memoirs by participants of the April 2 uprising and gives detailed reconstructions of the fighting, while the civilian movement which actually dislodged Martínez is rarely mentioned. The only book on the revolution of 1944 devotes thirty-five pages to the events of April 2–4, another twenty-two to the trials and executions of a number of the participants, and eight to a woefully inaccurate and incomplete account of the general strike.[9]

The first Russian Revolution of 1905 is not commonly understood as nonviolent. Indeed, it was accompanied by a great deal of politically motivated violence, mostly in the form of assassinations and peasant riots. On October 17, 1905, however, it was not violence that forced Tsar Nicholas II of Russia to take an unprecedented and, for him, repugnant step.[10] When Nicholas created Russia's first representative assembly, or Duma, he did so in response to a massive general strike, which has been described as one of the most complete in history, and a campaign of public defiance of civil laws that mobilized nearly the entire urban population of Russia.[11]

In addition to strikes, the nonviolent methods employed in this movement included the holding of political banquets during which petitions were drafted; mass demonstrations, processions, and demonstration funerals; the withholding of taxes; the usurpation of governmental prerogatives by illegal bodies; defiance of censorship laws; refusal of conscription; and the refusal of troops to carry out orders. Most of these methods were used in an improvised fashion. In the course of the struggle, new organizations such as unions, soviets, or workers' councils, and illegal political parties with a variety of orientations were formed. These gained invaluable experience during the revolution, and many of them persisted after it had run its course. Labor unions, for example, won the right to exist legally as a result of the struggle and continued to function openly for several years.

The Duma, which Nicholas called for in his manifesto of October 17, represented the first legal limitation on the autocratic power of the tsar. Its creation did not by any means constitute a complete victory over the tsarist system, but it was certainly a major step toward the disintegration of that system.[12]

The Danish response to occupation by Nazi Germany from 1940 to 1945 employed various forms of social, political, and economic noncooperation to preserve the integrity of Danish life and institutions in the face of a concerted attempt to integrate them into Hitler's New Order. Open resistance was not initially condoned by the Danish government, which remained nominally in power until August 28, 1943. Instead, the civil service and government officials who retained their positions worked to mitigate the effects of the occupation on the Danish people.

In this period, resistance mainly took the form of *schweikism*, or obstructionism disguised as apparent cooperation.[13] Government officials, for example, concealed increases in food production from the German authorities, leaked information about repressive actions to the intended victims, and generally slowed down orders which might have hampered other resistance activities.[14] German concerts were boycotted in favor of community songfests featuring traditional Danish music. German soldiers and their collaborators were ostracized. Danish national symbols and pro-Allied symbols became widely used as a means of expressing opposition at comparatively little risk.[15] Subtle forms of noncooperation prevented Nazi penetration of Danish governmental institutions for three years, during which time a psychological climate conducive to open resistance, by both violent and nonviolent means, was developed.

In August of 1943, an industrial strike movement, accompanied by widespread sabotage, provoked a crisis. Government officials resigned rather than implement the severe repressive measures demanded by German authorities. The Danish government dissolved, leaving no legitimate authority in its place and removing the legal barrier to open resistance. Among the most notable achievements of the nonviolent branch of the resistance was the rescue of approximately seven thousand Danish Jews from Nazi persecution by means of clandestine evacuation routes to Sweden, thus frustrating the implementation of Hitler's "final solution."[16] Later, early in the summer of 1944, the German occupation authorities gave in to demands to revoke a series of repressive measures when they found that they could not control a general people's strike in Copenhagen, although they had killed over one hundred Danes in the attempt to do so.[17]

It is important to note the catalytic role played by violent sabotage in eliciting the repression which stimulated the governmental crisis of August 1943. This illustrates the sometimes complex relationship between violent and nonviolent sanctions when they are used in the same conflict by the same protagonists.[18] The degree to which the two types of sanctions are, or are not, compatible under specific circumstances is a matter which has yet to receive serious and systematic study.[19]

In these three cases, nonviolent sanctions achieved a great deal. These examples do not, however, lead to the conclusion that nonviolent sanctions offer a ready-made panacea to those looking for a means of waging conflict. Indeed, examination of the outcomes brings to light the limitations of these and many similar movements.

While the Danish resistance made Germany's military and economic exploitation of Denmark less efficient than it would otherwise have been, neither the nonviolent sanctions nor the combination of violent and nonviolent sanctions stopped that exploitation. The opposition to Martínez failed in its attempt to establish democratic government in El Salvador, which soon succumbed to a new military dictatorship. Similarly, analysts of the 1905 general strike in Russia have pointed out that the coalition of forces which frightened the tsar into issuing the manifesto of October 17 did not act effectively to consolidate its new position. Instead, it became embroiled in its own internal struggles for power and ideological leadership. It was unable to respond with a unified program when the autocracy began to renege on promised reforms, to limit the powers of the Duma, and to invoke harsh repressive measures in the months that followed.[20]

When violent sanctions fall short of achieving their objectives we do not usually conclude that violence has been tried and found wanting. We ask what conditions favored the winner and what did the loser do wrong. Nonviolent struggle should be judged by the same standards. Given the nature of the forces involved in the examples above, there is no reason to think that the nonviolent protagonists would have achieved more with violent sanctions. We can, on the other hand, see their weaknesses. In each case nonviolent sanctions were improvised under harsh conditions with little or no advance preparation on the part of those using them. The Salvadoran opponents of Martínez had no strategy for pursuing longer-range goals beyond his resignation, and the opposition to the tsar suffered from lack of agreed-upon leadership and mechanisms for decision making.

Analysis of these and other cases of nonviolent struggle ought to suggest ways in which nonviolent sanctions could be made more effective, just as military strategists learn from the study of past victories and defeats. Over the past three decades a small group of researchers has begun a systematic study of nonviolent sanctions which should lead to a much better understanding of both their limits and their potential.[21]

POTENTIAL OF NONVIOLENT SANCTIONS

Nonviolent sanctions are already used with great regularity and proficiency in certain types of conflicts. Both sides in most labor disputes, for example, are skilled in the use of a variety of coercive yet nonviolent methods for attaining their ends. Domestic protest movements and civil rights movements in many countries rely heavily on nonviolent sanctions to advance their causes. The question before us now is whether, on the basis of historical experience and creative new thinking, it is possible to extend deliberately the range of issues and problems for which they are relevant and to which they can be applied with confidence.

It has been suggested that nonviolent sanctions might provide the basis of an alternative means of national defense.[22] This possibility was recently explored in a three-year study conducted by Britain's Alternative Defence Commission. The Commission's report, *Defence without the Bomb*, argues that British national security would be enhanced by a reduced role in NATO, unilateral nuclear disarmament, and the adoption of a two-tiered defense system, combining elements of both conventional military defense and prepared nonviolent resistance by civilians. The sixteen-member commission felt that conventional coastal and anti-aircraft defenses could extract a high entry price from a hypothetical invader, and that this might have some dissuasive power. Should an invasion be accomplished, however, the best defense might be achieved by withholding any form of cooperation from the opponent and waging a protracted resistance against the invaders by exclusively nonviolent means.[23]

For many small countries, any degree of armed resistance against their prospective opponents might be futile, if not suicidal. For these countries, a purely "civilian-based defense" may well offer the best alternative to surrender, on the one hand, and devastating armed conflict against much larger powers, on the other.[24] Such a defense policy would entail, in times of national crisis, the transformation of all of society's ordinary institutions and organizations into resistance organizations, thus denying the opponents effective political control and ultimately forcing them to withdraw. Naturally, the adoption of a civilian-based defense policy would imply considerable knowledge of, and confidence in, the nonviolent sanctions that would be its principal weapons.

Nonviolent sanctions are also being looked at with renewed interest by people who find themselves faced with various forms of social, political, and economic oppression. The assertion that armed struggle is the only effective method of changing or removing oppressive regimes is open to question. As the cases described above demonstrate, even the most repressive governments are dependent to some degree on the cooperation and acquiescence of the people they rule. When this cooperation is withdrawn in a systematic way, the power base of the oppressive authorities may erode very quickly. A struggle of this type inevitably involves violent repression against those wielding the nonviolent sanctions. Thus, participants must organize themselves at the outset to endure hardships and to continue the resistance despite repression, as they would have to do in a violent struggle. Nonviolent struggles are currently being waged in a number of repressive states, including Poland, Chile, and the Philippines. Nonviolent sanctions might also play a meaningful role in many other societies if their dynamics were better understood.

AN AGENDA FOR EDUCATORS

Developing the potential of nonviolent sanctions requires much more empirical research on their successes and failures, as well as theoretical work on questions of strategy and tactics. This is a task for institutions of higher learning. At the present time, Harvard University's Program on Nonviolent Sanctions in Conflict and Defense is the only program in the world, of which the authors are aware, that is specifically dedicated to research in this field, and it has only two full-time researchers. A handful of students have produced useful case studies as theses and dissertations, but many more are needed.

One reason for the paucity of research is lack of attention to nonviolent sanctions in the instructional programs of colleges and universities. While the World Policy Institute's curriculum guide, *Peace and World Order Studies*, does not necessarily give a complete picture of what is offered, it is probably representative. Of the thirty-one undergraduate peace studies programs surveyed, only eight appear to offer one or more courses on nonviolent action.[25]

The need is not simply to increase course offerings, however. As educators at all levels have become sensitive to the presence of race and gender stereotypes in what is taught—often implicitly rather than explicitly—we should ask how the existing curriculum perpetuates the assumption that violence "works" and how it treats the role of nonviolent sanctions in human life. A critical examination of curriculum guides, textbooks, and audiovisual materials from this point of view would show us where the deficiencies are and what is needed in the way of new materials. To our knowledge no such study has been proposed or undertaken. This is new subject matter for most teachers, which again argues for course offerings on nonviolent sanctions in colleges and universities, as well as in in-service training programs.

Education is not only what goes on in schools. A total of perhaps two-dozen informal study groups have used either a draft study guide on civilian-based defense or *U.S. Defense Policy: Mainstream Views and Nonviolent Alternatives*, which gives substantial attention to civilian-based defense.[26] The fall 1984 catalogue of the Pittsburgh Peace Institute offers an imaginative workshop on "The Nonviolent Defense of Pittsburgh." Interest in such adult education offerings is clearly growing and presents a challenge for the development of more and better materials.

To meet this interest, library holdings on nonviolent sanctions must be expanded. There is an urgent need for the translation of the best literature into languages other than the original, and for publication of new literature as it is developed.

The entertainment industry also has a role to play. Nonviolent struggle is drama. Its history abounds in stories of courage, suspense, and victory against formidable odds. Yet for every *Gandhi*, how many fantasies like *Red Dawn* unrealistically glorify violence? Why should films and television not bring us the excitement of, say, the rescue of the Danish Jews from Nazi persecution? And why should fiction not explore the as yet untried possibilities of the eminently human power of nonviolence?

We began by citing the threat to human survival posed by the technology of organized violence. That threat poses a challenge to educators, and central to the challenge is the need to help people envision credible alternatives to armed conflict. The development of nonviolent sanctions points the way to one such alternative.

Notes

1. This assessment of the problem, and much of the analysis which follows, draws heavily on Gene Sharp's *Social Power and Political Freedom* (Boston: Porter Sargent, 1980), ch. 9 and 11 in particular.

2. This point was first made by Walter Lippmann in "The Political Equivalent of War," *Atlantic Monthly*, Aug. 1928, p. 181.

3. Stoessinger, *Why Nations Go to War* (New York: St. Martin's Press, 1978), p. 123. Emphasis added.

4. Stoessinger, *Why Nations Go to War*, pp. 227–231.

5. Stoessinger, *Why Nations Go to War*, p. 136.

6. Sharp, *Social Power and Political Freedom*, p. 289.

7. For a list of eighty-five major cases, see Sharp, *Exploring Nonviolent Alternatives* (Boston: Porter Sargent, 1971), pp. 115–123.

8. For a detailed reconstruction and analysis of this case, see Patricia Parkman, "Insurrection Without Arms: The General Strike in El Salvador, 1944" Diss. Temple University, 1980.

9. Francisco Morán, *Las jornadas cívicas de abril y mayo de 1944*. (San Salvador: Editorial Universitaria, Universidad de El Salvador, 1979), pp. 61–96, 105–127, 127–136.

10. By the Julian calendar, used in Russia until 1918, thirteen days behind the Gregorian calendar used in the West.

11. Alan Moorhead, *The Russian Revolution* (New York: Harper, 1958), p. 58.

12. Only Peter Ackerman's "Strategic Aspects of Nonviolent Resistance Movements," Diss. Tufts University, 1976, and Sharp's, *The Politics of Nonviolent Action* (Boston: Porter Sargent, 1973), pp. 78–79, treat the specifically nonviolent character of this revolution.

13. This technique takes its name from the bungling soldier in Jaroslav Hasek's *The Good Soldier Schweik* (Harmondsworth: Penguin, 1951). This is a reprint of the posthumously published work, which Hasek had not completely finished at the time of his death in 1923.

14. Paul Wehr, "Aggressive Nonviolence," in *Response to Aggression*, ed. Arnold P. Goldstein, Edward G. Carr, William S. Davidson II, and Paul Wehr (New York: Pergamon Press, 1981), p. 485.

15. Jeremy Bennett, "The Resistance Against the German Occupation of Denmark 1940–1945," in *Civilian Resistance as a National Defence*, ed. Adam Roberts (Baltimore: Penguin Books, 1969), pp. 187–189.

16. Wehr, "Aggressive Nonviolence," p. 488. It is estimated that only 450 of Denmark's 8,000 Jews were actually apprehended.

17. Wehr, "Aggressive Nonviolence," pp. 489–490.

18. There is a lively discussion in the literature as to whether sabotage is by definition violent, and whether it is ever compatible with nonviolent struggle. See esp. Sharp, *The Politics of Nonviolent Action*, pp. 608–611; and Bennett, "The Resistance Against the German Occupation of Denmark 1940–1945," pp. 190–197. In this context, we refer primarily to bombings at industrial and military sites.

19. In addition to the sources cited above, further material on nonviolent resistance in Denmark can be found in Jorgen Haestrup's *European Resistance Movements, 1934–45: A Complete History* (Westport: Meckler, 1981).

20. Ackerman, "Strategic Aspects of Nonviolent Resistance Movements," pp. 371–376.

21. See esp. the work of Sharp, Adam Roberts, Theodor Ebert, Johan Galtung, Anders Boserup, and Andrew Mack on this subject. Boserup and Mack's *War without Weapons* (New York: Schocken, 1975) provides a useful bibliography of the major works.

22. The National Conference of Catholic Bishops, to cite one example, called for the development of nonviolent means of national defense in its 1983 pastoral letter, *The Challenge of Peace: God's Promise and Our Response* (Washington: United States Catholic Conference, 1983).

23. The Alternative Defence Commission, *Defence Without the Bomb* (London, Taylor & Francis, 1983), pp. 11, 204–205, 243.

24. Sharp, *Social Power and Political Freedom*, p. 232 ff., offers a definition and thorough discussion of this policy.

25. Barbara J. Wein, ed., *Peace and World Order Studies* (New York: World Policy Institute, 1984), pp. 629–667. Sample syllabuses can be found on pp. 70–126, although these are not all clearly focused on nonviolent sanctions as an alternative form of power.

26. Bob Irwin, *U.S. Defense Policy: Mainstream Views and Nonviolent Alternatives (A Macro-Analysis Seminar Manual)* (Waltham, MA: International Seminars on Teaching for Nonviolent Action, 1982).

Questions

1. How great a role does cultural conditioning play in the common acceptance of violence as an acceptable way of resolving conflicts? Give examples from your everyday experience.

2. Why do the authors say that violence is overrated? Do you agree or disagree? State your reasons.

3. What were some of the factors in the limited success of the three nonviolent movements cited by the authors?

4. What is the authors' assessment of peace studies programs? How could they be strengthened?

5. What role does the entertainment industry play in the promotion of the cult of violence? Give examples from your own experience.

8

Is There a Future for Nonviolence in Central America?

Dan R. Ebener

This article originally appeared in *Fellowship*, October–November 1983.

The author, who is director of the New Covenant Justice and Peace Center in Omaha, traveled to Nicaragua in the summer of 1983, where he and 150 others held a "nonviolent vigil and prayer service" in the war zone. Local residents considered the North Americans as a "peace shield" against the military activities of the U.S.-supported contras.

While in Nicaragua, Ebener asked the Rev. Ernesto Cardenal, Minister of Culture in the Sandinista government, whether non-violence had a future in that war-torn country. Cardenal's reply was a qualified one, not denying the value of non-violence but supporting his government's use of force in the present "armed struggle."

The author says he came away from Nicaragua with a fresh perspective on pacifism and non-violence. To a pacifist, any resort to arms is unjustified. This places the author in an uncomfortable position. He asks himself: "Can pacifists take sides in a revolution?" He replies that he stands firmly "in solidarity with the poor people who do take up arms in revolutionary struggle." Whether this compromises his basic principles is for him and his colleagues to answer.

Ebener witnessed a people at war. The stance of the Sandinistas is closer to the "just war" principles propounded by Thomas Aquinas than to the classical pacifist position. Nevertheless, the author notes some gains: the abolition of the death penalty and social programs aimed at the elimination of hunger and disease. Subsequent to Ebener's visit, elections were held in Nicaragua which were given a clean bill of health by many European observers. He notes that Nicaragua "is recovering from 17 years of revolutionary war and 100 years of rebellion." And he denies that Nicaragua has become a communist country.

Ebener recognizes that, in talking about non-violence to oppressed people, "we take the risk of sounding like the oppressor." Perhaps because the situation in Nicaragua is so intractable and the words of U.S. pacifists are likely to have little effect, he turns his gaze to the United States. "Pac-

ifists in the U.S.," he says, "should begin a nonviolent revolution here against U.S. policies that are creating the situation that perpetuates violence for the people there."

The author places his hopes in the comunidades de base *(grassroots communities) in Nicaragua to keep alive the philosophy and practice of non-violence. He appeals to the citizens of North America to mitigate the violent policies of their own governments. One senses that he does not answer his own question because, as a foreigner, he is not the one to give the answer.*

I asked that question of Rev. Ernesto Cardenal, Minister of Culture for the new government in Nicaragua.

"There were many nonviolent means used during the revolution," he answered. "Strikes, fasting, boycotts, taking over churches and schools, and peaceful marches were all vital to the revolution. Armed struggle was just one part. The arms we now have are due to the invasion. They are needed to defend the population: women, children—all the people." At first, I thought that the Jesuit priest had not understood my question. But later I realized that he had answered from his own frame of reference. Nonviolence is seen by many Central Americans as a luxury. Violence to protect one's land and people is seen as a necessity.

Travelling in Nicaragua in July 1983, I heard this argument repeatedly. From the Commandant of the armed forces to the leaders of the Christian grassroots communities, we heard the same message: "We want peace. We do not want unnecessary bloodshed. But if we must fight, we will. And we will win . . . But we want peace." A willingness to fight is matched by the sincere desire for peace. Nicaraguans have learned firsthand what war means. The long and bitter revolutionary war in Nicaragua continues today largely because the US is providing military aid to the counter-revolutionaries—the *"contras"*—who are now trying to overthrow the Sandinista government.

To protest US military and economic policies against Nicaragua, and to call for a peaceful end to the fighting on Nicaragua's borders, I joined Action for Peace in Nicaragua. Organized by the Carolina Interfaith Task Force on Central America, the action included 150 religious North Americans from thirty-two states. In Jalapa, a Nicaraguan border town that recent fighting has turned into a war zone, we held a nonviolent vigil and prayer service. Local residents and church leaders who joined us said that while we were there our bodies were acting as a "peace shield" against further invasion by the *contras.*

During this brief stay in Nicaragua, I looked at pacifism and nonviolence in an entirely new light. Pacifists will oppose US intervention whether they support Nicaragua or not. Because Nicaragua's revolution has embraced the taking of arms, most pacifists are in doubt about supporting the present Nicaraguan government. The question of nonviolence in a Central American context has already become a major question for many FOR members. At least one in our group came home feeling she could no longer consider herself a pacifist.

The wedding of liberation theology to the just war theory has led many church leaders, both in Central and South America, to support the taking up of arms in the revolutionary struggles. While I do not support the taking up of arms myself, I feel that I must stand firmly in solidarity with the poor people who do take up arms in revolutionary struggle. This position raises serious questions for me, such as: Can pacifists take sides in a revolution? Is it possible to support the poor in their struggle for liberation without endorsing their revolution? Can we support the revolution without endorsing the government?

Looking first at Nicaragua, it is shocking to witness the degree to which that country has been militarized. Signs of the US war against Nicaragua were all around us during our visit. The first person I met at the Managua airport was a US reporter who had been hit in the face by shrapnel while travelling with the *contras*. Billboards on the streets, posters at the airport, and paintings in the churches depict the central role guns have played and still are playing in the Sandinist revolution. It was common to see soldiers, many of them teenagers, armed with machine guns and pistols in front of government buildings, on the streets and near the bridges on the road to Jalapa. The civilian population is also armed. In the countryside near Jalapa, we saw peasants standing guard with rifles while co-workers cultivated the fields. They scanned the fields for any sign of *contras*, who reportedly have been kidnapping farmers out of the fields, giving them the choice either to join the *contras* or be killed. The area where we held our vigil was surrounded by bomb shelters, foxholes, and a Sandinist fortress.

At a political rally we attended in Jalapa, even the small children had looks of fear and anger as they chanted patriotic slogans and stood in military salute. Priest and general alike cited scripture and quoted Thomas Aquinas in calling for Christian participation in the war against the *contras*. So high are the fears of US escalation in the war on the Nicaraguan border that the government of Nicaragua now appears to be calling for a military draft, with no option for conscientious objection.

On the other hand, many forms of militarism have been abolished by the new Nicaraguan government. Since the Sandinist revolution took power in July 1979, Nicaragua has abolished the death penalty, established some degree of political pluralism, developed a national health and immunization program, reduced illiteracy, and almost eradicated the severe hunger and starvation that has plagued this country for generations. Still, more people continue to die in Central America from hunger and disease than from the spilling of blood.

We will never know what conditions would exist in Nicaragua if it were not for the present border invasions. But we must admit that our government's military strategy in Central America looms as the major factor in Nicaragua's present military preparedness. Nicaragua is recovering from eighteen years of revolutionary war and 100 years of rebellion.

Judging from what we saw in July 1983, the Sandinist revolution has brought about vast improvements upon the miseries of the past. Federal land has been distributed to thousands of peasant families. Education and health care are seen as human rights, available free to everyone. Federal housing projects are relocating victims of the 1972 earthquake, the revolutionary war, and the 1982 floods. The Institute for Food and Development reported in 1982 that "food self-sufficiency" was at hand in Nicaragua. (The current economic and military war has temporarily nullified this, causing shortages of food as well as medical supplies.)

Despite its weaknesses and shortcomings, the Nicaraguan revolution may become a model for other Latin American countries. The charge that Nicaragua is a Communist country is unfair. The openness of the society, the political pluralism, and the experiments in a mixed economy are all signs that Nicaragua enjoys many freedoms that do not exist in Soviet-bloc countries. During our stay in Nicaragua, we met with government officials, opposition leaders, peasants, bankers, church leaders, and even mothers of some of the victims of the recent fighting on the border. We were free to talk to people on the streets, to express our opinions, and to discuss problems within the Nicaraguan government. We raised questions with the Sandinistas about their handling of the economy, their mistreatment of the Miskito Indians, their censorship of *La Prensa*, and the delay in holding national elections. While they were not persuaded by our arguments, they were open to criticism and even willing to admit some of their mistakes. Self-criticism is not a common virtue in government leaders. It was refreshing to see it in Nicaragua.

Charges that Nicaragua is being aided by the Soviet Union and Cuba do have some basis in truth. With the US maneuvering thousands of troops in Honduras, stationing nuclear-armed battalions in the Caribbean, and financing the *contras* in the war on the Nicaraguan border, the Sandinistas have great cause for alarm. They have turned to many countries for help, not only Soviet-bloc countries, but also some US allies. Leaders in the San-dinist government stressed that they are not interested in going from US satellite status to becoming a satellite of the USSR. After fighting a revo-lution for independence, they do not wish to be aligned with either su-perpower.

When pacifists talk about nonviolence to people who have been op-pressed and hungry for many years, we take the risk of sounding like the oppressor. Reagan, Somoza, and Marcos say they are for "peace." When speaking of peace in Central America, we must first speak of justice and liberation. Without justice, poverty will continue to be the initiator of vi-olence. Without liberation, those who act for justice will continue to be repressed. As one labor organizer in Nicaragua put it, "I am struggling for peace, but not peace with hunger."

When North American pacifists begin to have more impact on US pol-icy, nonviolent struggle will become a more attractive and more possible option for the people of Central America. Rather than criticizing the weak-nesses of the people of Central America for turning to violence, pacifists in the US should begin a nonviolent revolution here against the US poli-cies that are creating the situation that perpetuates violence for the people there.

The Christian *comunidades de base* (grassroots communities) in Nicaragua, and throughout Latin America, hold the key to nonviolent revolution. One observer described their work in Brazil as "the greatest nonviolent movement of the century." Increasingly, these communities are adopting nonviolence as a force for revolutionary change. The grass-roots communities we visited in Nicaragua teach people of faith to live according to the gospel, to interpret the gospel message into their daily lives, and to act accordingly. In Nicaragua, these Christian communities play a central role in the evolving revolution.

Peasants in Central America support the revolutionary cause by open-ing their homes to soldiers and refugees and by performing works of mercy. They feed, clothe, shelter, pray with, and give medical attention to their comrades. It is for these acts that many peasants have been killed in the senseless massacres we read about in the US. Through their deeds, *campesinos* learn more about nonviolence than most North American pac-ifists will ever learn, risking their lives daily by performing acts of kind-ness.

If we take the time to listen to the poor in Latin America, we will hear that the most important step North American pacifists can take is to stop US military and economic intervention in their countries. Put simply, to side with the poor in Latin America means to oppose US policies in that region.

Questions

1. Does the author answer the questions he proposes in the title of his article? If so, how? If not, why not?

2. Are there ways in which one can "stand in solidarity" with the poor who take up arms without ourselves condoning violence?

3. Do you think the author shows consistency with his pacifist principles? Why, or why not?

4. In what ways can those who oppose the American government's policy toward Nicaragua make their influence felt?

5. Do you think non-violence has a future in Central America? Why, or why not?

9
A Latin American Response

Mano Barreno

This article originally appeared in *Fellowship*, October–November 1983.

The author, an Ecuadoran theologian, answers Dan Ebener's question (see previous article) by comparing Nicaragua to the victim of rape. Fairly or not, he finds an implication that the victim is somehow to blame for the act. At the least, the subject may not be timely to the Nicaraguan people struggling for survival. And yet, could not the same be said of the people of India under the colonial domination of England?

Barreno pursues the rape analogy with a review of the colonial history of the American continent at the hands of Europeans. He arrives at the concept of "institutional violence" enunciated by the Latin American bishops at Medellín in the 1960's. At that pivotal conference, the bishops made use of the "just war" theory to support "revolutionary insurrection" under certain conditions. Thomas Jefferson did no less in the Declaration of Independence. Even Archbishop Oscar Romero, a proponent of non-violence who was killed by a death squad in El Salvador, is quoted approving "the legitimate right of insurrectional violence."

By putting themselves on the side of the oppressed, the Latin American hierarchy and their co-religionists could be hardly expected to rule out all forms of violent struggle. The pacifist tradition in the Catholic Church is not that all-pervasive. The author states that those people who fight for liberation "do not want the death of those in power, but their conversion." Such a conclusion finds historical support in the Christian tradition, but it is the tradition of the "just war," not that of absolute non-violence.

Dan Ebener's question to Ernesto Cardenal—Is there a future for nonviolence in Central America?—is like asking a recovering victim of rape if there is a future for nonviolence in his/her life. It implies that the victims are to blame and comes from looking at violence and nonviolence with the eyes of the violent: the rich and powerful. This may explain the eagerness to sell nonviolence to the poor in Central America.

I will try to explain the Latin American Church's position on violence and nonviolence as it has embraced the perspective of those who are victims of violence and, often, of the nonviolence stance.

The rape of the American continent by the Europeans five centuries ago was only the beginning of the ongoing ethnocide of its inhabitants, the robbery of their lands and the destruction of their culture, their dignity, and their future. Cruel servitude was forced on the people to bring huge profits to the capitalist world that was born in England.

Today, most of these profits go to the US, leaving behind malnutrition, starvation, and death for the local populations. The US imposes an economic policy on Latin America that causes extreme poverty (structural *oppression*) and which is impossible to maintain without *repression* and terror. Repression and terror in Central America have reached a level of cool genocide. The local armies and death squads, trained, equipped, and guided by the US, persecute, torture, and assassinate Central Americans by the tens of thousands to silence their cries for justice and destroy the victorious people's revolution in Nicaragua.

The Medellín Conference of Bishops, in 1966, denounced the structural oppression and the repression that keeps it in place in Latin America as an "injustice which cries to heaven," and a "sinful situation." The fruit of that sin is death, the death of the Latin American people: either sudden death by violence or slow death from hunger or sickness. These two kinds of violence were seen by the bishops as belonging to the very essence of the capitalist system. In fact, they described the system itself as an "institutionalized violence," which causes the "temptations to violence" in Latin America. The rigid control of the victims by this system gets to the point where any deviation from the standards set by the capitalist society is grounds for labeling the victims "violent," "subversive," or "terrorist."

That is why the nonviolence stance called for by some US peace groups arouses suspicion. Could it be that nonviolence is one of the reactions permitted the victims by the system to prevent a radical change of its structures? Could nonviolence become an ideology that serves and protects the capitalist system?

The Latin American bishops seemed to suspect that it could. They did not blame the victims. They put the responsibility for the temptation to use violence to overcome the *institutionalized* violence in Latin America on those who support and benefit from the status quo. Those who exploit the poor are the cause of the victims' reaction, even if it is violent, for they created the victims as such. The bishops opened the doors for more options for the oppressed in the struggle for justice and liberation. While they urged the impoverished to use peaceful means in this struggle, they also stated that:

Revolutionary insurrection can be legitimate in the case of evident and prolonged tyranny that seriously works against the fundamental rights of the people, and that damages the common good of the country, whether it proceeds from one person or from clearly unjust structures.

By adding the existence of "unjust structures" as a legitimate reason for "revolutionary insurrection," the bishops extended that option to most of Latin America. The late Archbishop Oscar Romero applied this principle to the Salvadoran struggle in these words:

Christians are not afraid of combat. They know how to fight, but they prefer the language of peace. However, when a dictatorship seriously violates human rights and attacks the common good of the nation, when it becomes unbearable and closes all channels of dialogue, of understanding, of rationality—when this happens, the Church speaks of the legitimate right of insurrectional violence.

What the Latin American Church is saying through its practices and the documents of its bishops is that the victims have the right and the duty to defend themselves—even using violence—against the oppressor, whether individual or unjust structures. That is the theological principle. But the method, the selection of appropriate means (violent, nonviolent or both) is not a theological question; it belongs to the virtue of prudence, which is a political matter—according to Thomas Aquinas. It is to be decided by the oppressed themselves, in their own particular situation.

The Latin American Church arrived at this statement about the use of violence in a prophetic way. The bishops put themselves on the side of the oppressed and were able to see the world through the eyes of the victims. What they saw and felt through those eyes is reflected in the document.

Today the Latin American Church has gone far beyond simply legitimizing the insurrectional violence of the victims; it is lined up on the side of the poor in their struggle. There the Church is discovering, in a concrete way, what the bishops wrote in the Medellín document: that the revolutionary struggle of the poor is a liberation struggle, inspired and led by Jesus Christ as his very mission:

This struggle is an act of justice to the oppressed, based on love and it is liberating. The repressive struggle to dominate the impoverished and maintain the sinful structures of the capitalist system is unjust, enslaving, and sinful; it aims to eliminate those who strive for liberation. That is why we have the martyrs and the death of Jesus. Those who struggle for liberation do not want the death of those in power, but their conversion. That is why the blood of Jesus falls on the Romans, not to kill them but to save them.

Questions

1. Do you think the author is fair in his implication that Dan Ebener's question (see previous article) presupposes guilt on the part of the victim? Give your reasons.

2. Is "insurrectional violence" the only possible response to the "institutional violence" found in certain countries? What are some alternatives?

3. Why do aspects of the peace movement in democratic countries arouse suspicions among the poor in dictatorial regimes?

4. Do you agree that the revolutionary struggle of the poor in Latin America and elsewhere is "inspired and led by Jesus Christ as his very mission"? Why, or why not?

5. The author equates the early Christian martyrs with those who are fighting today for liberation. Do you agree or disagree with this comparison? Give your reasons.

10

The Precarious Road:
Nonviolence in the Philippines

Peggy Rosenthal

This article originally appeared in *Commonweal*, June 20, 1986.

The popular revolution that overthrew dictator Ferdinand Marcos of the Philippines in February 1986 astounded the world—and the Filipino people themselves. It all seemed so easy—and it was practically bloodless. Peggy Rosenthal, an author and a student of non-violence, sketches the history of the non-violent movement in this island nation. Her conclusion is that the toppling of Marcos was neither easy nor accidental.

Rosenthal gives much of the credit for training of non-violent activists to Hildegard Goss-Mayr and her husband Jean Goss, veterans of the International Fellowship of Reconciliation, who conducted intensive seminars in the Philippines in 1984. Hildegard Goss-Mayr in turn attributes the radical change in the political situation to the change of heart (conversion) of Benigno Aquino during his imprisonment under Marcos. Aquino's assassination in August 1983 was, in her words, "the blood of the martyr that bears fruit." The mass demonstrations following Aquino's shooting had all the potential for violent civil war, and it was into this turbulent scene that the Goss-Mayrs were invited by several Catholic religious groups. By stressing inward change as a necessary prelude to effective action, the trainers were able to help "peasants, political opposition leaders, labor union leaders, bishops and churchworkers" to put aside their differences and to unite for the peaceful overcoming of injustice.

The author also cites the work of Richard Deats, a Methodist minister, who conducted non-violent seminars among Filipino Protestants, as the Goss-Mayrs had done among Catholics. When Marcos called his "snap" election for February 1986, AKKAPKA, the newly formed non-violent movement of the Philippines under Father Jose Blanco, moved quickly to get out the vote, to protect the integrity of the ballot boxes and to set up "Tent Cities" for prayer, fasting and non-violent training in ten densely populated areas.

Rosenthal praises the role of the Catholic Church's Radio Veritas for coordinating the resistance and for broadcasting passages from such non-

violent leaders as Gandhi, Martin Luther King, Jr. and Jesus in his Sermon on the Mount. The gradual transformation of the Philippine hierarchy from a supporter of the status quo to an outspoken proponent of peaceful change—largely through the efforts of Bishop Francisco Claver—is a story in itself.

Finally, the author sees in Corazon Aquino, the slain leader's widow, the embodiment of the non-violent leader who truly wishes to help the people instead of acquiring power. As the title of this article implies, the road to full liberation is not without dangers. Social and economic problems, many of them dating back centuries, need to be addressed by the new administration in the same popular, non-violent manner by which the overthrow of Marcos was accomplished. This "second step," to quote Hildegard Goss-Mayr, requires "a total transformation of society."

During February of this year, spectators around the world watched nonviolence at work in the Philippines: on television we saw masses of unarmed people blocking tanks, soldiers accepting flowers from nuns, military and church leaders urging soldiers to refuse orders to shoot their fellow citizens. And soon we saw that nonviolence had indeed worked. With almost no bloodshed, and none caused by the opposition, a dictator was forced from power and the popularly elected choice became president. In one particular instance, we actually saw nonviolence succeed.

But how did it work? What were the dynamics of this powerful force for overcoming oppression? What steps of preparation made the success possible? What went on behind the scenes we saw? Can it last?

Someone uniquely qualified to answer these questions is Hildegard Goss-Mayr. She and her husband, Jean Goss, were in Manila during the first two weeks of February, meeting for regular strategy sessions with Mrs. Aquino and Cardinal Sin. They were also in the country in 1984, teaching active nonviolence to Filipinos who in turn undertook a nationwide education program in nonviolent action. Beyond their experience in the Philippines, for over twenty years the Goss-Mayrs have initiated and participated in nonviolent liberation struggles in Latin America and elsewhere.

Jean Goss was born in France in 1912. Hildegard Mayr was born in Austria in 1930, the daughter of a founder of the International Fellowship of Reconciliation (IFOR). After their marriage in 1958, they went as representatives of IFOR to several Eastern Bloc countries. They lobbied at the Second Vatican Council for an endorsement of nonviolent peacemaking, and succeeded in getting the first official church support of conscientious objection written into *Gaudium et Spes*. They spent most of 1962 to 1977 in Latin America, sent by the IFOR to teach nonviolence as a revolutionary force. Their influence on the nonviolent liberation movement in Latin America is indisputable: two of the movement's leaders, Dom Helder Camara and Nobel Peace Prize winner Adolfo Perez Esquivel, attribute their understanding of nonviolence to personal encounters with the Goss-Mayrs.

It was because of their Latin American experience that the Goss-Mayrs were invited to the Philippines in 1984 to help develop a nonviolent opposition to Marcos. But this development is best described in Hildegard Goss-Mayr's own words. I was priviliged to hear her talk and to interview her last April at a retreat in Groton, Massachusetts. The quotes that follow are from that occasion.

Hildegard—everyone calls her by her first name—agrees with other commentators that the public drama of mass nonviolent resistance to Marcos began in August 1983 with the spontaneous demonstrations of outrage at Benigno Aquino's assassination. But "it is not so well known," she says, that behind this event lay a decisive private drama: "Ninoy Aquino, while he was in prison, underwent a radical change— a kind of conversion" to nonviolence. When first imprisoned by Marcos, Aquino "was an opposition politician, certainly an honest person, but, like all politicians, trying to get power." Through reading the Gospel and Gandhi while suffering the conditions of imprisonment, he came to see "that to be a politician does not mean to try to get quickly as much power as you can, but it means to serve the people" at whatever cost to oneself.

Ninoy Aquino knew, when he decided in 1983 to return from the United States to the Philippines, that the cost might be his life. But "this gift of the life of Ninoy," as Hildegard puts it, was "the blood of the martyr" that bears fruit: it "encouraged thousands and thousands of others to overthrow the fear that had kept them passive, and to come out on the streets to demand that martial law be discontinued and human rights be respected."

The immediate result of these spontaneous mass demonstrations in the autumn of 1983 was, however, further repression by Marcos, as well as further strengthening of the Communist New People's Army (NPA), whose counterviolence offered the most powerful and organized opposition to the government's injustice. It was into this situation of polarized violence that Hildegard and Jean Goss-Mayr were invited to come by some Filipino religious communities who saw the urgent need for a well-organized nation-wide nonviolent campaign.

The Goss-Mayrs arrived in the Philippines in February 1984. After traveling around the country, they concluded "that it was very late to come into the situation with nonviolence," because of the deeply entrenched violence on both sides:

> We felt it was late, but we felt on the other hand that there were people really searching for the nonviolent alternative. And I think one thing that made us decide to accept this challenge was when, on the last day that we spent on this first visit, the brother of Ninoy Aquino came to see us. He was one of those who had been organizing these demonstrations after the assassination of his brother. And he said to Jean and myself: "A few days ago the arms merchants visited us and said to us, 'Do you think that with a few demonstrations you will be able to overthrow this regime? Don't you think you need better weapons than that? We offer them to you. Make up your mind.'" And then he said, "You see it is providential that you have come just at this point of time, because ever since this visit I am unable to sleep. Do I have the right to throw our country into major civil war? What is my responsibility as a Christian politician in this situation? Is there really such a thing as nonviolent combat against an unjust system like that of Marcos?"
>
> So Jean and I said, "At least you could try. You don't lose anything if you try with nonviolence. But you must make up your mind, and if you do, you must prepare yourself for nonviolent resistance. Nonviolence is not something that you do spontaneously and without preparation. No— you have to prepare yourself inwardly, because nonviolent methods are the fruit of a vision of man that we have. If you want to have seminars of preparation, let us know, and we are willing to come back."

A few weeks later the Goss-Mayrs were invited back. They returned that summer for six weeks, giving seminars on nonviolent liberation to a variety of people: peasants, political opposition leaders, labor union leaders, bishops, churchworkers, including nuns and priests and laypeople. In all these seminars, as in the ones the Goss-Mayrs have led throughout the world, the focus was two-fold: analysis of the structures of oppression, and personal spiritual conversion. The violence in society and the violence in our own hearts cannot, the Goss-Mayrs insist, be separated.

An incident at one of the seminars shows the dynamics of spiritual conversion at work in political reconciliation. Among the seminar participants were political opposition leaders and also peasant leaders:

> the peasants would not speak with the politicians. They said, "We have no faith in the politicians. Even if they are from the opposition, they have betrayed us so often, we have no faith." The people were very divided. One group would not relate to the other. So one evening when we celebrated the Eucharist together, Father Blanco, a Jesuit priest, distributed the host immediately after the consecration. Everybody

held the host, consecrated, right in his hand. And Father Blanco said, "Now, this host is bread. This body of Christ is our bread. This love of His—how do we live up to it? Let us now break this bread that we have in our hand, and bring one part of the host to those with whom we have not yet spoken in our seminar." And we experienced that the peasants would bring the host to the politicians, and politicians to the peasants. And we saw leaders from the labor unions with 400,000 members breaking down in tears, because they said, "So far we have only been educating the workers in polarization, and not in a work to overcome really the injustice—in the hearts and minds of those who carry responsibility." These seminars were not just training people in a methodology. But they really meant for each one of us a deep change, a conversion.

After the Goss-Mayrs completed their six weeks of seminars, an American, Richard Deats, Interfaith Director of the Fellowship of Reconciliation (FOR), went to the Philippines to lead three more weeks of nonviolent training sessions. Deats, a Methodist who had taught social ethics at Union Theological Seminary in the Philippines for thirteen years, focused his workshops on the Filipino Protestant community, since the Goss-Mayrs had worked primarily with Catholics. Out of the nine weeks of FOR seminars, AKKAPKA—the nonviolent movement of the Philippines—was formed. Under the energetic leadership of Father Blanco and a staff that soon grew to nine, AKKAPKA set right to work on building base communities and on giving in-depth seminars on active nonviolence to key groups of people around the country. Forty such seminars were held in thirty provinces during AKKAPKA's first year (autumn 1984–85).

Then when Marcos, at the end of 1985, unexpectedly announced the "snap" election for February 7, 1986, AKKAPKA changed its strategy. Discontinuing the general nonviolent education seminars, it concentrated on three projects: encouraging people to vote from their consciences, without fear and without accepting bribes; helping to train people in nonviolent defense of the ballot boxes (half a million people were in fact trained, and did defend the boxes without weapons when Marcos's forces tried to steal them); and setting up "Tent Cities," tents for prayer and fasting and nonviolent training located in ten highly populated areas.

The Tent Cities operated from mid-January until the end of the election crisis, so Hildegard Goss-Mayr was able to observe them when she returned to the Philippines at the beginning of February. Her assessment is that they were instrumental in the eventual success of the nonviolent campaign:

> One tent was set up right in the banking center in Manila, where the financial power of the regime was concentrated. There in a little park, this big prayer tent was set up. And around this prayer tent, people who

promised to fast and pray would, day and night, have a presence and carry within the fast and with the prayer the whole revolutionary process. And I think we cannot emphasize this enough: that in this whole process, there was always this unity—of outward nonviolent action against the unjust regime and of that deep spirituality that gave the people the strength later on to stand up against the tanks and to confront the tanks—this force of fasting and prayer. And in the celebrations of the Eucharist, they would point out that we are not fighting only against flesh and blood, we are fighting against the demons of richness and exploitation and hatred that we have to cast out from our people—from ourselves, from the military, from Marcos and his followers. And that we must use this arm together with the organized nonviolent resistance. . . . I think it makes a great difference, where in a revolutionary process, where people are emotionally very, very taken in, as you can understand—whether you promote hatred and revenge, or whether you help the people to stand firmly for justice but at the same time not to let themselves be taken in by the hatred of those who stand with the oppressor: not to become like the oppressor, but to stand for justice and to love your enemy to the extent that you want to liberate him, you want to win him, you want to draw him in, and you don't want his destruction but his liberation.

This message being delivered in the prayer tents was simultaneously being communicated by the Catholic radio station, Radio Veritas, which played an indispensable role in the nonviolent campaign. Not only did Radio Veritas coordinate the whole resistance, broadcasting continual reports of what was happening, but around the clock it also read passages of Martin Luther King, Jr., the Sermon on the Mount, and Gandhi, urging people to follow these examples.

While this public education in—and practice of—nonviolence was going on at prayer tents and over the radio, Mrs. Aquino and Cardinal Sin and the Goss-Mayrs were meeting privately to prepare "scenarios" of nonviolent response to various possibilities that might develop. "And the scenario of which everybody was most afraid," Hildegard says, "was that the army would split. . . . Then a great deal of bloodshed could be foreseen." In fact the army did split, and "Marcos did give the order to those who were still loyal to him to crush the dissident part of the army." But because Aquino and her advisors had prepared themselves for this possibility, they were ready with their response:

Radio Veritas immediately called people to fill up the street, to stand in front of the tanks, to speak to the soldiers. And for journalists to take films of those soldiers who would shoot on the people. No soldier wants to see a film in which his face is personally shown shooting on the people. And there were few in the beginning. But more and more and more, and finally you know there were several hundred thousand, who spent a whole weekend in the road blocking the tanks so that they could not move into the dissident groups—speaking to the soldiers and saying, "You are one of us; you belong to the people; come back to the group to whom you really belong."

These are the scenes of mass nonviolent action that we all saw. As crowd scenes, they were the most dramatic. But in the preceding weeks we had also watched other actors playing leading roles in the developing drama: Mrs. Aquino calling in campaign speeches for reconciliation instead of revenge; the Catholic Bishops' Conference issuing two crucial statements, one (on January 26) just before the election and one (on February 14) just after it, condemning the government's cheating as a "conspiracy of evil" and endorsing "the nonviolent struggle for justice" as the way to resist this evil "by peaceful means—in the manner of Christ." And just as behind the nonviolent people's power lay AKKAPKA's preparatory work, behind both Mrs. Aquino's and the bishops' calls for active nonviolence lay years of preparation and growing commitment.

Mrs. Aquino's commitment to nonviolence came out of personal suffering. According to Richard Deats, during the seven years of her husband's imprisonment she shared fully in his "dark night of the soul"; and "that tremendous encounter with suffering and oppression and finally assassination" gave her a deep identification with the Filipino people in their suffering under Marcos. Hildegard agrees: "Cory was not a person who wanted to be president, who wanted to have power, who wanted to make herself the first person in the nation. She's very authentic in that sense: that when she accepted, under the pressure of the people, under the demand of the church, to be a candidate for president, she did it because she knew she had to serve the people."

The story behind the bishops' dramatic election-crisis endorsement of nonviolent action is longer. It begins with Francisco Claver, S.J., who—as Bishop of Bukidnon in the 1970s—became committed to active nonviolence as the only legitimate Christian response to the violence of both the government and the NPA. Claver gradually gathered a growing number of like-minded bishops, who for fifteen years have been reflecting together on how to help their people in the light of the Gospel, studying the responses of bishops in comparable places like Brazil, and encouraging specific acts of nonviolent resistance in their dioceses when faced with government harassment and killings. Claver's group numbered between twenty and thirty (out of a Bishops' Conference of 104) by the time he brought them to meet with the Goss-Mayrs in 1984 and then again with Richard Deats in 1985. Under the influence of Claver's group, the Bishops' Conference of the Philippines issued increasingly strong statements against government oppression in the last few years. Their election statements are "not the first," says Hildegard approvingly. "There has been a process going on, similar to what happened in some Latin American countries, that a few bishops understand [nonviolence] and they believe that their brothers in Christ can understand also, if they witness."

This picture of the Filipino bishops gradually converting each other to active nonviolence over the years, combined with the visibly effective actions of the church hierarchy during the crisis (Cardinal Sin's Victory Mass for Mrs. Aquino, priests in all the churches reading from the pulpit the bishops' call for mass resistance), makes it look as if the leading role in the successful nonviolent liberation was played by the hierarchy rather than by the people. Yet Mrs. Aquino's celebration speeches attributed the success to "people's power." The question of who, behind the scenes, was the greater force on whom—the people or the church hierarchy—is a matter of interpretation; and Hildegard Goss-Mayr's view is complex. She sees Bishop Claver ("certainly one of the pillars of nonviolence") as a major force. And she appreciates the historic significance of the bishops' February 14 letter: "I think it is the first time, at least in present history, that a bishops' conference in writing asked people to go into nonviolent action and into civil disobedience as the way that the Gospel proposes to us in order to overcome the unjust system." But while stressing that "it was very important that in this last phase the church as an institution, the bishops, gave its full support to the nonviolent struggle," she sees the direction of influence precisely that way: the bishops giving support to a struggle already in process, "approving what the people had already lived." With a laugh she adds, "I think it is the people who converted the bishops!"

Although she enjoys this picture of conversion from the bottom up, Hildegard Goss-Mayr also sees its serious implications. Her voice sounds pained when she criticizes the church for not taking the lead in defense of human rights during the early years of martial law. "A small part of the church" did stand from the beginning "on the side of the people and work for social justice. . . . But the majority of the church leadership and of the middle class people were linked to the regime. And I think we must be truthful and say that it was similar to Latin America: that the church as an official institution was for too long—for much too long—linked to those in power." Much of the responsibility for the growth of the NPA lies, she insists sadly, with "the cowardice of large sections of the official church. People cannot remain passive under certain circumstances. And wherever the moral authorities, whether it is the Christian churches or other moral authorities, do not give a lead in a nonviolent resistance," people "will have to take counterviolence."

The church, then, bears some blame for the polarized violence which made the Goss-Mayrs pessimistic in 1984 about the possibilities of nonviolence. And even now, while Hildegard rejoices in what the Filipino church and people were able to do together through "the transforming power of nonviolence," her initial concerns remain. "There is as yet not enough preparation. . . . You cannot say that the whole nation is educated in nonviolence."

In her concern about the continued precariousness of the situation, Hildegard is careful about the language she uses in referring to the February drama. Bishop Claver, in recent articles in *America,* has called it "the February revolution." When I asked Richard Deats whether he thought "revolution" was an accurate term, he made a useful distinction; yes, he said, "in the sense that a revolution is a rapid change, a rapid turnover, and what happened was that a twenty-year reign of a dictator was ended." But "it is not a thorough, complete revolution in the sense of a total transformation of society. What is before us now is the second phase: addressing the deep social and economic problems such as the landlessness and the deep poverty." Hildegard Goss-Mayr's assessment is equally cautious. While believing firmly in nonviolence as a revolutionary force, and referring often to "the revolutionary process" in the Philippines, she calls the February events "the recent liberation struggle." And even that phrase she repeatedly qualifies by insisting that it was "only a first step":

> What is before the Filipino people now is at least as difficult, if not more difficult. Because it will need perseverance. And it will need a continued conversion of those who still adhere to the old regime, who still have important places in the provinces: to dismantle the private armies of the landlords; to carry out a land reform so that the mass of the people can live in dignity on the land: to negotiate with the Moslem minority; to negotiate with the NPA, so that perhaps they will be willing to put down their arms and to become one of the democratic parties in the country; to rebuild the economy of the country. Many very difficult steps.

Questions

1. What qualified the Goss-Mayrs to conduct non-violent seminars in the Philippines? Which aspect of their previous experience was likely to have been especially helpful?

2. Why was Benigno Aquino's change of heart so important to the future of the non-violent movement his death inspired?

3. What role did religious faith play in the unity of various elements of the opposition?

4. The article does not mention the defection of the army's chief of staff and the foreign minister to the opposition camp. How might their influence in the new government affect the future?

5. What are some of the problems that lay ahead for the Philippines?

SECTION FOUR

Other Forms of Conflict Resolution

1
The Art of Negotiating

Gerard I. Nierenberg

This article originally appeared in *The Art of Negotiating*, Hawthorn, 1968.

Negotiation, though a part of the non-violent action process, is a field unto itself. Far more organizations and people are likely to engage in negotiations to achieve their goals than are willing to resort to "self-suffering" and direct action. Since it is a more accessible activity than ahimsa, *it deserves a separate treatment.*

Gerard I. Nierenberg is a leading theoretician, practitioner and trainer in the field of negotiation. The following selection, taken from his 1968 book, The Art of Negotiating, *is still highly relevant. Everything he says flows from his first sentence: "In a successful negotiation everybody wins." Negotiation is not a game, he insists, because a game has clear rules, intense competition, a winner and a loser. It is not war, which results in a defeated or dead foe. Negotiation must be entered into on a mutually cooperative basis, in which each party expects "to reach cooperative goals." No one gets the whole cake.*

The competitive attitude does have a place in negotiating, as it focuses and integrates the energies of both parties. But instead of the plus and minus of a zero-sum game or mathematics, a successful negotiation can leave both parties with something of what they seek. A "total victory" by one side "contains the seed of its own destruction." The author gives examples from the world of sports and labor-management agreements to illustrate his point.

"The negotiator must learn when to stop," says Nierenberg, or else the reaction "can become uncontrolled and destructive." He gives an example from his own experience when he pushed too hard and came within a hair's breadth of losing everything. If even experts like the author can make such a mistake, others less skilled should take note.

The author concludes as he began, emphasizing cooperation, common interests, the behavioral process and the fact that everybody must win something. These principles should be kept in mind as the other readings that follow explore other facets of negotiation and its cousin, arbitration.

In a successful negotiation *everybody* wins.

NOT A GAME

Negotiating has often been compared to a game. A game has definite rules and a known set of values. Each player is limited in the moves he can make, the things he can and cannot do. True, some games have a greater element of chance than others, but in every game a set of rules governs the behavior of the players and enumerates their gains and losses. In games the rules show the risks and rewards. However, rules of this sort are not available in the unbounded life process of negotiation. In negotiating, any risks that are known have been learned from broad experience, not from a rule book. In a life situation the negotiator ordinarily has little or no control over the complex variables, the innumerable strategies, that the opposer may bring into the struggle. Even more difficult is to know the value structure upon which the opposer bases his strategy.

To look upon negotiation as a game to be played is to enter into the bargaining in a purely competitive spirit. With this attitude, the negotiator strives against other individuals for a goal which he alone hopes to attain. Even if he could persuade an opposer to "play" such a negotiating game, he would run the risk of being the absolute loser rather than the winner. In post-World War II Japan, some businessmen required that their employees study military strategy and tactics as a guide to successful business operations. How many of these employers realized that comparing business with war was only a metaphor? How many saw that the goal of a successful business deal is not a dead competitor?

The objective should be to achieve agreement, not total victory. Both parties must feel that they have gained something. Even if one side had had to give up a great deal, the overall picture is one of gain.

Negotiation, then, is not a game—and it is not war. Its goal is not a dead competitor. A negotiator ignores this point at his own peril.

A classic example is the recent history of the newspaper business in New York City. Bertram Powers, head of the printers' union, became nationally known as a man who "drives a hard bargain." With the aid of a couple of paralyzing strikes, the printers in New York achieved what seemed to be remarkable contracts. Not only did they obtain higher wages, but the newspapers were forbidden to institute such money-saving practices as the automated setting of market tables.

The printers won their points at the negotiating table—because they held out to the end. But the newspapers were forced into an economic straitjacket. Three major newspapers merged and finally, after another long strike, folded, leaving New York with one evening and two morning papers—and leaving thousands of newspaper people with no place to work. The negotiation was "successful," but the patient died.

"COOPERATIVE EGOTISM"

Think of negotiation as a cooperative enterprise. If both parties enter the situation on a cooperative basis, there is a strong likelihood that they will be persuaded to strive for goals that can be shared equally. This does not mean that every goal will be of the same value to the participants. But it does mean that there is greater possibility for each participant to reach successful cooperative goals.

However, the competitive attitude need not be abandoned. It serves as an integrating process, a rivalry that coordinates the activities of individuals. A single side of a scissors by itself cannot cut. Competition that permits each man to measure his competence or means against the other's—and to be rewarded proportionally—is really a cooperative achievement.

A great impetus to reaching an accord is the search for common interest levels. Franklin D. Roosevelt stated: "It has always seemed to me that the best symbol of common sense was a bridge." However, let us add what Robert Benchley says: "It seems to me that the most difficult part of building a bridge would be the start."

Always be on the alert to convert divergent interests into channels of common desires. In exploring these channels, both parties to the negotiation may be stimulated by the idea of sharing common goals. These goals are reached by finding mutual interests and needs, by emphasizing the matters that can be agreed upon, and by not dwelling on points of difference. . . .

There are many advantages to the cooperative approach. Results can be greater and the solution more lasting. Children are taught that one plus one is two and two minus one is one. Throughout their lives most people are inclined to apply arithmetical principles in their judgment of what is desirable or undesirable. It is not difficult, then, to understand the person who applies the "I win, you lose" (plus/minus) arithmetical concept to his negotiations. He is merely using simple equations in his judgment of human behavior.

However, these equations do not apply to all human efforts. Cooperative human efforts can be cumulative when ideas, rather than material goods, are exchanged. If you and I exchange ideas, where each of us had one idea we now each have two, and thus one plus one equals four. Certainly no one has lost by this transaction. It is possible that in making other people wealthier, happier, and more secure you will have more of your own needs satisfied. This is, in fact, an ideal result of any negotiation.

Many negotiations conducted in a highly competitive manner have ended in what seemed to be a complete victory for one side. The alleged winner was in possession of everything he wanted and the loser had suffered a humiliating defeat. However, such a "settlement" will rarely stay settled. Unless the terms arrived at have been advantageous in some way to the "loser," he will soon seek means of changing the settlement. Unlike a game, there is no "end" to a life negotiation situation. . . . An overwhelmingly one-sided settlement breeds trouble and in the end will only prove to be a great waste of time and effort. It contains the seed of its own destruction. Yet rigidly competitively oriented people often wonder why they can never seem to conclude anything. They say they work hard, but luck or life never seems to break for them. Something always goes wrong.

This should not be surprising. We could complete few tasks without the complete cooperation and assisting efforts of others. Who would drive an automobile if he could not rely on other people to comply with traffic regulations?

There are other advantages to the cooperative approach. Results can be greater, solutions more lasting.

A few years back a well-known professional athlete wanted more money in his yearly contract. For several seasons he had attempted to do his own negotiating but had failed to achieve what he considered a satisfactory settlement. Although the athlete was a man of considerable wealth and intelligence, he was shy and, by his own confession, no match for his hard-driving general manager. Furthermore, the general manager had an ace up his sleeve—the "reserve clause" that makes it impossible for an athlete to move from one team to another.

The manager invariably forced the ball player to sign for less than he deserved. The athlete had become so demoralized that he conducted negotiations with this man solely by letter. He felt defeated before he even started to negotiate.

Then an agent approached the athlete. He suggested a solution. True, the "reserve clause" precluded any threat of playing for another team. However, there was nothing to keep the player from dropping out of sports.

Despite the athlete's shyness, he had a pleasant personality and was not bad looking. People with far less in the way of presence have made it in show business. Negotiations were begun with an independent film producer. There was talk of a five-year contract.

Now, suddenly, the pressure was on the general manager. The fans would react adversely if the star left the team, and business would drop off. The athlete negotiated an enormous increase. The next season other members of the team used the same techniques. They pitilessly "held up" the manager for as much as the traffic would bear.

Had the manager been satisfied to negotiate, rather than dominate, he would have directed his efforts toward the cooperative goal of improving the club rather than toward resisting just demands. The lesson to be learned is, never press for the "best" deal and thereby corner your opponent. As Edna St. Vincent Millay observed, "Even the lowly rat in adversity has courage to turn and fight."

REACHING A LIFE BALANCE

Few negotiations proceed smoothly. I have participated in literally thousands of negotiations, and no two are ever alike. Sometimes a client managed to secure close to 100 per cent of the pie—when he was bargaining from a position of strength. At other times I have been forced to negotiate with almost all the strength massed on the opposite side of the table. In such a case one has to be content with salvaging as much as possible from the situation.

Negotiating is give and take. However, each side is watching the opposer for any clue to his prejudices that may provide a negotiating advantage.

It is fascinating to observe two master negotiators battling it out. As a rule they are able to arrive at a settlement very quickly. They go directly to the heart of the problem and waste no time on extraneous matters. Each side, after an initial period of probing and feeling out the other, promptly realizes that he is dealing with a master and that a quick solution is forthcoming. Many labor strikes could actually be settled at a first or second meeting but for political or economic reasons, the agreement is not verbalized until a later date.

However, when the bargaining is conducted with all the coolness of professional gamblers at a poker game, this is merely a surface mannerism. In actuality, experts do not play a negotiating game. They are adept at the art of compromise and accommodation. They are fully aware of the necessity for finding a common ground of interest, and they avoid the pitfalls of a competitive I-must-win-the-game attitude. At the earliest possible moment in the negotiation, each side manages to convey to the other its maximum concessions and the minimum concessions expected in return. This is not done explicitly, but subtly, by innuendo and deliberate tip-offs. Such skills and techniques, arrived at through long experience and training, enable the master negotiators to reach a satisfactory settlement. Examples of this type of negotiation are seen daily in the United Nations. However, remember that the final decisions are not within the control of these professionals. They act as agents for their individual governments and cannot effect satisfactory settlements to world problems by themselves.

WHEN CONTROLS BECOME UNCONTROLLABLE

Sometimes, when an opponent seems "on the run," there is a temptation to push him as hard as possible. But that one extra push may be the one that breaks the camel's back.

Simply stated, one of the first lessons the negotiator must learn is when to stop. Negotiation, like alcohol, does not conform to the simple mathematical principles we learned as children. It's that little extra "one for the road" that can kill you. There is a critical point in negotiation beyond which the reaction—like that of an atomic pile—can become uncontrolled and destructive. An example may be found in the extensive research that was conducted into the causes of unscheduled work stoppages—strikes, accidents, unavailability of supplies—occurring a few years ago in the coal mines around Manchester, England. It was found that when the group size in the individual work force exceeded a critical number, the stoppages occurred.

So the negotiator's aim should never be "just one more." He must sense when he is approaching the critical point—and stop short of it. All parties to a negotiation should come out with some needs satisfied.

This can't happen when one of the parties is demolished.

It's all too easy to lose sight of this principle. In the heat of negotiation, one can be carried away.

Once I was retained by a client who was the last tenant in an office building scheduled to be demolished. The new owner planned a skyscraper in place of this four-story building. All the other tenants had moved out. My function, in addition to protecting my client's rights, was to work out a solution acceptable to both parties.

The landlord recognized that, to get my client out of the building, he would have to pay money. His question was, "How little?" The landlord first approached me personally. (In my opinion, this was a mistake. Later we will take up the value, in certain situations, of bargaining through an agent who has only limited authority.)

"How much do you want?" the landlord asked. "I'm sorry," I replied. "You are the one who is buying. I am not selling." This placed the burden of opening the negotiations upon him. So far so good. We both recognized that my client was in a very strong position. He had two years to go on his lease, and the landlord needed to get started immediately.

The opening offer indicated the landlord's willingness to pay moving expenses and the differential in rent. I declined to get into anything other than the cash figure he was offering—"How much?" After some byplay he offered $25,000. I refused even to consider it. He left the office.

The landlord's next tactic was delay. But this worked against him, because my client was perfectly willing to stay put. When delay did not work, the next approach came through the landlord's attorney. I told the attorney that when he came up with a figure that was in the "ball park," we would negotiate. "Fifty thousand," he said. "Not in the ball park," I replied.

Approaches continued, with the offer getting higher. I never named a figure until the final stages. But I did do some homework, figuring out what the landlord had paid for the building, what it would cost him to keep the building vacant, what it would cost him to hold the mortgage commitments until the end of my client's lease.

I came up with a figure of a quarter of a million dollars. Knowing that this was speculation, and not wanting to squeeze the last dollar, I cut this in half. The landlord's lawyer was forced to bid against his own figure and finally settle for $125,000. It seemed to me that this was a solution that satisfied everyone.

However, I was in for a surprise. When the landlord's lawyers delivered the check, a young attorney said to me, "Five dollars more and you might have had a crane hit the building." The crane was on the property, and it just might have struck the old building—"accidentally"—so that it would be declared a hazard that had to be torn down. In that case my client might have gotten nothing. . . .

My client was vulnerable. If I had realized how close I was to the top figure, I would have settled at a lower price. The danger of going too far is not worth the risk. . . .

Successful negotiations are not sensational. No strikes, law suits, or wars occur. Both parties feel that they have gained something. Even if one side has to give up a great deal, the overall picture is one of mutual gain.

To sum up thus far: negotiation is a cooperative enterprise; common interests must be sought; negotiation is a behavioral process, not a game; in a good negotiation, everybody wins something.

Questions

1. How does negotiation differ from a "game"?

2. Does negotiation eliminate the need for competition? Explain. What positive qualities does competition bring out in a negotiator?

3. Why does the negotiator who "wins everything" really lose?

4. Do you think both sides in such international conferences as the Geneva arms reduction talks follow Nierenberg's principles? In what ways do they not?

5. Give an example from your own experience in which you negotiated well or badly.

2

Communication and Conflict— Management Skills: Strategies for Individual and Systems Change

Neil H. Katz and John W. Lawyer

This article originally appeared in *National Forum,* Fall 1983.

Like the U.S. cavalry riding to the rescue, Katz and Lawyer were brought into a conflict-ridden school problem. Unlike the cavalry, the authors—a professor at Syracuse University and the head of Henneberry Hill Consultants—brought with them peaceful ways of change.

After extensive interviews, they proposed a collaborative (win/win) model of action based on "trust, honesty and mutual respect" in the course of a two-day, off-site seminar. Out of this emerged a transition team to meet weekly throughout the school year, temporary task forces to deal with specific problems and a skills training course for all parties to the negotiations.

The authors define communication as "an exchange of meaning between persons that allows each to influence the other's experience." They lay stress on conflict management, a process which reveals the existence and causes of basic disagreements, followed by problem-solving methods in a manner that respects the rights and feelings of everybody. To bring out the best ("actualizing values") in the participants, Katz and Lawyer concentrate on developing a set of skills: instrumental (competence); interpersonal (generosity); imaginal (generation of ideas); systems (relating parts to the whole).

The skills training course runs from 30 to 36 hours and covers six areas: information sharing, reflective listening, problem solving, assertiveness, conflict management and skill selection. Examples illustrate the uses to which these skills are put. The authors also go into detail on how they conduct these sessions so as to increase their effectiveness.

As a consequence of such training programs, organizations usually experience a growth in the quality and quantity of work done, better use of resources, a spirit of cooperation, improved planning and other desirable outcomes. In the particular school system studied, the atmosphere im-

proved markedly. The same might be said for other organizations, large and small, that devote similar efforts to peaceful change.

Smarting from two painful contract negotiations, the teachers' association, administrative staff, and board of education in a large public school system were confused about what to do next. They faced yet another round of negotiations, this time in an atmosphere of heightened alienation, with each group holding the others accountable for the difficult situation in which they found themselves as individuals and as a school system.

At this point, the system's superintendent invited us as consultants to help the school move from its present adversarial (win/lose) model of dealing with conflict to a collaborative (win/win) model based on trust, honesty, and mutual respect.

Our response was to begin by conducting an organizational diagnosis. This involved one-on-one interviews with members of the executive committee of the teachers' association, with a sampling of the teachers, with the school's administrative staff, and with the school board members. After analyzing the resulting data, we decided to engage the members of the board of education, the administrative staff, and the executive board of the teachers' association in a two-day, off-site experience. Its design involved activities that would help surface the conflict, heal some of its scars, and develop a concrete action plan to bring about systemwide change, leading to a collaborative model of dealing with differences. The action plan involved three phases:

1. The creation of a transition team to facilitate change in the system toward win/win outcomes. Its membership consisted of two persons each from the board of education and the administrative staff as well as four persons from the teachers' association. This group agreed to meet weekly throughout the school year.

2. The creation of temporary task forces to deal with specific problems identified in the off-site experience. Their work is coordinated by the transition team.

3. Skills training in communication and conflict management, presented in both a five-day design offered during the summer or a two-weekend design offered during the school year. All members of the school's administrative, teaching, and noninstructional staff, and the board of education were invited to participate.

As a consequence of these efforts—specifically employing methods to enhance communication and conflict-management skills to bring about significant change in individuals and in organizations—this school system is moving rapidly toward a collaborative model of managing disputes. It is a model that allows all involved parties to experience positive outcomes, with their basic individual needs and interests satisfied.

Before considering the specifics of the content and process of communication and conflict-management skills training such as that offered in the polarized school system discussed above, we must briefly examine the basic concepts involved and the broader principles of values acquisition in which the skills training is grounded.

In our work, we define communication as an exchange of meaning between persons that allows each to influence the other's experience. Communication takes place at both conscious and unconscious levels. Conflict management is the process of becoming aware of a conflict, diagnosing its nature, and employing an appropriate problem-solving method to enable the persons involved to get their own needs met without infringing on the rights of others (that is, to simultaneously achieve their personal goals and enhance their relationships). As constructive techniques are engaged to manage conflict, feelings of self-confidence, competence, self-worth, and power increase, thereby enhancing the overall capacity of the system to respond to conflict in positive ways.

We believe that positive change can occur in a system when a significant number of its members are functioning at a level of development that enables them to make decisions based on an internal set of moral (other-regarding) principles rather than looking outside themselves for guidance and direction. This presupposes that the people in the system are largely engaged in the pursuit of their personal needs to be themselves, direct their own lives, and express creative insight. It also presupposes that their physical needs for safety and security as well as their needs for acceptance, affirmation, approval, and achievement are largely met. When people are developmentally able to make decisions independently, they can choose to meet not only their own needs but the needs of the system which includes other people as well.

Achieving this level of development requires that the system's members acquire such values as assertion, empathy, mutual accountability, flexibility, honesty, expressiveness, and initiation. Brian Hall and Helen Thompson, in their book *Leadership Through Values* (New York: Paulist Press, 1980), have defined values as priorities we choose and act upon that creatively enhance our own lives and the lives of those around us. Our lives are, in fact, motivated by values.

Integrating and actualizing values in our lives requires the development of skills (a skill being defined in this context as an internalized ability to actualize a value in behavior). For integrated development to occur, growth must take place in four skill areas:

- Instrumental skills: the ability to act with intelligence, using both mind and body to be competent in a chosen endeavor.
- Interpersonal skills: the ability to act with generosity and understanding toward others, which flows from self-knowledge, together with ability to represent one's experience to another with accuracy and clarity.
- Imaginal skills: the ability to initiate new ideas and use data-based information to develop new concepts and courses of action, including the ability to create by integrating instrumental and interpersonal skills in innovative ways.
- Systems skills: the ability to plan and design changes in whole systems and act based on a capacity to see how the parts relate to the whole. These skills combine a blend of imagination, sensitivity to others, and competence and they help to integrate instrumental, interpersonal, and imaginal skills.

For personal and systems growth to occur, members of the system must develop these skills in an integrated way and incorporate them into their everyday behavior.

The learning experience in communication and conflict management we have developed provides participants the opportunity to refine and integrate these skills. It focuses on the following specific interpersonal and imaginal skills that, when mastered, will enable the participants to communicate and manage conflict effectively and participate productively in systems change:

- Expressing and sharing emotions.
- Expressing anger and resentment in nonharmful ways.
- Identifying and expressing their own and others' thoughts and feelings accurately in both interpersonal and group settings.
- Using imagination, fantasy, and reflection.
- Listening to others attentively, with empathy and respect, thereby hearing and understanding more clearly what others are communicating.
- Enabling others to see and hear themselves accurately.
- Articulating needs, interests, and personal goals clearly.
- Clarifying and solving problems.
- Using creativity to imagine new and innovative outcomes for problems.
- Asserting in a straightforward manner to ensure that their basic human rights are secured without infringing on the rights of others.
- Affirming others for the positive impact they have had on the participants.
- Remaining calm under stress and in high-anxiety situations.

- Settling disputes involving both needs and values in constructive, resourceful, and collaborative ways.
- Negotiating differences in interests.

The specific skills listed above are grouped into the following six skill areas, designed for presentation during a 30- to 36-hour learning experience:

Information sharing. This involves expressing one's thoughts and feelings to another with clarity and accuracy and helping another do likewise. It involves representing one's experience to another without deleting, generalizing, or distorting information. Information sharing is enhanced by improving one's ability to establish and maintain rapport through increased sensory acuity, appropriate pacing, and selecting a manner of communicating that effectively mirrors the other's frame of reference.

Reflective listening. This entails following the thoughts and feelings of another and understanding what the other is saying from his or her point of view. It involves respectfully hearing both the thoughts and feelings of the other and then expressing (reflecting) them succinctly to him or her in one's own words to capture the essence of what the other is communicating. This skill is fundamental in constructive communication and is an essential ingredient in effective problem solving, assertion, and conflict management.

Problem solving. The ability to clarify another's problem and then use a problem-solving process to help the other generate a number of possible creative outcomes and select and commit to a constructive solution is an important skill for participants to develop.

Assertion. Everyone must develop the ability to express his/her thoughts, feelings, and opinions without infringing on the rights of another. Assertiveness involves achieving one's personal goals without damaging one's relationship with the other or injuring his or her self-esteem. Participants learn to formulate and send assertion messages that enable them to get their needs and interests met in effective ways.

Conflict management. Conflict management is a process of diagnosing a conflict situation and engaging the appropriate problem-solving approach to generate a solution that satisfies the interests of all parties involved. The learning experience introduces two strategies for producing mutually acceptable outcomes: one for conflicts involving mutually exclusive needs, goals, means, and scarce resources and another for conflicts involving fundamental differences in values, beliefs, and preferences.

Skill selection. We have found that it is also important to know when to use which skill.

In the ordinary communication situation, the feeling or energy level of both persons involved in the relationship is normal, with both usually being able to adequately represent their experience. Information-sharing skills are especially useful in this situation to prevent the generalization, distortion, or deletion of information.

The second situation is where another person has a problem or a pressing need or is feeling a particularly high level of positive or negative energy on an issue. In this case, the skills of reflective listening and problem solving are required. Within this area, three specific applications emerge. The first involves reflective listening where the problem or issue presented has no solution—for example, the death of a loved one. In this instance, reflective listening skills provide an accepting and supportive presence to the other person. The second application occurs when a person is presenting a problem or need for which a solution is possible. By using reflective-listening skills, one can commit to be with the other person as he or she discusses the pressing issue. In talking the matter through, the other can acquire new insight and become able to move directly to his or her own solution. A third application involves a situation where a person has correctly identified a problem but is unable to resolve the matter and is seeking assistance. In this case, both reflective listening and problem-solving skills are used to appropriately help the other.

A third situation emerges when you are the one who has a problem or a pressing need or you are experiencing especially high emotional energy or strong feelings about an issue. In this case, the skill of assertion is most appropriate.

In the fourth situation, the parties involved are experiencing strong feelings regarding opposing needs or values, requiring the skills of conflict management.

In short, knowing when to use which of these skills requires the ability to carefully observe from moment to moment where the energy in the relationship is and identify who has the pressing need. Once one is clear about who has the high energy or a pressing need, one can more readily select the appropriate skill.

In presenting communication and conflict-management skills, we have adapted an approach developed by Allen Ivey called microskill training. Ivey divides skills into small components, called microskills, which can more easily be presented and acquired than a skill in its entirety. In learning to play tennis, for example, we might first learn to hold the racket, then to place the ball, and finally to serve the ball using the racket. The skill components are acquired and added one-by-one, so that finally the entire skill area is mastered.

In our work we believe that the process used in training is fundamental to success in the acquisition of skills. We have found that effective delivery of communication and conflict-management skill learning involves the following process elements:

Modeling. Modeling the use of the skills we teach throughout the learning experience is critical to skill development. Each question is appropriately paraphrased. Each challenge is carefully heard nondefensively, using reflective listening skills.

Theory presentation. Each skill is introduced in simple language, using visual aids and examples from our personal and professional lives. The examples enable participants to relate the skill to real-life experience.

Demonstration. Each skill presented is demonstrated, usually using a volunteer participant who offers to share with us a concrete problem to enable everyone to see the skill in use in a real-life situation. Each demonstration is critiqued to extract maximum learning from the experience.

Practice. Since we believe that skills are acquired through use, a good portion of the learning experience involves skill practice. For skill-practice sessions, we use a small-group model involving three persons. In a reflective-listening practice, for instance, Person A describes a real-life concern or problem while Person B listens using the skill; Person C observes the process and leads a critique at the end of the session.

Feedback. Following each segment of the learning experience, we invite feedback about both its process and its content, in the belief that every learning experience is enhanced by periodic reflections and conversations around those aspects of the training that are going well and those that need to be adjusted in order to facilitate the participants' skill development. During those times set aside for discussion, each person is invited to share his or her thoughts and feelings about the experience as it is progressing.

The workbook. The workbook performs two functions: It provides a reference for material presented in the learning experience, and it includes written exercises that allow participants to practice responses to communication situations. These exercises are especially useful in the reflective listening and assertion components of the learning experience.

Personal documentation. At the beginning of each segment of the learning experience, participants are invited to write their current perspectives on the particular subject being presented. Later, after learning has occurred, participants are invited to capture another perspective, compare the two, and identify the new insights acquired.

Role-plays. Role-playing exercises are presented to permit effective skill practice in the conflict-management section of the learning experience. In each role-playing exercise, two roles are established—one for a skilled party and the other for an unskilled party. The role-plays allow participants to practice conflict-management skills in a safe, supportive environment.

In our consulting experience, we have found when individuals undertake training in communication and conflict-management skills, the systems in which they function experience significant improvement in the effectiveness of their members and their organization. As appropriate reflective listening, problem solving, assertion, and conflict-management skills are used, individuals communicate and deal with differences more constructively. Moreover, the health of the entire system is enhanced, as measured by improvements in such factors as:

• Overall performance of individuals and work groups, in terms of both quality and quantity of output;

• Organizational efficiency: the relationship of resources used by the organization to the quality of the product or services produced;

• Cooperation and coordination between individuals and work groups;

• Action planning and decision making, in terms of quality and timeliness;

• Organizational effectiveness: the degree to which the organization reaches its goals;

• The organization's climate and the level of morale and creativity exhibited by its members.

In short, the acquisition of communication and conflict-management skills empowers individuals with concrete strategies that enable them to help one another and attend to their own needs and interests in ways that enhance their self-esteem and improve their interpersonal relationships. More constructive interactions then impact favorably on the performance of the organization as a whole.

The school system we described at the beginning of this article has already experienced some of these benefits. As more and more people in the system have completed the basic communication and conflict-management learning experience, the quality of their interactions and the performance of the school as a whole has improved. Conflicts that were previously handled in adversarial terms are now being addressed in collaborative ways, with attempts being made to negotiate disputes so that all parties involved experience win/win outcomes with their basic needs and interests met. Skill training in communication and conflict management has indeed been the foundation of this system's broad-based change effort.

Questions

1. What are the advantages and disadvantages of bringing outside consultants into a dispute?

2. The authors give their definition of "communication." Can you think of any others?

3. What steps would you recommend to keep "conflict management" from being manipulated in favor of one party?

4. How would you react to the statement that all the authors are doing is putting common sense into fancy language? State your reasons.

5. The article speaks of feedback as part of the learning process. Define feedback and explain its significance.

3
The Techniques of Nonviolent Action

Gene Sharp

This article originally appeared in *Exploring Nonviolent Alternatives*, 1970.

The largely non-violent revolution in the Philippine Islands in February 1986 demonstrates how even a powerful autocrat like Ferdinand Marcos could be toppled when the people and their organizations rise up against him. In this excerpt from his 1970 book, Gene Sharp, a proponent and tactician of non-violent popular action, explains some of the basic principles of this strategy. It is significant that the U.S. Catholic bishops, in their 1983 pastoral letter, "The Challenge of Peace: God's Promise and Our Response," call for the training of citizens in "peaceable non-compliance" as a means of deterring an invading force.

Sharp distinguishes between military and non-violent action. He describes the purpose of military action as that of "inflicting heavy destruction" on an enemy. Non-violent action, on the other hand, seeks "to deny the enemy the human assistance and cooperation which are necessary if he is to exercise control over the population."

The author points out that a ruler—even a dictatorial one—must depend on the populace for such services as business, transportation, the bureaucracy and the police to make his rule effective. He further explains that the strategy consists of non-cooperation in those matters in which they are expected to obey and the performance of actions they are not expected to do. He insists that this is action, not inaction, passivity, submission or cowardice. Sharp also says that the strategies he recommends are different from pacifism, although he does not explain how. Perhaps the answer may be found in the fact that such actions may be motivated by religious or ethical motives, or purely pragmatic ones.

Sharp states that there are no less than 197 forms of non-violent action. He puts them into three categories: non-violent protest and persuasion, non-cooperation and non-violent intervention.

In the first category, he lists such things as marches, picketing, "haunting" officials, public meetings, distribution of literature and even humorous pranks. One thinks of the partially successful but ultimately defeated actions by members of the Solidarity Union in Poland.

The second category involves non-cooperative actions such as social and economic boycotts, strikes of all sorts and political non-cooperation. These are designed to deny the oppressor the ordinary activities of governance. For success, Sharp warns, sufficient numbers of people must take part.

The third method, non-violent intervention, challenges the opponent more directly, through sit-ins, fasts, non-violent obstruction and parallel government. Assuming "fearlessness and discipline," he says that relatively small numbers of people may have a "disproportionately large impact."

Such actions, states the author, may lead to conversion of the opponent, who may "come around to a new point of view." Failing this, the opponent may decide "to grant the demands of the nonviolent activists in a situation where he still has a choice of action." "Nonviolent coercion" goes beyond the first two steps. The ruler's power begins to disintegrate and he is no longer able to control the situation. This is eventually what happened to Marcos, though not without the help of the army.

Sharp states that repression may actually function as a "jiu-jitsu" tactic, in which the opponent is thrown off balance and manages to alienate the main population. If repression produces large numbers of adversaries to the regime "it will have clearly rebounded against the opponent."

The unique value of Sharp's analysis is that it provides suitable alternatives to submission and open warfare. However, it requires clear-headed leadership and discipline among the followers, qualities that are hard to maintain in many instances.

It is widely believed that military combat is the only effective means of struggle in a wide variety of situations of acute conflict. However, there is another whole approach to the waging of social and political conflict. Any proposed substitute for war in the defense of freedom must involve wielding power, confronting and engaging an invader's military might, and waging effective combat. The technique of nonviolent action, although relatively ignored and undeveloped, may be able to meet these requirements, and provide the basis for a defense policy.

ALTERNATIVE APPROACH TO THE CONTROL OF POLITICAL POWER

Military action is based largely on the idea that the most effective way of defeating an enemy is by inflicting heavy destruction on his armies, military equipment, transport system, factories, and cities. Weapons are designed to kill or destroy with maximum efficiency. Nonviolent action is based on a different approach: to deny the enemy the human assistance and cooperation which are necessary if he is to exercise control over the population. It is thus based on a more fundamental and sophisticated view of political power.

A ruler's power is ultimately dependent on support from the people he would rule. His moral authority, economic resources, transport system, government bureaucracy, army, and police—to name but a few immediate sources of his power—rest finally upon the cooperation and assistance of other people. If there is general conformity, the ruler is powerful.

But people do not always do what their rulers would like them to do. The factory manager recognizes this when he finds his workers leaving their jobs and machines, so that the production line ceases operation; or when he finds the workers persisting in doing something on the job which he has forbidden them to do. In many areas of social and political life comparable situations are commonplace. A man who has been a ruler and thought his power secure may discover that his subjects no longer believe he has any moral right to give them orders, that his laws are disobeyed, that the country's economy is paralyzed, that his soldiers and police are lax in carrying out repression or openly mutiny, and even that his bureaucracy no longer takes orders. When this happens, the man who has been ruler becomes simply another man, and his political power dissolves, just as the factory manager's power does when the workers no longer cooperate and obey. The equipment of his army may remain intact, his soldiers uninjured and very much alive, his cities unscathed, the factories and transport systems in full operational capacity, and the government buildings and offices unchanged. Yet because the human assistance which had created and supported his political power has been withdrawn, the former ruler finds that his political power has disintegrated.

NONVIOLENT ACTION

The technique of nonviolent action, which is based on this approach to the control of political power and the waging of political struggles, has been the subject of many misconceptions. . . .

The term nonviolent action refers to those methods of protest, noncooperation and intervention in which the actionists, without employing physical violence, refuse to do certain things which they are expected, or required, to do; or do certain things which they are not expected, or are forbidden, to do. In a particular case there can of course be a combination of acts of omission and acts of commission. . . .

While it is not violent, it is action, and not inaction; passivity, submission, and cowardice must be surmounted if it is to be used. It is a means of conducting conflicts and waging struggles, and is not to be equated with (though it may be accompanied by) purely verbal dissent or solely psychological influence. It is not pacifism, and in fact has in the vast majority of cases been applied by nonpacifists. The motives for the adoption of nonviolent action may be religious or ethical, or they may be based on considerations of expediency. Nonviolent action is not an escapist approach to the problem of violence, for it can be applied in struggles against opponents relying on violent sanctions. The fact that in a conflict one side is nonviolent does not imply that the other side will also refrain from violence. Certain forms of nonviolent action may be regarded as efforts to persuade by action, while others are more coercive.

METHODS OF NONVIOLENT ACTION

There is a very wide range of methods, or forms, of nonviolent action, and at least 197 have been identified. They fall into three classes—nonviolent protest and persuasion, noncooperation, and nonviolent intervention.

Generally speaking, the methods of nonviolent protest are symbolic in their effect and produce an awareness of the existence of dissent. Under tyrannical regimes, however, where opposition is stifled, their impact can in some circumstances be very great. Methods of nonviolent protest include marches, pilgrimages, picketing, vigils, "haunting" officials, public meetings, issuing and distributing protest literature, renouncing honors, protest emigration, and humorous pranks.

The methods of nonviolent noncooperation, if sufficient numbers take part, are likely to present the opponent with difficulties in maintaining the normal efficiency and operation of the system; and in extreme cases the system itself may be threatened. Methods of nonviolent noncooperation include various types of social noncooperation (such as social boycotts), economic boycotts (such as consumers' boycott, traders' boycott, rent refusal, and international trade embargo), strikes (such as the general strike, strike by resignation, industry strike, go-slow, and economic shutdown), and political noncooperation (such as boycott of government employment, boycott of elections, administrative noncooperation, civil disobedience, and mutiny.

The methods of nonviolent intervention have some features in common with the first two classes, but also challenge the opponent more directly; and, assuming that fearlessness and discipline are maintained, relatively small numbers may have a disproportionately large impact. Methods of nonviolent intervention include sit-ins, fasts, reverse strikes, nonviolent obstructions, nonviolent invasion, and parallel government. . . .

Just as in military battle weapons are carefully selected, taking into account such factors as their range and effect, so also in nonviolent struggle the choice of specific methods is very important.

MECHANISMS OF CHANGE

In nonviolent struggles there are, broadly speaking, three mechanisms by which change is brought about. Usually there is a combination of the three. They are conversion, accommodation, and nonviolent coercion.

George Lakey has described the conversion mechanism thus: "By conversion we mean that the opponent, as the result of the actions of the nonviolent person or group, comes around to a new point of view which embraces the ends of the nonviolent actor." This conversion can be influenced by reason or argument, but in nonviolent action it is also likely to be influenced by emotional and moral factors, which can in turn be stimulated by the suffering of the nonviolent actionists, who seek to achieve their goals without inflicting injury on other people.

Attempts at conversion, however, are not always successful, and may not even be made. Accommodation as a mechanism of nonviolent action falls in an intermediary position between conversion and nonviolent coercion, and elements of both of the other mechanisms are generally involved. In accommodation, the opponent, although not converted, decides to grant the demands of the nonviolent actionists in a situation where he still has a choice of action. The social situation within which he must operate has been altered enough by nonviolent action to compel a change in his own response to the conflict; perhaps because he has begun to doubt the rightness of his position, perhaps because he does not think the matter worth the trouble caused by the struggle, and perhaps because he anticipates coerced defeat and wishes to accede gracefully or with a minimum of losses.

Nonviolent coercion may take place in any of three circumstances. Defiance may become too widespread and massive for the ruler to be able to control it by repression; the social and political system may become paralyzed; or the extent of defiance or disobedience among the ruler's own soldiers and other agents may undermine his capacity to apply repression. Nonviolent coercion becomes possible when those applying nonviolent action succeed in withholding, directly or indirectly, the necessary sources of the ruler's political power. His power then disintegrates, and he is no longer able to control the situation, even though he still wishes to do so.

NONVIOLENT ACTION VERSUS VIOLENCE

There can be no presumption that an opponent, faced with an opposition relying solely on nonviolent methods, will suddenly renounce his capacity for violence. Instead, nonviolent action can operate against opponents able and willing to use violent sanctions, and can counter their violence in such a way that they are thrown politically off balance in a kind of political jiu-jitsu.

Instead of confronting the opponent's police and troops with the same type of forces, nonviolent actionists counter these agents of the opponent's power indirectly. Their aim is to demonstrate that repression is incapable of cowing the populace, and to deprive the opponent of his existing support, thereby undermining his ability or will to continue with the repression. Far from indicating the failure of nonviolent action, repression often helps to make clear the cruelty of the political system being opposed, and so to alienate support from it. Repression is often a kind of recognition from the opponent that the nonviolent action constitutes a serious threat to his policy or regime, one which he finds it necessary to combat.

Just as in war danger from enemy fire does not always force front line soldiers to panic and flee, so in nonviolent action repression does not necessarily produce submission. True, repression may be effective, but it may fail to halt defiance, and in this case the opponent will be in difficulties. Repression against a nonviolent group which persists in face of it and maintains nonviolent discipline may have the following effects: it may alienate the general population from the opponent's regime, making them more likely to join the resistance; it may alienate the opponent's usual supporters and agents, and their initial uneasiness may grow into internal opposition and at times into noncooperation and disobedience; and it may rally general public opinion (domestic or international) to the support of the nonviolent actionists; though the effectiveness of this last factor varies greatly from one situation to another, it may produce various types of supporting actions. If repression thus produces larger numbers of nonviolent actionists, thereby increasing the defiance, and if it leads to internal dissent among the opponent's supporters, thereby reducing his capacity to deal with the defiance, it will clearly have rebounded against the opponent.

Questions

1. How does military action differ from non-violent action? Do you think this distinction holds up in real situations? Why, or why not?

2. Do you think that non-violent action is different from pacifism? If so, in what ways? Are the two compatible or incompatible? Explain.

3. Briefly describe conversion, accommodation and non-violent coercion, as used by the author. In which situations is each most appropriate?

4. What does Sharp mean by describing non-violent action as "a kind of political jiu-jitsu?

5. Can you think of any situations besides the peaceful revolution in the Philippines where non-violent action has led to the removal of repressive regimes?

4
You Be The Arbitrator

American Arbitration Association

Each case story is a capsule version taken from a real case administered under the Voluntary Labor Arbitration Rules of the Association, and each was reported in AAA's monthly award reporting service, Summary of Labor Arbitration Awards. *Naturally, this brief, popular presentation does not permit full analysis of all the important details involved in the case. These stories should therefore be used not for in-depth examination of the issues, but as a training aid to give the reader an opportunity for a quick, superficial judgment. A synopsis of the decision by the arbitrator in the real case will be found at the end of this chapter.*

Most educators find "You Be the Arbitrator" useful for the practical insight it affords into day-to-day problems arising in the application and interpretation of collective bargaining agreements. The popular format helps stimulate discussion, and the student, whether in the academic environment or in industry, is brought to see that issues must be resolved within a general contractual framework.

Teachers, training specialists and discussion leaders naturally apply their own methods in using this pamphlet. Some consult the source (the Summary of Labor Arbitration Awards) *for a somewhat more comprehensive analysis of the case. Others may want the full text of the arbitrator's award, which can be purchased from AAA's Publications Department at 30 cents per page. (The typical labor arbitration award and opinion is about ten pages long.)*

No exact statistics are available, but it appears that a rather large percentage of those who read these stories, regardless of how limited their experience might be, come to the same conclusion the arbitrator reached in the real case. One can only speculate as to the reason. Perhaps it is that, underlying the many complicated and often difficult problems of contract interpretation, the arbitrator's task calls for plain common sense, of which an abundance is found among "amateurs" as well as professional arbitrators.

307

THE CASE OF THE HUMANE DEMOTION

John V. was promoted to a better job, which he performed compe-
tently as far as quality was concerned. But he never produced enough,
mostly because he just couldn't or wouldn't resist the temptation to chat
with everyone within earshot. Unfortunately, his work required him to be
in constant touch with other employees, which made matters worse. The
foreman spoke to John about this fault many times. In fact, the company
was later able to produce a dossier showing oral reprimands and even
warnings to the union.

Finally John was demoted to a lower-rated job, in a more isolated
area. The difference in pay was not great—only five cents an hour. But a
grievance was filed promptly. "You can't demote a man all of a sudden
without warning," the shop steward said. "You have a disciplinary system
that calls for oral warnings, written warnings, and other disciplinary action, but you never used it."

"If we followed the letter of that disciplinary system," the personnel
manager replied, "John would have been tossed out long ago. By demoting
him, we're being more humane. We're preserving his job."

Eventually the case went to arbitration. Suppose you were the arbitrator. How would you rule?

THE CASE OF WHO CAME FIRST

One Friday in February 1956, two men appeared at the personnel
office of an appliance manufacturing company looking for work. Both were
hired and instructed to start the following day. One was assigned to the 7
a.m.–4 p.m. shift, the other to the 4 p.m.–11 p.m. shift. Some years later,
the two men were still with the company but on the same shift. Work became slack and employees had to be laid off in accordance with plant-wide
seniority. It became a question of letting one of the two go. The man notified that he was to be laid off happened to be the one who had started on
the first shift. This led to a grievance.

"It's true the other man and I were hired on the same day and started
work on the same Monday," he argued. "But I started on an earlier shift.
That gives me an edge over him."

"Not at all," answered the personnel manager. "The contract defines
seniority as starting on the employee's original 'date of hire.' You two men
have identical seniority. I can select either one of you for layoff when your
date of hire is reached on the seniority list."

Eventually the case went to arbitration. Suppose you were the arbitrator. How would you rule?

THE CASE OF THE INNOCENT VICTIM

Tom K., a laborer in a nonferrous foundry, was picked up by the police one day on suspicion that he had passed a bad check during a night of overindulgence in a tavern. Bail was set, but Tom didn't have the money. He was kept in jail until his case was tried. The tavern owner withdrew charges; Tom was acquitted.

But that was not the end of his troubles. When Tom showed up for work, he was told he had been fired for unauthorized absence. "I couldn't help it," he explained. "They held me in jail until the trial. Besides, I was found not guilty. What kind of justice are you handing out when you fire an innocent man?"

"You may have been found innocent as far as the law is concerned," answered the company, "but the contract gives us the right to discharge men who are absent without good reason. Your reasons for absence aren't excusable. Besides, why didn't you get in touch with us right away and let us know the situation?"

Eventually the case went to arbitration. Suppose you were the arbitrator. How would you rule?

THE CASE OF THE NEAT NUT

Joe Lupo, a mechanic in a machine-building plant, came to work one day and found that someone—probably a fellow employee—had tampered with his tool box and broken the hinges. This would have been mildly distressing for anyone, but for Joe it was a calamity. As everyone in the shop knew, he was very fussy about the orderliness of his tools.

Unable to repair the tool box, Joe bought a new one and presented the bill to the company. "The contract requires all employees to furnish their own tools," he said. "That makes the company liable for damages and losses on company property."

The general foreman refused to okay the bill. The matter went through all the steps of grievance procedure without agreement. Finally, the union demanded arbitration.

Management appeared before the arbitrator, but the preliminary question of arbitrability was the main issue. The company's position was that the dispute was not arbitrable because there was nothing in the contract to require the company to reimburse employees for such damages. The union answered that the grievance was made arbitrable by the fact that employees were required to provide their own "tools of the trade" and by the fact that the company had reimbursed employees for losses in the past.

Eventually the case went to arbitration. Suppose you were the arbitrator. How would you rule?

THE CASE OF THE OVERTIME HOGS

Toward the end of the year, the foreman of a small appliance assembly department decided to keep his men on overtime to complete orders for the Christmas trade. There were 30 employees under his supervision, and he offered each of them five hours' overtime during a certain week. It didn't occur to him that a plan so obviously fair to all could ever possibly be the basis of a union grievance. But a grievance nevertheless resulted.

"Ten of these men are probationers," the shop steward reminded the foreman. "A right to share in overtime is not one of the privileges of seniority," the foreman replied. "As long as we give all employees an equal opportunity we're conforming to the agreement."

Eventually the case went to arbitration. Suppose you were the arbitrator. How would you rule?

THE CASE OF THE "SICK" MEN

Management of a furniture plant suspected that employees were pretending sickness to escape unpleasant tasks. It seemed that every time one of those assignments came up, the man who was supposed to do it would go to the first aid room with a headache or some other complaint not easy to diagnose and get a pass to leave the plant.

To control the situation, a new rule was established. It required an employee with such a pass to get a doctor's certificate of "fitness to work" before he could return. The union didn't protest.

One day, however, two men, after completing their regular eight-hour shift, begged off continuing for eight hours more with the excuse that they were "too tired and sick."

Their foreman wouldn't let them start next day without doctors' certificates. They got the statements, but the union filed a grievance.

Eventually the case went to arbitration. Suppose you were the arbitrator. How would you rule?

THE CASE OF THE FIRST-TIME LOSER

In negotiating a new contract with the union, management of an industrial equipment company insisted on a strong clause to cope with a serious problem of workers absenting themselves without calling in. The parties agreed to a series of penalties, ranging from reprimand for the first offense to discharge after the fifth violation.

Some months later, one employee failed to show up for work on a Monday and stayed out all week without getting any message to the personnel office. At the end of the fifth day, he was notified of his discharge as a fifth offender. When the union learned of this, a grievance was filed.

"Fifth offender nothing," said the shop steward. "The five days of absence were consecutive—one offense. The grievant can get a reprimand, that's all."

"Show me where the contract says that consecutive days of absence count as one day," replied the company. "He committed five offenses and got what the contract says was coming to him."

Eventually the case went to arbitration. Suppose you were the arbitrator. How would you rule?

THE CASE OF THE EDUCATED FOREMEN

The first problem following delivery of computers to an eastern company was to educate foremen and supervisors in their use. Management's solution was to close down the entire plant for a day so that all foremen and supervisors concerned with the new equipment could be sent to the computer manufacturer for a brief but intensive course of instruction. No doubt the supervisory staff was paid for this time, but hourly-rated employees were not. This led to a grievance.

"This is a lockout," the business agent said. "There's work to be done, and the employees are willing to do it. You can close the plant if you want to, but you have to pay them for the time."

"Since when?" the industrial relations director demanded to know. "Our contract does not contain a guaranteed workweek. We can close the plant if we have a good reason, and training supervisors is the best of reasons. If a senior man lost time while a junior worked, you would have a case. But we laid off the whole bargaining unit for one day, so you have no basis for objecting."

Eventually the case went to arbitration. Suppose you were the arbitrator. How would you rule?

THE CASE OF THE LATE SLEEPER

Thanksgiving day was a paid holiday in an auto parts manufacturing company. Management decided that the plant might just as well be closed the next day too. But one man, a maintenance mechanic, was ordered to report on Friday.

The mechanic had overeaten on Thanksgiving, then overslept on Friday. The result was that he punched in an hour and a half late for his holiday maintenance work in the plant.

The lateness wasn't held against him as a matter of discipline, but when he got his next paycheck he saw he wasn't paid for the holiday. "The union contract requires that you work the full regularly scheduled workdays surrounding the holiday as a condition for receiving holiday pay," the plant manager explained. "You forfeited holiday pay by reporting late."

The mechanic didn't think this was fair—neither did the shop steward.

Eventually the case went to arbitration. Suppose you were the arbitrator. How would you rule?

THE CASE OF THE UNWILLING TRAVELER

A company manufacturing electronic equipment often had to send its repairmen to distant cities to help install or repair pieces of apparatus. Some of the repairmen were glad to do this kind of work, others were reluctant to travel. When a union contract was negotiated, it was therefore agreed that "no employee will be required to go on an out-of-plant assignment unless he voluntarily accepts such assignment."

One summer, when management decided to add to the repair crew, the plant manager was very careful to hire a man who said he would like to travel. For several months, the new repairman worked in the plant, with no travel assignments coming his way. When the first out-of-plant assignment did come up, the repairman refused it.

"I know I agreed to travel," he admitted. "But that was before my wife had a baby. It's not convenient now and I refuse."

"If you won't travel you're not conforming to the terms of your employment," answered the personnel manager. "I'm giving to you two weeks' notice of dismissal beginning right now."

Eventually the case went to arbitration. Suppose you were the arbitrator. How would you rule?

THE ARBITRATORS' AWARDS

Caution: These awards do not indicate how other arbitrators might rule in apparently similar cases. Arbitrators do not follow precedents. Each case is decided on the basis of the contract, evidence, past practice and other facts involved.

THE HUMANE DEMOTION—John was ordered back on the

higher-rated job. The arbitrator admitted that this might result in John's dismissal altogether, because he was now officially warned that discharge would follow if he continued to perform less than the proper quantity of work. But this was the risk John must take. This conclusion, the arbitrator pointed out, followed from the fact that John was able to do his job properly. If he lacked ability the problem would not have been a disciplinary one and a different outcome would be indicated.

WHO CAME FIRST—The arbitrator wrote: "Dictionary definition and industrial usage agree that date of employment refers to the calendar day and not to the hour or minute when the employee began work." And so the grievance was denied.

THE INNOCENT VICTIM—The arbitrator wrote: "If the grievant had been found guilty, one might argue that he brought this period of imprisonment on himself and that his imprisonment was not a just cause for absence within the meaning of the contract. However, this cannot be validly argued in the face of the grievant's acquittal." But since Tom didn't do all he could to notify the company of his reason for absence, reinstatement was directed without back pay.

THE NEAT NUT—The arbitrator dismissed the grievance on the grounds that the dispute was not arbitrable. He wrote: "I cannot relate, directly or indirectly, the practice upon which the union relies to any express provision of the contract . . . I cannot decide a controversy entirely upon practices and customs outside of the obligations assumed in the written agreement."

THE OVERTIME HOGS—Reading the contract as a whole, the arbitrator said that the right to share in overtime was no more linked to seniority than was the right to a paid holiday. Both were privileges that accrue to employees, regardless of their length of service. The company won the case.

THE "SICK" MEN—The company was upheld in its right to promulgate the rule, but was not sustained in its application in this case. The proper application of the rule, the arbitrator said, was to discourage malingering. It even could be invoked to discourage refusal of reasonable overtime assignments. But there was nothing in the contract or the practice in this shop to require employees to work sixteen hours at a time.

THE FIRST-TIME LOSER—The arbitrator upheld the union. "The basic purpose of the warning system," he wrote, "is to advise the employee of his unsatisfactory behavior." If the grievant had been notified of the lesser forms of discipline, it would have been different. As it was, the five days counted as one offense and the discharge was reduced to a reprimand.

THE EDUCATED FOREMEN—Management won. The arbitrator said this was no lockout within the "normal meaning" of the word, because there had been no dispute between the parties and management was not trying to use economic pressure against employees in order to accomplish some purpose. Although the company might have managed the training some other way, he concluded, the manner it chose was within its "exclusive responsibility," and it was not for him to direct some other form of training.

THE LATE SLEEPER—The arbitrator observed that the holiday clause required work on the "full scheduled workdays" before and after the holiday. As the plant was shut down on the Friday in question, except for one man, it was not a "regularly scheduled" day within the meaning of the contract. The tardiness could not be used to deprive the man of holiday pay.

THE UNWILLING TRAVELER—The arbitrator sympathized with the company's position but said: "As the collective bargaining agreement is presently written, the company is obliged to abide with the vagaries of its employees. It was within the repairman's contractual rights to proceed as he did."

Questions

1. Explain the difference between arbitration and negotiation.

2. Is arbitration limited to labor-management disputes? Can you think of any international body that employs voluntary arbitration of disputes? Name a recent example.

3. How did your answers compare with those given at the end of the article? In the cases where you gave a different reply, were you convinced by the "official" answer? Why or why not?

4. What are the strengths and weaknesses of voluntary arbitration?

5
Conflict Resolution:
Isn't There a Better Way?

Warren E. Burger

This article originally appeared in *National Forum*, Fall 1983.

The former Chief Justice of the United States Supreme Court is a voice that cannot be ignored. When he asks whether our civil administration of justice has become obsolete, the problem must be serious indeed. To some extent, the roots of the problem—"in fees, expenses and waste of time"—go back to the adversarial (win/lose) tradition in which lawyers have been trained, according to Burger.

"Only very few law schools," says Burger, "have significant focus on arbitration." Even fewer, in his informed view, emphasize the art and skills of negotiation. Such "non-judicial" routes to conflict resolution could help ease the backlog of litigation as "Americans are increasingly turning to the courts for relief from a range of personal distresses and anxieties." Burger also recommends a "third" approach (in addition to arbitration and negotiation) exemplified in the administrative process used under the workers' compensation acts.

Justice Burger builds his case for "non-judicial" settlements by citing the growth of litigation in the federal district courts over a forty-year period at a rate six times that of the nation's population increase. And the rate is nearly tripled in the Court of Appeals over a shorter period as more litigants want a "second bite of the apple."

The justice points to the natural competitiveness of lawyers and business executives "to win using every tactic available." The time consumed, he says, runs "not weeks or months, but years" with corresponding expenditure of money.

The cases Burger suggests moving to the "non-judicial" process of mediation and arbitration include "divorce, child custody, personal injury, landlord and tenant cases and probate of estates." He gives historical examples of arbitration from the days of Homer in ancient Greece to the seventeenth century Dutch and other colonial procedures in America. He seeks to allay lawyerly fears of loss of business by reminding such advocates that they "are not excluded from that process."

Recent developments give Justice Burger some reason for hope. He lists the advantages of arbitration in terms of expertise, the absence of stress, cost and limitation of abuses. To be effective, he cautions, arbitration "should be final and binding." He notes with approval a recent step taken by the American Bar Association but calls for bolder moves. While praising the ABA, at whose 1982 convention in Chicago he delivered this address, Burger proposes a "commission of distinguished leaders" to study and recommend a wide-ranging series of steps to get many forms of litigation out of the courts and into a system "aimed at delivering justice in the shortest possible time and at the least expense."

The obligation of our profession is, or has long been thought to be, to serve as healers of human conflicts. To fulfill our traditional obligation means that we should provide mechanisms that can produce an acceptable result in the shortest possible time, with the least possible expense and with a minimum of stress on the participants. That is what justice is all about.

The law is a tool, not an end in itself. Like any tool, our judicial mechanisms, procedures, or rules can become obsolete. Just as the carpenter's handsaw was replaced by the power saw, and his hammer was replaced by the stapler, we should be alert to the need for better tools to serve the ends of justice.

Many thoughtful people, within and outside our profession, question whether that is being done today. They ask whether our profession is fulfilling its historical and traditional obligation of being healers of human conflicts and whether we are alert in searching for better tools. Although it may be too much to say that we lawyers are becoming part of the problem instead of the means to a solution, I confess there is more to support our critics than I would have thought 15 or 20 years ago.

LITIGATION AND THE ADVERSARY TRADITION

I address the administration of justice in civil matters, which shares with criminal justice both delay and lack of finality. Even when an acceptable result is finally achieved in a civil case, that result is often drained of much of its value because of the time-lapse, the expense, and the emotional stress inescapable in the litigation process.

Abraham Lincoln once said: "Discourage litigation. Persuade your neighbors to compromise whenever you can. Point out to them how the nominal winner is often a real loser—in fees, expenses, and waste of time." In the same vein, Judge Learned Hand commented: "I must say that, as a litigant, I should dread a lawsuit beyond almost anything else short of sickness and of death."

I was trained, as many of you were, with that generation of lawyers taught that the best service a lawyer could render a client was to keep away from the courts. Obviously that generalization needs qualifying, for often the courts are the only avenue to justice. In our search for "better ways," we must never forget that.

Law schools have traditionally steeped the students in the adversary tradition rather than in other skills of resolving conflicts. And various factors in the past 20–25 years—indeed increasingly—have combined to depict today's lawyer in the role of a knight in shining armor, whose courtroom lance strikes down all obstacles. But the emphasis on that role can be carried too far. Only very few law schools have significant focus on arbitration. Even fewer law schools focus on training in the skills—the arts—of negotiation that can lead to settlements. Of all the skills needed for the practicing lawyer, skill in negotiation must rank very high.

It is refreshing to note that the dean of a new law school recently said he hoped the school would play a leading role in preparing lawyers to find fresh approaches to resolving cases outside the courtroom. He said:

> The idea of training a lawyer as a vigorous adversary to function in the courtroom is anachronistic. With court congestion and excessive litigiousness drawing increasing criticism, it is clear that lawyers in the future will have to be trained to explore nonjudicial routes to resolving disputes. (Dean Charles Halpern, Law School, City University of New York.)

This echoed the theme of the 1976 Pound Conference of which this Association was a cosponsor. Obviously two of those "non-judicial routes" are arbitration and negotiation, and it is very encouraging to find a new law school opening with this fresh approach. A third approach is greater use of the techniques of the administrative process exemplified by the traditional workmen's compensation acts. The adversary process is expensive. It is time-consuming. It often leaves a trail of stress and frustration.

One reason our courts have become overburdened is that Americans are increasingly turning to the courts for relief from a range of personal distresses and anxieties. Remedies for personal wrongs that once were considered the responsibility of institutions other than the courts are now boldly asserted as legal "entitlements." The courts have been expected to fill the void created by the decline of church, family, and neighborhood unity.

Possibly the increased litigiousness that court dockets reflect simply mirrors what is happening worldwide. The press, TV, and radio, for hours every day, tell us of dire events in Asia, Africa, Europe, and Latin America where there is seething political, social, and economic turmoil. It is not surprising that our anxieties are aggravated and we have a few problems of our own.

In 1975, Professor John Barton of Stanford cautioned that:

> As implausible as it may appear, . . . increases over the last decade suggest that by the early 21st century—18 years hence—the federal appellate courts alone will decide approximately 1 million cases each year. That bench would include over 5,000 active judges, and the Federal Reporter would expand by more than 1,000 volumes each year.

We do not need to accept this scholar's perception to know that the future prospects are neither comfortable nor comforting.

COSTS OF LITIGATION

Our litigation explosion during this generation is suggested by a few figures: from 1940 to 1981, annual Federal District Court civil case filings increased from about 35,000 to 180,000. This almost doubled the yearly case load per judgeship from 190 to 350 cases. The real meaning of these figures emerges when we see that federal civil cases increased almost six times as fast as our population.

From 1950 to 1981, annual Court of Appeals filings climbed from about 2,800 to more than 26,000. The annual case load per Circuit judgeship increased from 44 to 200 cases. That growth was 16 times as much as the increase in population. A similar trend took place in the state courts from 1967 to 1976, where appellate filings increased eight times as fast as the population, and state trial court filings increased at double the rate of population growth.

It appears that people tend to be less satisfied with one round of litigation and are demanding a "second bite at the apple," far more than in earlier times.

We, as lawyers, know that litigation is not only stressful and frustrating, but expensive and frequently unrewarding for litigants. A personal injury case, for example, diverts the claimant and entire families from their normal pursuits. Physicians increasingly take note of "litigation neuroses" in otherwise normal, well-adjusted people. This negative impact is not confined to litigants and lawyers. Lay and professional witnesses, chiefly the doctors who testify, are also adversely affected. The plaintive cry of many frustrated litigants echoes what Learned Hand implied: "There must be a better way."

A common thread pervades all courtroom contests: lawyers are natural competitors and once litigation begins they strive mightily to win using every tactic available. Business executives are also competitors and when they are in litigation they often transfer their normal productive and constructive drives into the adversary contest. Commercial litigation takes business executives and their staffs away from the creative paths of development and production and often inflicts more wear and tear on them than the most difficult business problems.

We read in the news of cases that continue not weeks or months, but years. Can it be that the authors of our judicial system, those who wrote constitutions 200 years ago, ever contemplated cases that monopolize one judge for many months or even years? A case recently terminated has been in court 13 years, and has largely occupied the time of one judge for half that time, with total costs running into hundreds of millions of dollars.

I doubt the Founding Fathers anticipated such results. That these cases are infrequent is not the whole story. In 1960, there were only 35 federal trials that took more than one month. By 1981, these protracted cases multiplied five times, and that is not the end of the story. All litigants standing in line behind a single protracted case—whether it is a one-month, a three-month or a longer case—are denied access to that court. This becomes more acute if that litigant cannot recover interest on the award, or is allowed interest at 8 percent while paying double or more on a home mortgage or other debts.

MODERN APPLICATION OF ARBITRATION

We must now use the inventiveness, the ingenuity, and the resourcefulness that have long characterized the American business and legal community to shape new tools. The paradox is that we already have some very good tools and techniques ready and waiting for imaginative lawyers to adapt them to current needs. We need to consider moving some cases from the adversary system to administrative processes like workmen's compensation or to mediation, conciliation, and especially arbitration. Divorce, child custody, adoptions, personal injury, landlord and tenant cases, and probate of estates are prime candidates for some form of administrative or arbitration processes.

Against this background I focus now on arbitration, not as the answer or cure-all for the mushrooming case loads of the courts, but as one example of "a better way to do it."

If the courts are to retain public confidence, we cannot let disputes wait two, three, or five years to be disposed of, as is so often the situation. The use of voluntary private binding arbitration has been neglected. Lawyers in other countries, who admire the American system in general, are baffled that we use arbitration so little and use courts so much.

There is, of course, nothing new about the concept of arbitration to settle controversies. The concept of mediation and arbitration preceded by many centuries the creation of formal and organized judicial systems and codes of law. Ancient societies, more than 25 centuries ago, developed informal mechanisms, very much like mediation and arbitration, to resolve disputes.

In the time of Homer, for example, the community elders served as civil arbitrators to settle disputes between private parties. By the fourth century B.C., this practice was a settled part of Athenian law. Commercial arbitration was a common practice among Phoenician traders and the desert caravans of Marco Polo's day, and later in the Hanseatic League.

An early use of arbitration in America was of Dutch origin. In 1647, in what is now New York City, an ordinance created the "Board of Nine," which arbitrated minor civil and mercantile disputes. In colonial Connecticut, Pennsylvania, Massachusetts, and South Carolina, various arbitration mechanisms were established to deal with debt or trespass and boundary disputes. As early as 1682, the Assembly of West New Jersey enacted a law which provided:

> And for the preventing of needless and frivolous Suits. Be it Hereby Enacted . . . that all Accounts of Debt . . . of Slander . . . and Accounts whatsoever not exceeding Twenty Shillings, . . . Arbitration of two [neutral] Persons of the Neighbourhood, shall be tendered by some one Justice of the Peace who shall have Power to summon the Parties. . . .

Despite the early use of arbitration in this country, and despite legislative efforts to expand that process in this country, two strong adversaries emerged: first, some judges, fearing that arbitration would deprive them of their jurisdiction, jealously guarded their powers and resisted arbitration; second, lawyers, mistakenly fearing that arbitration would adversely affect their practice, zealously pursued court litigation. Ironically, experience has shown that litigants can secure acceptable arbitration results and lawyers are not excluded from that process.

More than 50 years ago the American Bar Association had a large part in drafting the United States Arbitration Act, which called for binding arbitration to cut delay and expense. Yet for all that early support of arbitration, it has not developed as an alternative to adversary litigation in the courts. Old attitudes and old habits die hard.

RECENT DEVELOPMENTS

It is often difficult to discern the precise time when new developments occur relating to the human condition, but I think that for at least the past 20 years there has been a slowly—all too slowly—developing awareness that the traditional litigation process has become too cumbersome, too expensive, and also burdened by many other disadvantages.

In 1976 we took note of these growing problems in commemorating the 70th Anniversary of Roscoe Pound's indictment of the American judicial and legal systems. That Conference brought arbitration sharply into focus. In opening the Pound Conference, I urged that we make a "reappraisal of the values of the arbitration process. . . . " The American Bar Association responded promptly to the Pound Conference and there are now committees taking a fresh look at alternative means of dispute resolution. Our President, David Brink, has given the broad subject priority status.

What we must have, I submit, is a comprehensive review of the whole subject of alternatives, with special emphasis on arbitration. It is now clear that neither the federal nor the state court systems are capable of handling all the burdens placed upon them. Surely the avalanche that is bound to come will make matters worse for everyone.

I do not suggest in any sense that arbitration can displace the courts. Rather, arbitration should be an alternative that will complement the judicial systems. There will always be conflicts which cannot be settled except by the judicial process.

Let me suggest some of the important advantages in private arbitration, especially in large, complex commercial disputes:

- Parties can select the arbitrator, taking into account the special experience and knowledge of the arbitrator.
- A privately selected arbitrator can conduct all proceedings in a setting with less stress on the parties; confidentiality can be preserved where there is a valid need to protect trade secrets, for example.
- Arbitration can cope more effectively with complex business contracts, economic and accounting evidence, and financial statements. A skilled arbitrator acting as the trier can digest evidence at his own time and pace without all the expensive panoply of the judicial process. (To operate a U.S. District Court with a jury costs approximately $350.00 per hour.)
- Parties to arbitration can readily stipulate to discovery processes in

a way that can control, if not eliminate, abuses of discovery processes.

One example of an effective statutory, although not binding, arbitration program is found in Pennsylvania. The impact upon court backlogs in that state has been significant. In Philadelphia, in the first two years after the jurisdictional level was increased to $10,000, the entire civil calendar backlog was reduced from 48 months to 21 months. In 1974, more than 12,000 of approximately 16,000 civil cases were resolved through arbitration.

Several federal courts have experimented with similar procedures established under local rules that refer certain types of civil suits seeking damages, in some cases up to $100,000, to an arbitration panel of three attorneys. The results indicate that arbitration could well shorten the disposition of most cases by two to four months, and that the counsel in the cases hold a generally favorable view of the procedure. Perhaps most important, preliminary evidence suggests that arbitration may reduce by as much as half the number of such cases that otherwise would go to trial.

We must, however, be cautious in setting up arbitration procedures to make sure they become a realistic alternative rather than an additional step in an already prolonged process. For this reason, if a system of voluntary arbitration is to be truly effective, it should be final and binding, without a provision for de novo trial or review. This principle was recognized centuries ago by Demosthenes, who, in quoting the law, told the people of Athens:

> [W]hen [the parties] have mutually selected an arbiter, let them stand
> fast by his decision and by no means carry on appeal from him to another
> tribunal; but let the arbiter's [decision] be supreme.

Anything less than final and binding arbitration should be accompanied by some sanctions to discourage further conflict. For example, if the claimant fails to increase the award by 15 percent or more over the original award, he should be charged with the costs of proceedings plus the opponent's attorney fees. Michigan is one of the states that has experimented with this kind of sanction and such programs deserve close study.

THE ABA PROGRAMS

The Association has taken a positive step by broadening the jurisdiction of the "Special Committee on Resolution of Minor Disputes" and it is now designated the "Special Committee on Alternative Means of Dispute Resolution."

That was a good step, but with all deference, I suggest we need more. Either the existing committee should be altered or an enlarged commission should be created. Such a commission could well include not only distinguished leaders of the Bar, but also distinguished representatives of business and other disciplines.

The Association should now proceed carefully with an indepth examination of these problems. This cannot be done routinely or casually. Rather, it must be done on the scale of the 1969 monumental work of the American Law Institute experience of such groups as the American Arbitration Association.

If there are objectors, as there may be, to broadening arbitration, objections will serve to sharpen the analysis of the alternatives and guide us in making arbitration effective.

For 200 years, our country has made progress unparalleled in human history. We have done this by virtue of a willingness to combine ancient wisdom with innovation and with what was long called "Yankee ingenuity."

The American Bar Association has been a leader in virtually every major improvement in the administration of justice in the past quarter of a century. During my tenure in office, alone, their support made possible the Institute for Court Management, the Circuit Executives for Federal Courts, the Code of Judicial Conduct, the National Center for State Courts, expanded continuing education for lawyers and judges, and training of paralegals. All of these were aimed at delivering justice in the shortest possible time and at the least expense.

This proposal could well be another major contribution to make our system of justice work better for the American people.

Questions

1. Why should the Chief Justice be concerned about the time and expense involved in litigation?
2. What factors in the past twenty-five years "have combined to depict today's lawyer in the role of a knight in shining armor"? What factors tend to portray the lawyer as a villain?
3. What does Burger mean when he says that "the courts have been expected to fill the void created by the decline of church, family and neighborhood unity"?
4. What effect does the competitive nature of our national ethos have on litigation and foreign policy?
5. Why does Burger insist that arbitration should be "final and binding"?

6
The Coming Evolution in Court-Administered Arbitration

Robert Coulson

This article originally appeared in *Judicature*, February–March 1986.

Robert Coulson, president of the American Arbitration Association, polishes his crystal ball and predicts a bright future for court-administered arbitration in state and federal court systems. In this respect, he provides a positive response to Justice Burger's plea for a "better way" (see previous article). Successful experiments in mandatory arbitration in small civil disputes, he contends, have made the judicial community sit up and take notice. Just how this evolutionary process will occur is the subject of the present article.

"The primary influence," he says, "will come from the bar." Indeed, lawyers have already shown themselves willing to act as arbitrators on court-annexed panels for little or no fee. With the inevitable increase in arbitration costs, Coulson forecasts that pressure will build for a shift from a panel of three lawyers to a single court-appointed arbitrator. He also foresees the time when lawyer-arbitrators will become so skilled in this novel procedure that they will make the transition from the arbitrator's role to that of the mediator. (See following article for the distinction between arbitration and mediation.)

Based on thousands of cases in the private (non-judicial) sector, Coulson finds mediation to be the alternative of choice 75% of the time. He envisions special training programs in mediation for selected lawyers, a movement that may perhaps lead to the creation of a new profession—that of Certified Public Mediator. "Mediation," he says, "is the sleeping giant of alternative dispute resolution." In certain types of disputes, the author has found that mediation has distinct advantages over arbitration. For all these reasons, Coulson is bullish on court-administered arbitration and mediation.

Prophets have enjoyed a lackluster record in recent years. Nevertheless, I am prepared to forecast that court-administered arbitration programs will flourish in both state and federal court systems and that they will change in fundamental ways, and for the better.

Mandatory court-annexed arbitration programs for relatively small civil disputes have been a major, recent reform in the American civil justice system. As news of this experiment percolates through the judicial community, court after court has been contemplating the installation of some such alternative dispute resolution system. Numerous judicial conferences on the subject have been scheduled in recent years where advocates for court arbitration have argued that this is an idea whose time has come.[1] Indeed, I am one of those enthusiasts.

My experience with the voluntary processes of the American Arbitration Association, moreover, convinces me that evolutionary pressures will inevitably change the structure of these court programs. Similar pressures have influenced the various rules and procedures of the AAA.

The primary influence, as would be expected, will come from the bar. At present, lawyer-arbitrators on court-annexed panels have been willing to serve as volunteers or for whatever nominal fee may have been established by local court rule or by the legislature. There will be steady pressure to increase such fees. Some of the programs have already had to raise the level of compensation.[2] When the arbitrators are paid several hundred dollars per case or some amount that covers their overhead approaching their normal professional billing rate, the cost of such programs must increase, perhaps becoming prohibitive.

At that point, there will be pressure on courts to use a single arbitrator, rather than the panel of three. Such a change may also be required to accommodate to the impediment that some busy lawyers will no longer be willing to serve as arbitrators on matters which they regard as relatively trivial, below their level of expertise. (Many civil disputes being arbitrated under these programs require the arbitrators to put a price on personal or property damages and do not require sophisticated legal skills.) Thus, both economic and professional factors will nudge such programs towards using a single arbitrator.

Another tendency is likely to present itself. Now, arbitrators are instructed to evaluate the case. They are warned not to attempt to mediate a settlement. That instruction seems sound because the program uses a rotating panel of lawyers, most of whom do not have mediation skills.

But as lawyer-arbitrators become experienced with these programs, and particularly when they serve frequently as sole arbitrators, they may become activists. Rather than serving as relatively passive arbitrator-evaluators, they may participate more actively in settlement negotiations—in effect, becoming mediators. In part, this may occur because they are encouraged to do so by the parties' attorneys.

Our experience with somewhat similar programs in the private sector indicates that trial attorneys, when selecting between binding arbitration and professional mediation, select mediation more than 75 per cent of the time. This observation is based on our experience with thousands of cases where representatives of the AAA have been authorized by insurance companies to offer that option to claimant attorneys.[3]

True, the setting is somewhat different in a court program. AAA representatives are offering the choice of binding arbitration before an experienced trial attorney or mediation with a trained, professional lawyer-mediator. Nevertheless, the preference expressed by claimant attorneys towards mediation appears consistently throughout the United States.

If a similar preference becomes reflected in court-administered programs where attorneys are offered the choice between arbitration (evaluation) or mediation, the courts may be persuaded to provide mediation as an option. Then, they may need to identify lawyers who are qualified and prepared to serve as mediators. Perhaps a selected group of lawyers will require specific training in mediation skills.

In my recent book, *Professional Mediation of Civil Disputes,*[4] I suggested that the creation of a profession of Certified Public Mediators would offer lawyers an alternative career, in addition to providing the courts with an attractive, off-budget, auxiliary service. If my expectation about the evolution of court-administered arbitration is accurate, mediation programs will appear in the courts in coming years. If lawyers prefer mediation, as our experience in the private sector would indicate, there is no reason for courts not to offer that service.

Many members of the bar are acquiring experience and training as mediators and are looking for fields in which to practice those skills.[5] Mediation is the sleeping giant of alternative dispute resolution. Again, AAA experience would confirm that notion. In cases actually mediated under the AAA's insurance alternative dispute resolution program, nine out of 10 are settled. This compares favorably with the settlement record of court-administered arbitration programs.

Moreover, the quality of the mediation process is better than court-administered arbitration where the award is based on a perfunctory presentation by the parties and an evaluation by a panel of three non-specialized lawyers. In mediation, the parties have an opportunity to discuss the issues at their leisure, reaching an agreement that reflects a mutually acceptable compromise. The clients themselves are more involved in mediation than they would be in an arbitration hearing.

I believe that court-administered arbitration programs will evolve inevitably towards mediation. The mediators will be lawyers who have become specialists in dispute resolution. They will operate under the overall supervision of the local courts. This will constitute one long step towards a new profession of Certified Public Mediators.

Notes

1. Burger, *Isn't There a Better Way?*, 68 A.B.A.J. 247 (1982); Salem, *The Alternative Dispute Resolution Movement: An Overview*, 40 *Arbitration* J. 9 (Sept. 1985).

2. *Court-Annexed Arbitration in the State Trial Court System,* Statement by Deborah R. Hensler, Institute for Civil Justice, The Rand Corporation, prepared for Senate Judiciary Committee Subcommittee on Courts, February 1, 1984, at 7.

3. American Arbitration Association ADR Insurance Program caseload statistics for October 1, 1984 through October 31, 1985.

4. Coulson, *Professional Mediation of Civil Disputes* (New York: American Arbitration Association, 1984).

5. American Bar Association, Special Committee on Alternative Means of Dispute Resolution. *Alternative Dispute Resolution: Who's in Charge of Mediation?* (Washington, D.C.: 1982).

Questions

1. Identify the evolutionary pressures that the author considers likely to change the structure of court programs.

2. Why does Coulson say the primary impetus for change will come from lawyers (the bar)?

3. Why are arbitrators advised at present not to attempt to mediate settlements? How is this situation expected to change?

4. What steps would be required to turn lawyer-arbitrators into mediators?

5. Name the advantages that mediation has over arbitration.

7
Arbitration vs. Mediation— Explaining the Differences

John W. Cooley

This article originally appeared in *Judicature*, February–March 1986.

There are many pathways to peace and the just settlement of disputes. Arbitration and its cousin mediation are two of the most effective tools available for bringing about solutions to human conflict. Yet, as the author—a lawyer and a former U.S. magistrate—declares, "an amazing number of lawyers and business professionals are unaware of the differences between arbitration and mediation." He finds this confusion understandable.

Even history is no sure guide, according to Cooley, because the two words have been used interchangeably. And the distinction between arbitration and mediation has not been much clarified in modern times, as can be seen by looking at the terminology in current labor relations statutes. Even libraries get into the act with imprecise cross-references to arbitration and mediation.

Cooley puts the distinction between the two means of resolving disputes into its simplest terms: "Arbitration involves a decision by an intervening third party or 'neutral'; mediation does not." He amplifies on this by describing arbitration as a "left brain" or "rational mental process" (analytical, logical, administrative); and mediation as a "right brain" or "creative process" (intuitive, artistic, symbolic, emotional). "The arbitrator," he explains, "deals largely with the objective; the mediator, the subjective."

Moreover, the two processes are usually employed to settle different types of disputes. Arbitration works best, says the author, when there is no reasonable likelihood of a negotiated settlement and the disputants will not have a continuing relationship. Mediation is employed in exactly the reverse conditions. "Mediation occurs first," he explains, "and if unsuccessful, resort is made to arbitration."

Cooley launches into the history of the arbitration process and the various stages it involves (initiation, preparation, prehearing conferences, the hearing and decision-making). To this he compares the stages of me-

diation (initiation, preparation, introduction, problem statement, gener-
ation and evaluation of alternatives and selection of alternatives). He adds:
"A mediator's patience, flexibility and creativity throughout this entire
process are necessary keys to a successful solution."

Drawing on legal precedents, Cooley further explains the differences
between the two processes in terms of function and power. He concludes
with the assertion that the benefits of arbitration and mediation "are just
beginning to be recognized by lawyers and business professionals alike."
His lucid explanation of the entire matter is likely to assist both legal
professionals and litigants to become more comfortable with the two meth-
ods of dispute resolution.

An amazing number of lawyers and business professionals are unaware of the differences between arbitration and mediation. Their confusion is excusable.

In the early development of the English language, the two words
were used interchangeably. The *Oxford English Dictionary* provides as
one historical definition of arbitration: "to act as formal arbitrator or um-
pire, to mediate (in a dispute between contending parties)." The Statutes
of Edward III (1606) referring to what today obviously would be called a
commercial *arbitration* panel, provided: "And two Englishmen, two of
Lombardie and two of Almaigne shall (be) chosen to be mediators of questions between sellers and buyers."[1]

Modern labor relations statutes tend to perpetuate this confusion. As
one commentator has observed:

> Some statutes, referring to a process as "mediation" describe formal
> hearings, with witnesses testifying under oath and transcripts made, re-
> quire reports and recommendations for settlement to be made by the
> neutral within fixed periods, and either state or imply the finality of the
> "mediator's recommendations." In one statute the neutral third parties
> are called, interchangeably, mediators, arbitrators and impasse panels.[2]

The Federal Mediation and Conciliation Service (note the absence of
"arbitration" in its title) performs a basic arbitration function by maintaining a roster from which the Service can nominate arbitrators to the parties
and suggest "certain procedures and guides that [the Service believes] will
enhance the acceptability of arbitration."[3]

The National *Mediation* Board (emphasis added) performs important
functions in the promotion of arbitration and the selection of arbitrators for
the railroad and airline industries.[4]

Libraries also assist in perpetuating the arbitration/mediation definitional charade. Search under "mediation" and you will invariably be referred to "arbitration." In the midst of this confusion—even among congressional draftsmen—it is time to explain the differences between the processes.

The most basic difference between the two is that arbitration involves a *decision* by an intervening third party or "neutral;" mediation does not.

Another way to distinguish the two is by describing the processes in terms of the neutral's mental functions. In arbitration, the neutral employs mostly "left brain" or "rational" mental processes—analytical, mathematical, logical, technical, administrative; in mediation, the neutral employs mostly "right brain" or "creative" mental processes—conceptual, intuitive, artistic, holistic, symbolic, emotional.

The arbitrator deals largely with the objective; the mediator, the subjective. The arbitrator is generally a passive functionary who determines right or wrong; the mediator is generally an active functionary who attempts to move the parties to reconciliation and agreement, regardless of who or what is right or wrong.

Because the role of the mediator involves instinctive reactions, intuition, keen interpersonal skills, the ability to perceive subtle psychological and behavioral indicators, in addition to logic and rational thinking, it is much more difficult than the arbitrator's role to perform effectively.[5] It is fair to say that while most mediators can effectively perform the arbitrator's function, the converse is not necessarily true.

Besides these differences the two processes are generally employed to resolve two different types of disputes. Mediation is used where there is a reasonable likelihood that the parties will be able to reach an agreement with the assistance of a neutral. Usually, mediation is used when parties will have an ongoing relationship after resolution of the conflict. Arbitration, on the other hand, is generally appropriate for use when two conditions exist: there is no reasonable likelihood of a negotiated settlement; and there will not be a continuing relationship after resolution.[6]

If the two processes are to be used in sequence, mediation occurs first, and if unsuccessful, resort is made to arbitration.[7] Viewed in terms of the judicial process, arbitration is comparable to a trial and mediation is akin to a judicial settlement conference. They are as different as night and day.[8] The differences can best be understood by discussing them in terms of the processes of arbitration and mediation.

THE ARBITRATION PROCESS

Arbitration has had a long history in this country, going back to procedures carried over into the Colonies from mercantile England. George

Washington put an arbitration clause in his last will and testament to resolve disputes among his heirs. Abraham Lincoln urged lawyers to keep their clients out of court and himself arbitrated a boundary dispute between two farmers. Today, arbitration is being used more broadly for dispute settlement both in labor-management relations and in commercial transactions.

Aside from its well-known use in resolving labor disputes, arbitration is now becoming widely used to settle inter-company disputes in various industries, including textile, construction, life and casualty insurance, canning, livestock, air transport, grain and feed and securities.[9]

Simply defined, arbitration is a process in which a dispute is submitted to a third party or neutral (or sometimes a panel of three arbitrators) to hear arguments, review evidence and render a decision.[10] Court-annexed arbitration, a relatively new development, is a process in which judges refer civil suits to arbitrators to render prompt, non-binding decisions. If a particular decision is not accepted by a losing party, a trial *de novo* may be held in the court system. However, adverse decisions sometimes lead to further negotiation and pre-trial settlement.[11]

The arbitration process, court-annexed or otherwise, normally consists of six stages: initiation, preparation, prehearing conferences, hearing, decisionmaking, and award.

Initiation. The initiation stage of arbitration consists of two substages: initiating the proceeding, and selecting the arbitrator. An arbitration proceeding may be initiated either by: submission; "demand" or "notice;" or, in the case of a court-annexed proceeding, court rule or court order.

A submission must be signed by both parties and is used where there is no previous agreement to arbitrate. It often names the arbitrator (or method of appointment), contains considerable detail regarding the arbitrator's authority, the procedure to be used at the hearing, statement of the matter in dispute, the amount of money in controversy, the remedy sought and other matters.

On the other hand, where the description of a dispute is contained in an agreement and the parties have agreed in advance to arbitrate it, arbitration may be initiated unilaterally by one party serving upon the other a written "demand" or "notice" to arbitrate.

However, even where an agreement contains a "demand" or "notice" arbitration clause, parties sometimes choose also to execute a submission after the dispute has materialized. In the court-annexed situation, a lawsuit is mandatorily referred to an arbitration track and the parties must select an arbitrator from a court-maintained roster or otherwise by mutual agreement.[12]

Several types of tribunals and methods of selecting their membership are available to parties who wish to arbitrate. Parties may choose between the use of a "temporary" or "permanent" arbitrator. They can also choose to have single or multiple arbitrators. Since success of the arbitration process often hinges on the expertise of the tribunal, parties generally select a tribunal whose members possess impartiality, integrity, ability and experience in the field in which the dispute arises. Legal training is often helpful but not indispensable.

Information concerning the qualifications of some of the more active arbitrators is contained in the *Directory of Arbitrators*, prepared by the Bureau of National Affairs, Inc., and in *Who's Who* (of arbitrators) published by Prentice-Hall, Inc. Also, the Federal Mediation and Conciliation Service (FMCS), the National Mediation Board (NMB) and the American Arbitration Association (AAA) provide biographical data on arbitrators.[13]

Preparation. The parties must thoroughly prepare cases for arbitration. Obviously, a party must fully understand its own case to communicate effectively to the arbitrator. Depending on the nature of the case, prehearing discovery may be necessary and its permissible extent is usually determined by the arbitrator. The advantages of simplicity and utility of the arbitration mode normally weigh against extensive discovery. During this stage, the parties also enter into fact stipulations where possible.[14]

Ordinarily, most or all of the arbitrator's knowledge and understanding of a case is based upon evidence and arguments presented at the arbitration hearing. However, the arbitrator does have some "preparation" functions. Generally, where no tribunal administrator (such as AAA) is involved, the arbitrator, after accepting the office, designates the time and place of the hearing, by mutual agreement of the parties if possible. The arbitrator also signs an oath, if required in the particular jurisdiction, and determines whether the parties will have representation, legal or otherwise, at the hearing.[15]

Prehearing conferences. Depending on the complexity of the matter involved, the arbitrator may wish to schedule a prehearing conference, which is normally administrative in nature.[16] Briefing schedules, if necessary, are set on motions attacking the validity of claims or of the proceeding. But generally, briefing is minimized to preserve the efficiency of the process. Discussion of the underlying merits of claims or defenses of the parties is avoided during a prehearing conference. *Ex parte* conferences between the arbitrator and a party are not permitted.[17]

The hearing. Parties may waive oral hearing and have the controversy determined on the basis of documents only. However, an evidentiary-type hearing in the presence of the arbitrator is deemed imperative in virtually all cases. Since arbitration is a private proceeding, the hearing is not open to the public as a rule but all persons having a direct interest in the case are ordinarily entitled to attend.

A formal written record of the hearing is not always necessary; use of a reporter is the exception rather than the general practice. A party requiring an interpreter has the duty to arrange for one. Witnesses testifying at the hearing may also be required to take an oath if required by law, if ordered by the arbitrator, or on demand of any party.[18]

Opening statements are made orally by each party in a brief, generalized format. They are designed to acquaint the arbitrator with each party's view of what the dispute is about and what the party expects to prove by the evidence. Sometimes an arbitrator requests each party to provide a short written opening statement and issue statement prior to the hearing. Occasionally, a respondent opts for making an opening statement immediately prior to presenting initial evidence.[19]

There is no set order by which parties present their cases in arbitration, although in practice the complaining party normally presents evidence first. The parties may offer any evidence they choose, including personal testimony and affidavits of witnesses. They may be required to produce additional evidence the arbitrator deems necessary to determine the dispute. The arbitrator, when authorized by law, may subpoena witnesses or documents upon his or her own initiative or by request of a party. The arbitrator also decides the relevancy and materiality of all evidence offered. Conformity to legal rules of evidence is unnecessary. The arbitrator has a right to make a physical inspection of premises.[20]

The parties make closing arguments, usually limited in duration. Occasionally, the arbitrator requests post hearing briefs. When this occurs, the parties usually waive oral closing arguments.[21]

Decisionmaking. When the issues are not complex, an arbitrator may render an immediate decision. However, when the evidence presented is voluminous and/or time is needed for the members of an arbitration panel to confer, it might require several weeks to make a decision.

The award is the arbitrator's decision. It may be given orally but is normally written and signed by the arbitrator(s). Awards are normally short, definite, certain and final as to all matters under submission. Occasionally, they are accompanied by a short well-reasoned opinion. The award is usually issued no later than 30 days from the closing date of the hearing. When a party fails to appear, a default award may be entered.[22] Depending on the nature of the award (i.e., binding), it may be judicially enforceable and, to some extent, reviewable. The losing party in a court-annexed arbitration is entitled to trial *de novo* in court.

THE MEDIATION PROCESS

Mediation is a process in which an impartial intervenor assists the disputants to reach a voluntary settlement of their differences through an agreement that defines their future behavior.[23] The process generally consists of eight stages: initiation, preparation, introduction, problem statement, problem clarification, generation and evaluation of alternatives, selection of alternative(s), and agreement.[24]

Initiation. The mediation process may be initiated in two principal ways: parties submit the matter to a public or private dispute resolution organization or to a private neutral; or the dispute is referred to mediation by court order or rule in a court-annexed mediation program.

In the first instance, counsel for one of the parties or, if unrepresented, the party may contact the neutral organization or individual and the neutral will contact the opposing counsel or party (as the case may be) to see if there is interest in attempting to mediate the dispute.

Preparation. As in arbitration, it is of paramount importance that the parties to a dispute in mediation be as well informed as possible on the background of the dispute, the claims or defenses and the remedies they seek. The parties should seek legal advice if necessary, and although a party's lawyer might attend a typical nonjudicial mediation, he or she normally does not take an adversary role but is rather available to render legal advice as needed.

The mediator should also be well-informed about the parties and the features of their dispute and know something about:

- the balance of power;
- the primary sources of pressure exerted on the parties;
- the pressures motivating them toward agreement as well as pressures blocking agreement;
- the economics of the industry or particular company involved;
- political and personal conflicts within and between the parties;
- the extent of the settlement authority of each of the parties.

The mediator sets the date, time and place for the hearing at everyone's convenience.[25]

Introduction. In the mediation process, the introductory stage may be the most important.[26] It is in that phase, particularly the first joint session, that the mediator establishes his or her acceptability, integrity, credibility and neutrality. The mediator usually has several objectives to achieve initially. They are: establish control of the process; determine issues and positions of the parties; get the agreement-forging process started; and encourage continuation of direct negotiations.[27]

Unlike a judge in a settlement conference or an arbitrator who wields the clout of a decision, a mediator does not, by virtue of position, ordinarily command the parties' immediate trust and respect; the mediator earns them through a carefully orchestrated and delicately executed ritual of rapport-building. Every competent mediator has a personal style. The content of the mediator's opening remarks is generally crucial to establishing rapport with the parties and the respectability of the mediator and the process.

Opening remarks focus on: identifying the mediator and the parties; explaining the procedures to be followed (including caucusing),[28] describing the mediation function (if appropriate) and emphasizing the continued decisionmaking responsibility of the parties; and reinforcing the confidentiality and integrity of the process.[29] When appropriate, the mediator might invoke the community and public interest in having the dispute resolved quickly and emphasize the interests of the constituents in the successful conclusion of the negotiations.[30]

Finally, the mediator must assess the parties' competence to participate in the process. If either party has severe emotional, drinking, drug, or health problems, the mediator may postpone the proceeding. If the parties are extremely hostile and verbally abusive, the mediator must endeavor to calm them, by preliminary caucusing if necessary.[31]

Problem statement. There are essentially two ways to open a discussion of the dispute by the parties: Both parties give their positions and discuss each issue as it is raised; or all the issues are first briefly identified, with detailed exposition of positions reserved until all the issues have been identified. The second procedure is preferred; the first approach often leads to tedious time-consuming rambling about insignificant matters, sometimes causing the parties to become more entrenched in their positions.[32]

Generally, the complaining party tells his or her "story" first. It may be the first time that the adverse party has heard the full basis for the complaint. The mediator actively and empathically listens, taking notes if helpful, using listening techniques such as restatement, echo and non-verbal responses. Listening is the mediator's most important dispute-resolving tool.[33]

The mediator also:

• asks open-ended and closed-ended questions at the appropriate time and in a neutral fashion;

• obtains important "signals" from the behavior and body movements of the parties;

 • calms a party, as necessary;

 • clarifies the narration by focused questions;

 • objectively summarizes the first party's story;

- defuses tensions by omitting disparaging comments from the summary;
- determines whether the second party understands the first party's story;
- thanks the first party for his or her contribution.

The process is repeated with the second party.[34]

Problem clarification. It is in this stage that the mediator culls out the true underlying issues in the dispute. Often the parties to a dispute intentionally obfuscate the core issues. The mediator pierces this cloud-cover through separate caucuses in which he or she asks direct, probing questions to elicit information which one party would not disclose in the presence of the other party. In a subsequent joint session, the mediator summarizes areas of agreement or disagreement, being careful not to disclose matters which the parties shared with the mediator in confidence. They are assisted in grouping and prioritizing issues and demands.[35]

Generation and evaluation of alternatives. In this stage, the mediator employs two fundamental principles of effective mediation: creating doubt in the minds of the parties as to the validity of their positions on issues; and suggesting alternative approaches which may facilitate agreement.[36] These are two functions which parties to a dispute are very often unable to perform by themselves. To carry out these functions, the mediator has the parties separately "brainstorm" to produce alternatives or options; discusses the workability of each option; encourages the parties by noting the probability of success, where appropriate; suggests alternatives not raised by the parties and then repeats the three previous steps.[37]

Selection of alternative(s). The mediator may compliment the parties on their progress and use humor, when appropriate, to relieve tensions; assist the parties in eliminating the unworkable options; and help the parties determine which of the remaining workable solutions will produce the optimum results with which each can live.[38]

Agreement. Before the mediation is terminated, the mediator summarizes and clarifies, as necessary, the terms of the agreement reached and secures the assent of each party to those terms; sets a follow-up date, if necessary; and congratulates the parties on their reasonableness.

The mediator does not usually become involved in drafting a settlement agreement. This task is left to the parties themselves or their counsel. The agreement is the parties', not the mediator's.[39]

A mediator's patience, flexibility and creativity throughout this entire process are necessary keys to a successful resolution.

THE "NEUTRAL'S" FUNCTIONS

To fully appreciate the differences (or the similarities) between the two processes, and to evaluate the appropriate use of either process, it is instructive to focus on considerations which exist at their interface—the function and power of the "neutral." This is a particularly important exercise to acquire a realistic expectation of the result to be obtained from each process.

The arbitrator's function is quasi-judicial in nature and, because of this, an arbitrator is generally exempt from civil liability for failure to exercise care or skill in performing the arbitral function.[40] As a quasi-judicial officer, the arbitrator is guided by ethical norms in the performance of duties. For example, an arbitrator must refrain from having any private (*ex parte*) consultations with a party or with an attorney representing a party without the consent of the opposing party or counsel.[41]

Moreover, unless the parties agree otherwise, the arbitration proceedings are private and arbitrators must take appropriate measures to maintain the confidentiality of the proceedings.[42] It has generally been held that an arbitrator may not testify as to the meaning and construction of the written award.[43]

In contrast, a mediator is not normally considered to be quasi-judicial, unless he or she is appointed by the court as, for example, a special master. Some courts have extended the doctrine of immunity to persons termed "quasi-arbitrators"—persons empowered by agreement of the parties to resolve disputes arising between them.[44] Although the law is far from clear on this point, a very persuasive argument may be advanced that mediators are generally immune from lawsuits relating to the performance of their mediation duties where the agreement under which they perform contains a hold-harmless provision or its equivalent.

In absence of such contractual provision, it would appear that a functionary such as a mediator, selected by parties to perform skilled or professional services, would not ordinarily be immune from charges of negligence but rather is required to work with the same skill and care exercised by an average person engaged in the trade or profession involved.[45]

Of course, weighing heavily against a finding of negligence on the part of a mediator is the intrinsic nature, if not the essence, of the mediation process which invests the parties with the complete power over their destiny; it also guarantees any party the right to withdraw from the process and even to eject the mediator during any pre-agreement stage.[46]

Also, in contrast to arbitrators, certain ethical restrictions do not apply to mediators. Mediators are permitted to have *ex parte* conferences with the parties or counsel. Indeed, such caucuses, as they are called, are the mediator's stock-in-trade. Furthermore, while one of the principal advantages of a privately-conducted mediation is the non-public or confidential nature of the proceedings, and although Rule 408 of the Federal Rules of Evidence and public policy considerations argue in favor of confidentiality, the current state of the law does not provide a guarantee of such confidentiality.[47] However, in most cases a strong argument can be made that the injury from disclosure of a confidential settlement proceeding is greater than the benefit to be gained by the public from nondisclosure.[48]

Finally, unlike the arbitrator, the performance of whose function may be enhanced by knowledge, skill, or ability in a particular field or industry, the mediator need not be an expert in the field which encompasses the subject of the dispute. Expertise may, in fact, be a handicap, if the parties look wrongly to the mediator as an advice-giver or adjudicator.[49]

COMPARATIVE POWER

The arbitrator derives power from many sources. The person may be highly respected in a particular field of expertise or widely renowned for fairness. But aside from these attributes which emanate from personal talents or characteristics, the arbitrator operates within a procedural and enforcement framework which affords considerable power, at least from the perspective of the disputants. Under certain circumstances, arbitrators may possess broad remedy powers, including the power, though rare, to grant injunctive relief.[50] They normally have subpoena power, and generally they have no obligation to anyone, not even "to the court to give reasons for an award."[51]

In general, a valid arbitration award constitutes a full and final adjustment of the controversy.[52] It has all the force and effect of an adjudication, and effectively precludes the parties from again litigating the same subject.[53] The award can be challenged in court only on very narrow grounds. In some states the grounds relate to partiality of the arbitrator or to misconduct in the proceedings, such as refusal to allow the production of evidence or to grant postponements, as well as to other misbehavior in conducting the hearings so as to prejudice the interests of a party.[54]

A further ground for challenge in some states is the failure of the arbitrator to observe the limits of authority as fixed by the parties' agreement—such as determining unsubmitted matters or by not dealing definitely and finally with submitted issues.[55] In Illinois, as in most states, a judgment entered on an arbitration award is enforceable "as any other judgment."[56] Thus, from a systemic perspective, the arbitrator is invested with a substantial amount of power.

In striking contrast, with the exception of a special master appointed by the court or a neutral appointed by some governmental body, the mediator has little if any systemic-based power. Most if not all of a mediator's power is derived from experience, demonstrated skills and abilities, and a reputation for successful settlements.

Any particular mediator may wield power by adopting a particular role on what might be described as a continuum representing the range of strengths of intervention: from virtual passivity, to "chairman," to "enunciator," to "prompter," to "leader," to virtual arbitrator.[57] The mediator who can adopt different roles on this continuum, changing strategies to fit changing circumstances and requirements of both the disputants and himself, is inevitably more effective in accumulating and wielding power which is real, yet often not consciously perceptible by the disputants themselves.[58]

Since, in the ordinary case, the result of the mediation process is an agreement or contract not reduced to a court judgment,[59] the result is binding on the parties only to the extent that the law of contracts in the particular jurisdiction requires. And to the same extent, the result is enforceable by one party against another. As a practical matter, where a party breaches an agreement or contract which is the product of mediation and the agreement is not salvageable, prudence would seem to dictate that in most cases the underlying dispute—and not the breach of agreement—should be litigated.

SUMMARY

It is clear that both the functions and the levels of power of the arbitrators and mediators are dramatically different. Counsel must assess the nature of the dispute and the personalities of the disputants prior to determining which process, arbitration or mediation, has the best chance to achieve a successful resolution of the particular conflict.

For example, arbitration would probably prove to be the better dispute resolution choice where the dispute involves highly technical matters; a long-standing feud between the disputants; irrational and high-strung personalities; and no necessity of a continued relationship after resolution of the conflict.

On the other hand, mediation may prove to be the most effective choice where disputants are stubborn but basically sensible; have much to gain from a continued relationship with one another; and conflict resolution is time-critical.

Table 1 **A comparison of arbitration/meditation processes**

Arbitration	Meditation
1. Initiation Submission Demand or notice Court rule or order Selection of arbitrator	**1. Initiation** Submission Court rule or order Assignment or selection of mediator
2. Preparation Discovery Prehearing conference Motions Stipulations Arbitrator's oath Arbitrator's administrative duties Arbitrator does not seek out information about parties or dispute	**2. Preparation** Usually, no discovery Parties obtain background information on claims, defenses, remedies Mediator obtains information on parties and history of dispute Usually, no mediator oath
3. Prehearing conference Administrative Scheduling No discussion of underlying merits of claims or defenses No *ex parte* conferences	**3. Introduction** Mediator: Conducts *ex parte* conferences, if necessary, for calming Gives opening descriptive remarks Develops trust and respect Emphasizes importance of successful negotiations Helps parties separate the people from the problem
4. Hearing Not generally open to public Written record, optional Witnesses and parties testify under oath **Opening statement** Made orally Sometimes also in writing **Order of proceedings and evidence** Complaining party usually presents evidence first Arbitrator may subpoena witnesses Evidence rules relaxed Arbitrator rules on objections to evidence; may reject evidence	**4. Problem statement** Confidential proceeding, no written record Parties do not speak under oath Issues identified Issues discussed separately; stories told Mediator listens; takes notes Mediator asks questions; reads behavioral signals Mediator calms parties; summarizes stories; defuses tensions Mediator determines whether parties understand stories Mediator usually has no subpoena power

Table 1 **A comparison of arbitration/meditation processes** *(continued)*

Arbitration	Meditation
Closing arguments Oral arguments normally permitted for clarification and synthesis Post-hearing briefs sometimes permitted	**5. Problem clarification** Mediator: Culls out core issues in caucus Asks direct, probing questions Summarizes areas of agreement and disagreement Assists parties in grouping and prioritizing issues and demands Helps parties focus on interests, not positions
5. Decisionmaking If issues non-complex, arbitrator can issue an immediate decision If issues complex, or panel has three members, extra time may be required	**6. Generation and evaluation of alternatives** Mediator: Creates doubts in parties' minds as to validity of their positions Invents options for facilitating agreement Leads "brainstorming;" discusses workability; notes probability of success of options
	7. Selection of alternative(s) Mediator: Compliments parties on progress Assists parties in eliminating unworkable options Helps parties to use objective criteria Helps parties determine which solution will produce optimum results
6. Award Normally in writing, signed by arbitrator(s) Short, definite, certain and final, as to all matters under submission Occasionally a short opinion accompanies award Award may be judicially enforceable or reviewable	**8. Agreement** Mediator: Summarizes and clarifies agreement terms Sets follow-up date, if appropriate Congratulates parties on their reasonableness Usually does not draft or assist in drafting agreement Agreement is enforceable as a contract and subject to later modification by agreement

Arbitration and mediation are two separate and distinct processes having a similar overall goal (terminating a dispute), while using totally different methods to obtain dissimilar (decisional vs. contractual) results. These differences are best understood by viewing the processes side-by-side in Table 1.

The benefits of arbitration and mediation to litigants, in terms of cost and time savings, are just beginning to be recognized by lawyers and business professionals alike. It is hoped that this discussion of the arbitration and mediation processes and their differences will help lawyers feel more comfortable with these two methods of dispute resolution and to use them to their clients' advantage in their joint pursuit of swift, inexpensive, simple justice.

Notes

1. Robins, *A Guide for Labor Mediators* 6 (Honolulu: University Press of Hawaii, 1976).

2. *Id.*

3. Elkouri and Elkouri, *How Arbitration Works* 24 (Washington, D.C.: BNA, 3rd ed. 1973).

4. *Id.* at 25.

5. As one American professional mediator put it, the mediator "has no science of navigation, no fund inherited from the experience of others. He is a solitary artist recognizing, at most, a few guiding stars and depending mainly on his personal power of divination." Meyer, *Function of the Mediator in Collective Bargaining*, 13 *Indus. & Lab. Rel. Rev.* 159 (1960).

6. In labor relations arbitrations, of course, condition (2) is normally not present. Labor disputes are generally divided into two categories: rights disputes and interest disputes. Disputes as to "rights" involve the interpretation or application of existing laws, agreements or customary practices, disputes as to "interests" involve controversies over the formation of collective agreements or efforts to secure them where no such agreement is yet in existence. Elkouri and Elkouri, *supra* n. 3, at 47.

7. Because of ethical considerations, the arbitrator and mediator normally are different persons. It should also be noted that mediation is frequently effective when it is attempted, with the concurrence of the parties, during the course of an arbitration with a neutral other than the arbitrator serving as the mediator. Often the unfolding of the opponent's evidence during the course of arbitration leads to a better appreciation of the merits of their respective positions and hence an atmosphere conducive to settlement discussions.

8. The stark distinction between mediation and arbitration was well made by a professional mediator who became chairman of the New York State Mediation Board: "Mediation and arbitration . . . have conceptually nothing in common. The one [mediation] involves helping people to decide for themselves, the other

involves helping people by deciding for them." Meyer, *supra* n. 5, at 164, as quoted in Gulliver, *Disputes and Negotiations, a Cross-cultural Perspective*, 210 (New York: Academic Press, 1979).

9. Cooley, *Arbitration as an Alternative to Federal Litigation in the Seventh Circuit, Report of the Subcommittee on Alternatives to the Present Federal Court System, Seventh Circuit Ad Hoc Committee to Study the High Cost of Litigation*, 2 (July 13, 1978).

10. *Paths to Justice: Major Public Policy Issues of Dispute Resolution, Report of the Ad Hoc Panel on Dispute Resolution and Public Policy*, Appendix 2 (Washington, D.C.: National Institute for Dispute Resolution, October, 1983).

11. *Id. See also Evaluation of Court-Annexed Arbitration in Three Federal District Courts* (Washington, D.C.: Federal Judicial Center, 1981).

12. Cooley, *supra* n. 9, at 4, Elkouri and Elkouri, *supra* n. 3, at 183–86. Domke on Commercial Arbitration. §§14:00–14:05 (Rev. Ed. 1984). Arbitrators, if chosen from a list maintained by an arbitration organization or court-maintained roster, are normally compensated at the daily rate fixed by the organization or the court. Arbitrators selected independently by the parties are compensated at the daily or hourly rate at which they mutually agree. In such cases, the parties equally share the expense of the arbitrator's services.

13. Elkouri and Elkouri, *supra* n. 3, at 24–25.

14. Elkouri and Elkouri, *supra* n. 3, at 197; (for preparation checklist *see* pp. 198–199); Domke, *supra* n. 12, §§24:01 and 27:01.

15. *Id.*

16. Some of the matters which might be discussed at a prehearing conference are: whether discovery is needed and, if so, scheduling of same; motions that need to be filed and briefed or orally argued, and the setting of firm oral argument and hearing dates.

17. Cooley, *supra* n. 9, at 4–5; Elkouri and Elkouri, *supra* n. 3, at 186–90.

18. Cooley, *supra* n. 9, at 5.

19. Elkouri and Elkouri, *supra* n. 3, at 224–25.

20. Cooley, *supra* n. 9, at 5; Elkouri and Elkouri, *supra* n. 3, at 223–28.

21. Elkouri and Elkouri, *supra* n. 3, at 225.

22. Cooley, *supra* n. 9, at 6.

23. Salem, *Mediation—The Concept and the Process*, in *Instructors Manual for Teaching Critical Issues* (1984, unpublished). *See generally* Simpkin, *Mediation and the Dynamics of Collective Bargaining* 25 (BNA, 1971). Court-annexed mediation is a process in which judges refer civil cases to a neutral (mediator or master) for settlement purposes. It also includes in-court programs in which judges perform the settlement function full-time.

24. *See generally* Ray, *The Alternative Dispute Resolution Movement*, 8 *Peace and Change* 117 (Summer 1982). The process of mediation and the roles and strategies of mediators have been generally neglected in studies of negotiation. As one author remarked, "Mediation still remains a poorly understood process." Gulliver, *supra* n. 8.

25. Meagher, "Mediation Procedures and Techniques," 18–19 (unpublished

paper on file in the Office of the General Counsel, FMCS, Washington, D.C.). Mr. Meagher is a former commissioner of FMCS.

26. The success of the introductory stage is directly related to two critical factors: (1) the appropriate timing of the mediator's intervention, and (2) the opportunity for mediator preparation. A mediator's sense of timing is the ability to judge the psychological readiness of an individual or group to respond in the desired way to a particular idea, suggestion or proposal. Meagher, *supra* n. 25, at 5, *see also* Maggiolo, *Techniques of Mediation in Labor Disputes* 62 (Dobbs Ferry, NY: Oceana Publications, 1971). The kinds of preparatory information needed by the mediator are discussed in the text *supra*. In many instances, such information is not available prior to intervention and thus it must be delicately elicited by the mediator during the introductory stage.

27. Meagher, *supra* n. 25, at 26–27. Wall, *Mediation, An Analysis, Review and Proposed Research*, 25 J. *Conflict Res.* 157, 161 (1981).

28. Caucusing is an *ex parte* conference between a mediator and a party.

29. Meagher, *supra* n. 25, at 28; Maggiolo, *supra* n. 26, at 42–44.

30. *Id.*

31. Ray, *supra* n. 24, at 121; Maggiolo, *supra* n. 26, at 52–54.

32. Meagher, *supra* n. 25, at 30; Maggiolo, *supra* n. 26, at 47.

33. Ray, *supra* n. 24, at 121; Salem, *supra* n. 23, at 4–5; Robins, *supra* n. 1, at 27; Maggiolo, *supra* n. 26, at 48–49.

34. Ray, *supra* n. 24, at 121.

35. *Id.* at 121–22; Meagher, *supra* n. 25, at 57–58; Robins, *supra* n. 1, at 43–44; Maggiolo, *supra* n. 26, at 49–50.

36. Maggiolo, *supra* n. 26, at 12. Other basic negotiation principles which some mediators use to advantage throughout the mediation process are found in Fisher and Ury, *Getting to Yes* (New York: Penguin Books, 1983). Those principles are: (1) separate the people from the problem; (2) focus on interests, not positions; (3) invent options of mutual gain; (4) insist on using objective criteria.

37. Ray, *supra* n. 24, at 122. Meagher, *supra* n. 25, at 48–49, describes additional techniques of "planting seeds," "conditioning," and "influencing expectations."

38. Ray, *supra* n. 24, at 122.

39. *Id.*

40. Domke, *supra* n. 12, §23:01, at 351–53.

41. *Id.* §24:05, at 380.

42. *Id.*

43. *Id.* §23:02, at 355.

44. See Craviolini v. Scholer & Fuller Associated Architects, 89 Ariz. 24, 357 P.2d 611 (1960), where an architect was deemed to be a "quasi-arbitrator" under an agreement with the parties and therefore entitled to immunity from civil liability in an action brought against him by either party in relation to the architect's dispute-resolving function. *Compare* Gammell v. Ernst & Ernst, 245 Minn. 249,

72 N.W.2d 364 (1955), where certified public accountants, selected for the specific purpose of making an examination and of auditing the books of a corporation to ascertain its earnings, were held not to have acquired the status of arbitrators so as to create immunity for their actions in the performance of such service, simply because the report was to be binding upon the parties.

45. Domke, *supra* n. 12, §23:01, at 352–53.

46. As two professional mediators have poignantly commented: "Unlike arbitration and other means of adjudication, the parties retain complete control . . . If they do not like the mediator, they get another one. If they fail to produce results, they may end the mediation at any time." Phillips and Piazza, *How to Use Mediation*, 10 *A.B.A.J. of Sect. of. Lit.* 31 (Spring, 1984).

47. *See* Grumman Aerospace Corp. v. Titanium Metals Corp., 91 F.R.D. 84 (E.D. N.Y. 1981) (Court granted a motion to enforce a subpoena *duces tecum* involving a report prepared by a neutral fact-finder on the effects of certain price-fixing activities). *See generally* Restivo and Mangus, *Alternative Dispute Resolution: Confidential Problem-Solving or Every Man's Evidence? Alternatives to the High Cost of Litigation*, 2 *Law & Bus. Inc./Ctr. for Public Resources*, 5 (May, 1984). Parties can assist the preservation of confidentiality of their mediation proceedings by reducing to writing any expectations or understanding regarding the confidentiality of the proceedings and by being careful to protect against unnecessary disclosure both within their respective constituencies and the outside world, *id.* at 9.

48. *See, e.g.*, NLRB v. Joseph Macaluso, 618 F.2d 51 (9th Cir. 1980); Pipefitters Local 208 v. Mechanical Contractors Assn. of Colorado, 90 Lab. Cas. (CCH) ¶ 12,647 (D. Colo. 1980).

49. Phillips and Piazza, *supra* n. 46, at 33.

50. In re Ruppert, 29 LA 775, 777 (N.Y. Ct. App. 1958); In re Griffin, 42 LA 511 (N.Y. Sup. Ct. 1964). *See generally* Elkouri and Elkouri, *supra* n. 3, at 241–51.

51. Domke, *supra* n. 12, §29:06, at 436.

52. Donoghue v. Kohlmeyer & Co., 63 Ill. App. 3d 979, 380 N.E.2d 1003, 20 Ill. Dec. 794 (1978).

53. Borg, Inc. v. Morris Middle School Dist. No. 54, 3 Ill. App. 3d 913, 278 N.E.2d 818 (1972).

54. Domke, *supra* n. 12, §33:00, 463.

55. *Id.* In Illinois, the court's power to vacate or modify arbitration awards is narrowly circumscribed. *See Ill. Rev. Stat.* ch. 10, ¶¶ 112, 113 (1981).

56. *Ill. Rev. Stat.* ch. 10, ¶ 114 (1981).

57. Gulliver, *supra* n. 8, at 220.

58. *Id.* at 226.

59. Where a settlement agreement is reduced to a judgment, for example, through intervention and assistance of a special master, the "consent judgment" is generally enforceable, if necessary, before the court in which the consent judgment is entered.

Questions

1. Explain in your own words the differences between arbitration and mediation.
2. What kinds of skills does the mediator need that the arbitrator does not require?
3. What are the main features of the decision-making stage of arbitration?
4. How does the generation and evaluation of alternatives work in mediation?
5. Give some of the roles a mediator may adopt to help settle disputes.

8
Mandatory Mediation of Divorce: Maine's Experience

Lincoln Clark and Jane Orbeton

Figure 1: Divorce mediations January through June 1985
Type and Disposition

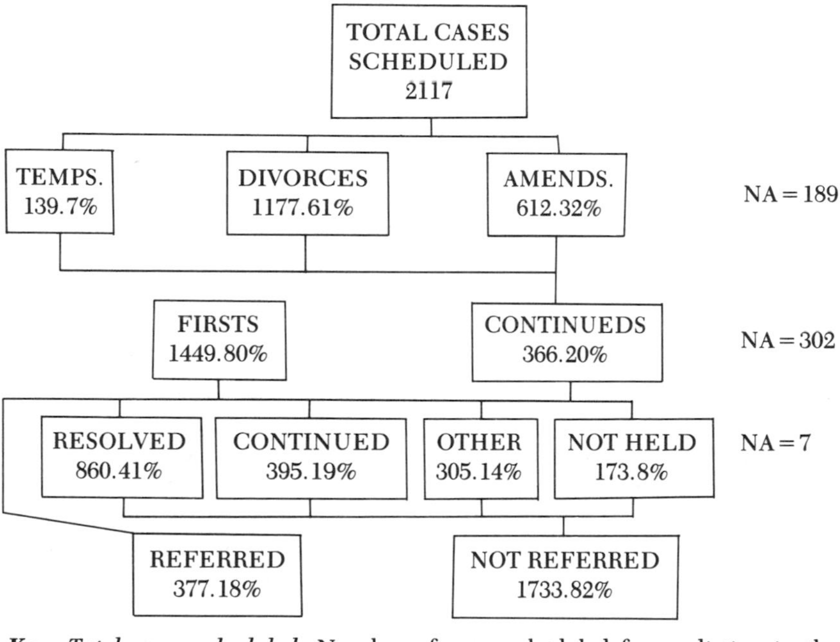

```
                    ┌─────────────────┐
                    │  TOTAL CASES    │
                    │  SCHEDULED      │
                    │     2117        │
                    └─────────────────┘

  ┌──────────┐      ┌──────────┐      ┌──────────┐
  │ TEMPS.   │      │ DIVORCES │      │ AMENDS.  │    NA = 189
  │ 139.7%   │      │ 1177.61% │      │ 612.32%  │
  └──────────┘      └──────────┘      └──────────┘

            ┌──────────┐        ┌──────────────┐
            │ FIRSTS   │        │ CONTINUEDS   │    NA = 302
            │ 1449.80% │        │   366.20%    │
            └──────────┘        └──────────────┘

  ┌──────────┐ ┌──────────┐ ┌────────┐ ┌──────────┐
  │ RESOLVED │ │CONTINUED │ │ OTHER  │ │ NOT HELD │  NA = 7
  │ 860.41%  │ │ 395.19%  │ │305.14% │ │ 173.8%   │
  └──────────┘ └──────────┘ └────────┘ └──────────┘

        ┌──────────┐        ┌──────────────┐
        │ REFERRED │        │ NOT REFERRED │
        │ 377.18%  │        │  1733.82%    │
        └──────────┘        └──────────────┘
```

Key: *Total cases scheduled:* Number of cases scheduled for mediation in the month. **Temps:** Contested temporary motions pending divorce. **Divorces:** Contested divorces. **Amends:** Contested post-divorce amendments. **NA:** Cases with data not available. **Firsts:** First mediation. **Continueds:** Second (or more) mediations. **Resolved:** All issues resolved. **Continueds:** Further mediation. **Other:** Cases to be resolved by parties. **Not held:** Party(ies) did not appear. **Referred:** Cases for trial with issues estimated to take more than $1/2$ hour of judge's time to resolve. **Not referred:** Sum of Resolved, Continued, Other, Not Held.

Voluntary mediation of divorces has been utilized in Maine and in other states for several years. Mandatory mediation of divorces in which child custody or visitation is a contested issue was introduced in California in 1981[1] and in Maine in 1984.[2] Maine's statutes, based on the laws of California and other states, were passed after public hearings that included testimony of judges and members of the Court Mediation Service on their experience with voluntary mediation. Also influential were the report of the Commission to Study Child Custody and testimony given by members of the commission. The legislature, concerned over how best to protect the interests of children in divorce, decided on mandatory mediation.

Maine's statute provides for mandatory mediation of all contested cases in which the parties have minor children. Mandatory mediation also applies to unmarried parents seeking an order on parental rights and responsibilities and child support.[3] It applies to judicial separation,[4] and to parties seeking temporary, permanent, and post-divorce orders.[5] In Maine, mediation is a step in the domestic relations process, an opportunity for the parties to try one more time to settle the issues in their legal action before a trial in court.

The case that is settled proceeds to an uncontested hearing on the basis of the agreement. The case that is not settled may return to mediation again, may be negotiated toward settlement outside mediation or may proceed to a contested trial. Parties in cases that have not settled have frequently thanked the mediators for the opportunity to talk with their spouses and with the mediators. Parties in cases which have settled have left mediation with a plan for the future that they fashioned, and that can serve as a foundation from which to parent cooperatively. It was these goals which the Maine legislature was seeking when they instituted mandatory mediation.

The number of cases handled by the Court Mediation Service is approaching 5000 per year, of which about 4000 are contested divorce actions. There are 60 mediators serving all 50 of Maine's district and superior courts. Complete agreements are reached in a single mediation session in 41 per cent of all divorce cases. Another 19 per cent are continued to a second or third mediation. Fourteen per cent are resolved after the mediation by the parties without the participation of a judge or a mediator. Eight per cent were withdrawn by the parties (see Figure 1). The remaining 18 per cent go to the court for trial.

The Court Mediation Service is governed by Maine statutes and the policies of the Court Mediation Committee. This committee, chaired by the chief justice, is composed of four judges, the state court administrator, and the director of the Court Mediation Service.

Maine's Court Mediation Service is distinctive in that it has become completely financed by the state's Judicial Department. In addition to divorces, it handles a wide variety of other types of cases—small claims, landlord-tenant, and major civil litigation cases. The mediator decides whether the case should be continued for further mediation or referred to court for trial. Mediators recruit, nominate, train, assign and evaluate other mediators. The scheduling of mediations is done cooperatively with clerks of court.

START-UP PROBLEMS

That there were several problems at the beginning of mandatory mediation was no surprise. There were a flood of cases and an insufficient number of trained mediators, many attorneys were unfamiliar with mediation, there was a lack of rooms for mediations, and parties failed to appear or cancelled. The first few months following the passage of the statute in July 1984 were hectic. Now, less than a year later, scheduling systems and operating procedures are running quite smoothly and rarely must a case wait more than a month for a mediation date.

Many prospective participants were apprehensive about mandatory mediation. The mediators themselves feared recalcitrance of parties to participate actively. They now report no significant difference in the degree of cooperation of the parties between mandatory and voluntary mediation. Some parties simply accept mediation as a required step in the procedure to obtain a divorce; more seem to welcome mediation as an alternative to a trial in court.

Attorneys' fears that concessions or compromises in mediation might prejudice ongoing litigation have diminished. Some attorneys have reported that they are negotiating more agreements—a desirable trend that is reducing the number of contested cases. Mediation is particularly useful when parties with their attorneys cannot resolve their differences by negotiation. More and more attorneys are expressing appreciation when mediators offer creative proposals to break impasses blocking negotiation. Polls of attorneys report no noticeable overall effect on legal costs—lower when mediation succeeds, higher when it fails.

COMPARING STATES

While both Maine and California have legislated mandatory mediation, there are many significant differences. In California, mediation is restricted to custody and visitation issues. In Maine, all disputed issues must be mediated if the parties have minor children and also when there are no minor children if so ordered by a judge. The broader range of issues covered in Maine's mediation stems from the conviction that many issues in a divorce affect the children. Where the children will live, which parent gets the family residence, how the mortgage will be covered, who will get the family car, who will pay the overdue doctor's bills and whether there will be support payment are subject to mediation.

Mediators in California may exclude attorneys from the mediation session where the mediator deems exclusion of counsel to be appropriate or necessary. In Maine, attorneys are encouraged to participate and, indeed, they may not be forced to leave the mediation. Practice and procedures vary with the mediator, the court, and the region in Maine with regard to the manner in which attorneys participate. Sometimes they are present for the entire mediation, sometimes they are present for part or they consult with their clients before a final decision is made. The choice is made by the party and attorney together. Most attorneys participate cooperatively with the parties and the mediator to work out an agreement. In addition, attorneys are an essential resource when legal issues arise since the mediators are cautioned not to give any legal opinions or advice.

In California, as of January 1, 1984, all mediators were required to have a masters degree in psychology, social work, marriage, family and child counseling or psychotherapy. The backgrounds of Maine's mediators are very heterogeneous. In addition to counselors, they include retired business executives, chaplains, college presidents, community service leaders, professors, school teachers, social workers, a Navy captain, a probation officer, and attorneys not engaged in the practice of domestic relations.

We disagree with the tendency in many states, and the special interest pressures in other states and in Maine, to establish mandatory background qualifications in the absence of any tested evidence of their relevance. We have not found any correlation between mediator background and performance; much more important than professional background are attributes which can only be judged subjectively. A series of interviews can attempt to determine if the prospective mediator is a paragon who can elicit and propose creative solutions (paramount because mediation is most useful when neither the parties nor their attorneys could negotiate a solution), is impartial, empathetic, able to control emotional outbursts, and facilitate communication between the parties and attorneys. The recruitment problem is further compounded by lack of agreement on how to measure performance. We think the mediator is truly successful if he or she initiates a process that results in the parents undertaking to resolve their common child rearing problems after they are separated—but we do not know how to measure this. Clearly "Who will be a good mediator?" is no easier to answer than "Who will be a good judge?"

The California statute declares the mediation proceedings to be private and confidential. It also provides that communications from the parties to the mediator are deemed to be official information and are therefore inadmissible in court. In Maine, the privacy of mediation is insured by an amendment to the Maine Rules of Evidence: "Evidence of conduct or statements by any party or mediator at a court-sponsored domestic relations mediation session is not admissible for any purpose."[6]

Mediators in California may make a recommendation to the court as to custody or visitation of the child or children and may recommend mutual restraining orders. When an agreement has not been reached, the mediator may recommend that the court order an investigation of the family prior to a contested hearing. Mediators in Maine do not have authority to report or make such recommendations to the court. It is felt that this limitation on the power of the mediators enhances their role as impartial catalysts for settlement and increases the trust which the parties feel toward the mediators.

FINE TUNING

An amendment to the statutes passed March 31, 1985 remedied two problems encountered with the statute of July 25, 1984—delays in motions pending and the absence of sanctions for failure to make a good faith effort to mediate or to appear.[7]

There are three possible court divorce proceedings: a temporary order, called a "motion pending;" the divorce; and a motion to amend the divorce decree. The statute mandates mediation in all three of these stages. There are situations described in some motions pending, however, which, for the sake of the family, warrant an immediate decision by a judge. The amendment authorized a judge to hear a motion pending on any issue for which good cause for temporary relief has been shown. The parties then go to mediation on any remaining issues.

The statute provides that "when agreement through mediation is not reached on any issues, the court must determine that the parties made a good faith effort to mediate the issues before proceeding with a hearing." It may prove difficult to enforce that provision. Nevertheless, the legislature's Judiciary Committee rejected the idea of removing the "good faith" requirement from the statute—parties should mediate in good faith.

Sometimes a mediation cannot be held because one party, usually the defendant, fails to appear. The resulting additional costs, inconvenience, and time lost are resented by the participants who have kept their appointment. While one absence is usually "forgiven," repeated absences of a party may be brought to the attention of the court. If the court finds that either party failed to make a good faith effort to mediate or failed without good cause to appear for mediation after receiving notice of the scheduled time for mediation, an appropriate sanction may be applied. The court may order the parties to submit to mediation, dismiss the action or any part of the action, render a decision or judgment by default, or assess attorney's fees and costs.

THE FUTURE

In addition to divorces the Court Mediation Service has also been handling over a thousand small claims cases a year and the volume is quite certain to increase. Possible new directions are mediations of probate, guardianship and child protection proceedings, infractions of building codes and zoning ordinances, boundary disputes, and more landlord-tenant cases.

The expansion of mediation in Maine is due to so many factors that perhaps it can only be explained by the cliché that it is an idea whose time has come. But it would not have started without the support of the Maine Bar Association and the sponsorship of the Judicial Department; it would not have grown so rapidly without competent mediators and the statutory action of the legislature. Inquiries show the widespread national interest in Maine's innovative efforts to reduce adversarial confrontations in court.

Notes

1. California Civil Code §4607.
2. 19 Maine Revised Statutes §214, 581 and 752 (1984).
3. 19 M.R.S.A. §214 (1984).
4. 19 M.R.S.A. §581 (1984).
5. 19 M.R.S.A. §752 (1984).
6. Rule 408, Maine Rules of Evidence.
7. Chapter 53, Public Laws of 1985.

Questions

1. Why did Maine begin its divorce mediation program with child custody cases?
2. Do you think that mediation helped the parties reach settlement even in the cases in which they proceeded to trial? Why, or why not?
3. How does Maine's law differ from California's? Which do you think is better? Be specific in your answer.
4. What amendments were added to Maine's original law? Why were they seen as needed?
5. Why do you think an article on divorce was included in this volume?

9
Arbitration:
An International Wallflower

Robert Coulson

This article originally appeared in *National Forum*, Fall 1983.

Robert Coulson, president of the American Arbitration Association, raises his voice for the settlement of disputes between nations by means of arbitration. He refers to the widespread practice even today of resolving international commercial problems by this means. In view of arbitration's success in cases where it has been used, Coulson wonders why "impartial, binding arbitration of nonbusiness disputes between nations (has) become an international wallflower."

For one thing, he says, arbitration provides "a rational alternative to the threat of force" as exemplified by the Algerian Accords which settled monetary claims between the United States and Iran. Like Burger, Coulson has recourse to historical examples of arbitration, which were "discarded" during the Civil War and "overwhelmed" by World War I. He cites with approval the non-violent efforts of Gandhi and Martin Luther King, Jr.

Given the troubles of the American delegation to the United Nations, Coulson reflects on the common public attitude: "In America, real men don't mediate." Such "macho" attitudes, he says, make the future dim for international arbitration. He appeals for "a more acute understanding of the mutual dependence of all peoples" in accordance with concepts of international justice.

Coulson admits that high hopes for the Permanent Court of Arbitration set up at the Hague earlier in the century have not lived up to expectations. But he says that multinational cooperation has worked in communications, air travel and space. Coulson suggests that "the potential causes of war (economic and social differences) could be the subject of mediation (non-binding) or arbitration (binding)." In the dance of nations, he concludes: "It is time to invite arbitration to the party."

Long before laws were memorialized or formal courts of justice were created, people resorted to arbitration for the resolution of disputes. For adjusting obscure tribal discords, for settling sordid business squabbles among dusty traders, for resolving border disputes between angry nation-states, arbitration was the remedy of choice throughout the ancient world. (See also Warren E. Burger's article for further documentation of this historical precedent.)

Today, multitudes of business controversies are resolved by arbitration in preference to court litigation. In the United States, arbitration tribunals resolve a substantial percentage of commercial cases because many executives are convinced that such tribunals composed of their peers will make informed decisions. Elsewhere in the world, arbitration is frequently used for both domestic and transnational business disputes. Arbitration clauses are placed in virtually all contracts between Western corporations and socialist foreign trade organizations. In international commercial transactions, where neither party wants to submit to the other's courts, the parties' use of arbitration clauses in contracts has become almost universal. The convenience and informality and privacy of arbitration appeal to business firms and their attorneys.

Arbitration is used in the United States for a wide variety of noncommercial matters. Arbitrators resolve labor-management grievances and collective-bargaining impasses. They settle minor criminal matters. They adjust family disputes. They have even been installed in correctional institutions to settle confrontations between inmates and the prison administration.

In arbitration, a neutral person or panel is selected to hear the parties and, having gained an understanding of the dispute, that person is authorized to issue a binding award. Most legal systems recognize the arbitration process and enforce parties' agreements to arbitrate and give force and effect to any award rendered by the arbitrator. Arbitration provides a practical, alternative, dispute-resolution process.

One party to an arbitration may be a government entity. In labor arbitration, the "employer" may be a local municipality, county, state, or even a federal agency. In building construction, the "owner" may be a governmental agency. In international commercial arbitration, the contract may pit a multinational investment firm against a foreign state or instrumentality. A substantial body of law has developed around the question of whether government entities can submit their disputes to arbitration and whether, once having done so, such a party can repudiate its agreement. With relatively few exceptions, courts have held governments to their agreements.

International commercial arbitration has become a well-recognized mode of settlement of international trade and investment disputes. The United Nations Convention on the Recognition and Enforcement of Foreign Arbitral Awards has only confirmed this trend. In view of the broad acceptance of arbitration as a method for resolving commercial disputes, one must wonder why arbitration seems to have lost its early popularity as a method for fixing other disagreements between nations. Why has impartial, binding arbitration of nonbusiness disputes between nations become a wallflower?

From time to time, arbitration continues to be used to fix some international border, particularly where the participants are minor powers. The impasse over the United States employees held by Iran was resolved by the Algerian Accords which created an arbitration tribunal to process monetary claims. Arbitration clauses are frequently inserted in international conventions, dealing with quasi-commercial matters. But, in general, arbitration has not been selected as the remedy of choice in international affairs. Why not?

I will discuss some problems that seem to stand in the way of a broader use of arbitration for resolving disputes between nations. At the outset, arbitration is regarded as a "soft" or "weak" form of dispute settlement. Military force, in contrast, is highly regarded by the major powers. Arbitration provides a rational alternative to the threat of force. Unfortunately, arbitration has become identified with pacifism in the political mind. In the United States, the peace movement always played a relatively minor role in national politics. For example, an American Peace Society was founded in 1828 but was virtually swept aside by the Civil War. In that frenzy of hostilities, rational alternatives were discarded for fear that they would weaken the public's commitment to armed conflict.

In the postwar period, arbitration had another passing vogue. In 1874, both houses of Congress passed a resolution that arbitration clauses be incorporated in treaties. Arbitration groups were formed to encourage the idea: the National Arbitration League (1882), the Christian Arbitration Association (1886), and the Lake Mohonk Conference (1895-1916). The American Arbitration Association, itself, received inspiration from such efforts and continues its support of research in the field of international arbitration.

World War I overwhelmed whatever chance there might have been for arbitration to replace the major powers' reliance upon the threat of violence, supplemented by diplomacy. From time to time, world leaders came to the surface, like Gandhi, who espoused arbitration and nonviolence, or Martin Luther King, Jr., who created a social movement using similar ideas. Both men were representatives of a large, emerging population, confronting a powerful national interest. For their time and purpose, arbitration provided an appropriate part of their strategy. The justice of their cause was so persuasive that an impartial tribunal would be likely to decide in their favor.

Encouraging the United States to make broader use of arbitration agreements presents a different challenge. On many issues, Americans find themselves in the minority. The General Assembly of the United Nations is not always an accurate guide to world opinion, but our experience there has been unfortunate. Our wealth and potential power make us the envy of other nations, creating a climate that does not encourage us to submit vital issues to arbitration tribunals selected from the nationals of other countries. American leaders may legitimately doubt whether the public would support the submission of important matters to a neutral tribunal. Our society seems committed to adversarial competition. The American public expects to win; to field a winning team; to overwhelm its enemies. What politician would act in denial of such expectations?

Some internationalists believe that, through better communication, by building trust and trying to understand mutual needs, it becomes possible to resolve international disputes through mediation. In mediation, a skillful third party helps the parties to reach their agreement through bilateral negotiations. But, as someone succinctly stated at a recent conference, "In America, real men don't mediate." The machismo of our leaders and of our mass media limits the potential of third-party intervention. In those areas where it has become part of the system, such as labor relations for local and state employees, the use of arbitration results from statutory law. As long as nations refuse to relinquish their autonomous power to defend vital interests through force, the future of international arbitration seems dim.

Arbitration has become popular in international commercial agreements, because the parties can select their own system of dispute settlement, avoiding national courts that one or another may suspect of bias. In international political disputes, national leaders may find it difficult to trust anyone's impartiality. And yet we find examples of such trust as Iran and the United States agreeing to arbitrate substantial investment claims.

At home, the federal government is reluctantly willing to arbitrate labor disputes with its own workers. Congress encourages mediation through the Community Relations Service and, in labor relations, through the Federal Mediation and Conciliation Service.

Federal courts are experimenting with court-annexed arbitration and with mediation by court masters. In all of these developments, one perceives a recognition that alternative, dispute-resolution methods such as arbitration can play a greater role in resolving public controversies.

Adherence to arbitration is inspired by a vision of international disputes being determined in accordance with concepts of international justice, rather than under the threat of force. The mechanics of the process are no problem: arbitration agreements can be made a part of multinational conventions or of bilateral agreements between any two nations. In order to achieve that goal, our leading citizens must be prepared to set aside national prejudices and learn to look at conflicts as citizens of the world. That commitment is not shared by many politicians, most of whom tend to believe that the United States demands such total loyalty that national security must be the primary concern of government and of every citizen. To them, it may seem disloyal for a United States citizen to serve as an impartial arbitrator in an international matter. It takes great intellectual and moral stamina for an American to say that loyalty to humanity and to justice and to the world community should exceed national allegiance. The broader use of impartial arbitration for disputes between nations may require a more acute understanding of the mutual dependence of all peoples. National sovereignty stands in the way of any meaningful allegiance to legal principles accepted by the world community, enforced by impartial arbitrators.

Some United States nationals may be capable of rising above such a national bias. But whether United States nationals can act as impartial arbitrators in situations where the security interests of the United States are concerned is, at least, questionable. As a populace, we have not been encouraged to think of ourselves as citizens of the world.

In about 600 B.C., a controversy between Athens and Megara over possession of the island of Salamis was submitted to an arbitration tribunal consisting of five Spartans, who assigned the island to Athens. Could we believe that any five Americans would have been invited to decide the Falkland Islands' dispute? Americans have earned a reputation as nationalists. With few exceptions, we probably deserve that label.

The Permanent Court of Arbitration at The Hague was established by international conferences in 1899 and 1907. High hopes were current that the Court would provide machinery for preventing future wars. Periodic wars have disabused the world of that expectation. Likewise, the League of Nations and the United Nations have not insured world peace. On the other hand, in areas where multinational cooperation is essential—communications, air travel, space, etc.—conventions and international compacts have been entered into and include mechanisms for resolving disputes through impartial arbitration. The use of arbitration may spread from these limited applications to become the channel for more dramatic confrontations between nations. The pending Convention on the Law of the Sea, for example, is replete with arbitration provisions, although it seems unlikely that the United States will sign it.

The need for defining and implementing a concept of international justice seems increasingly apparent. Burdened by evergrowing military budgets, fearful in the face of threats of violence, and in some cases incapable of providing for basic human needs, the citizens of the world can no longer cope with the present and can articulate no realistic plan for the future. In the absence of precise, operational principles for conflict resolution—substantive principles of justice and fairness—impartial arbitration has demonstrated its value for deciding business controversies and its potential for resolving the pragmatic problems stemming from interconnecting world technology.

Many of the potential causes for war arise from economic or social differences that could be the subject of mediation or arbitration. Trade issues or controversies over raw materials or the rights of minority groups have frequently been the crux of such disputes. By submitting these kinds of issues to impartial dispute resolution, nations may have one last clear chance to escape the horrors of military control. The rule of law, backed by arbitration, may provide the only visible alternative to world government. The modest experiments in international arbitration that are now operating could be expanded. Arbitration might become an active participant in the dance of nations, calling partners together, forging some rational future arrangements for the world community. It is time to invite arbitration to the party.

Questions

1. Why does the author say that arbitration has become "an international wallflower"? Can you think of military clashes in recent history which could have been avoided by arbitration?

2. Why is the prevailing American view one that seeks to impose its will by force? How does this compare with the high degree of religious observance in this country?

3. Would it be unpatriotic for an American judge to rule against his country in an international dispute? What is your definition of patriotism?

4. Name a recent case before the Permanent Court of Arbitration (World Court) in which the United States was involved. What happened?

5. The author states that the rule of law, using arbitration, may be the only alternative to world government. Give your critique of this opinion.

10
Getting to "Yes"
in a Nuclear Age

Roger Fisher

This article originally appeared in *Getting to 'Yes': Negotiating Agreement without Giving In*, 1981.

Roger Fisher, a Harvard University specialist in international affairs, observes in his 1981 article that current U.S. foreign policy seeks peace through belligerent behavior toward the Russians. He bids us to consider how America reacts when the Soviets do the same thing. One-sidedness, he says, makes the superpower negotiators much like drug addicts unable to shake their addiction.

Before World War II, Fisher says, "Political power was directly related to military power." With the atom bomb, this is no longer the case. He envisions the problem of getting agreements to be more psychological than military: "the balance between the consequences they see in saying 'yes' and the consequences they see of saying 'no'." In Table 1, Fisher lays out these consequences in regard to Russia's response to martial law in Poland.

The author argues that cutting off communication with the Soviets actually decreases our ability to influence their behavior. Also important is how we negotiate. At some length, he contrasts "hard" and "soft" negotiating stances, and compares them with what he calls "principled negotiation." (See Tables 2 and 3.) Since "principled negotiation" is his brain child, he dwells on it at length, calling it an attempt to "change the game." It involves: (1) separating the people from the problem; (2) focusing on interests, not positions; (3) generating a variety of possibilities before deciding what to do; (4) insisting that the result be based on an objective standard.

Each of these four principles is subject to three stages in negotiation: analysis, planning and discussion. The finished product, in Fisher's view, "typically results in a wise agreement." He cites the success of Salt I and even the unratified Salt II agreement which have generally been observed by both superpowers. As with international conventions that pertain to shipping, it is advance knowledge, convergence of interests and mutual understanding that count for more than the legally binding nature of an agreement.

The political and military intentions of the Soviet Union are of utmost concern to American officials. Since World War II, a central task of United States foreign policy has been to influence Soviet decisionmaking. To this end the United States has employed a variety of approaches, ranging from arms limitation agreements and the expansion of East-West trade, to economic sanctions, geopolitical confrontations, and the pursuit of nuclear superiority.

Recently, the United States has been looking especially hard to do something. Faced with a continuous Soviet arms buildup, the military domination of Afghanistan, the presence of Cuban and East German forces in Africa, the potential invasion of Poland, and Soviet failures to comply with the human rights provisions of the Helsinki Accords, Washington has taken a decidedly military approach toward influencing the Soviet Union. Strategic and theatre-level nuclear forces have been upgraded toward a first-strike capability; "rapid deployment" forces have been expanded; overall military spending has been vastly increased. There also has been tough talk about American resolve and willingness to fight a nuclear war, variously accompanied by public denunciations, a boycott of the Olympics, and on-again/off-again grain embargoes. And all too often, Washington has placed tight restrictions on communication. We have tended not only to hang up the phone, but to cut the line. For nine months the United States had no ambassador in Moscow. At every level, contacts with Soviet officials have tended to be stiff, peremptory, and minimal.

The underlying assumption is clear enough: the way to make the Soviets more peaceful is for the United States to behave more belligerently. The idea is that by engaging in a massive military buildup, and threatening to use it, we will scare the Soviet Union into being more peaceful.

But let us stop and think. How do we react when the Soviets build more weapons and threaten us? Do we ask ourselves whether U.S. policies have looked unduly aggressive? Do officials suggest that we show restraint by slowing down our military spending and behaving in more peaceful ways? No. When the Soviets build SS-20 missiles by the score, we become more bellicose. And we step up our military spending.

Knowing how we react, common sense tells us how the Soviet Union will react to our bellicosity. We react belligerently to the fact that the Soviets outspent the United States during the past decade by some $300 billion for military purposes. We should well understand why the Soviet Union reacts similarly to the fact (equally true) that during that same decade we and our NATO allies outspent the Soviets and their allies by some $280 billion for military purposes.

Of course, throwing our arms away cannot be expected to cause the Soviets to lie down like lambs, no more than the United States would do so were the Soviet Union to pursue the same course. But now that each of us has more than enough military hardware to serve as a deterrent, now that both sides have roughly comparable military forces (all the talk about a "missile gap" or a "window of vulnerability" to the contrary notwithstanding), more U.S. weapons will hardly cause the Soviets to produce less.

In sum, the suggestion that being more belligerent will cause the Soviets to behave less belligerently is contrary to both experience and common sense. And the companion notion that we make the world safer for the United States by acquiring weapons that make it more dangerous for the Soviet Union is far worse. So far as nuclear war is concerned, we are in the same boat. We cannot make our end of the boat safer by making the Soviet end more likely to tip over. And to diminish Soviet confidence in the physical security of their nuclear forces only increases the pressure to use them.

Thus, while the original international problem for which we got our nuclear weapons was fear of aggression by another Hitler, the cure has now become more dangerous than the disease. Like drugs to which we have become addicted, our nuclear weapons have become habit-forming and dangerous. Designed to protect us from other countries that legitimately give us cause for concern, they themselves have become a threat to national survival; and a failure to appreciate this blunt fact indicates a failure to comprehend the radical change from the days when there were only conventional weapons available. We can boldly say: "Better dead than Red." But, honestly, each of us would prefer to have our children in Havana, Belgrade, Beijing, Warsaw, or Leningrad today than in Hiroshima or Nagasaki when the nuclear bombs went off. A general nuclear war would be far more damaging to our national interest than even the most outrageous political domination.

I

Before World War II, superior military force was persuasive indeed. Defensively, if a country had the clear physical ability to protect itself, then others could be persuaded not to attack: since an attack would fail, why try? Offensively too, if a country had the clear ability physically to impose its will and to produce the result it desired, then why resist? In an era which considered both colonialism and war legitimate, the political cost of imposing a desired result was likely to be modest. The power to bring about a result by self-help if negotiations should fail made it far more likely that a weaker country would agree to the result requested by a stronger country. A country that could not prevent a given result by fighting might just as well agree without a fight. Political power was directly related to military power.

Despite our nuclear age, some military weapons still do enhance the power to persuade. Having enough "smart" anti-tank weapons helps persuade an adversary not to launch a tank attack. A strong physical barrier, a mine field, an anti-submarine net, or anti-aircraft batteries may effectively persuade an opposing country not to attempt a particular military action. Such weapons deter action because they have the power to prevent it. Offensively, too, where the desired result is to occupy and maintain control over nearby territory, the physical power to do so greatly enhances a State's negotiating power. The situation of Israel and the Golan Heights is a case in point.

But in the world today, most foreign policy objectives—particularly those of the United States and the Soviet Union toward one another—cannot be accomplished by military means. There is no way we can physically impose freedom upon the Soviet Union, and no way they can physically impose their values upon us. We cannot physically impose self-government on some country that does not have it. The United States has found that its possession of vast military forces has not given it the power to persuade Vietnam, Libya, South Africa, Syria, or Iran to make the decisions we want them to make. And the Soviet Union has discovered that the billions of rubles it has spent on arms have not given it the power to influence others either. Ten years ago, Egypt had 17,000 Soviet troops. Today those troops have been expelled and American and Egyptian troops conduct joint maneuvers.

This point—that the power to persuade and military power are no longer necessarily synonymous or coextensive—is especially important in the context of nuclear confrontation. The consequences of a nuclear war would be catastrophic. And they would be worse for some countries than for others. But unless a real prospect of nuclear war appears on one side of the choice a country faces, the consequences of a nuclear war are irrelevant to that choice. For example, as we press the Soviet Union to bring about an end to martial law in Poland, the Soviet Union might see their choice as depicted in Table 1. If this is the way the Soviet Union sees its choice, our military weapons, including our nuclear weapons, are irrelevant to their decision. Equally so our nuclear superiority has been irrelevant to our negotiations with Iran over the hostages, to our efforts to persuade Israel to stop building settlements in the West Bank, to our

Table 1
Today's Context: Where Military Power Is Not the Power to Persuade

QUESTION: SHALL WE, THE SOVIET UNION, PRESS FOR THE END OF MARTIAL LAW IN POLAND?	
If "Yes"	If "No"
− We accept full responsibility for the mess in Poland.	+ We limit our responsibility for Poland.
− We risk instability in Eastern Europe.	+ Eastern Europe is likely to remain stable.
− We antagonize Poland nationalists of all kinds in the military, in Solidarity, in the Church, and in the Party.	+ We buy time.
	+ We stand up to the United States.
− Both the economy and the political situation are likely to become worse.	+ The Polish Army may bring the situation under control.
− We look weak in backing down to a US demand.	+ We limit our confrontation with the Poles.
	+ We keep our options open (we can always do something later if it appears desirable).

efforts to moderate Libya's behavior, or to persuade our European allies to support sanctions against the Soviet Union.

True, our nuclear weapons do serve one important function. They make it extremely dangerous for the Soviet Union to do outrageous things such as bomb Pearl Harbor or New York, or land forces in Florida or Britain, or try a blitzkrieg attack across Western Europe. But once we have enough strategic forces to make any such action extremely risky, additional nuclear forces do not improve our negotiating position on the daily problems we have with the Soviet Union and with other governments of the world. If having a superior power to destroy gave one the power to persuade, then the Soviet Union—and the rest of the world, for that matter—would have been dancing to our tune for the last 30 years.

In sum, diplomatic success today depends less upon what can be produced by physical means than upon what takes place in somebody else's head; "our" success depends upon "their" decision. And in all such cases the critical balance is not the balance of destructive power, but, rather, the balance sheet of the presently perceived choice: how do the consequences of "their" deciding as "we" wish compare in their minds with the consequences of not doing so? The critical balance, in other words, is not that between our military force and the force on the other side, but the balance between the consequences they see of saying "yes" and the consequences they see of saying "no."

Of course, beyond an analysis of Soviet decisionmaking, we can see that our choice also is subject to influence. Indeed, the major case for an enormous strategic weapons buildup rests on the premise that those weapons will protect us against a Soviet demand that is backed up with a nuclear threat. But just as a large number of nuclear weapons provides no protection against attempted extortion by a lone terrorist, they cannot protect us from attempted extortion by a Soviet leader who might be equally indifferent to the fate of others. The outcome of such attempted blackmail is not determined by counting potential casualties; the numbers are all but irrelevant. In such an exchange of unprincipled threats, the advantage goes to the leader who is least concerned with human life, is more ruthless, is more willing to gamble for high stakes, is less vulnerable to criticism by a free press, and has fewer constituents to whom he must later answer. But there is no way in which our acquiring additional nuclear warheads will make it wise policy for an American President to compete in ruthlessness with a leader of the Soviet Union.

Our ability to influence the Soviet Union depends, then, upon our ability to affect the way they see a future choice, independent of the nuclear threat; and this is as true in the realm of arms control and disarmament as it is in any other. To persuade the Soviet Union to agree to meaningful arms limitation and reduction proposals, we need to formulate and present a series of choices where each time the consequences of deciding as we would like are more attractive to them as well as to us than their proceeding down the road toward a deteriorating relationship.

II

Of the many variables that enhance such negotiating power, one of the most important is effective two-way communication. If we are to change Soviet minds, we need to know what is on those minds; we need to listen. Whatever Soviet officials may try to conceal, the more extensive our discussions, the more we can listen "between the lines," the better will be the intelligence we can glean.

There are those who favor breaking or reducing diplomatic relations as a response to outrageous conduct. They suggest that talking under such circumstances looks "soft," that it implies approval, and that actions speak louder than words. Actions do speak loudly. But our purpose is not simply to express ourselves. It is to affect Soviet behavior, and to this end communication is more powerful if it is two-way, precise, and continuous. To close down the Soviet purchasing office, to suspend talks on wheat sales and merchant marine matters, or to reduce scientific exchange, tends to decrease our ability to influence the Soviet Union, not increase it. Such actions suggest that we are enemies no matter what the other side does, thus eliminating any incentive for change. With continuous talks, however, we learn more and there is more time for good ideas to prevail. We also avoid the unfortunate result that if stopping talks is used to signal disapproval, then resuming talks—as we did over wheat sales—implies approval, it implies for instance, that Soviet conduct, even in Afghanistan, is not so bad after all.

The model for good communication is not a "high-noon" confrontation between gunslingers, but the kind of intensive talks that produced the treaty banning atmospheric nuclear tests. We exert influence most effectively when the other side knows exactly what is expected, why it is legitimate, and what we will do next. These are conditions that are hard to meet without talking extensively and in detail. We can be just as firm in a meeting as elsewhere—and a great deal clearer. Our negotiating power is enhanced by maintaining the maximum amount of two-way communication at all levels. Without effective two-way communication there is no successful negotiation.

III

Another key variable to successful negotiation is how we negotiate. Our purpose is to work out with the Soviet Union a way to live together on this precarious globe. We want to clarify existing restraints and develop additional ones because it is in our mutual interest to do so. But to increase the chance of our devising wise restraints in time to avoid disaster, we should stop bargaining over positions as though haggling over the price of a rug; we should use a method more likely to serve our shared interests. The process of negotiation itself is critical.

The traditional mode of conducting a two-party international conference is well illustrated by the SALT—now START—process, and has three key features:

Decide first, talk later. Each side unilaterally develops and decides upon its proposed solution before talking with the other side.

Argue about positions. Most of the discussion among negotiators is devoted to explaining and defending one's own one-sided position and attacking that of the other side.

Make concessions slowly. As time goes by, one side or the other reluctantly makes a small concession to keep the talks from breaking down.

This is a poor method of negotiating.

First, this approach is unlikely to produce optimal results: with it more time is spent arguing over extreme positions than in trying to develop creative solutions. When negotiators bargain over positions, they tend to lock themselves into those positions. The more often they restate a position and defend it against attack, the more committed they become to it. The more they try to convince the other side of the impossibility of changing their opening position, the more difficult it becomes to do so. Egos become identified with positions. There develops a new interest in "saving face"—in reconciling future action with past positions. This process makes it less and less likely that any agreement will wisely reconcile the parties' original concerns.

The danger that positional bargaining will impede a negotiation was well illustrated by the breakdown of talks under President Kennedy for a comprehensive ban on nuclear testing. A critical question arose: how many on-site inspections per year should the Soviet Union and the United States be permitted to make within the other's territory to investigate suspicious seismic events? The Soviet Union finally agreed to three inspections. The United States insisted on no less than ten. And there the talks broke down—over positions—despite the fact that no one understood whether an "inspection" would involve one person looking around for one day, or a hundred people prying indiscriminately for a month. The parties had made little attempt to design an inspection procedure that would reconcile the United States's interest in verification with the desire of both countries for minimal intrusion.

As more attention is paid to positions, less attention is devoted to meeting the underlying concerns of the parties. Agreement becomes less likely. Any agreement reached may reflect a mechanical splitting of the difference between stated positions rather than a solution carefully crafted to meet the legitimate interests of the parties. The result is frequently an agreement less than satisfactory to each side than it could have been.

Second, this "bazaar" or "haggling" approach to negotiation tends to be extremely inefficient; it takes a lot of time. The United States devoted a full year to producing preliminary agreement among Army, Navy, Air Force, State Department, Arms Control Agency, and White House officials, as well as our NATO allies, merely on an opening SALT/START position—which everyone knew had no chance of being accepted by the Soviet Union. Now, over the months and years ahead, we will have to get similar agreement on each of many concessions arising from this maximum position.

Bargaining over positions creates incentives that stall settlement. In positional bargaining we try to improve the chance that any settlement reached be favorable to us by starting with an extreme position, by stubbornly holding to it, by deceiving the other party as to our true views, and by making small concessions only as necessary to keep the negotiation going. The same is true for the other side. Each of those factors tends to interfere with reaching a settlement promptly. The more extreme the opening positions and the smaller the concessions, the more time and effort it will take to discover whether or not agreement is possible.

The standard minuet also requires a large number of individual decisions as each negotiator decides what to offer, what to reject, and how much of a concession to make. Decisionmaking in this fashion is difficult and time-consuming at best. Where each decision not only involves yielding to the other side but the possibility of having to yield further, a negotiator has little incentive to move quickly. Dragging one's feet, threatening to walk out, stonewalling, and other such tactics become commonplace. They all increase the time and costs of reaching agreement as well as the risk that no agreement will be reached at all.

Finally, in addition to producing unwise agreements and to being time-consuming, positional bargaining is politically costly, endangering ongoing relationships. During the entire process there is an incentive for everyone to be stubborn, hoping that someone else will yield first. In the East-West context, the contest of will that this process involves can be expected to exacerbate relations not only with the Soviet Union but among our allies as well.

Each negotiator asserts what he will and won't do. The task of jointly devising an acceptable solution becomes a battle. Each side tries through sheer will power to force the other to change its position. "We're not going to give in. If you want to limit or reduce arms, it's our way or nothing." Anger and resentment often result as one side sees itself bending to the rigid will of the other while its own legitimate concerns go unaddressed.

Positional bargaining thus strains and sometimes shatters the relationship between the parties. This has happened between the United States and the Soviet Union on numerous occasions, and the world is not a safer place for it.

On the other hand, being "nice" is no answer either. Many people recognize the high costs of hard positional bargaining, particularly on the parties and their relationship. They hope to avoid them by following a more gentle style of negotiation. Instead of seeing the other side as adversaries, they prefer to see them as friends. Rather than emphasizing a goal of victory, they emphasize the necessity of reaching agreement. In a soft negotiating game the standard moves are to make offers and concessions, to trust the other side, to be friendly, and to yield as necessary to avoid confrontation.

Table 2 illustrates two styles of positional bargaining: soft and hard. Most people see their choice of negotiating strategies as between these two styles. Looking at the table as presenting a choice, should the United States or the Soviet Union be a soft or a hard positional bargainer?

The soft negotiating game emphasizes the importance of building and maintaining a relationship. Within families and among friends much negotiation takes place in this way. The process tends to be efficient, at least to the extent of producing results quickly. As each party competes with the other in being more generous and more forthcoming, an agreement becomes highly likely. But the agreement may not be wise. Any negotiation primarily concerned with the relationship runs the risk of producing a sloppy agreement.

Table 2

PROBLEM

Positional Bargaining: Which Game Should You Play?

SOFT	HARD
Participants are friends.	Participants are adversaries.
The goal is agreement.	The goal is victory.
Make concessions to cultivate the relationship.	Demand concessions as a condition of the relationship.
Be soft on the people and the problem.	Be hard on the problem and the people.
Trust others.	Distrust others.
Change your position easily.	Dig in to your position.
Make offers.	Make threats.
Disclose your bottom line.	Mislead as to your bottom line.
Accept one-sided losses to reach agreement.	Demand one-sided gains as the price of agreement.
Search for the single answer: the one *they* will accept.	Search for the single answer: the one *you* will accept.
Insist on agreement.	Insist on your position.
Try to avoid a contest of will.	Try to win a contest of will.
Yield to pressure.	Apply pressure.

Further, pursuing a soft form of positional bargaining makes us vulnerable to someone who plays a hard game of positional bargaining. In positional bargaining, a hard game dominates a soft one. If the hard bargainer insists on his position while the soft bargainer insists on agreement, the negotiating game is biased in favor of the hard player. Any agreement reached will be more favorable to the hard positional bargainer than to the soft one.

IV

Fortunately, the "bazaar" approach to negotiation is not the only way to seek agreement. If we do not like the choice between hard and soft positional bargaining, we can change the game.

A more efficient and effective approach to negotiation, a method explicitly designed to produce wise outcomes efficiently and amicably, is called principled negotiation or negotiation on the merits. Based on the principle of talking first and deciding later, it can be boiled down to four basic points.

These four points define a straightforward method of negotiation that can be used under almost any circumstance. Each point deals with a basic element of negotiation, and suggests what you should do about it.

People: Separate the people from the problem.
Interests: Focus on interests, not positions.
Options: Generate a variety of possibilities before deciding what to do.
Criteria: Insist that the result be based on some objective standard.

The first point responds to the fact that human beings, including representatives of national governments, are not computers. We are creatures of strong emotions who often have radically different perceptions and have difficulty communicating clearly. Emotions typically become entangled with the objective merits of the problem. Taking positions just makes this worse because people's egos become identified with their positions. Hence, before working on the substantive problem, the "people problem" should be disentangled from it and dealt with separately. Figuratively if not literally, the participants should come to see themselves as working side by side attacking the problem, not each other. Hence the first proposition: Separate the people from the problem.

The second point is designed to overcome the drawback of focusing on stated positions when the object of a negotiation is to satisfy underlying interests. Since any norm we might later agree upon must be in the interests of the Soviet Union and the United States, we should learn as much as possible about Soviet needs and wants, and we should make sure that Moscow is equally clear about ours. We should ignore any declared position except as evidence of some underlying interest. Compromising between positions is unlikely to produce an agreement which will effectively take care of the human needs that lead people to adopt those positions. The second basic element of the method thus is: Focus on interests, not positions.

The third point responds to the difficulty of designing optimal solutions while under pressure. Trying to decide in the presence of an adversary narrows one's vision. Having a lot at stake inhibits creativity. So does searching for the one right solution. A major aim, therefore, is to invent, without commitment, different ways of possibly reconciling conflicting interests. We can offset the constraints of pressured circumstance by setting aside designated occasions within which to think up a wide range of possible solutions that advance shared interests and creatively reconcile differing interests. During the SALT I talks, two members of each delegation (called "the wizards" by the Russians) used to meet for the purpose of creative brainstorming, understood to be without commitment on behalf of either government. Some such process is extremely valuable, permitting the Soviet Union and the United States to devise norms of behavior, both for weapons and for military-political activity, that are in the interest of each country to respect so long as the other is demonstrably doing so. Hence the third basic point: Before trying to reach agreement, invent options for mutual gain.

Some negotiators obtain a favorable result simply by being stubborn. To allow that to happen rewards intransigence and produces arbitrary results. It is possible to counter such a negotiator by insisting that his single say-so is not enough and that any agreement must reflect some fair standard independent of the naked will of either side. This does not mean insisting that the terms be based on the standard we select, but only that some fair standard determine the outcome. In negotiating arms limitations, there are many possible objective standards to assure fairness or rough equivalence in arms reductions, in force levels, or in military vulnerability. By discussing such criteria rather than what the parties are willing or unwilling to do, neither party need give in to the other; both can defer to a fair solution. Hence the fourth basic point: Insist on using objective criteria.

The method of principled negotiation is contrasted with hard and soft positional bargaining in Table 3, which shows the four basic points of the method in boldface type. With a good understanding of each other's interests, with multiple options that have been designed to meet them, and with the principle of reciprocity as a guide, there is an optimal chance that negotiators can produce recommendations for official decision.

It is important to note also that the four basic propositions of principled negotiation are relevant from the time one begins to think about negotiating until the time either an agreement is reached or a decision is

Table 3

PROBLEM Position Bargaining: Which Game Should You Play?		SOLUTION Change the Game— Negotiate on the Merits
SOFT	**HARD**	**PRINCIPLED**
Participants are friends.	Participants are adversaries.	Participants are problem-solvers.
The goal is agreement.	The goal is victory.	The goal is a wise outcome reached efficiently and amicably.
Make concessions to cultivate the relationship.	Demand concessions as a condition of the relationship.	Separate the people from the problem.
Be soft on the people and the problem.	Be hard on the problem and the people.	Be soft on the people, hard on the problem.
Trust others.	Distrust others.	Proceed independent of trust.
Change your position easily.	Dig in to your position.	Focus on interests, not positions.
Make offers.	Make threats.	Explore interests.
Disclose your bottom line.	Mislead as to your bottom line.	Avoid having a bottom line.
Accept one-sided losses to reach agreement.	Demand one-sided gains as the price of agreement.	Invent options for mutual gain.
Search for the single answer: the one *they* will accept.	Search for the single answer: the one *you* will accept.	Develop multiple options to choose from; decide laters.
Insist on agreement.	Insist on your position.	Insist on objective criteria.
Try to avoid a contest of will.	Try to win a contest of will.	Try to reach a result based on standards independent of will.
Yield to pressure.	Apply pressure.	Reason and be open to reasons; yield to principle, not pressure.

made to break off the effort. That period can be divided into three stages: analysis, planning, and discussion.

During the analysis stage one is simply trying to diagnose the situation—to gather information, organize it, and think about it. Negotiators will want to consider the people problems of partisan perceptions, hostile emotions, and unclear communication, as well as to identify their interests and those of the other side. They will want to note options already on the table and identify any criteria already suggested as a basis for agreement.

During the planning stage negotiators deal with the same four elements a second time, both generating ideas and deciding what to do. How do they propose to handle the people problems? Of their interests, which are most important? And what are some realistic objectives? They will want to generate additional options and additional criteria for deciding among them.

Again during the discussion stage, when the parties communicate back and forth, looking toward agreement, the same four elements are the best subjects to discuss. Differences in perception, feelings of frustration and anger, and difficulties in communication can be acknowledged and addressed. Each side should come to understand the interests of the other. Both can then jointly generate options that are mutually advantageous and seek agreement on objective standards for resolving opposed interests.

To sum up, in contrast to positional bargaining, the principled negotiation method of focusing on basic interests, mutually satisfying options, and fair standards typically results in a wise agreement. The method permits reaching a gradual consensus on a joint decision efficiently without all the transactional costs of digging in to positions only to have to dig out of them. And separating the people from the problem allows dealing directly and empathetically with the other negotiator as a human being, thus making possible an amicable agreement. If all this is possible, an actual commitment becomes less important. The provisions of SALT I have expired and those of SALT II never have come into effect. Yet, except for the dismantling provisions, both the Soviet Union and the United States are respecting those terms. Even nonbinding norms can establish a modus vivendi. As with an unmarried couple sharing an apartment, it may be easier for both countries to live together than to enter into major commitments.

We and the Soviet Union have good reason to be skeptical about each other's intentions. Yet however high our level of mutual distrust, we share an enormous interest in avoiding a calamitous collision. On the high seas the danger of ships colliding is reduced through international agreement on a system of signals and evasive turns. What matters is not that the signals are legally binding but that they have been worked out in advance and have become well understood.

The danger of a military collision between the Soviet Union and the United States is both far more dangerous and far more difficult to avoid. The fact that we distrust each other makes joint planning for crisis management both more important and more urgent. As disastrous as any nuclear war would be, it would be tragic indeed to have a nuclear war which both sides wanted at the last minute to avoid, but didn't know how. Maintaining effective two-way communication and adopting techniques of principled negotiation in the pursuit of common interests are among the first prerequisites for overcoming mutual distrust and avoiding such a calamity.

Questions

1. Why does Fisher say that cutting off contacts with the Soviets does little to influence them to move in our direction?

2. How can U.S. policymakers "read between the lines" to determine Soviet intentions?

3. Why does the author compare most international negotiations with "haggling over the price of a rug"? Why does he find this method counterproductive?

4. How does "principled negotiation" differ from "hard" and "soft" negotiation?

5. What would be one example of an objective standard on which to evaluate the results of a negotiation?

11
Ideological Convergence of the U.S. and U.S.S.R.

Gordon L. Anderson

This article originally appeared in *International Social Science Review*, 1985.

Is there hope for world peace through social science? Gordon Anderson, an editor at the International Journal of World Peace, *thinks there is. Insofar as Roger Fisher's contribution in the preceding article was an application of social science, Anderson complements it by a backward and forward look at ideology and "science."*

Anderson notes that traditional Western wisdom has taken a top-down approach. To this, he contrasts the statistical and behavioral approaches of the social sciences, illustrating in Figure 1 the different ways these two systems arrive at truth. Anderson expresses guarded confidence that someday Soviet and Western researchers may arrive at the same conclusions following agreed-upon methods.

Social scientists in the West, he says, have gone through several stages, from a brash "reductionism" which alienated many advocates of traditional wisdom, to a "hands-off" approach which was criticized as being too timid, to a gradual acceptance in recent years. Today, many social scientists are emboldened to proclaim (1) the inadequacy of the nation state, (2) the inadequacy of the "rational man" model of decision-making, and (3) the possibility of the integration rather than the continuation of conflict. Anderson predicts that traditional wisdom and social science will perform complementary functions in arriving at useful political goals.

As for the Eastern bloc, the author takes Marx himself for a bottom-up thinker whose writings eventually became a new "strand of wisdom," or ideology. Along came Lenin who "espoused Marx's bottom-up approach to knowledge but applied Marx in a top-down manner." Stalin tightened the screws on freedom of thought, and it was not until the mid 1950s that "we find historical and cultural forces pushing the Soviets toward scientific criticism of inherited dogma." Starting almost from scratch, the Soviets have begun to make use of social science in a manner similar to that of the West.

Even though ideological polemics dominate the international atmosphere today, the author is hopeful that social science may increasingly provide a bridge between East and West, much as the disputatious churches of fifty years ago have moderated their differences through membership in the World Council of Churches.

The author's concluding recommendations, not surprisingly, are for the U.S. and the U.S.S.R. to increase their exchanges in the area of social sciences and that each nation's leadership take more account of the social sciences in their foreign policies.

Part of the mistrust between the United States and the Soviet Union which fuels the nuclear arms race is rooted in ideological differences. The author argues that common methods of research on common issues facing the two superpowers are leading to ideological convergence. Convergence does not appear to be the case, if one observes the harsh rhetoric exchanged between these nations in previous years. However, the next generation of social science scholars will approach ideological convergence. There is a precedent for this theory in the National Council of Churches in the USA, where past theological differences have become minimized as joint engagement of the same issues for over 50 years has led to theological convergence.

I. INTRODUCTION

The pressing problem of the nuclear arms race and the tension between the United States and the Soviet Union has been the subject of serious discussion by politicians, scholars, and citizens in both countries. Traditionally, nation-states have been viewed as sovereign entities which resolved their differences through war or treaties. The post-World War II situation has gradually changed that view. In the context of potential nuclear annihilation, war between the United States and the Soviet Union would end life as it is currently experienced. Nuclear war is an unthinkable way of resolving conflict. Treaties have also come to reveal limited usefulness as over 20 years of negotiations for arms limitations have failed to end the arms buildup by both superpowers. Without trust or mutual understanding, or by subordination to national interest, treaties have been breached, sometimes aggravating the international stress. Since World War II, the doctrine of deterrence temporarily ascended to the status of orthodox political thought. But this doctrine has recently been losing credibility because it does not halt proliferation of nuclear weapons to other countries. Further, young people who have grown up under the umbrella of deterrence have limited hope in the future. They suffer psychological distress and often live by a "live it up today for tomorrow may not come" attitude.

Recent studies in the field of international relations shed light on an alternative strategy to reduce tension between the superpowers. This is an attempt to work toward the reduction of the causes of the tension itself, rather than merely devising ways of defending oneself from another nation viewed as "the enemy." The basic hypothesis underlying this study can be described as follows: If two conflicting nations are to establish durable co-operation and reduce tension, then incremental integration would be more effective than attempts at comprehensive settlements (treaties).

In analyzing the theme of integration, it is useful to make distinctions between top-down and bottom-up approaches and between external and internal integration. In current international relations literature, there are several theories of integration which are top-down, bottom-up, or some mixture of the two directions. The federalist approach, which advocates a world government structure, is an example of a top-down theory of integration. The transactionalist approach is a bottom-up theory which advocates all kinds of human interchange and communication across borders. Soviet scientists meeting with United States scientists, cultural events, or the Olympics are examples of bottom-up integration. Functional and neo-functional approaches look at integration on an intermediary level. Examples are the International Labor Organization or the International Postal Union. "External integration" refers to structural and organizational integration. This means some people in the United States and some people in the Soviet Union would be related to the same law or authority. This structure can be applied from the top-down by force of treaty or be generated from the bottom-up by common practical needs. "Internal integration" refers to unity of thoughts and feelings shared by people in the two nations. Again, this can be forced on a people by rigid indoctrination and training programs; or, it can emerge as common responses and conclusions drawn by different peoples in a genuine quest for truth as in scientific study.

Much of the writing in international relations has been devoted to the spectrum from top-down to bottom-up external integration. Ideological differences have polarized the United States and the Soviet Union so sharply that reconciliation has been seen as impossible. This is especially true if "ideology," like religious beliefs, is forced top-down by rigorous indoctrination programs. The brutality marked by religious conversion at the point of a sword is a memory which most Westerners want to forget. The polemics exchanged by the superpowers, especially since the Soviet invasion of Afghanistan, seem to confirm the irreconcilability of the political philosophies of the United States and the Soviet Union. The cultures are viewed as eternally different. Ideological integration received some attention in the 1970's, but has rarely been discussed in the 1980's.

In the short run, ideological incompatibility may be the case but it is our thesis that this is not so in the long run. A larger historical overview of thought patterns reveals convergence. The common global challenges which confront the two superpowers will generate shared beliefs about the world and have a tendency to reduce the internal or ideological conflict between the superpowers. All this hinges, of course, on the condition that nuclear war does not break out in the short run. Our hypothesis about ideological integration reads as follows: For reduction of internal tension and increased integration with conflicting ideologies, the a priori, or naive, belief systems must be criticized and modified by a posteriori, or scientific, philosophy.

Hope for the reduction of the ideological tension between the two powers can be found in the increased input from the social sciences into government decisions in both systems. Section II traces this development within the United States and Section III describes its emergence in the Soviet Union. In Section IV these developments are analyzed and compared to the similar situation which has faced ecumenical activity of different religious bodies. It is noted that new supradenominational beliefs have emerged among once hostile religious denominations. Ernst Troeltsch's explanation for the basic epistemological process at work helps to clarify the development we witness. Finally, we conclude with some specific policy recommendations which can assist in the reduction of the ideological tension between the United States and the Soviet Union.

II. SCIENTIFIC POLITICAL PHILOSOPHY IN THE UNITED STATES

A. *The Top-Down Tradition*

The history of Western civilization is replete with top-down approaches to national politics. The Greeks and Romans laid strong foundations with the political decision-making authority resting in kings and emperors. The most influential Christian thinkers, Augustine, Aquinas, and Martin Luther, gave sanction to the top-down application of power by temporal rulers for the sake of social order. Obedience to the secular authority was taught to be a Christian virtue. Under these conditions it was difficult to develop any scientific political philosophy which might challenge the will of the ruler.

Following the demise of feudalism, the status of law became elevated and constitutional monarchies were favored. Calvin's Geneva was an early development of the modern period in political philosophy. The fullest development of the modern view is found in G. W. F. Hegel (1770–1831), who benefited from the accumulated thought of Machiavelli, Hobbes, Rousseau, and Kant. For Hegel, the law of the state was regarded as divine, as the incarnation of the Absolute Spirit as it unfolded in history: "The state is the realization of the ethical idea. . . . The state is the march of God through the world. . . . The state is the world which the spirit has made for itself. . . . Just as the spirit is superior to nature, so is the state superior to physical life. We must therefore worship the state as the manifestation of the divine on earth."[1]

Hegel's philosophy was compelling because it wedded traditional Christian ideas to Enlightenment philosophy in the context of the emerging nation-state system. He recommended the constitutional monarchy as the desired political order. Because Hegel viewed the state as the highest form of government, he concluded that disputes between nations must be settled by treaty or war. He glorified war as playing an ethical role in the unfolding drama of world history, the final court of justice. The Hegelian synthesis has influenced most modern political philosophy, whether it be German idealism, American realism, or Marxist-Leninism.

Early post-World War II political philosophy in the United States reflects the Hegelian political world view. Hans Morgenthau's classic work, *Politics Among Nations* (1948), depicts a world of sovereign nation-states with competing interests resolved by power. The federalist theory of world government is an attempt to expand the notion of a constitutional monarchy to the world level. The reverence for the top-down application of world law is reflected in Clark and Sohn's *World Peace Through World Law*. In all of these approaches, elites, diplomatic history, law, military power, and government structure provided the content of political philosophy. Though kings and princes had been outmoded and substituted by other forms of government, solutions to international tensions were still essentially top-down.

B. The Inherited Tradition as "Wisdom"

Although the study of politics inherited in this top-down context has been termed "political science," there have been serious questions more recently about how scientific this has really been. Traditionally, as with Aristotle, science employed reason and logic while observing phenomena. However, statistical methods developed in this century have placed new controls on observer biases. The methods of Thomas Aquinas, Kant, Hegel, or Marx, which rely on revelation, self-evident truths, or natural law as a basis for obtaining scientific conclusions, are now considered suspect by social scientists who use statistical methods as their research of human society and human behavior. The traditional method has been juxtaposed to the statistical methods by Charles McClelland in an article titled "International Relations: Wisdom or Science?" By "wisdom" McClelland referred to the traditional method of using reason, logic, and intuition in light of the received ideology when considering historical events. By "science" he meant the recent statistical or "behavioral" methods of the social sciences.

Figure 1 contains a set of diagrams which compare the traditional wisdom method of obtaining knowledge with the scientific approach as McClelland has defined it. While the processes can be diagrammed in parallel, the major emphasis of the scientific model is to control the influx of ideology, or unscientific beliefs.

The traditional wisdom model is culture-specific because it contains habits, beliefs, and the world view of the preceding generations. Each culture has developed different ways to view and act on the world. The observer is required to rationalize or justify observed phenomena in light of his received beliefs. For example, a Christian may explain one's poverty as a lack of faith in God while a Marxist might explain it as the result of capitalist oppression. History is full of examples of bloodshed resulting from wars fought over beliefs held as absolute, whether they purportedly led to political or to eternal salvation. Much of the struggle between the

Figure 1. Wisdom Versus Science

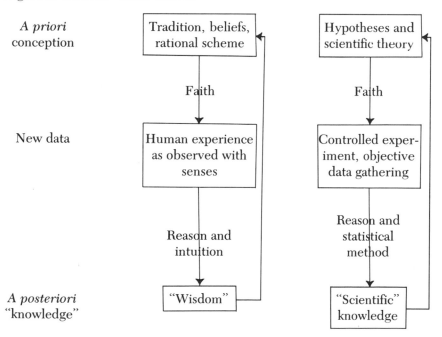

United States and the Soviet Union is rooted in this type of ideological conflict. These are top-down internal conflicts.

The scientific model, or the behavioral approach, is less culture-specific because the results obtained are based on an abstract (statistical) method with controlled conditions. Theoretically, a researcher in the United States and a researcher in the Soviet Union would reach the same conclusion if the same controlled procedure is followed.

C. The Rise of Scientism

The discovery and application of reliable scientific methods led to a hope that conventional wisdom, dogmas, and ideologies could be transcended. New doors were opened which allowed social scientists to apply more sophisticated research methods to all types of phenomena. Many diverse and disconnected areas were studied. Social science disciplines evolved and developed jargon confined to their own field. The error of reductionism which begat belief systems more potentially destructive than inherited wisdom was common in the infancy stage of the social sciences. The diverse "facts" discovered could not be integrated into any overarching world view, since any preexisting world view was methodologically excluded. Relating this problem to international relations theory in 1968, Neil Smelser concluded: "We do not at present have the methodological capacity to argue causally from a mixture of aggregated states of individual members of a system to a global characteristic of a system."[2] Psychologist Fred Greenstein echoed this statement, saying: "In part it is the reductionistic excesses of the past that account for the present lack of attention given by students of institutional processes to aggregation: there are too many horrible examples of the treatment of institutions as individuals writ large."[3]

Many social scientists initially kept their findings within the discipline and did not bring them to bear on political theory. Margaret Mead has said that anthropologists suffered severe disillusionment with government policies toward "primitive" people who are the traditional objects of study. They adopted the dictum "you can't advise an advisor." Elliot Aronson, a social psychologist, said many researchers used the excuse that social psychology was a young science when they ignored their political obligations.

The Vietnam War engendered harsh criticisms of the isolated studies of various disciplines. Lack of activism led David Horowitz to accuse the social sciences of a "bias towards the status quo," saying, "prostitution of the intellect has become so pervasive and profound that all but a small minority mistake it for academic virtue."[4] The cry went up to make scholastic research relevant to social action. This was what Ralph Pettman called the postbehavioral move from scientism to conciencism. At the American Political Science Association's 1969 meeting, President David Easton leveled several charges: that behavior science concealed an ideology of empirical conservativism; that technical jargon was building barriers; that the claim to scientific neutrality was a dangerous deception; and that academics have ignored their civic duties. The time had come for the social sciences to influence political thought.

D. Contributions of Social Sciences to Political Philosophy

The trend to go consciously beyond scientism in the 1970's has led to substantial contributions from the social sciences to political theory. There is an openness to interdisciplinary approaches to human problems; there is a trend toward correction of status quo political philosophy, and not thoughtless rejection of it; and there is a new sense of responsibility. Thus, the social sciences have contributed several insights which broaden traditional theory.

The most forthright assertion of the new researchers is the inadequacy of the traditional nation-state level of analysis. There is a new recognition of operative international systems, such as transnational economic organizations of cultural spheres. There is an increasing tendency to view the planet as one interrelated ecosystem. Also, psychology and social psychology have shown ways in which individual and group activities and beliefs affect national behavior. The state is not, as was earlier taught, viewed as an autonomous authority.

A second contribution to political theory is the insistence on the inadequacy of the "rational man" model of decision making. The high status traditionally accorded to human reason has been undercut by studies of the nonrational side of human behavior. Images, symbols, loyalties, ego-defense, habits, group dynamics, perception, and other noncognitive factors in decision making are studied. Further, it is now acknowledged contrary to what some philosophers might want to think, that our goal cannot and should not be to eliminate nonrational factors. It has been argued that the conscious attempt to be rational might result in one's being less rational. It has also been shown that conformity to social images and habits is often more beneficial than harmful. In short, every decision requires noncognitive, intuitive judgment, and to try to escape that fact can have negative consequences.

The third point which social science considers is the possibility of integration rather than continuation of conflict. This means that the balance of power theories are inadequate; they may provide an intermediary security function, but they are not part of the long-range goal of integration.

The possibility of interdependence is seen in nonwarring nations like the United States and Canada. Here it is not traditional top-down power relations which determine friendship between the nations.

Finally, the new social science approaches are open to new discoveries, to contingencies. They disdain absolutism or closed canons of ideological truth. Change, growth, process, and transition are conditions to be observed. The view of each nation as a steady-state "billiard-ball" is outmoded. As Margaret Mead has said: "It is no revelation to any field experienced anthropologist that everything is related to everything else."[5] And political scientist Karl Deutsch has concluded: "In world politics, we may learn to outgrow the fascination of a pseudo-conservatism which for thousands of years has trapped people into that futile path which ancient writers of Greek tragedies called koros, the hero's pride in success; hybris, tragic arrogance and overreaching; and, *ate*, the eventual madness of doom which drives the hero to rush towards self-destruction. Rather we may yet learn that only through growth, change, adaptation, and partial self-transformation can persons, groups, and peoples preserve their own identity so that true conservatism becomes possible."[6]

E. Where the Field Is Going

The postbehavioral era in international relations theory began with a call to integrate the theories of various disciplines and generate metatheories from the bottom up. In 1971 a popular international relations textbook suggested: "Students in such disciplines as sociology and psychology who study conflict will continue to center their efforts at least in part on conflict in the international context. Ideally, international relations provides a framework for an emerging discipline for the integration of concepts, propositions, and methodologies from many disciplines."[7]

What this young discipline was really trying to perform is the traditional role of religion or philosophy, in other words, develop an overall world view. Of course, this was a task for which the social scientists with their statistical methods were not equipped. The initial schism between the traditionalists and scientists, which led to an attempt to build up theories in a vacuum, apart from history, generated a new respect for those in the "wisdom" camp. Robert J. Lieber acknowledged: "Some of the best behavioral work has been informed by traditional problems or insights, and the resulting linkage of the two orientations produces work that is of real merit."[8]

J. David Singer sees an end, but a purpose to the wisdom-versus-science debate, realizing the two approaches complement each other: "If we modernists can master the substantive, normative and judgmental end of it as well as the traditionalists are mastering the concepts and methods at our end, convergence will be completed and the 'war' will not have been in vain."[9]

Currently, there is still a tendency to "impose order on eclecticism" or to pick and choose theories on an ad hoc basis. However, it seems clear that in the long run the political philosophy guiding international politics will be rooted in traditional knowledge and criticized and transformed by ongoing social scientific research.

III. SCIENTIFIC POLITICAL PHILOSOPHY IN THE SOVIET UNION

A. The Marxian "Scientific" Approach

While the roots of Marx's thought rely heavily on Hegel, Marx's project involved "standing Hegel on his head." Through the work of the left-wing Hegelian, Ludwig Feuerbach, Marx concluded that Hegel's "Absolute Spirit" was an abstraction from reality that one does better without. Marx did not believe that truth could be reasoned from the abstract but was present in the lives of real people. Consciousness was a reflection of activity, and practice was the criterion of knowledge and truth. Marx felt that traditional philosophy was out of touch with the common person; it reflected the consciousness of the philosopher who, by nature, was in a class alienated from the masses: "One of the most difficult tasks confronting philosophers is to descend from the world of thought to the actual world."[10] And "The philosopher, who is himself an abstract form of estranged man, takes himself as the criterion of the estranged world."[11]

Marx was concerned about the problems generated by the role of ideology and its illusory aspects. He was aware of the gulf between the ideology of the ruling class and that of the common worker when both used reason to explain their own world views. Marx's intent was to sever himself from the illusory aspects of philosophy which acted to justify an unjust situation which the oppressed faced. Because he used "ideology" to describe the negative aspects of "bourgeois" thought, Marx never used the phrase "scientific ideology" himself; this was a product of his interpreters. There is great debate among Marxists as to how much Marx actually presupposed an ideology as necessary for himself. For purposes of clarity, the more extreme view of rejection of ideology and reliance on practice as the sole criterion of truth is presented in Figure 2. This bottom-up approach is perhaps more consistent with Engels's interpretation of Marx than the view of Marx himself.

We must realize that what Marxists call "scientific" is quite different

Figure 2. Marx-Engels: Practice as Criterion of Truth

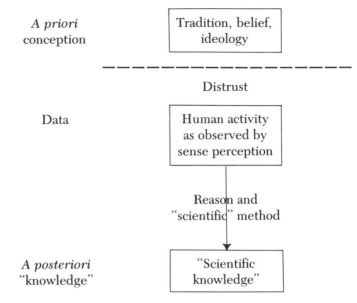

from the statistical approach of the social sciences in the United States. Marxism was developed in an earlier age, when Newtonian physics was accepted as truth. Marx and Engels placed excessive reliance on their own sense perception and judgment. As such, they reject inherited ideology but suffer from some of the same epistemological limitations as their predecessors. In this sense, it is the beginning of a new strand of "wisdom," untested by centuries of adjustment. Further, by claiming that "it is not the consciousness of men that determines their being, but their social being that determines their consciousness," Marx laid the foundation for universalizing his perceptions of a particular historical context.

B. Lenin's "Scientific Ideology"

Nikolai Lenin (1870–1924) was neither a philosopher nor a scientist. He was a lawyer. Yet, Lenin's *Materialism and Empirio-Criticism* (1908) is the only classic Soviet text on the theory of knowledge. This text, a polemic against critics of materialism, is written as a defense of the epistemology of Marx and Engels. While Lenin preached the basic tenet of Marxism, he was not so rigid as to believe that each context required the same form of socialism: "We think that independent elaboration of Marx's theory is especially essential for Russian socialists; for this theory provides only guiding principles, which, in particular, are applied in England differently than [*sic*] in France, in France differently than in Germany, and in Germany differently than in Russia."[12]

Because he allowed contextual interpretation of Marx, Lenin cannot be accused of rigid dogmatism, as he often has been. However, in practice in a particular context, the Soviet Union, it appears that Lenin de facto initiated dogmatism. Lenin openly professed a scientific and interdisciplinary approach to knowledge; yet, he did not do scientific analysis himself. Considering Marx to be a real scientist, Lenin set out to defend the truth of Marxism in terms of historical analysis. He was in practice more an apologist than a scientist. Since Lenin believed that Marx had provided the basics of "scientific ideology" which revealed the nature of oppression, he considered his task to get on with the revolution. In other words, Lenin espoused Marx's bottom-up approach to knowledge but applied Marx in a top-down manner.

The period following the revolution in the Soviet Union reveals no progress in epistemological development. Rather, there appears to have been a house-cleaning period in which all the "reactionary" views criticized in *Materialism and Empirio-Criticism* were banned and Lenin's work made the official state expression of the Marxist theory of knowledge. The social sciences fared no better. Moscow State University had a chair of sociology until 1924, but the Academy of the Social Sciences, attached to the Communist Party of the Soviet Union (CPSU), became the guardian of the field of sociology.

The Stalin era seems to have effectively stifled intellectual development of philosophy or the social sciences. Recent Soviet sources have little to say about the era, calling it "hero worship" or a "personality cult." Pavlov's *Theory of Reflection* (1936) is perhaps the most notable exception, but it had to be published under the pseudonym P. Dosev. As late as 1956, Leopold Labedz could write, "There is no Soviet counterpart of Western sociology." Ironically, Marx, who was a sociologist, had his own discipline virtually abolished in a "Marxist" country.

The top-down application of Marxist-Leninism is diagrammed in Figure 3. Note that whereas for Marx and Engels there is a total distrust in inherited ideology (Figure 2), or "naive realism," after the Soviet revolution total faith was placed in Marxist ideology and no new social science input was allowed. While Lenin opposed fideism, this is exactly what his revolution produced. In the first 40 years after the revolution, faith was placed in ideology and the world was explained in a method similar to Christian apology in the Middle Ages. One could say that Lenin and Stalin had succeeded in standing Marx on his head.

The possibility of internal integration of the philosophy of the United States and the Soviet Union under these circumstances is remote, indeed.

Figure 3. Lenin-Stalin: Faith in Marx's "Scientific" Ideology

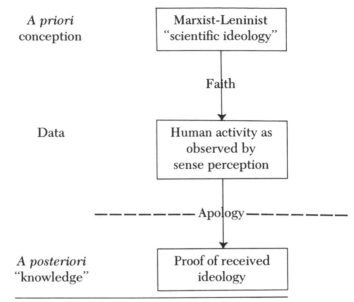

Fortunately, the end of the Stalin era marked the beginning of a new scientific approach to the study of international relations. It is from the mid-1950's that we find historical and cultural forces pushing the Soviets toward scientific criticism of inherited dogma.

C. The Rise of Soviet Social Sciences

Since psychology was the only visible social science discipline in the Stalin era, it was quite natural that leading forces in Soviet epistemology would be philosopher-psychologists. Pavlov's discoveries had been new and controversial. S. L. Rubinstein, an active Pavlovian in the 1950's, became the leading philosopher-psychologist with his classic works, *Being and Consciousness* (1957) and *On Thought and Paths of Its Investigation* (1958). Another important early work was M. N. Rutkevic's *Practice as the Base of Knowledge and Criterion of Truth* (1952). This latter work was both the clearest expression of Soviet doctrine and a threat to current official Soviet policy. These early writers were intelligent enough to become indispensable to the CPSU and yet they were perceived as enough of a threat so that official conferences were held condemning the writings of each. Their publications have remained modern classics and have occasionally been revived and declared official.

The 20th Congress of the CPSU, held in 1956, was a major turning point for the development of scientific political philosophy in the Soviet Union. At the meeting, Mikoyan asked who was available to engage in serious study of capitalism's contemporary state. The answer was no one. Not a single postgraduate had submitted a thesis in foreign policy in 1956. I. Galkin, dean of Moscow State University, stated: "Training of postgraduates in the field of international relations has stopped . . . at a time when we are in dire need."[13]

According to an American Soviet expert, William Zimmerman, there were not even the prerequisite facilities for scholars. "Aside from any qualitative standards, there were not even the most rudimentary boundary markers indicating the existence of a legitimate area of inquiry. There were no required courses on international relations, no textbooks, no reference books dealing with political parties of government bodies, no yearbooks of world events, no institutes concerned specifically with the study of international relations."[14]

At the 20th Congress, Mikoyan, representing the dominant Khushchevian position which advocated new development of the social sciences, stated the following: "It is not enough [that specialists merely affirm] that the course of history indicates that in the present stage of imperialism all Marxism-Leninism's basic tenets are invariably confirmed. [Instead they should concern themselves with] when, where, to what degree, and how this takes place."[15]

Rather than merely affirming the received ideology, the 20th Congress opened the door for sophisticated thinking about the ideology. Pressing needs in international relations forced the Soviet Union to develop the social sciences. Social sciences were forced into existence for the preservation of the status quo. The desires of the Congress were slow to materialize. First, there were no texts or qualified professors. Second, the traditional guardians in the fields of law and economics resisted any social science approach to international relations. Third, since previous study of sensitive foreign policy material could mean a trip to Siberia for the student, few students were prepared to jump at the new "opportunity." An example of the shortage which still existed in 1962 during the Cuban missile crisis is that no one in the Soviet Union had written a thesis on Cuba for seven years. By default, foreign policy remained top-down application of ideology.

In 1957 a New Institute of World Economy and International Relations was established by the Soviet government. Initially it was staffed by Marxist economists, but by the early 1960's it had become increasingly interdisciplinary and aware of several levels of analysis. A Soviet textbook dating from 1962 defined the field as follows: "International relations is the aggregate of economic, political, ideological, legal, diplomatic, military ties and interrelationships between peoples, between states and systems of states, between basic social, economic, and political forces and organizations acting in the world arena."[16]

Though we find in this definition an emphasis on the traditional foci of political science, the basic road for a complete interdisciplinary approach to the study of international relations was paved. This is consistent with the epistemology taught by Marx and Lenin even though it had not been applied by the political powers in the Soviet Union. Theoretically all the sciences should be involved in the study of anything. Indeed, this is how recent Soviet philosophers have connected the social sciences to the traditional disciplines. This recent Soviet viewpoint has allowed rapid progress in terms of both sophistication and political relevance in the past three decades.

The early 1960's were accompanied by a flowering of new institutes and journals. Information about other countries became available to scholars in the USSR for the first time since the revolution. Writings of the 1960's often contradict the traditional Soviet doctrine. The doctrines of inevitable war and class analysis, central to orthodox Marxism, became transmuted as "peaceful coexistence," détente, and policies of other nations became objects of study by a new class of Soviet scholars. Numerous Western works were translated and the vilification of Western scholars markedly decreased in the 1960's.

Khrushchev's ouster in 1964 temporarily slowed the liberalization of Soviet scholarship but the die had been cast. By 1963 some of the Western methods of social science were being used in Soviet research. An address given by a major CPSU spokesman on ideology characterized "attention to the methodological questions as a symbol of progress in Soviet science." He expressed dissatisfaction with the traditional Hegelian analysis of the state. It should be studied not by legal science but "on the plane of real activities"; not as the historians do but about "burning vital questions of the day."[17]

Game theory, computers, and probability were adopted by the new breed of Soviet specialist. All these innovations of social science techniques have served to critique and modify the received Marxist-Leninist world view. Increasingly, young Soviet scholars are employing "scientific political philosophy." William Zimmerman's 1967 analysis of Soviet perspectives concludes as follows: "All things considered, there has been a marked tendency for Soviet perspectives on international relations to converge with the American analysis."[18] This assessment seems accurate insofar as the megatrends are concerned. However, the ability for the upcoming generation to influence the CPSU has remained limited.

D. Creative Marxism-Leninism

The trends of the 1960's led the Soviets to desire to go beyond Marx, Engels, and Lenin. In 1963 the Central Committee of the Party encouraged P. N. Fedosev and Yu. P. Frantsev to make a statement regarding the liquidation of dogmatism: "Our task is now to proceed further and more daringly on the path laid for the historical science by K. Marx, F. Engels, and V. I. Lenin. For this purpose it is necessary to liquidate once and for all the consequences of the cult of personality in the area of the social sciences, including historical science. One of the worst consequences of the cult of personality was lowered prestige of the social sciences. This was done by placing the scientists, working in the area of social sciences in those days, into a situation which limited to the extreme their creative activity. Therefore it became widely believed that Soviet social scientists are capable only of either repeating citations of one and the same man, or restating the contents of these citations and without end commenting upon the directives these contained. The works of social scientists were filled with dogmatism alien to Marxist-Leninism."[19]

This quotation serves to confirm the thesis described in Figure 3 above that initial application of Marxism was top-down. The Soviets, by 1963, had become discontented with this kind of use of ideology. One of the most lucid descriptions of the program of the new Soviet "ideologians" comes from K. Ivanov, who stated that "in Lenin's works there is such a wealth of wisdom that each epoch will find something new in them."[20] This program resembles the project of theologians of the Christian Church who have been required to interpret creatively the Bible, the Church Fathers, and papal decrees. This is what Thomas Aquinas was involved in as he sought to make received "truth" compatible with the newly discovered scientific methods of Aristotle. Christians have called Jesus Christ judge, warrior, businessman, revolutionary, mother, and a host of other conflicting metaphors over the centuries. It was part of Feuerbach's goal to reveal the way in which individuals project themselves onto "truth." Now the wheel has gone another circle and the followers of Feuerbach's disciple, Marx, have tried to reconcile received canons of truth with the science of their day.

Recent critiques have not ended the guiding role played by ideology in the Soviet theory of knowledge, but they have inaugurated an era of creative interpretation. Leonid Brezhnev made this viewpoint official at the 25th Congress of the CPSU in 1975. Following is a section of Brezhnev's speech, which was refreshing to social scientists: "At the present stage of the country's development the need for further creative elaboration of theory has been growing. . . . The importance has been steadily growing of scientific research into cardinal problems of world development and international relations, the revolutionary process, the interaction and unity of its various streams, the relationship between the struggle for democracy and the struggle for socialism, and the contest of forces on the main issue of the day, the issue of war and peace. . . . The task of establishing a creative atmosphere in scientific work remains as important as ever. It goes without saying that the creative comparison of views should proceed on the basis of our Marxist-Leninist ideological platform."[21]

In 1977, Progress Publishers published a collection of articles on problems in Soviet philosophy which shows creative thinking in this area. The lead article by Fedoseyev, one of the most prominent philosophers, openly discusses the problem that relativity theory poses to traditional Marxism-Leninism. He demands a new and broader approach to problem solving. One writer, D. P. Gorsky, has invoked a semblance of Augustine's sensus literalis and sensus spiritualis as he reinterpreted the concept of practice as the criterion of truth to account for imaginary numbers: "Whereas in pre-scientific times the basic source of the multiplication of social experience was practice, man's activity in satisfying his immediate needs, the preservation and prolongation of his life (practice was the source of knowledge in the literal sense of the word), today the connection between knowledge and practice is becoming mediated. This indicates the constant increase in anticipatory forms of reflection of activity compared with the more direct forms. . . . Moreover, practice as the criterion of truth should not be interpreted crudely, that is to say, every scientific proposition must be applied in practice and confirmed by practice."[22]

V. Z. Kelle closes the volume with an epistemological summary. Ideology "contains definite guidelines for action," but "scientific ideology" is in constant flux, reflecting the "material conditions of life."[23] This allows for the transformation of the originally narrow tradition of Marxism-Leninism in light of the situation that the Soviets encounter.

Regardless of the difficulty that the old guard may have with "creative Marxism-Leninism," it has allowed for a renaissance to occur in Soviet social sciences which has put Soviet scholars on par with others. Younger scholars such as S. A. Egorov show an ability to grasp "state of the art" discussions of United States political scientists.[24] They show a capacity for introspection as well as analysis of other societies. They show wisdom in dialogue with Western scholars. Their dependence upon the teachings of Marx and Lenin is reduced.

While there is an increase in convergence in the way scholars in the United States and the Soviet Union view the world, the polemics of traditional ideological foundations dominate the postdétente era since the

Soviet invasion of Afghanistan. However, this new cold-war period precedes the death knell of the old ideological struggles. It is doubtful whether the younger generation of Soviet scholars could return to the dogmatism of the Stalin era just as it is doubtful whether US scholars will return to the dogmatism of Senator McCarthy. The sheer weight of pluralism among socialist nations parallels the plurality of denominations in Western Christianity. The current problems of crime, alcoholism, family life, and racism in the Soviet Union have forced citizens to modify any naive and utopian Marxist world view.

IV. HOPES FOR PHILOSOPHICAL INTEGRATION

A. *The Converging Trends*

Convergence in the political philosophies of the United States and the Soviet Union has been occurring on the political science level even though the inherited tradition and ideologies of the two nations are at odds. The trend in both nations has been to modify or transform inherited doctrine with theories generated from observance of current political reality. Since political scientists in both nations have been using many of the same quantitative methods of research and many of the same theories, such as game theory, and applying them to the same problems of nuclear deterrence, they finally reach many of the same conclusions. We can call the process going on in both nations "scientific philosophy" inasmuch as this involves transformation of the received world view upon analysis of new data. Convergence occurs in the stage referred to as a posteriori "knowledge" in Figure 4.

B. *The Role of Ideology*

"Ideology" is a word with both positive and negative connotations. In general it refers to one's inherited world view and belief system. The negative use of ideology is when it is forced upon people against their will or when it remains closed to transformation of analysis of human experience. The top-down enforcement of Marxism by Stalin is an example of the worst kind of use of ideology. Christian history, especially in the Middle Ages, is also full of such abuses of ideology. On the other hand, everyone, even a two-year-old child, holds a world view as a matter of course. As one's experience in the world broadens, one's world view should develop accordingly. It is enforced dogmatism which prevents this process from taking place that is culpable, not the holding of a naive world view.

One of the major errors in Marxism and the Enlightenment in general

Figure 4. Scientific Philosophy

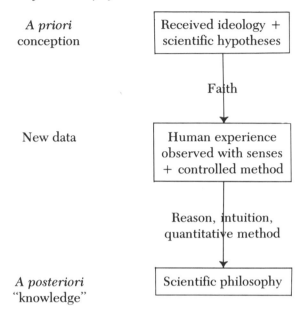

has been rejection of the inherited world view because inconsistencies with reality were observed. Starting over tabula rasa with the theories of the Enlightenment thinker, the Marxist being the prime example, is an arrogant attempt to control or guide the world with one's own view. However, habit and tradition developed almost unconsciously over centuries of human experience are very important in guiding human behavior. Social evolution involves many dimensions of life which transcend the rational. Most decisions are a combination of intuition and reason, intuition comprising the bulk of the decision-making process. This "intuition" is a product of human social experience. Tradition is ever present in science and reason. Thus, the Enlightenment attempt to reject tradition is really unscientific; rather, it is more an emotional reaction to those sectors of society which hold to tradition dogmatically. In his modern classic writing on tradition, Edward Shils concluded: "The renunciation of tradition should be considered as a cost of a new departure; the retention of traditions should be considered as a benefit of a new departure. . . . I wish to stress that traditions should be considered as constituents of worthwhile life. A mistake of historical significance was made in modern times by the construction of a doctrine which treated traditions as the detritus of the forward movement of society. It was a distortion of the truth to assert this and to think that mankind could live without tradition and simply in the light of immediately perceived interest or immediately experienced impulse or immediately excogitated reason and the latest stage of scientific knowledge or some combination of them. It was wrong however admirable the motives for the mistake and whatever benefits which the mistake helped to bring about."[25]

Another great sociologist and historian of religion is Ernst Troeltsch (1865–1927). While Troeltsch concerned himself with the plurality of world views among the denominations in Christianity, his inquiry led him to the same epistemological problem involved in the plurality of world views among nation-states. Troeltsch described the process of acquisition of knowledge as follows: "The simplest observational judgment, the most natural impulses of the will, the rules and customs traditionally passed down, all of these are taken by the naive man as absolute. . . . Absoluteness is a universal characteristic of the naive way of thinking.

"Equally universal, however, is the process that leads to limitation or dissolution of such naive conviction. Comparison . . . and the realization that one has to make adjustments in his initial, naive outlook has a shattering effect on absoluteness and paves the way for thinking. Freedom from this naive absoluteness is the essence of culture. . . . This process continues until all different kinds . . . have been juxtaposed, until all the contradictions and antitheses have been matched point for point in an effort to discover in these correlations an ultimate principle that make possible a unified and coherent account and assessment of the whole. In this way the naive world view changes into a scientific one. . . . Mature wisdom of thought signifies that reality as naively perceived is not denied but viewed in a higher context, and that different orders and dimensions in naively perceived reality are permitted to remain as they are if, despite the attempt to see them in context, they resist all synthesizing efforts and thus prove themselves incapable of being united. These principles are basic epistemology."[26]

Troeltsch did not only see the above process of obtaining "mature wisdom" as "basic epistemology," he also stated that the scientific transformation is accompanied by an "elevating and liberating effect." "It releases men from the narrowness, pettiness, and intolerance of the first way of understanding, vagueness and one-sidedness. It frees them for a dispassionate and comprehensive perspective, for generosity and gentleness of outlook, for tolerance and forebearance, and for firmness and clarity of conviction."[27]

According to Troeltsch, the scientific transformation of naive thought, or ideological thinking in its negative sense, into mature wisdom of thought also opens the way for tolerance and cooperation among those holding differing world views. If this is the case, then the increase of scientific transformation of the doctrines of the United States and the Soviet Union will lead to a greater foundation for cooperation between the two superpowers. While some strategists argue that the ideological powers that exist are too entrenched and too strong to be transformed, there is historical precedent for the convergence of the political philosophies of the United States and the Soviet Union. This is in the formation of the National Council of Churches in the United States.

C. Towards a Superseding World View

Wars between peoples of different religious persuasions have been the cause of some of the greatest bloodshed in history. This was one of the Enlightenment's chief criticisms of religion. Now the world witnesses a cold war based on secular political ideologies. The former may be religious and the latter political, but the similarities in ideological narrowness are great enough to warrant comparison between warring religious belief systems and warring political belief systems; both contain ideology in the negative sense which needs to be superseded by higher knowledge.

Originally, religious denominations in the United States were separated by state boundaries. Each colony had an established church. Any attempt to discuss doctrine drew heated emotional debate. There were witch hunts and heresy trials by adherents of majority religions against minority religions. The origin of cooperation took place in practical matters of concern to all churches. The ecumenical movement began when Christians of different denominations met together to discuss issues like slavery, alcohol, government regulations on missioning foreign lands, and so forth. When the first ongoing ecumenical conference was established, it was declared that "no resolution shall be considered which deals with theological or ecclesiastical questions that represent denominational differences."[28] After the association of denominations had existed for some years, a movement of Faith and Order developed among scientific-minded theologians who were able to discuss ideological issues in a nonviolent manner. It took the ecumenical movement, which later became known as the National Council of Churches (NCC), 50 years before its denominational hierarchy began to accept statements of the Faith and Order Commission as guiding principles for their own churches. How did this happen?

The shared experiences must be seen as the decisive unifying force. The responses developed to crises, such as slavery and labor reform, were shared responses which generated shared ideas. As all denominations suffered the effects of World War I, the response of German theologian Karl Barth influenced the theology of all the churches. A joint study on evangelism in 1932 led to common teachings by the members of the NCC on evangelism. After many years of this process, the denominations which at one time sparred with each other had more similarities than differences in their belief. They generated a common belief system which superseded the earlier and more narrow views. We might term this process "ideological epigenesis."

If we look at the relationship between the United States and the Soviet Union with the ecumenical movement in mind, there is indeed hope that convergence will occur; that ideological epigenesis will take place. There are certainly many world problems jointly shared by the two nations—limited natural resources, fear of nuclear proliferation to unstable nations, crime, cultural pluralism, North-South issues, and so forth. Scientific cooperation on these problems without reference to ideological differences could be quite useful. Political scientists in the two nations have already begun this process. The development of a common language of social science in approaching the study of international relations hastens the process of ideological epigenesis.

D. Policy Recommendations

On the basis of the trends outlined here, two immediate actions which can be implemented to further the reduction in US-Soviet ideological tension appear. First, it is recommended that government publications discussing science policy give due consideration to the social sciences as well as the hard sciences. There has been a tendency for the United States Congress to discuss scientific cooperation with the Soviet Union solely in terms of the physical sciences and technology. It is as though the social sciences were not really "sciences" in the eyes of the US government.

Secondly, it is recommended that foreign policy publications cite as much social-scientific evidence as possible, diffusing ideological and propagandistic elements in politics. This can reduce the perceived threat to the other nation. This can also diminish the quantity of politicized rhetoric in foreign policy discussions. Further, the United States' use of scientific research in policy materials should encourage Soviet decision makers to do likewise for reasons of credibility. This would increase the percentage of overlap of the world views of the two nations, reducing the inherent conflict in the naively received ideologies.

Notes

1. Georg F. W. Hegel, *The Philosophy of Right*, Chapter X, "The Philosophy of Law." Cited from W. Sahakian, *History of Philosophy*, New York: Barnes and Noble, 1968, pp. 196–201.

2. Neil Smelser, "Personality and the Explanation of Political Phenomena

at the Social-System Level: A Methodological Statement," *Journal of Social Issues*, No. 3, 1968, p. 123.

3. Fred Greenstein, *Personality and Politics*, New York: Norton, 1975, p. 121.

4. David Horowitz, "Billion Dollar Brains," *Ramparts*, May 1969.

5. Margaret Mead, "Changing Styles of Anthropological Work," *Annual Review of Anthropology*, 1973, p. 8.

6. Karl Deutsch, *The Analysis of International Relations*, Englewood Cliffs, New Jersey: Prentice-Hall, 1968, p. 290.

7. James Dougherty and Robert Pfaltzgraff, *Contending Theories of International Relations*, New York: Lippincott, 1971, p. 386.

8. Robert Lieber, *Theory and World Politics*, Cambridge, Massachusetts: Winthrop, 1972, p. 149.

9. J. David Singer, "The Incompleat Theorist: Insight Without Evidence," *Contending Approaches to International Politics*, edited by Knorr and Rosenau, Princeton: Princeton University Press, 1969, p. 86. Cited in *ibid*.

10. Karl Marx and Friedrich Engels, *Collected Works*, Moscow: Progress, 1976, Volume 5, p. 446.

11. *Ibid.*, Volume 3, p. 331.

12. V. I. Lenin, *Collected Works*, Moscow: Progress, 21, 1960–1970, Volume 4, pp. 211–212.

13. I. Galkin, "The Duty of Soviet Scholars," *International Affairs*, February 1956, p. 133.

14. William Zimmerman, *Soviet Perspectives on International Relations*, Princeton: Princeton University Press, 1969, pp. 31–32.

15. Leo Gruliow, editor, *Current Soviet Policies II: The Documentary Record of the 20th Party Congress and Its Aftermath*, New York: Praeger, 1957, p. 87.

16. The textbook is titled *International Relations Since World War II*, Moscow: Gospolitizdat, 1962, Volume 1, p. xxvi.

17. Leonid Il'ichev, "Methodological Problems of the Natural and Social Sciences," *Vestnik Akademii Nauk*, cited by Zimmerman, *op. cit.*, pp. 62–63.

18. *Ibid.*, p. 282.

19. P. N. Fedoseyev, *History and Sociology*, pp. 6–7.

20. K. Ivanov, "The National Liberation Movement and the Non-Capitalist Path of Development," *International Affairs*, September 1964, p. 35.

21. *Building a New Society: The 25th Congress of the Communist Party of the Soviet Union*, edited by Smith, Laibman, and Bechtel, New York: New World Review, 1977, pp. 59–60.

22. D. P. Gorsky, "Social Practice and Scientific Knowledge," *Philosophy in the U.S.S.R.*, Moscow: Progress, 1977, p. 162.

23. V. Z. Kelle, "Ideology as a Phenomenon of Social Consciousness," *ibid.*, p. 265.

24. S. A. Egorov, "Principal Research Directions in U.S. Political Science in the 1970's," *Soviet Law and Government*, Summer 1980, pp. 61–77.

25. Edward Shils, *Tradition,* Chicago: University of Chicago Press, 1981, p. 330.

26. Ernst Troeltsch, *The Absoluteness of Christianity and the History of Religions,* Richmond, Virginia: John Knox Press, 1971, pp. 132–135.

27. *Ibid.*

28. Samuel McCrea Cavert, *Church Cooperation and Unity in America,* New York: Association Press, 1970, p. 37.

Questions

1. Name some strengths and weaknesses of the top-down approach to international affairs.

2. Do the same for the bottom-up approach.

3. What are some advantages and dangers that may result when the social sciences seek to influence political thought? Why is the Vietnam War instructive in this regard?

4. Trace the movement of Communist thought from Marx to Lenin to the post-Stalinist period. Does the current trend among the social sciences in the U.S.S.R. give you hope for eventual convergence with Western perceptions? Why or why not?

5. Is the gradual convergence of beliefs among the members of the World Council of Churches a suitable model for expectations that the same process will be followed by the superpowers? Give your reasons.

SECTION FIVE

World Order

1
Foreign Aid and U.S. National Interests

George Shultz

This article originally appeared in *Current Policy No. 457* U.S. Department of State, February 24, 1983.

Realism, strength and negotiation are the foundations of the conduct of American foreign policy, according to Secretary of State Shultz. In his address to the Southern Center for International Studies, the Secretary enunciates President Reagan's policy "to reduce a decade's accumulation of doubt about U.S. commitments and staying power."

Realism, he says, involves calling aggression, chemical and biological warfare and economic problems by their right names, "whether it happens to be in a country that is friendly to us or not." Shultz's interpretation of strength begins with military force, but he qualifies that by saying that "military strength rests on a strong economy." In this connection, he cites the control of inflation, increased productivity and a rising standard of living as American accomplishments. Above all, he invokes the importance of maintaining confidence in "our own beliefs and ideals." In regard to negotiations, he makes reference to American efforts toward "saving the city of Beirut from complete destruction," in addition to trying to resolve the difficulties in such places as Kampuchea (Cambodia), Afghanistan and southern Africa. He expresses the wish that the U.S. be conceived "as part of the solution and not part of the problem."

With this background, Shultz turns to relations with the third world. His two basic assumptions are that economic growth in the developing nations is essential to a strong American economy and that the same applies to security and peace in these countries. With statistical evidence, he asserts that, until the recent recession, the third world accounted for forty percent of U.S. exports—a factor in saving American jobs. He concedes that the worldwide recession of 1982 has hurt the U.S. economy and adds that American dependence on third world countries for strategic minerals and other goods emphasizes the interrelatedness of the world economy. To this he pledges his Administration to fight for the reduction of trade barriers and to oppose protectionism.

In regard to peace and security, the Secretary asserts that the main challenges in recent years have come from unrest and warfare in third world countries, a development he blames on "the Soviet Union and its allies." Like his predecessors going back to World War II, Secretary Shultz emphasizes the need for military support for friendly countries around the world. Complementing such activities are U.S. foreign aid programs which, he is quick to say, are not a "giveaway." This too places the Reagan Administration, in its stated goals, in the mainstream of U.S. postwar foreign policy.

In conclusion, Shultz compares the small amount spent each year on foreign aid with the amount Americans spend on luxuries. Above all, he calls for perseverance so that "we will be able to brighten the future for ourselves and for others throughout the world."

A speech such as today's provides an opportunity for me to use a wide-angle lens. Although the broad picture is ever in our mind, the day-to-day business of the State Department generally finds us using not the broad brush but the jeweler's glass as we examine the myriad individual issues on which our foreign relations turn. So today I want to begin by opening the lens full scope. I will describe the fundamental tenets which underlie President Reagan's foreign policy.

Then I'd like to turn the lens down in two successive notches: first, a moderate turn to discuss the importance to our foreign policy of the more than 100 developing countries of the Third World—Asia, Africa, and South America.

Finally, I plan to focus way down and—in this time of tight budgets—discuss the funds which the United States must expend to achieve its objectives. Contrary to popular opinion, the currency of foreign affairs is not cookies. It takes resources—modest but sustained, applied credibly over time—to secure international peace, foster economic growth, and help insure the well-being of each of our citizens. But we'll start with the broader view.

FUNDAMENTAL TENETS OF U.S. FOREIGN POLICY

Since his inauguration 2 years ago, President Reagan has sought to revitalize U.S. foreign policy. He is resolved to reduce a decade's accumulation of doubt about the U.S. commitment and staying power. Our watchwords in doing this are four ideas:

First, we start with realism.

Second, we build our strength.

Third, we stress the indispensable need to negotiate and to reach agreements.

Fourth, we keep the faith. We believe that progress is possible even though the tasks are difficult and complex.

Let me take each of these very briefly in turn. I'm very conscious of them, because as I get caught up in the day-to-day details of foreign policy and go over to the White House to discuss my current problems with the President, he has the habit of bringing me back to these fundamentals. And I believe they are truly fundamental.

Realism. If we're going to improve our world, we have to understand it. And it's got a lot of good things about it; it's got a lot of bad things about it. We have to be willing to describe them to ourselves. We have to be willing if we see aggression to call it aggression. We have to be willing if we see the use of chemical and biological warfare contrary to agreements to get up and say so and document the point. When we see persecution, we have to be willing to get up and say that's the reality, whether it happens to be in a country that is friendly to us or not.

When we look at economic problems around the world, we have to be able to describe them to ourselves candidly and recognize that there are problems. That's where you have to start, if you're going to do something about them. So, I think realism is an essential ingredient in the conduct of our foreign policy.

Strength. Next, I believe is strength. We must have military strength, if we're going to stand up to the problems that we confront around the world and the problems imposed on us by the military strength of the Soviet Union and the demonstrated willingness of the Soviet Union to use its strength without any compunction whatever.

So, military strength is essential, but I think we delude ourselves if we don't recognize—as we do, as the President does—that military strength rests on a strong economy; on an economy that has the capacity to invest in its future, believe in its future—as you do here in Atlanta; an economy that brings inflation under control and that stimulates the productivity that goes with adequate savings and investment and has given us the rising standard of living and remarkable economic development that our country has known. But more than that, we have to go back to our own beliefs and ideals and be sure that we believe in them. And there is no way to do that better than to live by them ourselves. So, we have to maintain our own self-confidence and our own will power and our own notion that we are on the right track to go with the strength in our economy and our military capability.

Negotiation. Of course, beyond this, if we are realistic and we are strong, I believe it is essential that we also are ready to go out and solve problems, to negotiate with people, to try to resolve the difficulties that we see all around the world—not simply because in doing so we help the places where those difficulties are but because in doing so we also help ourselves, we further our own interests. So, negotiation and working out problems has got to be a watchword for us, and we do that all around the world. I think it is no exaggeration to say that the efforts of the United States resulted in saving the city of Beirut from complete destruction. We are active in trying to resolve difficulties in Kampuchea. We have called attention to the problems in Afghanistan. We're working in southern Africa in a most difficult situation to bring about a resolution of the Namibia issues, and so on around the world. But I like to think that the United States must be conceived of as part of the solution and not part of the problem. That's where we want to be standing.

Finally, if we can achieve these things, if we can be strong enough so that people must take us seriously, and put our ideas forward in a realistic manner, then we will be able to solve problems and have some competence to be successful, and, if we're successful, certainly the world can be better.

RELATIONS WITH THE THIRD WORLD

Against that background, let me turn to the problems of the Third World and our dealings with them and our stake in doing so successfully. Many of our citizens still see the developing countries as accessories to our basic interests. But over the past two decades, these countries have increasingly moved to the front of the stage where issues of peace and prosperity are played out. I believe this trend has assumed such proportions that I can advance two fundamental propositions.

First, there will be no enduring economic prosperity for our country without economic growth in the Third World.

Second, there will not be security and peace for our citizens without stability and peace in developing countries.

Let me explain these propositions. For the past 15 years, until the current recession took its toll, the developing countries as a whole have been growing more rapidly than the United States and Europe. As they have grown, they have become increasingly important as customers and suppliers for ourselves and other industrial nations.

In 1980, developing countries purchased about 40% of U.S. exports—more than bought by Western Europe, Eastern Europe, the

Soviet Union, and China combined. These countries have accounted for more than half the growth in U.S. exports since 1975. At this juncture, approximately 1 out of every 20 workers in our manufacturing plants and 1 out of every 5 acres of our farmland produce for Third World markets. I might say that 2 out of every 5 acres of our farmland produce for export. That's how interrelated our farm community is with the international community.

The current worldwide recession has vividly—if painfully—highlighted these relationships. In the past several years, growth rates in the developing countries have dropped from over 5% per year to around 2%. Partly as a result, our exports to these countries—which were increasing at more than 30% a year in the late 1970s—have tapered off. For example, in the first 8 months of 1982, U.S. exports to Mexico dropped 26%; to Chile, 59%; and to Thailand, 25%. According to estimates, every $1 billion decline in U.S. exports erases 60,000–70,000 U.S. jobs after multiplier effects are taken into account. There's a direct correlation. Today some of the workers in our unemployment lines and some of the businesses and farms on the auction block are living, if unwanted, proof that the well-being of our citizens is linked to the well-being of citizens in the Third World.

On the other side of the trade ledger, the developing countries supply about 40%–45% of the goods which we import for our factories and consumers. Although we are richer in minerals than most industrialized countries, the Third World supplies more than half the bauxite, tin, and cobalt used by U.S. industry. For some 11 other strategic metals and minerals, the developing countries supply more than half of our imports. For some natural products, such as rubber, coffee, cocoa, and hard fibers, the Third World supplies everything we use.

This intertwining of the European and our economy with those of the Third World will increase in the 1980s and 1990s. As the recession fades, we can expect the faster growing countries—particularly in Asia but also in South America—to resume their role as engines of growth in the world economy. They will open up new opportunities for our exports and jobs for our citizens. We have an abiding interest in fostering this growth.

It is for this reason that we are joining with other industrial nations to add funds to the International Monetary Fund. These funds are critical to helping debt-plagued developing countries make painful but unavoidable adjustments in their economies and thereby resume healthy growth rates. We have a direct stake in their success.

For this reason, also, we resist—and call on all Americans to resist—pleas for further protectionism. Putting up barriers to imports will only result in losing markets for our exports and paying higher prices for goods. Resorting to protectionism as an antidote to recession is like turning to alcohol to ward off the cold. It may feel good at first, but it shortly becomes corrosive. The tonic for our ills is noninflationary growth, not stiff draughts of old Smoot-Hawley.

Beyond the demands of economies, the Third World is fundamental to our aspirations for security and peace. Since 1950, most of the major threats to international stability, and the chief opportunities for expansion of the Soviet Union's political reach, have come in the Third World. The headlines have rung with now familiar names: Korea in 1950; Dienbienphu in 1954; Suez, Cuba, and more recently Iran, Angola, Afghanistan, Kampuchea, El Salvador, and Ethiopia.

A study by the Brookings Institution has identified no fewer than 185 incidents in developing countries since the end of World War II when U.S. military forces were used in situations which threatened our political or economic interests. As we speak today, 1,200 Marines are on duty in Lebanon helping again to patch the torn fabric of peace.

The point is clear. The fault line of global instability runs strongly across the continents of the Third World. This instability is inimical to our security in many ways. Small incidents can flare into larger conflagrations and potentially into confrontations between the superpowers. Korea and Cuba teach this lesson well.

More subtly, the Soviet Union and its allies are able to feed on political instability. Some of the most significant uses by the Soviets of military power since World War II have been in the developing world. The Soviet deployment of a deepwater navy, an airlift capacity, and mobile ground forces has given them the ability to intervene when they perceive opportunities.

In addition, the Soviet Union supports 870,000 troops in North Korea—60% more than maintained by South Korea. It bankrolls the Vietnamese Army, which has positioned 180,000 troops directly on the border of Thailand. It supports about 40,000 Cuban troops in Angola, Ethiopia, and Mozambique. In 1981, the Soviet Union supplied about three times as many tanks, aircraft, and artillary pieces as did the United States.

We cannot ignore these realities as they challenge our national interests. Strategically, some of the least secure Third World countries are sources of critical raw materials or lie astride sealanes which carry our military forces and world commerce. The premier example is the Persian Gulf. About 32% of the free world's oil supplies is pumped there. The region is vital to the economic and political security of Europe, Japan, and the United States. It is in our interest to build stability in this region and thereby help assure access to those supplies.

As a parenthetical remark, I want to mention my belief that the recent decline in oil prices—and the possibility of further declines—will spur the free world's economic recovery. For some countries—such as Venezuela and Mexico—cheaper oil surely means tougher times. But it will be good for most of us. I have seen one illustrative estimate that a decline in oil prices to $20 per barrel would boost real growth rates in the industrial countries by up to 1.5%. A less steep decline would have proportionately positive effects. So, I have the sense that as people contemplate the declines in oil prices, there's a tendency for people to wring their hands about what happened to this or that business or financial institution or country— and there are problems and we need to look at them, all right. But let's not forget the main point, it's going to be good for us and good for economic growth, which we need.

The job of building our security also requires that we maintain military facilities and strengthen indigenous defense forces around the world. This includes U.S. bases in the Philippines and in Turkey, the Azores, Morocco, and other strategically placed countries.

The United States cannot defend its interests by operating out of the United States and Europe alone. We need the cooperation of countries in the Third World to grant transit, refueling, and base rights. Otherwise, while we may wish to build up a rapid deployment force, we will be unable to deploy it without Third World friends who will allow us to use their facilities. We must be prepared, in turn, to help these key countries achieve their aspirations for security and economic growth. This is not just a short-term proposition. The process of mutual cooperation weaves ties of interdependence and friendship which will redound to our benefit in years to come.

It goes without saying that the least desirable method for preserving our strategic interests and insuring stability in the developing countries is by sending in U.S. forces. The 185 incidents which I mentioned earlier represent, in essence, 185 failures to resolve problems by more measured means. If we are to reduce incidents in the future, we need a significant program—sustained over time—to secure peace and economic well-being in regions vital to our security.

U.S. SECURITY AND DEVELOPMENT COOPERATION PROGRAM

In fact, we have such a program. It is called the U.S. Security and Development Cooperation Program. Although our Administration has clarified its goals and sharpened its focus, it is essentially the same program endorsed by every U.S. President since Harry Truman. It's sometimes called foreign aid and all too often depicted as a giveaway. But that is a misnomer. The program's purpose is to create those conditions of growth, security, and freedom in developing countries which serve the fundamental interests of each U.S. citizen.

Let me give some examples of how it works. Our highest priority in this program is bringing peace to the Middle East. Because of the ties between the United States and Israel, a crisis in this region has always placed us in the center of a potentially serious world confrontation. This has been so for more than 25 years. Achieving a lasting peace in the Middle East will not only benefit each and every citizen in those lands but will ease one of the fundamental threats to world peace and our own security.

Making peace there means more than holding talks, as vital as these are. Sustained economic growth is needed in Egypt, Israel, and Jordan. Lebanon needs to open roads, restore electrical service, restart its economic engines, and resume its place as a stable and friendly nation in that part of the world. These countries also need to be able to defend themselves against those they see as aggressors. In this circumstance, we and other nations provide both economic and military aid. This aid is indispensable to the peace process.

Another program—with particular bearing here in the south—is the President's Caribbean Basin initiative. Some of you have dealt directly with the consequences of poverty, political turmoil, and Soviet/Cuban interventionism near our shores. These have come in human form—off airplanes and out of boats—to present in person their claims for a better deal. For the south, the need to help the Caribbean and Central American nations grow economically and build democratic institutions is not an abstract issue. It is one which can directly affect your economy and society.

Another part of our program is helping curb the rampant population growth which underlies much of the Third World's poverty and threatens our planet's resource base. The arithmetic is inexorable. Before World War II there were more than 2 billion people in the world. Now there are 4.3 billion. Even though growth rates have slowed in recent years, 17 years from now, in the year 2000, there will be 6 billion. If we act effectively, the world population may stabilize at between 12 and 16 billion in the last half of the next century. That's 12–16 billion people to feed, clothe, and provide jobs for.

To bring it closer to home, Mexico currently has 62 million people. If they are able to lower their birth rate to the two-children-per-family level in the first 20 years of the next century, they will have "only" about 250 million people when their population stops growing.

Faced with these numbers, the United States provides direct technical advice and training to 27 countries to assist them to mount voluntary family planning programs. It's been an effective effort. We have a deep interest in continuing it.

Similarly, we provide funds for U.S. agricultural universities to help developing countries grow more food. Although there are food surpluses now, population increase, plus growth in the world economy, means that food production in the developing countries must keep growing at 3%–4% per year, or we may all face shortages and rising prices again by the end of the decade.

So with U.S. funds, Mississippi State is introducing improved seed in Thailand. The University of Florida is increasing crop production in Ecuador. Auburn is working in Jamaica and Indonesia on fish production. It is in all our interests that these universities, and others across our agricultural heartland, continue with our support to devote some of their considerable talents to building secure food supplies in the world.

Let me give one more example, this time on the security side. A glance at a map indicates the importance of Turkey to our strategic interests. It sits like a wedge between the Soviet Union, the Middle East, and the western flank of the Persian oil fields. With Iran and Iraq in turmoil, the importance of an economically and militarily strong Turkey has increased. In the last few years, the Russians have increased the size of their forces stationed north of Turkey.

Hence, we and other countries of Europe, led by the Germans, are helping the Turks spur their economy and replace obsolete tanks and other equipment in their armed forces. The cost to us of assisting Turkey maintain strong defense forces between Russia and the Middle East is less than one-sixth of the cost of maintaining U.S. soldiers overseas for the same purpose.

These are examples of how an investment of our resources contributes to the well-being and security of each of us in this room. The cost is modest. For the coming fiscal year, the amounts we've requested from the Congress for the examples I've given work out as follows for each U.S. citizen:

For building peace in the Middle East .... $12.35 per person
For the Caribbean Basin .... $3.84 per person
For curbing population growth................... 92¢ per person
For building secure food supplies.............. $3.15 per person
For helping Turkey .... $1.78 per person

The total request for all our security and economic assistance programs in the developing countries is $43.91 per person.[1] By contrast, we Americans spend $104 per person a year for TV and radio sets, $35 per person per year for barbershops and beauty parlors, $97 per person per year for soap and cleaning supplies, and $21 per person per year for flowers and potted plants.

I'm not belittling any of these expenses. That's not my intent. They're part of our commerce, which provides us with jobs as producers and satisfies us as consumers. I am simply trying to establish some relative values.

Every American must understand that it's necessary to spend a fraction of our collective resources to secure our most precious goals of freedom, economic well-being, and peace. An esteemed son of Georgia and predecessor of mine, Dean Rusk, said it succinctly: "Freedom is not free."

PROGRESS IS POSSIBLE

Let me close by opening my lens back up and reverting to the fourth of the tenets which guide our conduct of foreign affairs: namely, our conviction that progress is possible. We Americans have lived for over 40 years in a tumultuous world in which we have pursued four basic goals:

First, building world peace and deterring war—above all, nuclear war which would threaten human existence;

Second, containing the influence of nations which are fundamentally opposed to our values and interests—notably the Soviet Union and its allies;

Third, fostering a growing world economy and protecting U.S. access to free markets and critical resources; and

Fourth, encouraging other nations to adopt principles of self-determination, economic freedom, and the rule of law which are the foundation stones of American society.

In these endeavors, we have had some signal successes. Some formerly troubled countries of the world—for instance, the countries of East Asia—are now relatively strong and prosperous. Western Europe, a cock-

---

1. The figures cited are derived by dividing the Administration's FY 1984 request for development assistance, PL 480, economic support funds, military education and training program, military assistance and foreign military grants by the U.S. population of approximately $230 million. The figures *do not include* foreign military sales guaranteed loans which are extended at market or near-market rates to foreign governments. These loans by law are not included in the U.S. budget.

pit of warring nationalities for a century, has been at peace for 37 years. Progress has been made in fundamental areas affecting the mass of mankind: better health, longer life expectancy, more schooling, increased income. We have a chance in the coming year to make major strides in fashioning peace in the Middle East.

Americans as a people are pragmatists, suspicious of grand assurances or easy promises. But I'm convinced that if we persevere—proceeding realistically, backed by strength, fully willing to negotiate and search for agreement—we will be able to brighten the future for ourselves and for others throughout the world.

Questions

1. If the basic principles of U.S. foreign policy, as enunciated by Secretary Shultz, are consistent with those of previous Administrations, how do you explain the partisan debates about foreign policy in Congress?

2. Do you think Shultz's statement on realism in foreign policy can be taken at face value? Give examples.

3. Does Shultz's assertion of U.S. economic growth in the post-war period stand up to scrutiny? Why, or why not?

4. The Secretary puts the blame for unrest in the third world squarely on the shoulders of the U.S.S.R. How might the Russians respond to this charge?

5. Shultz calls for military and economic support for friendly countries. Can you think of any qualifications to that statement?

2
Redefining National Security

Lester R. Brown

This article originally appeared in *Nuclear Times*, June 1986

Lester Brown of the Worldwatch Institute, a Washington think tank, sheds light on a factor not discussed in the previous article—the emergence of Japan as an economic superpower. The principal reason for this emergence is not hard to find: Japan spends less than one percent of its Gross National Product on the military while the U.S. lavishes seven percent and the U.S.S.R. pours fourteen percent of its GNP into armaments. For many countries, he says, the era of guns-and-butter has come to an end.

Brown repeats, in concise form, some of the economic woes facing both military superpowers as recorded by Dumas in Section One. While the U.S. and the Soviets suffer economic setbacks for their weapons expenditures, Brown fears that too little attention is paid to such major matters as third world debt, the international financial system and the deterioration of the world's natural resources.

Yet he finds some hope in the fact that military expenditures are actually going down in such countries as China, Argentina and Peru. Brown does not go so far as to predict that other countries will follow suit, but there is no doubt where his heart is. In the nettlesome area of superpower arms reduction, "the likelihood of reducing tensions may be improving." Even in the Soviet Union, he discerns signs that pragmatism may win out over ideology.

Future world leadership for both the U.S. and the U.S.S.R., he says, "may now depend on reducing military expenditures to strengthen their faltering economies."

Preoccupied with each other, the United States and the Soviet Union have apparently failed to notice that global geopolitics are being reshaped in a way that defines security more in economic than in traditional military terms. Now, quite apart from the positive contributions of the peace movement, worsening economic conditions may become the key motivation for reversing the militarization of the past generation.

412

Throughout most of the post-war period, an expanding economy permitted the world to have more guns and more butter. For many countries, however, this age has come to an end. Governments can no longer both boost expenditures on armaments and deal effectively with the forces that are undermining their economies.

The choices now are between continued militarization of the economy and restoration of its environmental support systems; between continued militarization and attempts to halt growth of the U.S. debt; between continued militarization and new initiatives to deal with the dark cloud of Third World debt. The world has neither the financial resources nor the time to militarize and to deal with these new threats to security.

DEBTS OF DESPAIR

"National security" has become a commonplace expression, a concept regularly appealed to. It is used to justify the maintenance of armies, the development of new weapon systems, and the manufacture of armaments. One-fourth of all the federal taxes in the United States and at least an equivalent amount in the Soviet Union are levied in its name.

Since World War II, the concept of national security has acquired an overwhelmingly military character, rooted in the assumption that the principal threat to security comes from other nations. Commonly veiled in secrecy, consideration of military threats has become so dominant that new threats to the security of nations—threats with which military forces cannot cope—are being ignored.

For the United States and the Soviet Union, the cost of the arms race goes beyond mere fiscal reckoning. It is draining their treasuries, weakening their economies, and lowering their positions in the international economic hierarchy. This long, drawn-out conflict is contributing to a realignment of the leading industrial countries, with Japan assuming a dominant position in the world economy. One of the keys to Japan's emergence as an economic superpower is its negligible military expenditures—less than one percent of its gross national product (GNP), compared with seven percent of the GNP in the United States and 14 percent in the Soviet Union.

The doubling of the U.S. national debt, from $914 billion in 1980 to $1,841 billion in 1985, is due more to the growth of military expenditures than to those of any other sector. The growing federal debt is mortgaging the country's economic future and, consequently, its position in the world economy.

An overvalued dollar and the lack of investment in new industrial capacity have dramatically altered America's position in world trade. As recently as 1975, the United States had a small trade surplus. In 1980, it registered a trade deficit of $36 billion. The trade deficit climbed to $70 billion in 1983, and to a staggering $150 billion in 1985.

This ballooning trade deficit and the associated borrowing abroad to finance the federal debt have cost the country its position as the world's leading international investor. While Japan's external holdings during this decade have grown from $12 billion to more than $120 billion, the net foreign assets of the United States have plummetted to *minus* $120 billion. Almost overnight, the United States has become a debtor nation—a precipitous, and unprecedented, fall from leadership.

This is a worrisome shift for a country whose international leadership role since World War II has derived in large part from its economic strength and prestige. The military expenditures that are weakening the United States economically are diminishing both its stature within the international community and its capacity to lead.

The Soviet Union, too, is paying a heavy price for its role in the arms race, retaining second-class economic status despite its wealth of natural resources. Military spending channels roughly one-seventh of the nation's resources to nonproductive uses. From the early 1950s through the late 1970s the Soviet economy grew at roughly five percent annually, a rate of expansion that brought progress on many fronts. Today, Soviet industrial growth has slowed to a crawl. In agriculture, less grain is being produced now than in the late 1970s.

While the United States and the Soviet Union have been preoccupied with each other militarily, Japan has been moving to the fore economically. By some economic indicators, it now leads both military superpowers. In a world where the enormous investment in nuclear arsenals has no practical use, the terms denoting leadership and dominance are shifting in Japan's favor. Governors and mayors in the United States now compete vigorously for Japanese investment. And Third World delegations seeking investment and technology from abroad regularly journey to Tokyo. For developing countries, the Japanese model is far more attractive than either the problem-ridden Soviet economy or the debt-ridden American one.

The U.S. economy is still twice as large as Japan's, and the country has a vastly superior indigenous resource base of land, energy fuels, minerals, and forest products. Nonetheless, a country that is a net debtor, borrowing heavily from the rest of the world, cannot effectively exercise economic or political leadership.

Unfortunately, the two superpowers that are perpetuating the arms race are not its only victims. To the extent that the arms competition diverts attention from the Third World debt that is weakening the international financial system, or from the ecological deterioration that is undermining the global economy, the entire world suffers. The extensive deterioration of national support systems and the declining economic conditions evident in much of the Third World pose threats to national and international security that now rival the traditional military ones.

HOPEFUL SIGNS

Yet, a few governments have begun to redefine national security, putting more emphasis on economic progress and less on buying arms. At a time when global military expenditures are rising, some countries are actually cutting military outlays. A handful are reducing them sharply, not only as a share of GNP, but in absolute terms as well. Among these are China, Argentina, and Peru.

As recently as 1972, China was spending 14 percent of its GNP for military purposes, one of the highest rates in the world at the time. Beginning in 1975, however, China systematically began to reduce its military expenditures, and except for 1979 has done so for the last eight years. By 1985, military spending had fallen to 7.5 percent of its gross national product.

There are indications that this trend may continue throughout the 1980s. In July 1985, Beijing announced a plan to invest $360 million over two years to retrain one million soldiers for return to civilian life. Such a move would cut the armed forces in China from 4.2 million in 1985 to 3.2 million in 1987, a drop of 24 percent. At the same time, the leaders in Beijing have stepped up the effort to restore and protect the economy's environmental support systems by increasing expenditures on agriculture, reforestation and desert reclamation. In effect, China is defining security in economic and ecological terms.

In Argentina, one of the first things that Raul Alfonsin did as newly elected president in late 1983 was to announce a plan to steadily lower military spending. When he took office there was broad public support for a reduction in arms expenditures, partly because of the ill-fated Falklands War, which undermined the military's credibility. By 1984, arms outlays had been cut to half the peak level of 1980, earning Alfonsin a well-deserved reputation for reordering priorities and shifting resources to social programs.

More recently, Peru has joined the ranks of those announcing plans to cut military expenditures. One of the first actions of President Alan Garcia on taking office in the summer of 1985 was a call to halt the regional arms race. Garcia is convinced of the need to reduce the five percent of Peru's GNP allotted to the military, a sum that consumed one-fourth of its federal budget. As an indication of his sincerity, President Garcia announced that he was cancelling half of an order for 26 French Mirage fighter planes.

Encouragingly, the reductions in military expenditures undertaken by these three governments were independent of any negotiated reductions in neighboring countries. China lowered military outlays unilaterally, despite its 3000 kilometer border with the Soviet Union, which has continued to increase its military might. Over the next few years, as governments everywhere face difficulties in maintaining or improving living standards, others may also choose to reduce military expenditures.

RESHAPING GEOPOLITICS

Understanding the new threats to security and economic progress will challenge the analytical skills of governments. Sadly, the decision-making apparatus in most governments is not organized to balance threats of a traditional military nature with those of an ecological and economic origin. Non-military threats are much less clearly defined. And national defense establishments are useless against them.

The key to demilitarizing the world economy and shifting resources is defusing the arms race between the United States and the Soviet Union. Whether this can be achieved in the foreseeable future remains to be seen. But as the costs of maintaining the arms race multiply, both for the superpowers and for the world at large, the likelihood of reducing tensions may be improving.

In East Asia, for example, traditional adversaries China and Japan appear to be in the process of establishing strong economic ties. In contrast to the United States, China appears to be abandoning military competition with the Soviet Union. With Japan showing little interest in becoming a military power, the stage is being set for peace in the region. Both countries have redefined security and reshaped their geopolitical strategies.

If ideology gives way to pragmatism, as it is doing in China, then the conflicts and insecurities bred by the ideological distinctions between East and West can lessen. If the Soviet Union adopts the reforms needed to get its economy moving again, a similar ideological softening may result. Turning more towards a market-oriented economy to allocate resources and boost productivity could not only restructure the Soviet economy, but also reorient Soviet politics. Although pragmatism has typically taken a back seat to ideology in the Soviet Union, the leaders have demonstrated that they can be pragmatic when circumstances require, as when they import grain from the United States, their ideological rival.

For the world as a whole, the past generation has seen an overwhelming movement toward militarization. Apart from the heavy claim on public resources, the East-West conflict contributes to a psychological climate of suspicion and distrust that makes the cooperative, international assessment of new threats to the security of nations next to impossible. China, Argentina and Peru may provide the models for the future. If demilitarization could replace militarization, national governments would be free to reorder their priorities, and could return to paths of sustained progress.

Ironically, for the United States and the Soviet Union, maintaining a position of leadership may now depend on reducing military expenditures to strengthen their faltering economies. Acting thus in their own interest, they could set the stage for demilitarizing the world economy. Once it starts, demilitarization—like militarization—could feed on itself.

Questions

1. What effect does militarization have on the world environment, the U.S. budget deficit and third world debt?
2. Name some threats to the security of the U.S. that cannot be coped with by the armed forces.
3. What are some consequences of the fact that the U.S. is now a debtor nation?
4. Is the author too optimistic in his estimate that the cost of the arms race may help reduce East-West tensions? Give your reasons.
5. What effects are the lowered military outlays by China likely to have on the U.S.S.R.?

3

Obtain the Possible:
Demand the Impossible

Robert Jay Lifton and Richard A. Falk

This article originally appeared in *Indefensible Weapons*, Basic Books, 1982.

Anti-nuclear sentiment is subject to peaks and valleys. The "nuclear freeze" movement of the recent past has seemingly receded from the public view, perhaps to be re-energized at a critical moment. Yet, as authors Lifton and Falk of Harvard University maintain, even the abolition of nuclear weapons would leave the world in danger so long as "national sovereignty and the war system remained." Nuclear powers, they remind us, would still retain the knowledge and technology to rearm, thus leaving suspicion in the minds of potential adversaries. They maintain that war itself (even "conventional" war) must remain the target of the anti-nuclear "Zen archer."

Rather than wait for the millennium to come to pass, the authors insist "there are many things we can do to make the world safer and saner." They recommend freezing the arms race, renunciation of first-use options, opposing the deployment of specific weapons systems, establishing nuclear-free zones and prohibiting flight testing of missiles and underground testing. Without underestimating the complexity of achieving even these limited goals, Lifton and Falk say that the anti-nuclear movement "will have to develop a politics of struggle and resistance if it hopes to achieve major results."

Bureaucracies both Eastern and Western are, they say, "more durable than either politicians or popular movements." The authors advise a strategy that combines tactical demands with essential long-range objectives. "Either without the other will collapse," they say. One possibility they see is a shift from "adventurous" nuclearism to a more moderate stance on the part of governments. While remaining skeptical of the outcome, the authors detect some signs of a "conversion of the elite" in the Reagan Administration.

Lifton and Falk seek to replace "peace through war" thinking with a more holistic world picture as a way of challenging the "mental armor of nuclearism." They would do this by highlighting "the immorality, illegal-

ity and illegitimacy of nuclear weapons and tactics." They go on to defend the limited steps recommended above. They take pains to deny that their holistic vision implies "covert support for the project of world government or for the formation of a superstate." While they recognize the dangers of the national security state (heightened by the nuclear dimension), the authors retain their faith in an "energetic citizenry" to put checks on the "secular absolutism" of at least the democratic states. They seem to feel that selfishness, not altruism, "would lead other countries to join with us in this process of nuclear renunciation."

In pressing for limited steps ("the possible") on the way to a peaceful world ("the impossible"), the authors urge anti-nuclear activists to remain in the game for the long haul "by regarding attitudes of reconciliation as a cardinal virtue alongside those of perseverance and commitment."

Participation in the surging popular movement of opposition to nuclearism is making many people more hopeful about the future. Yet this new hopefulness is often closely connected to an arousal of fear and anxiety, and is certainly fragile, being vulnerable to disillusionment. The present spirit of the antinuclear movement is captured by W. H. Auden's words:

"We who are about to die demand a miracle." Demanding a miracle is itself an affirmation of life, exhibiting, at the same time, an uplifting clarity about the gravity of the danger.

The miraculous applies to freeing the planet of nuclearism altogether. Such a prospect seems beyond the horizon of what is possible. Complete nuclear disarmament is not really plausible so long as leaders hold a Machiavellian world picture, and perhaps, so long as the organization of political life is based upon grossly unequal sovereign states competing militarily for scarce resources. Common sense illustrates the difficulty of achieving total nuclear disarmament in the world as we know it, even assuming good will on the part of the main governments, which it is misleading to assume either for ourselves or our adversaries. Suppose we imagine a situation in which nuclear disarmament had been agreed upon and implemented, but national sovereignty and the war system remained. It seems inconceivable that a government faced with the prospect of defeat in a major war, yet retaining the knowledge and technology to reconstruct nuclear weaponry would refrain under such conditions. Realizing this prospect, a government would assume that its adversary might try to evade the disarmament agreement at least to the extent of retaining a small hidden stockpile as a hedge against a rearmament race or nuclear blackmail. To prevent this evasion of a disarmament treaty, given the grave consequences at stake, would require a highly reliable system of verification, itself a nonnegotiable barrier to agreement, given the apprehensions associated with sovereignty. But more than this, since the bomb cannot be disinvented and since the technology will become more and more accessible, it must be supposed that any political actor faced with the prospect of defeat would revive at the onset of crisis its nuclear weapons option. When these considerations are understood, it becomes clear that war, in general, not nuclear weapons in isolation, must become the inevitable focus for any serious effort to overcome nuclearism. Like the Zen archer, the dedicated antinuclearist must aim above the target to strike the bull's-eye.

To get rid of war, however, requires a new type of world order, including a far stronger sense of human identity to complement and complete the various partial identities of nationalism, religion, race, and ideology. The end of war implies, in effect, the displacement of Machiavellianism by a holistic world picture.

For all these reasons, then, it seems impossible, as matters now stand, to achieve nuclear disarmament, despite its necessity. As long as nuclear weapons remain a central basis of national security, the danger of their use will condition our experience—at times mitigated, at other times, such as the present, magnified. Additionally, reliance on nuclear weapons inevitably concentrates antidemocratic authority in governmental institutions and builds such a strong permanent disposition to engage in ultimate war as to negate the atmosphere and structure of genuine peace. We can never taste real peace again until we find the means to eliminate nuclear weapons altogether.

Yet we need not wait. There are many things we can do to make the world safer and saner, thereby also creating opportunities for more fundamental changes to occur. We can greatly reduce the risks of nuclear war, as well as dramatically reduce the drain upon the world's precious resources. It is possible to foster a political climate in which leaders are induced to take steps, gradual and partial in character, but highly significant in their cumulative effect. The antinuclear movement, while finally demanding the impossible, is tactically focused on attainable goals: freezing the arms race, renouncing first-use options and limited war doctrine, opposing the deployment of specific weapons systems (for example, neutron bomb, Pershing II, cruise missile), establishing nuclear-weapons-free zones (such as the Indian Ocean, the Korean peninsula, Europe), prohibiting all further flight testing of missiles, and underground testing of warheads.

These tactical goals will themselves not be easy to attain. There are powerful, vicious, mystifying, and self-mystifying social forces tied up with the reign of nuclearism. Politicians are surrounded by advisors who contend that whatever danger of nuclear war exists is attributable to their enemy, and preserving "peace" depends on achieving nuclear superiority for oneself. There are, in other words, . . . powerful nuclear illusions that keep the arms race going and oppose by all available means popular demands for minimizing the dangers of nuclear war. Some nuclearists in and close to power centers will surely resort to a mixture of deceit, nominal accommodation, infiltration and provocation, and outright repression before giving way to democratic peace pressures. The antinuclear movement, without losing its enthusiasm, will have to develop a politics of struggle and resistance if it hopes to achieve major results. There is no assured way to get from here to there, even if there is defined in the relatively limited terms of stabilizing the role of nuclear weaponry.

Also, bureaucracies are unfortunately more durable than either politicians or popular movements. Politicians can respond to shifts in mood and might even be persuaded to implement serious antinuclear goals. We see that beginning to happen here and in Western Europe and Japan. It is an impressive tribute to the extraordinary vitality and strength of the antinuclear movement. Yet the roots of militarism are deeply embedded in the huge, implacable structures of governmental bureaucracy and reach out to encompass powerful, privileged sectors of the economy, including parts of the media. If past behavior is any guide, this faceless, durable bastion of nuclearism is certain to organize a variety of responses to the popular movement, perhaps even largely behind the backs of the main politicians, hoping to disillusion, or at least outlast, protest activity. Consider the following: Stalin was repudiated, but Stalinism remained, not exactly as before but essentially a regrouping of the same forces to maintain a basically repressive relationship between the Soviet state and the Soviet people. Bureaucracies are notoriously hard to reform so long as they remain intact.

Since popular movements are difficult to sustain (Americans being particularly prone to quick disillusionment), it is essential that its guiding spirits possess and impart a vision of what needs to be done, and how to do it. There is a special requirement present here, as well. To oppose nuclearism effectively does impose a difficult and special requirement that we connect tactical demands with a commitment to perseverance in pursuit of essential long-range objectives. Either without the other will collapse: the moral passion that gives grassroots politics its edge depends largely on an overall repudiation of nuclearism in any form, while the emphasis on attainable goals builds needed popular confidence that victories over nuclear forces are possible, that ordinary people can mobilize and wield decisive power, and that a path can be eventually found to overcome, once and for all, the nuclear menace.

Most current action within the peace movement is dedicated, whether deliberately or not, to stabilizing rather than eliminating nuclearism. The goal is to force a shift from certain adventurist forms of nuclearism (arms race, counterforce strategy, first-strike options, limited war and war-fighting scenarios) toward some variant of a defensive nuclear posture (nuclear weapons are retained, but their role is strictly limited to providing protection against nuclear blackmail and surprise attack by an enemy state).

Recalling the discussion of world pictures, it seems evident that the shift toward a more defensive nuclear posture can be achieved by stages and can partly rely on the methods of politics-as-usual, including the logic and dynamics of the Machiavellian world picture. It is not surprising, then, given the self-destructive dangers of adventurist nuclearism, that many prominent Machiavellian "realists" are beginning to lend their support to popular demands for greater moderation when it comes to nuclear weapons policy. These welcome defections from the upper ranks of policymakers greatly enhance prospects for influencing formal institutional policies. A stifling consensus is replaced by a political process consisting of pressures and counterpressures that reflect the interplay of special interest groups, social forces, and competing images of realism. At the center of dispute is the proper content of national self-interest and security requirements in relation to the various facets of nuclear weapons policy.

Only within the altered climate created by the popular movement do we find elite figures advancing their own proposals for moderation. In the late 1970s militarist forces within and without the governing structure had succeeded in dominating policy with a predictable heightening of East-West tensions and quickening of the arms race. Only the unexpected reactions of public opinion, alarmed about rising nuclear war risks, created a serious possibility of challenging nuclear adventurism at the level of national debate. The tricontinental peace movement now enables even mainstream politicians and journalists to consider openly, and even support, policies designed to move toward more moderate roles for nuclear weapons. At this point it is astonishing to observe even an avowedly militarist president clambering aboard the arms control bandwagon. It may well turn out to be an optical illusion. Strong grounds for skepticism remain. The Reagan forces could merely be riding out the antinuclear storm, hoping to calm things down enough to go forward with their basic thrust toward nuclear superiority and an interventionary foreign policy. It seems realistic, rather than cynical, to suppose that the current American leadership would like to place the onus of their arms race on Soviet shoulders so as to convey the sense that the United States has tried and failed, and now has no choice but to proceed with a further military buildup. However it may also be possible that the drive to remain in the White House will convince even confirmed cold warriors and superhawks that dramatic progress toward stabilizing nuclearism can alone bring them victory on the domestic scene. Everyone recalls that it was that impeccable anti-Communist, Richard Nixon, who in 1972 turned a conciliatory visit to Red China into a great electoral triumph. Ironies never cease. Now it may be the turn for an ardent militarist like Reagan to deliver the goods on arms control and world peace.

While it is important not to be duped by powerfully entrenched militarist interests, it is also desirable to be receptive to changes by leaders, however opportunistic their motivation. In one sense, the popular movement against nuclearism has achieved substantial success when it rewards peace-minded leadership at the ballot box. In fact, shifting the calculations of politicians is the most hallowed democratic method of reorienting policy and should be respected. Beyond even this kind of healthy pragmatism, however, lies a more genuine possibility of shifting the inner balance of feelings operative among our war-makers. Even the most ardent militarist admits that a nuclear war would be a disaster, and some part of his being must be touched by efforts to minimize these risks.[1] The distinctiveness of the nuclearist menace is that all of us, including even nuclearists and their families, are potential victims in the fullest sense. The kind of benefit that some derive from positions, power, wealth, and influence associated with present patterns of nuclearism would be forever destroyed by the personal tragedy brought about by nuclear war. Conversions among the elite have already taken place, and there must always be a readiness to welcome with open arms those who genuinely renounce nuclearism. In this central sense, the antinuclear movement, despite its destiny of struggle, has no permanent or inevitable enemies.

What blocks many from recognizing their own deeper affinities with the peace forces, aside from their preoccupation with defending special interests, are certain insulating thought-forms that have grown up over the centuries to bolster the militarism of the Machiavellian world picture, despite its growing absurdity as a rational ground for security. I have in mind here particularly the paradoxical idea, enchanting to foreign policy specialists and former national security advisors, that peace is most effectively pursued through preparation for war. This posture toward war and peace enables one to reconcile ethical and survival concerns with the most adventurist forms of nuclearism. As such, it inhibits a recognition of the dangers of the nuclear arms race, allowing at most tactical adjustments in response to political pressure. The contrary position taken by the antinuclear movement is that preparations for war are themselves a cause of war, that arms races have through international history displayed an overall tendency to heighten tensions, produce crises, and lead to wars.

I think it is particularly important to challenge the mental armor of nuclearism at this stage. For this reason, it seems useful to highlight the immorality, illegality, and illegitimacy of nuclear weapons and tactics.[2] Such an emphasis is also consistent with a series of United Nations General Assembly resolutions declaring that "the use or threat of use of nuclear weapons should . . . be prohibited, pending nuclear disarmament."[3] The most effective way to push ahead on this front is through a global insistence on a no-first-use policy pertaining to nuclear weapons, an insistence that earlier might have prevented a nuclear arms race altogether . . . , but even now could contribute greatly to a more stable world.[4] Such a step would make the crucial acknowledgment that these weapons can never be legitimately threatened or used for the ends of state power, however helpful it may seem in a particular set of circumstances. It would be beneficial to have such a declaration of no-first-use solemnized in a formal statement subscribed to by all governments. Part of the appeal of such a no-first-use arrangement is its simplicity: it is equal, easy to negotiate or can consist of unilateral declarations, requires no monitoring or verification, and contributes to overall security. The importance of this step is not only as an official statement of policy but also to persuade governments to abandon the forward or battlefield deployment of nuclear weapons, especially in Western Europe. A government of a superpower is unlikely to make a declaration of this sort in solemn form without adapting its war plans and deployment patterns.

Some Western specialists say that Europe, South Korea, or the Persian Gulf cannot be defended without threatening to respond to conventional attacks with nuclear weapons. There are many reasons to believe that the new conventional weaponry that is becoming available, including the latest in precision guided munitions and antitank technology, can meet defense requirements at current levels, or less, of expenditure. Contrary to the protestations of nuclearists, it is not necessary to militarize further other dimensions of domestic and world politics to compensate for taking this large step toward the stabilization of nuclearism. Note, also, that a no-first-use posture is fully compatible with a wide range of other arms control proposals, including the nuclear weapons freeze, prohibitions on new weapons systems and further testing, creation of nuclear-free zones, restraints on conventional weaponry, and a diplomacy of nonalignment for countries formerly allies of one or the other superpower.

Some critics complain that a no-first-use pledge is worthless, consisting of mere words, lacking any provision for sanctions, enforcement, or verification. Its verbal character, they argue, creates a one-sided trap for the more peace-minded states in the world, while placing no obstacle whatsoever in the path of an aggressor government. Here again the reasoning of defenders of the nuclear status quo seems poor. Except for possibly the United States, no other country has the slightest incentive other than in a situation in extremis to threaten or use nuclear weapons. If the United States were to adopt a no-first-use posture, it would certainly at the same time alter accordingly its contingency plans and capabilities, while the fear of what a beleaguered country might do if at the edge of survival and in possession of nuclear weapons seems almost irrelevant. Of course, no regime of restraint can promise perfect compliance. All rules of inhibition are susceptible to violation in any situation where political survival is deeply threatened, and yet even here, the situation would be no worse than what exists without the declaration. The importance of no-first-use thinking and practice is to discourage resolving crises by the temptation of recourse to nuclear threats. Even with a no-first-use orientation firmly in place, it will remain dangerous to press hard for military victory in conflicts touching on the vital interests of states that retain nuclear weapons or are closely aligned to such states. The Falklands/Malvinas War of 1982 vividly shows the helplessness of international society as a whole when the "honor" of sovereign states is drawn into question, especially if a military confrontation is popular at home and officials of the adversary governments are eager to distract criticism with an overseas sideshow. This helplessness has resulted in a stream of costly, senseless wars over the course of history, perhaps World War I being the clearest major instance in our century. No rule of conduct can hope to do more in a world of sovereign states than build a framework of inhibition that over time reshapes attitudes and expectations about the role of nuclear weapons, and by such alteration builds new possibilities for further denuclearization.

If moderate postures (that is, as a weaponry of ultimate recourse when total defeat is in prospect) evolve into purely defensive nuclear postures (that is, a weaponry retained only as protection against the nuclearism of others), then a fundamentally different situation would exist. True, even a defensive conception of nuclear weaponry might produce various forms of anxiety about whether the capabilities and intentions of the other side could not mount a successful disarming first strike (thereby destroying the hedge), and such speculation, possibly induced by maliciously false intelligence reports, could, if believed, create renewed pressures to resume the nuclear arms race despite the adoption of declarations of prohibition, freeze arrangements, and a host of other arms control measures. As long as the weaponry continues as an existing part of the security package then the structure of nuclearism, however contained, will cast its long shadow across our lives, posing in some form risks to human survival, impairing democratic relations between state and society, and, very likely, inducing a tensed reliance on nonnuclear militarism to offset the diminishing role of nuclear weaponry in an unchanged global political context. A central source of persisting anxiety will be the forward march of technology, making the weaponry of mass destruction more and more accessible to virtually all governments and discontented groups; the problems of proliferations will remain and jeopardize any international framework based on purely defensive conceptions. Furthermore, so long as the war system persists, a purely defensive posture for nuclear weapons would always be drawn into question whenever a government possessing nuclear weapons was facing the prospect of a major military defeat. Worthy and ambitious as is the shift to a purely defensive posture, it cannot hope to be entirely stable, and yet, as Jonathan Schell tirelessly underscores, the weaponry cannot be disinvented. We again confront here the apparent unresolvable tension between our need to get totally rid of this weaponry and the apparent impossibility of doing so. This tension expresses in clearest form the specific nature of the nuclear trap. History must be reversed, but history, by its nature, is irreversible.

Yet the finality of this formulation may itself be a trap set by ourselves, by our way of thinking. Nuclear weapons may "disappear" when other arrangements render them "irrelevant," when, for instance, the defense of our national boundaries relies no more on military capabilities than does the security of Pennsylvania in its relationship to New Jersey or Ohio. We get a glimpse of this possibility in the mutual relations of Western Europe countries since 1945 or of Canada and the United States in this century.

To overcome nuclearism, as such, requires quite a different sort of action than increasing the rationality and prudence of existing political leaders or of moderating institutional arrangements. It rests on the live possibility of establishing an orientation toward security that is not wedded to militarist strategies of geographical defense. It presupposes, in other words, supplanting the Machiavellian world picture with some version of a holistic world picture. Such a process would automatically transform the role and character of political institutions, eliminating a society's dependence on the existence of an enemy to achieve identity and coherence. A holistic world picture defines group coherence positively by a capacity to satisfy basic human needs of all people without damaging the biosphere or weakening reverence for nature. This holistic alternative is struggling in various ways to emerge in our thought and action, although as yet its influence seems weak and marginal, often expressing itself more in relation to ideas about diet and health than reshaping our sense of the political. It is important for the movement against nuclearism to grasp that realizing its goals is inseparable from the triumph over time of this holistic orientation. At this stage, this understanding may require nothing more substantive than a receptivity to such a possibility and a clarity about the desirability, yet limited horizons, of actions designed to diminish the dangers of nuclearism in its current forms.

There are a few additional orienting comments about action that flow from an acceptance of the long-range necessity for holistic politics.

CONTRA UTOPIANISM

A holistic vision does not imply a blueprint for the future, much less does it imply covert support for the project of world government or for the formation of a superstate; only in the process of gaining ascendency can the holistic world picture evolve appropriate institutional forms, but we can anticipate that they will not be reproductions on a global scale of the sort of governmental arrangements now associated with the sovereign state. Decentralization of power and authority will be paramount, as will efforts to coordinate economic, social, and cultural relations without reliance on bureaucratic oversight. New technologies for dispersed participation in shaping and sharing information may be one of the keys helpful for unlocking the future. Finally, the holistic prospect is not cut off from historical processes of evolution, as is the case with utopias that are posited as fully wrought solutions. We require a politics, as well as an imagery, of transformation.

CONTRA MILITARISM

Militarism is difficult to define clearly. It involves both a state of mind and a set of supportive societal arrangements. The essence of modern militarism is a comprehensive reliance on instruments of violence in the pursuit of national security. Militarism is also tied to technology. A militarist state of mind does far less damage, as a rule, under conditions of primitive technology, although even this direct assertion needs to be qualified. If, as is the case in the nuclear age, the consequences of militarism are catastrophic, then even the unabashed militarist is inhibited to a certain extent. Militarist guidance of foreign policy without any nuclear weaponry on the scene would undoubtedly have already produced World War III by now.

The rejection of militarism is wider than the rejection of nuclearism, but it is integral to it. And, in fact, the rejection of nuclearism without the substantial modification, if not outright rejection, of militarism is, finally, a futile project. Although nuclearism represents something that reaches far beyond the mere application of military technology according to the dictates of the Machiavellian world picture, its incorporation of specific weapons of war proceeded within this traditional framework. It may not be necessary, at least at the outset, to confront militarism with pacificism, but overcoming militarism will eventually depend on the existence of non-violent alternatives to achieve security for peoples and nations.[5] One important way to dilute militarism is to confine military capabilities and foreign policy to the strict circumstances of defensive necessity, as well as to draw distinctions between the defense of governments and of people. Of course, defense is an elastic concept, but my intention is to emphasize a real change of heart that seeks to restrict sharply the role of military weapons of all kinds.

The arrival of a sheriff in a western town during the early part of the last century brought a different kind of order only if the expectations about violence changed for most of the inhabitants. Without such a shift the new forms, and even capabilities, could not enhance security in the community and might indeed have produced a reliance on higher levels of violence on all sides.

Unless antinuclearism evolves in the wider setting of antimilitarism there is conjured up the prospect of a renunciation of the nuclear option combined with a vast buildup of conventional weaponry, a revival of the draft, an enormous peacetime army deployed around the world, thus creating an overall darkening prospect of major wars fought with weaponry of far greater savagery than used in World War II, as well as the persisting prospect of nuclear rearmament. The kind of popular momentum created by antinuclearism would, if it succeeded, also move naturally in an anti-militarist direction, questioning the ethics and viability of interventionary diplomacy and realizing the need to diminish those nonmilitary causes of war related to food and energy supplies, world poverty, and environmental decay.

CONTRA A NARROW AGENDA

There is a view frequently found among antinuclear activists that their concerns can be treated apart from others, arguing that the removal of the danger of nuclear war constitutes the necessary ground that must be achieved first if other social and political challenges are ever to be faced. This insistence on priority, however well conceived, tends to misunderstand the political conditions that must come to exist if an antinuclear movement is to achieve even limited success in both East and West. We need to consider what quality and quantity of social forces must be mobilized to challenge effectively the nuclear national security state in both superpowers. When we do this it becomes obvious, I think, that labor and minority discontent, peace activism by leading church groups, popular demands for liberty and social justice, and attacks on the corruptions and repressiveness of the bloated state create bonds of transnational dimension that can also easily become bearers of antimilitarist and antinuclearist sentiments. The success of Polish Solidarity, as most leaders in the European Nuclear Disarmament movement understood, would strengthen their prospects; its defeat would be demoralizing and debilitating, in part constituting a reassertion of the primacy of Soviet militarism and an uncertainty about whether a Western-centered movement for peace is not, in the end, self-defeating.

If antinuclearism succeeds in influencing policies of nuclear governments, it will be because it prevails through struggle, a struggle that includes the persuasiveness in debate of antinuclear forces. Persuasiveness is an important instrument to mobilize portions of the citizenry and to sow doubts in the nuclearist consensus, but it is by itself not nearly enough. Coalitions must be struck with social forces animated by discontent about the status quo. The nuclear national security state has grown into a powerful apparatus of coercion that can be and would be trained upon any opposition movement that threatened its dominion. The more broadly conceived the movement, the harder to break its will and morale.

It is pure illusion to suppose that there exists an apolitical and nonmilitant path to a nuclear-free United States or world. It is a further illusion to suppose that a political path can be discovered that is not beset by obstacles and struggle. Prospects for a nonviolent struggle toward these ends is likely to depend, in large part, on how broadly based and strongly motivated such an oppositional movement can become. In this regard, the particular characteristics of the movement need to be understood by its various segments. On the one side are the present fragments of the American political elite and generally conservative professionals, including doctors, lawyers, and engineers, who have formed their own antinuclear pressure groups. On the other side are present more militant groups that oppose nuclearism as part of a wider struggle against the modern state and its injustices. In between are an array of other orientations, including a wide variety of positions emanating from church activism on the nuclear issue. The capacity of the overall movement to grow more powerful and successful will depend greatly on the wisdom of its leaders, especially their ability to regard the diversity and multileveled character of the antinuclear movement as an expression of democratic vitality rather than as an indication of disunity and weakness.

CONTRA SECULAR ABSOLUTISM

Over time the modern state, even in societies proudest of their democratic identity, has adopted absolutist prerogatives and moved steadily in authoritarian directions. Nowhere is this tension between democratic creed and antidemocratic practice more evident than in relation to nuclear weapons diplomacy. The same leaders who insist that the major stake in international conflict is the fate of democratic governance have steadily eroded democratic content in the name of national security.

It is well to recall the early American antipathy to peacetime military establishments of any kind, phrased as opposition to so-called "standing armies." Even Alexander Hamilton, in so many ways an architect of governmental centralism, joined in the then prevalent belief that, as set forth in Federalist Paper No. 8, the standing armies of Europe and their perpetual readiness to engage in war "bear a malignant aspect to liberty and economy" for the country involved.[6] The founders of the American republic believed that advantages of geography and of political ideology would provide the United States with a general circumstance of security without militarism.

A similar disposition underlay, of course, the preoccupation with creating checks on possible abuse of presidential powers. The entire Constitution was drafted in light of the central doctrine of "the separation of powers" and the closely aligned notion of "checks and balances." The founders of our republic sought to avoid, above all else, a recreation in some new format of royalism and of leaders, who like the kings of old, could claim to rule by divine right. The American idea was to limit presidential authority by combining rules of substance with restraining procedures. Indeed, given the stern religious teachings of early America, including a preoccupation with original sin, the constitutional framework was conceived as a buffer against weakness and evil inherent in the human condition. The requirement that Congress participate in a declaration of war was specifically intended to prevent the president from having the power to commit the country unilaterally to war.

Over time there have been many encroachments on this conception of peacetime governance, a variety of accommodations to practical necessity without any formal adjustments by way of constitutional revisions. The avoidance of standing armies gave way to an expanding permanent military establishment. The Executive Branch claimed various privileges to keep national security information secret. The Congress and the public tolerated, even encouraged, a variety of recourses to armed force without prior declarations of war, American involvement in the Korean and Vietnam wars being the most spectacular instances.

All these tendencies helped to set the stage for the advent of nuclear weaponry that has put a permanent seal of inevitability on the imperial presidency. The nuclear national security state is a new, as yet largely unanalyzed, phenomenon in the long history of political forms. Being constantly ready to commit the nation (and the planet!) to a devastating war of annihilation in a matter of minutes on the basis of possibly incorrect computer-processed information or pathological traits among leaders creates a variety of structural necessities that contradict the spirit and substance of democratic governance: secrecy, lack of accountability, permanent emergency, concentration of authority, peacetime militarism, extensive apparatus of state intelligence and police. No king ever concentrated in his being such absolute authority over human destiny, not just in relation to his own people but for humanity as a whole. War as the sport of presidents has become the ironic, dreadful descriptive circumstance, an outcome brought about by the combined impact of the growth of statism and of the characteristics of the technology of war now available to leaders of the superpowers.

Indeed, nuclearism has caused a cultural, as well as a political and constitutional, breakdown. The unconditional claim by finite, fallible human beings to inflict holocaustal devastation on an unlimited scale for the sake of national interests and on behalf of any particular state is an acute variety of idolatry—treating the limited and conditional as if it were unlimited and unconditional. Our religious leaders have been slow to respond, complacent in their own secularism, and have tended to acquiesce in whatever powers the state claims for itself beneath the banner of national security. An encouraging recent sign is a dramatic weakening of deference to secular absolutism within the religious community when it comes to nuclear weapons policy. An increasing number of spiritual leaders with an array of denominational backgrounds are speaking out, to date mainly on the pernicious nature of nuclear weapons but also in strong support of individuals who stand apart from the state in a posture of resistance.

The erosion of democracy, while serious, is by no means final. In fact, if popular forces succeed in altering nuclear weapons policy it will have an overall revitalizing effect on our entire political process. Thomas Jefferson, always dubious about the capacity of constitutional arrangements ("a mere thing of wax"), put his trust for the maintenance of democratic vitality in "an energetic citizenry." One of the features of the nuclear national security state is to demobilize the citizenry as totally as possible on the most crucial questions facing the society. Only an energetic citizenry can hope to modify the political climate sufficiently to create space for new leadership and different directions of official policy. To combat nuclear militarism in the United States certainly requires an even more energetic citizenry reinforced by a cultural and religiously active appreciation that the authority of the state has degenerated into a new and acute species of idolatry.

At this time political analysts are in a position comparable to that of seismic specialists called upon to predict the intensity and date of an expected earthquake. There are many warning tremors. The political fault lines are so wide and deep that when it comes, the eruption could shake the strongest institutional foundations, but we cannot be sure whether this shattering of our order will come sooner or later, or what precise form it will take.

On a more concrete level, a distinction can be drawn between proximate goals that can be stated quite concretely and more distant goals that will have to be specified as they are approached. The essence of an antinuclearist orientation, given the realities of the world as we know it, involves a renunciation of the nuclear option combined with the retention of a limited number of nuclear weapons as an instrument of ultimate resort, confined in its potential role to a nuclear retaliation to a nuclear attack. The ethics and politics of this renunciation should help center a popular movement in the United States and would, I feel confident, find a resonant response elsewhere, including the Soviet Union. Such an expectation is not based on any perception of untapped altruistic energies being set loose. Quite the contrary. Selfishness would lead other countries to join with us in this process of nuclear renunciation, partly because it is the United States alone that has made such a strong investment over the years in maintaining the nuclear option against all challengers. I would not want to pretend that this dynamic of partial renunciation will come about easily. Its realization would represent a profound reversal of field with respect to the lineaments of security in the nuclear age.

If antinuclear sentiments take command, even more ambitious goals would then seem attainable: namely a determined assault on "the war system" in its totality, including national and transnational subsystems of special privilege, exploitation, and repression. In effect, the pursuit of humane governance is a goal on all levels of social organization from the family to the world. Such an animating vision may never be fully attainable, but its pursuit seems implicit in any serious engagement to work toward liberating our planet and our species from the nuclear curse that has been laid so heavily upon it.

Notes

1. There is a deep self-mystification that interferes with such awareness. Militarists continue to believe that the path to peace is to deter the other side by being even stronger and that the path to war is to tempt enemies to commit aggression.

This obsolete mind-set, which has elements of insight, needs to be understood, analyzed, and discredited as effectively as possible. As long as it dominates the thinking and feeling of policymakers and opinion-shapers, it will allow those in power to oppose peace forces in good faith. For an important attempt along these lines see Richard J. Barnet, *Real Security: Restoring American Power in a Dangerous Decade* (New York: Simon and Schuster, 1981).

2. For an extended discussion see Richard Falk, Lee Meyrowitz, and Jack Sanderson, "Nuclear Weapons and International Law," World Order Studies Program, Princeton University Center for International Studies Occasional Paper No. 10, 1981, pp. 1–80.

3. The most recent formulation is contained in G. A. Resolution 36/911, in Report A/36/751 (1981). It was adopted by a vote of 121 to 19, with 6 countries abstaining. The opposition included the United States and most of NATO, while both China and the Soviet Union voted in favor of the resolution.

4. For analysis to this effect see McGeorge Bundy, George F. Kennan, Robert S. McNamara, and Gerard Smith, "Nuclear Weapons and the Atlantic Alliance," *Foreign Affairs* 60 (1982):753–768.

5. For an important effort to rethink security and foreign policy see Robert C. Johansen, *The National Interest and the Human Interest* (Princeton, N.J.: Princeton University Press, 1980); Johansen, "Toward a Dependable Peace: A Proposal for an Appropriate Security System," World Order Models Project Working Paper No. 8 (New York: Institute for World Order, 1978).

6. Jacob E. Cooke, ed., *The Federalist* (Cleveland, Ohio: World Publishing Co., 1961), p. 44.

Questions

1. Why would the banning of nuclear weapons still leave the world in danger?

2. Are you convinced by Lifton's and Falk's argument that the anti-nuclear movement should work for limited goals? How likely are these goals to be attained—in the short run? in the long run?

3. Why are bureaucracies more durable than politicians or popular movements? How can their views be changed?

4. Describe in your own words the "holistic world picture" of the authors. How does this differ from world government?

5. Do you agree with the authors that self-interest would induce other nations to follow a U.S. lead in banning nuclear weapons? Explain.

4

The Lesser Evil over
the Greater Evil

Jeane Kirkpatrick

This article originally appeared in *Commentary*, November 1981.

Traditional morality has it that a good end does not justify an evil means and that, in certain cases, one may tolerate a lesser evil in order to avoid a greater evil. Jeane Kirkpatrick, U.S. Ambassador to the United Nations in the first Reagan Administration, looks at another dichotomy— that of human rights and the national interest. She finds no basic conflict here because the public good that defines the United States "is and has always been a commitment to individual freedom and a conviction that government exists, above all, for the purpose of protecting individual rights." She defines the purpose of foreign policy as that of "defending these rights or extending them to other peoples."

It is not in the acceptance of this principle, but in its application, that Kirkpatrick parts company with human rights advocates of the Carter Administration. She discerns a difference in the Carter years from the policy of its predecessors in that a "cultural revolution" resulted in the questioning of the morality of many aspects of U.S. foreign policy. In a sweeping statement, she declares: "As long as the United States was perceived as a virtuous society, policies that enhanced its power were also seen as virtuous." Under Carter, however, she declares that "morality now required transforming our deeply flawed society, not enhancing its power." The result of the Carter view "was a conception of human rights so broad, ambiguous and utopian that it could serve as the grounds for condemning almost any society."

Kirkpatrick criticizes the previous administration for its reluctance to condemn communist (totalitarian) regimes and a willingness to find fault with "authoritarian" recipients of U.S. aid—e.g., Central and South American countries, Iran under the Shah and South Africa. She accuses the Carter people of condemning government "repression" in these countries "while ignoring guerrilla violence." The result, she says, is a reduction of American influence throughout the world.

For her part, Kirkpatrick finds authoritarian (non-communist) regimes limited in the damage they can do to the people while the power of totalitarian (communist) regimes is unlimited. She sees the possibility of an evolution toward democracy in the authoritarians, a process she does not see happening in the totalitarians. For these and other reasons, Kirkpatrick exhibits "a steady preference for the lesser over the greater evil." While conceding that such policies will not make a perfect world, "at least they will not make the lives of actual people more difficult or perilous, less free than they already are."

Politics is a purposive human activity which involves the use of power in the name of some collectivity, some "we," and some vision of the collective good. The collective may be a nation, class, tribe, family, or church. The vision of the public good may be modest or grand, monstrous or divine, elaborate or simple, explicitly articulated or simply "understood." It may call for the restoration of the glory of France; the establishment of a Jewish homeland; the construction of a racially pure one-thousand-year Reich; the achievement of a classless society from which power has been eliminated. The point is that government act with reference to a vision of the public good characteristic of a people. If they are to command popular assent, important public policies must be congruent with the core identity of a people. In democracies the need for moral justification of political action is especially compelling—nowhere more so than in the United States. The fact that Americans do not share a common history, race, language, religion gives added centrality to American values, beliefs, and goals, making them the key element of our national identity. The American people are defined by the American creed. The vision of the public good which defines us is and always has been a commitment to individual freedom and a conviction that government exists, above all, for the purpose of protecting individual rights. ("To protect these rights," says the Declaration of Independence, "governments are instituted among men.") Government, in the American view, has no purpose greater than that of protecting and extending the rights of its citizens. For this reason, the definitive justification of government policy in the U.S. is to protect the rights—liberty, property, personal security—of citizens. Defending these rights or extending them to other peoples is the only legitimate purpose of American foreign policy.

From the War of Independence through the final withdrawal from Vietnam, American Presidents have justified our policies, especially in time of danger and sacrifice (when greatest justification is required), by reference to our national commitment to the preservation and/or extension of freedom—and the democratic institutions through which that freedom is guaranteed. Obviously, then, there is no conflict between a concern for human rights and the American national interest as traditionally conceived. Our national interest flows from our identity, and our identity features a commitment to the rights of persons. (Conventional debate about whether foreign policy should be based on "power" or morality is in fact a disagreement about moral ends and political means.)

It is true that the explicit moral emphasis on presidential pronouncements on U.S. foreign policy had declined in the decade preceding Jimmy Carter's candidacy, partly because of the diminishing national consensus about whether protecting human rights required (or even permitted) containing Communism even through war, and partly because of concern that moral appeals would excite popular passions and complicate the task of limiting the war in Vietnam. It is also true that Jimmy Carter shared this reticence and only reluctantly—and in response to pressure from Senator Henry Jackson—incorporated the human-rights theme into his presidential campaign.

Almost immediately, however, it became clear that the human-rights policies expounded and implemented by Jimmy Carter were different in their conception and their consequences from those of his predecessors. The cultural revolution that had swept through American cities, campuses, and news rooms, challenging basic beliefs and transforming institutional practices, had as its principal target the morality of the American experience and the legitimacy of American national interests. It was, after all, a period when the leading columnist of a distinguished newspaper wrote: "The United States is the most dangerous and destructive power in the world." It was a time when the president of a leading university asserted: "In twenty-six years since waging a world war against the forces of tyranny, fascism, and genocide in Europe we have become a nation more tyrannical, more fascistic, and more capable of genocide than was ever conceived or thought possible two decades ago. We conquered Hitler but we have come to embrace Hitlerism." It was the period when a nationally known cleric said: "The reason for the paroxysm in the nation's conscience is simply that Calley is all of us. He is every single citizen in our graceless land."

If the United States is "the most destructive power in the world," if we are "capable of genocide," if we are a "graceless land," then the defense of our national interest could not be integrally linked to the defense of human rights or any other morally worthy cause.

The cultural revolution set the scene for two redefinitions: first, a redefinition of human rights, which now became something very different from the freedoms and protections embodied in U.S. constitutional practices; and second, a redefinition of the national interest which dissociated morality and U.S. power.

As long as the United States was perceived as a virtuous society, policies which enhanced its power were also seen as virtuous. Morality and American power were indissolubly linked in the traditional conception. But with the U.S. defined as an essentially immoral society, pursuit of U.S. power was perceived as immoral and pursuit of morality as indifferent to U.S. power. Morality now required transforming our deeply flawed society, not enhancing its power.

In the human-rights policies of the Carter administration, the effects of the cultural revolution were reinforced, first, by a secular translation of the Christian imperative to cast first the beam from one's own eye, and, second, by a determinist, quasi-Marxist theory of historical development. The result was a conception of human rights so broad, ambiguous, and utopian that it could serve as the grounds for condemning almost any society; a conception of national interest to which U.S. power was, at best, irrelevant; and a tendency to suppose history was on the side of our opponents. (Of course, the Carter administration did not invent these orientations, it simply reflected the views of the new liberalism that was both the carrier and the consequence of the cultural revolution.)

Human rights in the Carter version had no specific content, except a general demand that societies provide all the freedoms associated with constitutional democracy, all the economic security promised by socialism, and all the self-fulfillment featured in Abraham Maslow's psychology. And it assumed that governments were responsible for providing these. Any society which did not feature democracy, "social justice," and self-fulfillment—that is, any society at all—could be measured against these standards and found wanting. And where all are "guilty," no one is especially so.

The judicial protections associated with the rule of law and the political freedoms associated with democracy had no special priority in the Carter doctrine of human rights. To the contrary, the powerful inarticulate predisposition of the new liberalism favored equality over liberty, and economic over political rights; socialism over capitalism, and Communist dictatorship over traditional military regimes. These preferences, foreshadowed in Carter's Notre Dame speech, found forthright expression in the administration's human-rights policy. UN Ambassador Andrew Young asserted, for example: "For most of the world, civil and political rights . . . come as luxuries that are far away in the future," and he called on the U.S. to recognize that there are various equally valid concepts of human rights in the world. The Soviets, he added, "have developed a completely different concept of human rights. For them, human rights are essentially not civil and political but economic. . . . " President Carter, for his part, tried hard to erase the impression that his advocacy of human rights implied an anti-Soviet bias. "I have never had an inclination to single out the Soviet Union as the only place where human rights are being abridged," he told a press conference on February 23, 1977. "I've tried to make sure that the world knows that we're not singling out the Soviet Union for criticism." In Carter's conception of the political universe, strong opposition to Marxist-Leninist totalitarianism would have been inappropriate because of our shared "goals." On April 12, 1978, he informed President Ceausescu of Romania that "our goals are also the same, to have a just system of economics and politics, to let the people of the world share in growth, in peace, in personal freedom."

It should not be supposed that under Carter no distinction was made between totalitarian and authoritarian regimes—for while the Carter administration was reluctant to criticize Communist states for their human-rights violations (incredibly, not until April 21, 1978 did Carter officials denounce Cambodia for its massive human-rights violations), no similar reticence was displayed in criticizing authoritarian recipients of U.S. aid. On the basis of annual reports required by a 1976 law, the Carter administration moved quickly to withhold economic credits and military assistance from Chile, Argentina, Paraguay, Brazil, Nicaragua, and El Salvador, and accompanied these decisions with a policy of deliberate slights and insults that helped delegitimize these governments at the same time it rendered them less open to U.S. influence.

President Carter's 1977 decision to support the mandatory UN arms embargo against South Africa; Secretary Vance's call, before a meeting of the Organization of American States in June 1979, for the departure of Nicaragua's President Somoza; the decision in 1979 to withhold U.S. support from the Shah of Iran; and President Carter's decision, in June 1979, not to lift economic sanctions against the Muzorewa government in Zimbabwe Rhodesia expressed the same predilection for the selective application of an "absolute" commitment to human rights.

Why were South American military regimes judged so much more harshly than African ones? Why were friendly autocrats treated less indulgently than hostile ones? Why were authoritarian regimes treated more harshly than totalitarian ones? Part of the reason was the curious focus on those countries that received some form of U.S. assistance, as though our interest in human rights were limited to the requirements of the 1976 Foreign Assistance Act; and part of the reason was the exclusive concern with violations of human rights by governments. By definition, guerrilla murders did not qualify as violations of human rights, while a government's efforts to eliminate terrorism qualified as repression. This curious focus not only permitted Carter policy-makers to condemn government "repression" while ignoring guerrilla violence, it encouraged consideration of human-rights violations independently of their context.

Universal in its rhetoric, unflagging in its pursuit of perceived violations—"I've worked day and night to make sure that a concern for human rights is woven through everything our government does, both at home and abroad" (Jimmy Carter, December 15, 1977)—the Carter human-rights policy alienated non-democratic but friendly nations, enabled anti-Western opposition groups to come to power in Iran, and totalitarians in Nicaragua, and reduced American influence throughout the world.

The Carter administration made an operational (if inarticulate) distinction between authoritarianism and totalitarianism and preferred the latter. The reason for its preference lay, I believe, not only in the affinity of contemporary liberalism for other secular egalitarian development-oriented ideologies (such as Communism) but also in the progressive disappearance from modern liberalism of the distinction between state and society. The assumption that governments can create good societies, affluent economies, just distributions of wealth, abundant opportunity, and all the other prerequisites of the good life creates the demand that they should do so, and provokes harsh criticism of governments which fail to provide these goods. The fact that primitive technology, widespread poverty, gross discrepancies of wealth, rigid class and caste structures, and low social and economic mobility are characteristic of most societies which also feature authoritarian governments is ground enough for the modern liberal to hold the existing governments morally responsible for having caused these hardships.

The same indifference to the distinction between state and society also renders the new liberals insensitive to the pitfalls and consequences of extending the jurisdiction and the coercive power of government over all institutions and aspects of life in society. It is, of course, precisely this extension of government's plans and power over society, culture, and personality that makes life in totalitarian societies unbearable to so many. Authoritarian governments are frequently corrupt, inefficient, arbitrary, and brutal, but they make limited claims on the lives, property, and loyalties of their citizens. Families, churches, businesses, independent schools and labor unions, fraternal lodges, and other institutions compete with government for loyalties and resources, and so limit its power.

Authoritarian governments—traditional and modern—have many faults and one significant virtue: their power is limited and where the power of government is limited, the damage it can do is limited also. So is its duration in office. Authoritarian systems do not destroy all alternative power bases in a society. The persistence of dispersed economic and social power renders those regimes less repressive than a totalitarian system and provides the bases for their eventual transformation. Totalitarian regimes, to the contrary, in claiming a monopoly of power over all institutions, eliminate competitive, alternative elites. This is the reason history provides not one but numerous examples of the evolution of authoritarian regimes into democracies (not only Spain and Portugal, but Venezuela, Peru, Ecuador, Bangladesh, among others) and no example of the democratic transformation of totalitarian regimes.

Authoritarian governments have significant moral and political faults, all the worst of which spring from the possession of arbitrary power. But compared to totalitarian governments, their arbitrary power is limited. Only democracies do a reliable job of protecting the rights of all their citizens. That is why their survival must be the first priority of those committed to the protection of human rights.

The restoration of the subjective conviction that American power is a necessary precondition for the survival of liberal democracy in the modern world is the most important development in U.S. foreign policy in the past decade. During the Vietnam epoch that subjective link between American power and the survival of liberal democratic societies was lost. Its restoration marks the beginning of a new era.

The first implication of that fact is that human-rights policies should be and, one trusts, will be, scrutinized not only for their effect on the total strategic position of the United States and its democratic allies—not because power is taking precedence over morality, but because the power of the U.S. and its allies is a necessary condition for the national independence, self-determination, self-government, and freedom of other nations. The human-rights policy of the Reagan administration has not been fully articulated, but the myriad concrete decisions made so far suggest that it will manifest the following characteristics:

First, clarity about our own commitment to due process, rule of law, democratic government and all its associated freedoms.

Second, aggressive statements in information programs and official pronouncements of the case for constitutional democracy. As the party of freedom we should make the case for freedom by precept as well as by example.

Third, careful assessment of all relevant aspects of any situation in another country in which we may be tempted to intervene, symbolically, economically, or otherwise. In Poland as in El Salvador we should be careful neither to overestimate our power to shape events according to our own preference, nor to underestimate the potential negative consequences of our acts.

Finally, a steady preference for the lesser over the greater evil.

Such policies will not make a perfect world, but at least they will not make the lives of actual people more difficult or perilous, less free than they already are. Conceivably, they might leave some people in some places more secure and less oppressed than they are today.

Questions

1. Do you agree with the author that "extending human rights to other peoples" is a necessary consequence of the public good? How would you relate your answer to your conception of the "national interest"?

2. Do you accept Kirkpatrick's statement that "as long as the U.S. was perceived as a virtuous society, policies that enhanced its power were also seen as virtuous"? If not, what qualifications would you make?

3. The author quotes several wholesale condemnations of the United States. Does the use of these quotations strengthen her case against President Carter's policies? Explain.

4. Is it your understanding that "human rights in the Carter version had no specific content"? Explain.

5. Does the author's quotations of President Carter give a complete picture of his attitude toward the Soviet Union? Cite examples.

5

America's Liberal Tradition

Charles William Maynes

This article originally appeared in *Commentary*, November 1981.

Taking issue with Jeane Kirkpatrick (see preceding article), Charles
William Maynes, editor of Foreign Policy magazine, argues for a liberal
American tradition that guides its foreign policy even when conservatives
are in power. Without claiming that the U.S. has always conducted policy
in a liberal way, he asserts that "a foreign policy that is in flagrant conflict
with that policy is in trouble." Even conservatives, he says, acknowledge
the liberal tradition by contending that, if we do not press too hard on
authoritarian regimes, they will "evolve in a democratic direction."
     In the short run, the author admits that emphasis on human rights
can hurt U.S. national interests, as occurred in Turkey and Argentina. But
he doubts that the American people, with its free press, would indefinitely
tolerate a Realpolitik that respects only power and ignores basic morality.
Whereas Kirkpatrick keeps power and morality at arm's length (as representing different categories of reality) Maynes sees them deeply interrelated at every stage of the process. "Foreign policy," as he conceives it, "is
basically the effort to manage the resulting tension between short-run policy needs (pragmatism) and long-run policy preferences (American values)."
     Maynes refuses to draw a sharp distinction between authoritarian and
totalitarian governments in terms of their evolutionary possibilities, the
severity of their repression and the differences between regimes under
each label. "(M)ust (we) place Yugoslavia and North Korea in the same pigeonhole?" he asks.
     The author also asks whether right-wing dictatorships always serve
U.S. interests better than left-wing dictatorships. He gives the Somoza
government as a case in point. In wartime, he remarks that countries cannot be overly choosy about their allies, but he denies that the U.S. is at
war with the U.S.S.R., as we were with Nazi Germany. Maynes acknowledges the "severe challenge to American interests" presented by the Soviet Union. But he is hopeful that "through logic, diplomacy and appeals
to common interest catastrophe could be avoided." Supporters of the

Reagan Administration who concentrate exclusively on "the present danger" would have the U.S. court South Africa and embrace reaction in Central America, he says. This, in his opinion, will not be accepted by the American people in the long run because they "remain adherents to the liberal tradition."

Much of the angry debate over U.S. human-rights policy overlooks one obdurate fact: America is a liberal country. It is not liberal in the sense that conservatives always lose elections. Numerous elections, including those in 1980, have shown that to be false. America is liberal in the sense that even conservative administrations are under pressure to pursue liberal political values.

America's behavior throughout the 20th century demonstrates just how strong the American liberal tradition is. Repeatedly, the country has been willing to sacrifice quite concrete commercial or security interests in order to respond to its liberal tradition. In 1911, when big business dominated American political life in a way it has seldom done since, the United States nonetheless abrogated its commercial treaty with Czarist Russia because of American outrage over the regime's treatment of its Jewish population. In the early 1920's, the vehemently anti-Communist Harding administration undertook a massive food program to feed the starving Russian people even though that move helped to save the new and hated Bolshevik regime. Under President Carter, although the U.S. relationship with Vietnam was one of intense hostility, the United States provided food to millions of starving Cambodians, a step that meant propping up the Vietnamese-supported puppet regime in Phnom Penh.

The existence of the liberal tradition does not mean that the U.S. always has liberal policies. It does mean that a foreign policy that is in flagrant conflict with that tradition is in trouble. The Reagan administration has recognized this point by shifting its stance on human rights. Although it earlier attempted to draw a distinction between human-rights abuses committed by authoritarian regimes and those committed by totalitarian regimes, it now contends it will have a single standard for all countries.

In short, the American liberal tradition of interest in the human rights of others is deeply rooted in the American body politic. It has manifested itself repeatedly throughout our history in both Republican and Democratic administrations. It is in this regard that Americans—whether conservative or radical—are in the end liberal.

Even the heated debates over the U.S. human-rights policy that have taken place in *Commentary* are a tribute to the strength of the U.S. liberal tradition. Many of *Commentary*'s authors want policy results different from those suggested by that tradition. But they are reluctant to call openly for a departure from that tradition. To defend unpopular recommendations, they are forced to argue counter-intuitively that in the Third World the best way to pursue democratic liberties is not to strike out for them directly but to support authoritarian regimes that allegedly will evolve in a democratic direction. Even if the immediate policy recommended violates the American liberal tradition, in other words, the underlying message is that the final result will conform to that liberal tradition.

The traditional American attitude toward human rights has acquired a new contemporary potency, however. The reason is modern-day ethnic politics. Today there is scarcely a nation on earth without some of its citizens or their descendants living in the United States. And in our system of government, with its checks and balances and with the unique power our Congress enjoys in the field of foreign policy, the more significant groups have had and will continue to have a major voice in the development of American foreign policy. In particular, they will be very concerned about the degree of political and economic welfare of their former countrymen or co-religionists. Inevitably, they will seize on the emotive power of the American liberal tradition and its support for democracy and the human rights that flow from that system of government to buttress their concern. Convincing other Americans that the issue is not simply a form of tribal loyalty to Israel or Cyprus or black South Africans but a form of liberal concern for democracy, self-determination, or common decency can only broaden the base of national support.

Can this approach lead to a conflict with U.S. national interest? The answer depends on the time-frame through which one is viewing the national interest. Certainly in the short run the conflict can be severe. The U.S. concern with human rights in the Soviet Union has troubled sensitive negotiations with that country in recent years. When non-Jewish Americans have based their support for Israel on the issue of self-determination and democracy, U.S. relations with oil-producing Arab states have been affected. Relations with South Africa have become increasingly strained because of U.S. attitudes toward the inhumane treatment of blacks in that country. Our bases in Turkey were closed down temporarily because we opposed Turkish suppression of self-determination in democratic Cyprus. Our influence with Argentina has fallen because of opposition to government-sanctioned slaughter of dissidents, real and imagined, in that country.

But those who shake their heads at this price in the American approach to foreign policy should ask themselves: what kind of foreign policy would we end up with over the long run if we were to follow the approach of clear-headed *Realpolitik* they advocate? Isn't our aim a policy that serves our interests and that commands popular support? And in that regard can one imagine the American people over the long run ever supporting a policy toward the Soviet Union that overlooks completely the fate of communities inside the Soviet Union that have so many ties to communities inside the United States? As long as we have a free press, could a policy of *Realpolitik* toward South Africa or Guatemala long survive the continued shocks of the expose of one human-rights outrage after another? Could any relationship with the Arab world be healthy that did not reflect the strong American support for a Jewish people expressing its democratic right of self-determination?

The reality for American foreign-policy "realists" is that their fellow citizens will not support a foreign policy over the long run that offends too frontally the American liberal tradition. Indeed, this is why the Begin government's attitude toward the Palestinians is so critical. For it is not clear that the traditionally warm relationship between the United States and Israel can survive the incorporation into Israel proper of the West Bank, with permanent political repression or expulsion of the Arab majority living there.

Given the American attitude, how should the U.S. handle the hard realities of international politics? In the short run the U.S. should deal on a pragmatic basis with both totalitarian and authoritarian regimes to protect U.S. security and welfare. It should buy key minerals from authoritarian South Africa. It should assist totalitarian China, at least with economic aid, to stand up to the Soviet Union. But over the long run it must be opposed to the political system of both authoritarian and totalitarian regimes, and it should not hesitate to say so. Our people will reject any short-run policy that ignores this long-run American preference. Foreign policy is basically the effort to manage the resulting tension between short-run policy needs and long-run policy preferences.

This observation about tension in any foreign policy is relevant to the contention that somehow authoritarian governments are better than totalitarian governments. Viewed closely, some of the distinctions drawn between the two seem weak at best. For example, it is not at all clear that one is more likely than the other to evolve in directions that we would like to see. There have been repeated efforts to gain political freedom in totalitarian Eastern Europe. Is it not likely that one day they will succeed? Would they not have succeeded already except for the intervention of the Soviet army, which may not be able to move so easily into non-contiguous areas?

Nor are all totalitarian states always more bloody than all authoritarian states. Few places have been more bloody than Guatemala in recent years.

Another major problem with the asserted distinction between

authoritarianism and totalitarianism is that both labels cover too vast a spectrum of countries to be meaningful. Is Mexico, authoritarian but relatively benign, to be placed in the same category as authoritarian El Salvador, in which political opponents are hunted down like some tagged member of the animal kingdom? If we accept, as many who draw this distinction do but I would not, that Communist states cannot change and remain forever totalitarian, then are we comfortable with the fact that we must place Yugoslavia and North Korea in the same pigeonhole? If we are forced to group such wildly different countries under the two labels, is the distinction not useless for policy purposes?

Nor is it always true—certainly in the longer run—that right-wing dictatorships serve U.S. interests better than left-wing dictatorships. Did Somoza of Nicaragua serve U.S. interests? As a right-wing foreign minister from a major Latin American country once explained to the Carter administration, Somoza's main achievement was to develop a plantation and to lose a country.

There is, however, one condition under which the distinction between authoritarianism and totalitarianism might acquire new significance, or at least be viewed in a new light. Suppose that the United States were now effectively at war with the Soviet Union. In wartime a country cannot always be overly selective in its choice of allies. Survival becomes the key issue and at virtually any price. Finland, after the Soviet attack in 1939, later accepted the support of Nazi Germany in an attempt to regain its territory. The Western allies did not hesitate to join hands with Stalin, a dictator of comparable moral degradation, in their effort to crush Hitler.

Are we at war? Some, including the editor of *Commentary*, Norman Podhoretz, in effect argue that we are. The Soviet Union is seen as "exactly" like Nazi Germany. It is seen as posing precisely the same kind of threat to American security and welfare. Whether intended or not, the equation of the Soviet Union with Nazi Germany is incendiary in its policy implications. Given our collective memory of World War II and the lessons we all believe we learned from the history of the 1930's, the evocation of Nazi Germany can only suggest inevitable and fairly immediate conflict. Negotiations begin to seem foolish. Even preemptive war might be in order. We would not want to make the mistake we made in the 1930's of letting the aggressor power choose the time and place of the inevitable attack. In any event, we should join with any allies we can find in combating this new menace, whose appetite, like that of Nazi Germany, cannot be sated. Against such a threat, some would also take action at home. The new chairman of the Senate Judiciary Committee has stated that Senator Joseph McCarthy was doing the right thing, only in the wrong way.

Few would deny that the Soviet Union poses a severe challenge to

American interests worldwide. Indeed, were the Soviet Union to invade Poland, the international situation would begin to resemble the summer of 1914 in its tensions and dangers. Vigorous military and diplomatic measures would become even more pressing than they are now. But even viewing the Soviet Union today in the way the rest of Europe viewed Imperial Germany in the summer of 1914 is very different from viewing the Soviet Union as the modern-day equivalent of Nazi Germany. In the former case, there could still remain some hope that through logic, diplomacy, and appeals to common interest catastrophe could be avoided. The margin of maneuver would be small but it would still allow some room for attention to be given to longer-run considerations. In the latter case, the margin for maneuver disappears altogether. The only value is survival, and the sole test of a foreign-policy relationship is whether it contributes to the pressing goal of survival.

Among the prominent supporters of the Reagan administration there are some who do see American options in the single blinding light of "the present danger" that now transfixes many of the contributors to *Commentary* in its high beam. These supporters would drive the administration to court South Africa, to embrace reaction in Central America, and to condone human-rights abuses so long as they are committed by our friends. They might even nod their heads approvingly when *New York Times* columnist William Safire writes: "What is 'winning' [in El Salvador]? Is it a military junta that kills the opposition but by its repressive nature produces more opposition that it becomes necessary to kill? If need be, yes— considering the aggressive totalitarian alternative. . . . "

The problem for those who espouse such a policy is that their fellow citizens will not accept it. The American people remain adherents to the liberal tradition. They fear the Soviet Union but they are not so terrified that they are willing to abandon long-standing American values. For that reason they have already rejected decisively the administration's initial hard-line and callous policy toward El Salvador. They will reject similar policies elsewhere. The Reagan administration would save itself much political gain if it acknowledged that there are some things that it cannot change and one of them is the basic liberal character of the country it governs.

Questions

1. How has the emergence of "modern-day ethnic politics" influenced American foreign policy? Is this good or bad for the national interest? Make any necessary distinctions in your answer.

2. Do you feel with the author that, in the long term, the American people

will not tolerate support for repressive regimes? Explain, giving examples.

3. Are the differences between totalitarian regimes so great as to rule out any consistent U.S. policy toward them? Give examples. Do the same in regard to authoritarian regimes.

4. Should the West view the Soviet Union today as comparable to Germany in 1939 or Germany in 1914? What are the differences, and what policy choices exist between the two situations?

5. The author appeals to the American people as the ultimate arbitrators of political morality. Is there another way to view the source of morality? Explain.

6
Scientists and the Peace Movement: Some Notes on the Relationship

Johan Galtung

This article originally appeared in *Bulletin of Peace Proposals*, #1, 1986.

As the founder of the International Peace Research Institute in Oslo, Johan Galtung has spent much of his professional life exploring the relation between peace activists and the scientific community. He notes the increasing tendency of scientists to ally themselves with political advocates of nuclear disarmament and other initiatives.

Will the scientists be "on top" of such popular-based movements or "on tap" to answer specific questions? he asks. Galtung comes out in favor of the democratic concept that "people should have the final say, not the experts." He calls for a partnership between the two groups. The role of scientific experts in popular movements, in his view, are: (1) data (the facts, within one's field of competence); (2) values (the consequences of actions in such areas as health and rational thought); (3) theories (the contribution of fresh ideas and policies).

Galtung asserts that the peace movement is in special need of the third form of assistance, observing that it "is good in criticism, not bad on empiricism, but very poor on constructivism, on designing desirable and viable alternatives." He warns against excessive optimism on the role of scientists because their rational arguments do not always lead to change and their statements tend to be ignored by authorities. He stresses the need for more than negative statements by peace activists: "Most people want vision, hope—not to be told that they are doomed."

Galtung thinks that scientists have much to learn from the peace movement: (1) they are exposed to new data; (2) they are exposed to an intense level of value commitment, which may force them to "do their homework"; (3) they are forced to be constructive and perhaps humbled in the process. He does not go so far as to predict that the joining of scientists to peace movements will result in a "happy marriage." But, despite all the pitfalls, he regards such a wedding as "a unique training in the values of democracy—and isn't that also what the peace movement is about?"

1. THE DEMOCRATIC INJUNCTION

We have recently witnessed a considerable increase in the size and the impact of the peace movement, even if the peace movement as an anti-missile movement in Western Europe has suffered a certain defeat, certainly to be expected when the deployment of the missiles nevertheless took place in fall 1983. We have for a long time had a rate of increase in the production of scientists (of all kinds, natural science, social sciences, humanities) possibly sooner or later approaching a saturation point. Naturally, there has been a spill-over from one to the other: scientists as such, physicians, physicists and engineers, social scientists of all kinds, historians, lawyers, theologians are making statements and aligning themselves in various ways with the broad popular movement to avert nuclear war. The interesting point is that they no longer do so as committed individuals only, accepting some very general principles, but try to bring their scientific expertise to bear on their position in favor of the peace movement and its causes. This is my point of departure.

I think there is a basic problem here that needs some exploration: What does it mean to the democratic character of a political process when scientists in great numbers join a popular movement, presumably as experts? Will they try to be in command of the movement, legitimizing a leadership position by reference to superior knowledge? Will they be experts on top, in other words, or be satisfied to remain experts 'on tap', counting one vote only if elections and votes are on the agenda, but at the same time making their knowledge-based insights available?

In a sense the answer is easy: in a democracy, as opposed to an expertocracy, people should have the final say, not the experts. It is pressure from the people rather than from the experts that should lead to course corrections, whether these corrections are carried out by the executive power directly or mediated through the pressures exercised by a popular assembly, parliament. Experts may err, and so may people. In war-peace issues the parliaments and governments of aligned member countries certainly err, if the experience from the past century is a valid guide. Offensive weaponry leads to arms races in offensive weapons; arms races tend to lead to wars. And the consequences of all these errors in the course charted for society as a whole are visited upon the people and not only on the military experts, parliamentarians and governmental bureaucrats. Hence the responsibility should also rest with the people. Societies are not constructed in such a way that only people high up pay the consequences; usually they get off more easily than the people in general. Nor should people abdicate from responsibility. Democracy is based on the principle of and by the people, simply because what happens may not only be for, but also against the people.

The peace movement is an expression of this sentiment. It is the obvious outcome of a situation where it is possible, like in the Federal Republic of Germany, to make a decision with extremely serious potential consequences, such as the deployment of the Euromissiles November 1983, with only a 55% majority in the parliament and probably with not more than 5% of the population at that time really supporting the decision. The peace movement not only stands for, or rather against, a certain course of action; it is also an expression of the democratic urge in large sections of the population to step in where they feel that experts, parliamentarians and bureaucrats fail. In other fields there may be discontent, but nevertheless a feeling that by and large the self-correcting mechanisms of the establishment are sufficient. In the field of security politics this is no longer the case, and the peace movement is one answer to the gap in credibility, even legitimacy.

From this it should follow that it would be very unwise for the peace movement to abdicate to its own experts, the scientists who join. The peace movement should not become an exercise in liberation from one set of experts, only to end up in the arms of another set, certainly with a position closer to that of the peace movement at some place, at some time, but otherwise not differing much from experts in general. The peace movement should keep its distance, listen to all experts carefully (including those from the Establishment), sift the chaff from the wheat, use the experts, and really squeeze them. But there should be no abdication; any leadership should be democratically elected, not selected because of some status in the knowledge hierarchy. It should be remembered that democracy is based on the faith that the insights of everybody concerned can be added up in some meaningful manner, particularly provided a dialogue has taken place, and that the expert's deep insight at some points in the spectrum of knowledge is compensated by the non-expert's intuitions over a wider range. Partnership is the way to democracy, which is neither 'parliamentocracy', nor 'expertocracy', nor 'populocracy'.

2. WHAT THE SCIENTISTS CAN CONTRIBUTE TO THE PEACE MOVEMENT

It seems to me that in a popular movement like the peace movement the scientists have three quite clear tasks, based on data, values and theories respectively.[1]

(1) Empirically, to give the data, the facts, in connection with policies

chosen or recommended. This, however, they should above all do within their range of competence, not trying to step outside that range, which is often quite narrow.

It is equally painful listening to a social scientist trying to behave like a nuclear scientist as it is listening to a nuclear scientist who believes that he is a social scientist, pontificating on peace and war. As a regular peace movement member he is, of course, free to do so—but then it should not necessarily be assumed automatically that his insights are particularly deep or valid. They may be, but that will have to be tested. The Pugwash movement, at some time dominated by the superpowers and the nuclear scientists, and particularly by superpower nuclear scientists, had some of this faith built into it, particularly in the first twenty years.

To this it may be objected that scientists are surrounded by an aura anyhow, and this can be utilized and capitalized upon by the peace movement. I doubt it. I think physicians are particularly effective when they pronounce themselves in their capacity as physicians and end up with conclusions underpinning positions taken by the peace movement; not when they pronounce themselves on any and all matters outside their field of competence. On the contrary, others would not fail to pay attention to such mannerisms, and may also make use of such pronouncements in order to illegitimize the specialists, even when they are clearly within their field of competence. Of course, that kind of debating trick will probably be made use of anyhow, and should not be taken too seriously. But the difficulty remains that when the scientists are inside their field of competence the novelty of what they say may not be acknowledged in any case, because people are so used to their positions, which are usually of a pessimistic kind, even apocalyptic. 'Nuclear winter' may be an example here.

(2) Critically, being explicit in their evaluation of courses of action, again within their field of competence. But at this point a new element enters: the scientists not only say what the consequences will be but also deplore them, speak out against them, utter clear warnings. To do so there has to be an element of value commitment, not only good data or reasonable predictions about the empirical consequences of a course of action. Some scientists are better trained in combining empirical projections with a value commitment than others; physicians bring in the supreme value of health, engineers the supreme value of (scientific and economic) rationality. Both commitments are much heralded in our civilization and bring in their wake no particular difficulties to the members of these professions. The same could be the case for peace, particularly when coupled with such other honor words as 'security' and

'freedom'—but we are not yet quite at that stage. However, some scientists have reached that point more than others and do criticize; they do engage in criticism.

It should be pointed out that when they do so they are not outside their realm of competence as scientists, provided they make the value-orientation they use reasonably explicit. The value to which they are committed is trivial, at least as long as we stay within the examples quoted above. What they do is simply to read off the consequences, on which they are presumably experts, on a screen with a value dimension on it. Actually, it is not even required of them that they believe in health, rationality or peace—all they do is spell out the consequences in these terms. If they want to make this very clear, all that is needed is to preface their statements with an 'if': 'If peace is what you want, then this course of action will probably rather bring you the opposite for the following reasons . . . ' Very simple, and doing so in no way interferes with their qualities as scientists. It is only unusual in the sense that many of them are trained in the university to believe that values and facts do not mix at all, in which case medical science and engineering would be impossible. Staying within their empirical field of competence, there should be no problem in this connection, explicitness being compatible with competence.

(3) Constructively, contributing new ideas, suggesting new policies. Here a new element is brought in as there is no longer any solid empirical base. The new courses of action would be located in the interface between theory and value, the values indicating the ends and the theories the means (of course a simplification since the two are rather interrelated). But physicians and engineers, like architects and medical people, are doing this every day, as an obvious part of their professional activities. Lawyers are doing so, often more with a view to preventing wrong courses of action than encouraging the right ones. Hence, this is not so revolutionary either and could safely be engaged in by many more people. Whether one does it well or badly is another matter.

In the three points just mentioned, there is a clear past-present-future dimension. The empirical approach would obviously have to be based on data from the past, since only the past yields data—although projections into the future may be entertained. A critical approach will usually be about current politics, and the scientist will become an actor in the political field. The constructive activity would be with a view to preparing blue-prints for tomorrow, inspiring the peace movement to new vistas.[2]

It goes without saying that some scientists are better at documentation, others at criticism, and still others at proposal-making. It is also obvious that the three activities do not exclude each other. They can be found in the same person, at least two of them if not all three (all three would demand much expertise in one scientist, and for that reason better obtained through dialogue processes in groups, collectively). The peace movement is in need of all three types of activities, singly and combined, which is just another way of saying that scientists are indispensable to the peace movement. Usually the peace movement is good in criticism, not bad on empiricism, but very poor on constructivism, on designing desirable and viable alternatives.

However, from this it does not follow that the peace movement will necessarily make more headway the more scientists there are. In fact, this might be an occasion to warn against two sources of excessive optimism:
—that in an open society rational arguments, and people's movements, will eventually lead to course corrections;
—that strong, warning statements by scientists will eventually lead to course corrections, or at least be heeded.

As to the first assumption we have reasonably open societies in Western Europe; there has been no scarcity of warning voices, nor any absence of movements and demonstrations. It has even been clearly brought to the attention of everybody that the majority of the population in the five Euromissile countries is against deployment. Yet deployment has happened, for the simple reason that however important peace issues are to many people, the peace movement has not yet succeeded in making peace the number one priority issue for the majority of the population. The moment that such is the case, people would vote in favor of a peace party even if that means choosing a party that does not favor the economic policy they themselves would like to see implemented. But that kind of voting hardly takes place to any significant extent today. On the contrary, I think Eastern European countries in general, and the Soviet Union in particular, could learn from the West that they have nothing to fear from the open society: just let people organize, write petitions and thick books, walk any number of kilometers in a straight line or in a circle, with or without torches. All one has to do is not to pay too much attention unless such demonstrations show up in parliament. And there, as the last resort, there is always the possibility of exercising strong idea power, exchange power, or threat power—convincing, buying, cajoling recalcitrant 'dissidents'. Very last resort: a military coup.

As to the second assumption, I am not convinced that science-based stern warnings, and pessimistic predictions, will really bring about change. Rather, I think there are reasons to believe that political establishments accept criticism the moment they see a constructive alternative that is acceptable to them for other reasons. In other words, criticism alone, however well it is backed up by empirical data, will not change the course of action, only marginally modify that course, as I can easily imagine in connection with the 'nuclear winter'. If the prediction is that a certain megatonnage will whirl so much dust into the atmosphere that sunshine will be blocked out with disastrous consequences, then one alternative would not be to ban nuclear war, but to go in for smaller bombs with lower yields, more dispersed, and precise enough to hit targets that do not generate too much dust in the atmosphere. But that was hardly what those emitting those warnings had in mind, nor the peace movement.

It is, therefore, the constructive alternative, coupled to a critical assessment of the current course of action, asserted forcefully and with a tinge of optimism, that probably will win out—if not in the shorter, at least in the longer run. And this also has something to do with the way in which policies are criticized and proposed. That negativism, criticism and pessimism do not necessarily attract more votes than a positive attitude, constructivism and optimism, can be clearly seen from some recent elections: Mondale vs. Reagan in the United States, November 1984 (and November 1980 against Carter also, for that matter); or Kohl vs. Vogel in the Federal Republic of Germany in March 1983 (another example would be the elections for the office of mayor of West Berlin, May 1985). What holds for such elections probably holds for politics in general, and may be one very important reason why the peace movement does not make a more significant breakthrough. When proposals are put forward these are usually in terms of limitation, cuts, 'freeze', disarmament and control—not about something new and expansive, even if it also has to be expensive. Which is just another way of saying that criticism, at least in change and progress-oriented societies like ours, has to be combined with constructivism, with new horizons—not only stopping action, back to status quo ante. Most people want vision, hope—not to be told that they are doomed.

What has just been said are some reasons why the fault may not necessarily be with society if the peace movement is not sufficiently listened to and its proposals are not accepted. There may also be something wrong with the whole style of the peace movement. Similarly, if the peace experts find that the peace movement does not accept their way of thinking in general, and their specific advice in particular, it may not necessarily be the fault of the peace movement. In a democracy scientists should never be arrogant relative to a popular movement, but they should not be submissive either. We have more than enough of submissive intelligentsia who for a salary/honorarium offer the 'advice' the weighty institutions in society want to hear anyhow. Similarly, nobody is served by 'scientists' who give up their precious capacity always to continue asking 'But is that really so?', and instead become the call girls of the tiny peace movement commissariat—differing from those kept by the establishment mainly in not even being paid. But, since the scientist can never predict where unceasing questioning will lead him, there may be conflicts of loyalty—part of the social dialectic.

3. WHAT THE SCIENTISTS CAN LEARN FROM THE PEACE MOVEMENT

The other side of the coin of the scientist/peace movement relationship is often forgotten: what the scientists get out of that relationship. I would like to mention three particular points, all of them from my own experience.

First, a scientist is exposed through the peace movement to new data, to combinations of events in the past, the present, and possibly also the future that he would hardly have come up against had he just been engaged in conventional library research. Of course, this is the case whenever a scientist enters some kind of consultancy relationship; the 'client' presents him with situations that are new, if not to the 'client', at least to the scientist. I can only mention the example that gave rise to my own book *There Are Alternatives:* I was questioned by one particular peace-moved person (my own son), 'Where in Europe is it safest to live in case an atomic war should break out?' In all academic settings, such general but basic questions are overshadowed by a plethora of specialised, less basic problems.

Second, the scientist is exposed to a more intense level of value commitment than he usually has himself. Also, he may be exposed to conflicting value commitments, at least if the movement is diverse enough. These values are held with an intensity that makes the problems much more pressing, particularly as there are demands for answers, rewards for good answers and some punishment for the scientist who hedges, who never comes out with anything like a clear answer. Suddenly the scientist realises not only that an answer is requested of him, and if he cannot come up with one, it is not necessarily because he is 'scientific' in the sense of not jumping to conclusions, but simply because he has not done his homework, so that he becomes able to jump to valid conclusions, if jump he must!

Third, the scientist is exposed to the need to be constructive, to propose some alternative and not only to use his knowledge to present and project data, possibly in a critical manner. Only parts of the peace movement will demand this constructive activity of him; most of the movement will be more than satisfied if he can help the movement buttress their essentially critical argumentation against establishment policies engaged in or proposed. The scientist can solve the problem by keeping away from such movements or parts of movements, or demand of them in advance that such pressures should not be exercised. But he will also find himself rejuvenated as a scientist by accepting the pressures, and perhaps become more humble, facing his inability to supply the goods demanded, trying to do something about it. What a challenge to face people who ask difficult, precisely because not 'academic', questions where knowledge of literature and quotations will get you nowhere!

These are high rewards for the scientist, although they are not in monetary terms. Of course they are only rewards for a scientist who feels some kind of basic alignment with the peace movement, its ideas and ideals. He cannot do as the establishment scientist who may be even repelled, or feel aversion in connection with establishment goals but comforts himself that at least he is well paid, his family well fed and clothed and sheltered, and that 'such is life' and 'if I don't do it, somebody else will' and 'I have a mortgage to pay'.

The peace movement might do well to understand that they can keep their scientists particularly happy, and also filter out the scientists less valuable to the movement, by maintaining a certain pressure on them to deliver intellectual goods and services. It is not a bad idea to have a scientist introduce a working group, but only if the questions have been relatively precise and well-formulated, and sufficiently difficult. If a general talk is needed, then a generalist rather than a specialist might be asked to deliver it; in fact, the opposite would be not only abuse but also bad utilization of the specific talents of a scientist.

4. CONCLUSION: A HAPPY MARRIAGE?

Not necessarily. To assume this is to be far too optimistic. There are plenty of scientists who feel hurt, even insulted, when 'common people' fail to accept their advice; there are very many 'common people' who much too easily accept what is said by a 'famous' expert. Much of this comes from a lack of inner faith in democratic ideas and ideals, a search for authority and the authority's search for somebody who accepts them in a more unquestioning manner than their colleagues are likely to do.

Further, scientists used to performing brilliantly when relating data to theories and vice versa may become very inadequate when asked just to present the data, relate the data to values critically, or relate the values to theories constructively. They are simply not trained in these activities and often do not even realize that something new is going on. They stick to their old ways, insensitive to the signals of apathy, incomprehension or protestations of irrelevance.

When, even in an open society, the critical prophesies pronounced by scientists and carried into every nook and cranny of society, on the backs of a broad-shouldered popular movement, are not sufficiently paid attention to, scientists might be inclined to blame the peace movement. The movement was not quantitatively big or qualitatively deep enough, or something like that. It may not occur to the scientists that their message was only half of what people want to hear and that the constructive half was missing. Moreover, however brilliant the scientists, they may not be very good at the game of politics and power play. The political establishment will pick those scientists, and take whatever they can use from any scientist which is consistent with their policies. Whatever is incompatible will not even be listened to, or if listened to not understood, or if understood not paid attention to, or if paid attention to used in the wrong way. Except for the very, very rare occasion.

Finally, the scientist, more likely than not, will view the relationship as a one-way relationship where the scientist is 'giving' something to the movement, for instance his valuable time—and he may be reflecting on the opportunity costs, articles not written, books not produced, lectures not given (honoraria not received). It may not occur to him that he perhaps receives more from the thousands or even millions in the movement than he is able or even willing to give, because he has been trained only to perceive experts as real people, and the rest as 'masses'. Listening too much to colleagues may have made him deaf to what others have to say. Hence, a unique training in basic values of democracy—and isn't that also what the peace movement is about?

Notes

1. See my *Methodology and Ideology*, Ejlers, Copenhagen 1977, Ch. 3 for an exploration of this theme.

2. My own book *There are Alternatives!* (German, English, Dutch, Spanish editions 1984; Norwegian, Swedish, Italian, Japanese editions 1985) is actually a mix of all three—how successful is another issue.

Questions

1. How might scientists abuse their authority when they take public positions on political issues?
2. Why must scientists be willing to learn as well as teach?
3. Why is the peace movement long on criticism of governments and short on constructive proposals?
4. The author thinks that the "nuclear winter" issue (Jonathan Schell in *The Fate of Earth*) has been overblown. Do you think he is right? Why?
5. What are some of the responsibilities of the scientist as a citizen?

7

Why the U.N. Is Worth Saving

Harvey J. Feldman

This article originally appeared in *The New York Times*, June 2, 1986.

The author of this article is not so quick to write off the United Nations as is the writer of the following article. As a defender of the world body's accomplishments, Harvey Feldman, vice-president of the Institute of East-West Security Studies in New York City, begins with the admission that much of the criticism is justified.

Since the United States, at the time of writing, accounts for more than half of the organization's unpaid bills (the price of two B-1 bombers), the author seeks to put the problem in perspective for domestic policymakers. Granting the excesses of the General Assembly, Feldman makes a case for its positive accomplishments, especially the resolutions by which human rights violations can be measured and condemned.

But the U.N., he reminds us, is not just the General Assembly. Feldman recalls, for those who may have forgotten, that the Security Council has dispatched peacekeeping forces to various world trouble spots. He cites the successes of the World Health Organization in eliminating such diseases as smallpox and the role of the International Atomic Energy Agency, which was catapulted into prominence by the Soviet nuclear catastrophe at Chernobyl in the spring of 1986. To these, one might add the accomplishments of the Food and Agriculture Organization and other, less publicized, organs of the world body.

Feldman criticizes a Congressional proposal for a weighted system of voting in the General Assembly as unilateral and unlikely to get enacted. Instead, he recommends an adjustment in the annual assessment formula for contributions to the world body, which might stand some chance of adoption. By reducing the U.S. contribution from twenty-five percent to twenty percent and requiring even the smallest member states to pay at least 0.5 percent, "the higher tab may heighten the responsibility of countries now getting something close to a free ride."

It is interesting and sad that the United Nations, which we helped found 40 years ago, is enduring a financial crisis that threatens to shut it down, and nobody seems much to care. Indeed, the fact that the General Assembly had to be called back into special session rated only the briefest mention in New York and Washington, and nothing at all most everywhere else.

The reason for the crisis is plain to see: a number of countries have not paid their bills. The leading debtors are the Soviet Union and Eastern European nations, which together owe $113.6 million, and the United States, which owes $253.5 million. These debts account for two-thirds of the outstanding arrears of $542 million.

As far as the United States is concerned, the problem is political, not fiscal. Most Americans, including members of Congress, equate the United Nations with the General Assembly and see it as a collection of mountebanks or worse, hurling invective at Uncle Sam while running up bills at his expense, and scapegoating Israel.

Over the years, the Assembly has indeed become an instrument of irresponsibility, particularly fiscal irresponsibility. One of the more egregious examples was the Assembly's decision, during the height of the African famine, to spend $70 million on a new conference center in Ethiopia. But it is also the Assembly that adopted the Declaration on the Elimination of All Forms of Religious Intolerance, as well as most of the other key instruments for human rights, and that debates torture and holds those governments practicing it up to universal scorn.

In any event, the General Assembly is only one part of a complex system, and neither the largest nor the most important part. Sometimes it seems to be the price one has to pay for the rest of the system—for the Security Council, which, in the exercise of its peacekeeping function, has dispatched troops to keep antagonists apart in Cyprus, Kashmir, Lebanon and elsewhere; for the World Health Organization, which essentially has eliminated smallpox from the planet; for the constellation of specialized agencies; for the High Commissioner for Refugees, caring for more than 10 million people worldwide; for the International Atomic Energy Agency, so much in the news since Chernobyl.

The system as a whole seems worth saving. The question is how to go about it.

Of the $250 million we owe, $40 million is a hangover from last year, and $210 million—the price of two B-1 bombers—is this year's bill. Congress, through an amendment sponsored by Senator Nancy Landon Kassebaum, Republican of Kansas, has instructed the Reagan Administration to withhold about $80 million of that unless the United Nations switches the system by which budgets are approved from a two-thirds majority to one in which votes on budgetary issues are weighted according to the amount of contribution.

To be sure, the present arrangement, under which a two-thirds majority can be put together by states that collectively pay less than 15 percent of the budget, is a sham. But the problem is that the two-thirds formula is enshrined in the United Nations Charter. Senator Kassenbaum is attempting to overturn a treaty by an amendment to a domestic appropriations bill—not exactly the way a great power ought to do things.

Nevertheless, the amendment, along with Gramm-Rudman-Hollings legislation, has done one thing marvelously well: it has caught the attention of the United Nations's members. We should now press for a total revamping of the scale of assessment, such that no country would pay less than one-half of one percent next year, and no country more than 20 percent (thus cutting the United States back from its current 25 percent). The higher tab may heighten the responsibility of countries now getting something close to a free ride.

Will this transform the General Assembly into the kind of mature, deliberative body we would like it to be? No, but then neither is the United States Congress. And Congress has had 200 years of working at it.

Basically, what it comes down to is this: is the United Nations system, even including the General Assembly, worth the price of two B-1 bombers to us? I think the answer is yes.

Questions

1. Is it right to blame the failures of the United Nations on the structure of the organization itself? Where else might one look for causes?

2. Do you think that this article and the succeeding one (see Brucan) are at odds on all points? Where might there be areas of convergence?

3. Do you think that a weighted system of voting in the General Assembly (based on percentage of annual contribution) is a good idea or a bad one? Explain.

4. Would a change in the annual assessment to the U.N. bring about a more responsible voting pattern in the General Assembly? Why, or why not?

5. What, in your opinion, has been the U.N.'s greatest contribution to world peace? What is its most far-reaching failure?

8

The Establishment of a World Authority: Working Hypotheses

Silviu Brucan

This article originally appeared in *Alternatives—A Journal of World Policy*, Fall 1982.

One should not expect from this article more than it purports to be— a series of working hypotheses. It is not a blueprint for world order, much less a roadmap on how to get there. But Silviu Brucan performs a service by analyzing past and current trends in order to describe (in however hazy a manner) what the future of a world community may be like.

By world order, the author means "a pattern of power relations among states capable of ensuring the functioning of international activities according to a set of rules—written and unwritten." It is his conviction that, even with the United Nations, such a pattern does not now exist. Yet he sees signs that there are changes in the air. In the midst of "general disorder prevailing now," he perceives nation-states entering a period of transition "from the international nation system to the emerging world system." In some ways, he echoes the insights of Pope John XXIII in his 1963 encyclical letter "Peace on Earth" cited earlier. Brucan's concern is that "such a drive has no conscious direction and rationality." He calls for a world authority to "control and direct its motion."

Brucan traces the history of international institutions from the Concert of Europe (1812–1914) to the League of Nations (1919–1939) to the United Nations (1945). The United States, he says, dominated this body until 1960, only to see its influence wane as newly independent nations, now numbering more than 150, took their seats in the General Assembly. Under the rule of "one nation, one vote," the Assembly consistently voted against perceived American and Western interests. Such a system, he says, "merely points up the gap between juridical principles and power realities." Frustration with the Assembly led the major powers to make their decisions outside the halls of the U.N. At this point, he feels that the U.N. has reached its "historical limits."

Labeling twenty years of superpower disarmament negotiations a failure, Brucan calls for "a strong and effective world institution (as) the only rational solution." He also faults the present world body for its inability to close the widening gap between rich and poor nations or to find a way to enforce its decisions.

Brucan's "working hypotheses" point out the areas in which research must be done: (1) He proposes a study of the transfer of power—partial and gradual—from nation-states to the new institution. (Whether this is feasible or likely he does not say.) (2) He distinguishes World Authority from world government in that he does not foresee the dissolution of nation-states. This is because the transfer of authority will be only partial. (3) The two major tasks of such a World Authority are peace maintenance and the restructuring of international economic relations, though it implies a world police force and a world tribunal. The remainder of Brucan's suggestions are the logical concomitants of these three principles. "Unless we assure people that they need not fear abuses from the World Authority," he says, "the political will for establishing the new institution is not likely to be forthcoming." He urges capitalist, communist and third world nations to "think anew and act anew."

INTRODUCTION

As we approach the end of the twentieth century, the world is entering a stage in which every major development—whether an essential resource becoming scarce, a social or political upheaval—seems to acquire such magnitude and involve consequences so ominous that new international arrangements are required to contain, control, and direct them. The globalization of the phenomena, processes, and problems besetting our world has turned the establishment of an international institution capable of controlling and managing them into the central question of world order.

In the 1960s, a world institution was proposed with the exclusive purpose of preventing a catastrophic nuclear war. Very soon, however, it became clear that such a partial approach is thoroughly inadequate. To build a new international institution one must deal with the whole, not with its parts; even the elimination of war is preconditioned on the solution to global economic and social problems that have proved unmanageable under present international organizations.

In fact, the general disorder prevailing now in various international activities informs us that we are on the threshold of a new era in the history of international relations. As I view this, we are going through a period of transition—from the international state system to the emerging world system. Whereas in the former, the nation-state is the prime mover and its inputs are predominant in shaping the system and determining its behavior, in the latter, it is the reverse effect of the world system that is beginning to prevail over its subsystems, adjusting them all to its own motion.

No longer is the nation-state functioning as a self-contained social system whose decisions are determined inside; outside factors now increasingly participate in national decisions and governments are totally inept in coping with them.

Apparently, international relations and transnational activities are growing so interdependent, so systemic, that the world system acquires a drive of its own. And since such a drive has no conscious direction and rationality, it is imperative that a world authority control and direct its motion. It is in that historical perspective that I intend to deal with the issue of the new world institution.

THE HISTORICAL CASE

Throughout history, international organizations or institutions have always mirrored the contemporary world power structure and the respective stage in the evolution of international relations. The issue now involves chiefly the management of power in international society and the ways and means of securing the smooth functioning of relations among its political units. Here, one must proceed from the fact that in the international arena there is no center of authority and power like the state in national society. Over the ages, this vacuum has been filled by various schemes substituting for a central power and endeavoring to perform in the international sphere order-keeping and integrative functions—if possible, through international organizations.

Such a necessity became particularly critical with the formation of the modern international system in the historical period in which the expansion of capitalism coincided with the making of nation-states in Europe—a symbiosis that left its mark on the whole system and its behavior. The capitalist mode of production gave an impetus to the extension of trade and to the creation of the world market, overcoming the isolation of countries and continents typical of the Middle Ages and feudalism. Nation-states provided the basic political units that would constitute the structure of the system.

Although not an international organization, the Concert of Europe (1812–1914) was the first comprehensive scheme for coordinated management of world order. It was based on the premise that each of the four or five participating European powers could enforce common decisions in its own sphere of influence. A classical balance-of-power scheme, the Concert of Europe was hailed as the "golden age of diplomacy" stretching over a century of "international order and stability." Yet, if one looks deeper into the matter, one finds that this Golden Age witnessed the imperialist conquest of Africa, Asia, and Latin America that kept the colonial powers so busy overseas that Europe remained necessarily peaceful for a while.

The League of Nations, endowed with a Covenant, an Assembly, a Council, and a Permanent Secretariat, constituted a radical departure from previous arrangements. It was a real organization with a legal personality, a structure, and agencies of its own. The League was a step forward in international society, responding to the growth of international activities after World War I. Its membership reached more than 30 nations, for the first time providing small nations with an opportunity to participate and be heard in an international forum. Yet, the League reflected the predominant position of Britain and France, allowing them to control the organization and to use it for their imperialist ends. Hence the Covenant did not specifically outlaw war—an expression of an epoch in which force was still considered the final arbiter of international conflict.

The United Nations is an organization much more democratic and universal in membership and more advanced in its principles. However, while most of the principles and purposes of the UN Charter reflect the new openings in world affairs after World War II, the mechanism of the governing structure of the UN bears the imprint of the power realities of 1945. The Big Five of the victorious coalition were given a privileged position as permanent members of the Security Council with a right to veto any resolution that did not suit their particular interests. The practical consequence has been that the UN is unable to take effective action whenever one of the great powers is directly or indirectly involved in a conflict. Thus, very few military outbreaks can be resolved by the UN, for we live in a world in which power is ubiquitous. What is more, as one author puts it: "In relations among the Great Powers, decisive for the maintenance of world peace, international organizations stand exposed to perpetual defeat."[1] The total impotence of the UN in halting the insane nuclear race is a case in point.

Since power relations are never static, the evolution of the UN has followed postwar shifts in the worldwide distribution of power. For the first 15 years, the United States, as the leader of both the Western world and of the Latin American nations, controlled more than two-thirds of the votes and could easily prevail over the group of socialist states in the General Assembly. By the end of the 1950s, a new political factor began to assert itself in the UN: as Latin American nations joined the Third World, the voting pattern within the UN shifted dramatically. In this respect, then, the UN has come a long way—from the "blunt truth that far more clearly than the League, the UN was essentially conceived as a club of great powers"[2] to the present state of affairs in which the great powers complain about the "tyranny of the majority."

From a strictly juridical angle, power simply does not exist in the UN. Article 2, paragraph 1 of the Charter solemnly proclaims: "The Organization is based on the principle of the sovereign equality of its members." The same principle is implicit in Article 18 which gives each member of the General Assembly one vote. To be sure, there are political analysts who take these provisions at face value as though world politics were guided by legal criteria and rules. Actually, international power relations are marked by great discrepancies, and the distribution of power in the real world merely points up the gap between juridical principles and power realities. Hence the theory of the "weighted vote" is essentially an attempt to eliminate this gap and to duplicate in the UN the power relations prevailing on the international scene.

The contrast between world law and world reality may well be the underlying reason why in recent years issues involving the great powers have been gradually removed from the UN. The major protagonists feel they are in a better position to promote their interests outside a setting that has become too egalitarian and democratic for power politics. Apparently, the nuclear stalemate outside the UN has been compounded by a political stalemate within the organization. On the one hand, to be effective, key UN decisions require the agreement of the great powers; on the other, neither the United States or the Soviet Union nor any combination of the major powers can any longer move the UN to act against the interests of the Third World.

This is a structural crisis that must be carefully examined. To begin with, while the drafters of the UN charter recognized the state of international relations after World War II and decided to codify it as an international state system functioning according to the principle of national sovereignty, their underlying assumption was that such a system could be run by an organization in which the great powers could act as coordinate managers of world order on the premise that each one would enforce UN decisions in its own sphere of influence. This basic constitutional assumption reflected the ideology of an epoch in which power realities were skillfully disguised in the liberal rhetoric of international law.

At the time of the Concert of Europe, four or five powers were able to apply such a scheme because there were actually very few sovereign states in the other continents: the colonial empires of the European powers practically covered the whole planet. Such a scheme, though gradually altered, continued to function in the years of the League and seemed still workable at the time when the UN was set up. It was not until the 1960s, when the political configuration of the world radically changed, that it became obvious that such a scheme could no longer work. Social revolutions in Eastern Europe, China, and elsewhere had considerably enlarged the number of countries dropping from the capitalist system. The national liberation movement expanded rapidly: almost 20 Arab states appeared, while in Africa and Asia dozens of new states arose over the ruins of the French, British, Dutch, and, lastly, Portuguese empires. Indeed, the number of sovereign political units around the world has multiplied to well above 150, and so has the membership of the United Nations.

And it is not only the map that looks different. Though the new states started with a backward economy and therefore have had to retain economic links with their former metropoles, the political activation of the mass population stimulated by independence, increasing education, and touches of modernization and industrialization, has resulted in a powerful thrust of national resurgence that has swept world politics. While it is true that this resurgent movement does not involve power in the traditional sense of the term, it has nevertheless produced a new international setting in which it is no longer possible for the major powers to run the world, or even to exercise effective control over their allies, partners, or clients. Actually, we are witnessing the most decentralized international system in modern history.

Perhaps the greatest merit of the UN lies in its capacity of accommodating the decolonization struggle and the support it gave the new nations in achieving statehood. In fact, the UN has helped extend the state system to all continents, making the system truly international. The UN Charter proved well drafted for this historical task while the organization displayed flexibility in adapting to its requirements.

Having accomplished this mission, the UN seems to have reached its *historical limits*. Apparently, the UN was neither conceived nor equipped to deal with the global problems that have come to the fore in recent years (the nuclear arms race and proliferation, development, world resources and the energy crisis, ecological deterioration, etc.), or with the economic and financial disorders that trouble the world today. These problems and tasks actually belong to new historical conditions so different from those which produced the UN. The very principle of sovereignty that made the UN system work and enabled it to successfully carry out the internationalization of the state system is now the single greatest barrier in coping with the problems now confronting the international community.

To sum up the historical case with the extension of the state system all over the world, international organizations can no longer work as instruments of great powers, nor can international organizations substitute for a center of authority whilst their activity depends on the political will of 150 member-states with conflicting interests, objectives, and views. A new type of international institution must now be established having the authority to plan, to make decisions, and to enforce these decisions.

WHY A WORLD AUTHORITY?

Ours is a world in which changes on the international scene are so rapid that decisions made today must be necessarily conceived in terms of tomorrow. This is even more so when the issue is a world institution designed to accommodate world developments in the decades to come.

The world of the next decades will be a "small world" in which the per capita GNP of the developed nations will still be 12 times that of the developing nations, even if the growth rates set by the UN for the year 2000 were achieved. The population of the developing nations, however, will be five times that of the developed world. Anyone who puts these two sets of figures together must realize that the explosion will not be limited to population. We will live in a world in which it will take about two or three hours to fly from Caracas to New York or from Lagos to London, a world in which the Bolivian or the Pakistani will see on television every night how people live in the affluent societies, a world in which there will be no suburbia for the rich to insulate themselves from the poor.

While the insane nuclear arms race will continue generating its own perilous moments in the drive for first-strike capability and military superiority (whatever that means in overkill terms), the world of the next decades will live and sleep with a balance of terror in the hands of 20 or so ambitious nations armed with atomic weapons, not to mention terrorist groups using atomic bombs for blackmail or ransom. With the shift of the superpower confrontation to the battlefields of the Third World, the arms race will continue to be exported to Africa, Asia, and Latin America, infecting a growing number of developing nations with militarism, dominance appetites, and regional policeman roles. As the pillars of the old order crumble one after the other, the world of the coming decades will look like New York, Tokyo, or Paris, without traffic regulations and policemen.

The present dislocations in the world market and the recurring disruptions in the monetary system, compounded by the chaos of oil prices, are but signals of a long period of instability ahead for the world economy. We can thus expect an equally long period in world affairs that will involve great dangers of military adventurism and neofascism caused by the desperate attempts of finance and corporate capital to hold on to its challenged positions. It is the belief of this writer that the remaining two decades of this century may go down in history as its most critical and explosive period. For never before have so many social and political contradictions requiring structural changes converged in a world so small and so capable of destroying itself.

Surely, the United Nations is not equipped to deal with problems of such nature and magnitude. A decision-making system with 150 independent participants is in itself a prescription for ineffectiveness in dealing with global problems. A strong and effective world institution is the only rational solution to the kind of global problems confronting us today. What else could break the war system by halting the arms race and reversing its trends while planning and managing the conversion to a peace economy without serious disruptions? Twenty years of disarmament negotiations have resulted in a complete failure. Military expenditures have reached monstrous proportions while nations, starting with the great ones, feel less secure than ever.

Within present international arrangements, nothing can stop the escalation of the nuclear arms race, the most aberrant product of power politics. The nuclear arms race seems very little affected either by rational economic arguments or by moral standards; it remains untouched by the most terrifying prospects and is stronger even than man's instinct for self-preservation. To keep the war system going, even "peace agreements" like that of Camp David are supposedly buttressed by arming to the teeth the two partners—Egypt and Israel; so-called arms controls treaties, like SALT II, are actually used as a springboard for a new escalation in armament expenditures.

Equally inefficient are the efforts by present international organizations to deal with development. Two "Development Decades" have elapsed under the UN's aegis, and the abysmal gap between the haves and the have-nots is growing wider. In the years since 1974, when the UN adopted the historic resolution on the establishment of a New International Economic Order, it has become all too clear that no significant headway will ever be possible without some sort of global planning and management designed to ensure that the transition toward a new order is not marred by disruptive competition and chaos for industrial nations and developing ones alike. Such global planning is inconceivable without a world authority.

Furthermore, even a partial agreement in North-South negotiations will come up against the issue of enforcement. Who will make sure that all the parties involved will observe the terms of the agreement? The real choice is between a world authority and the laws of the market, which systematically work in favor of the rich. As for the latter, global planning is also imperative if the industrial nations are ever to come out of their present economic and financial crises. Thus a world authority is a must for both.

In recent years, international UN conferences have brought to the fore the enormity of such world problems as the human habitat, population growth, transfer of science and technology, ecological deterioration and pollution, food, etc. They all point in the same direction: the need for global planning and management. To cite but one such problem, merely to build the physical infrastructure of the human habitat—houses, schools, hospitals, factories, new cities, etc.—required before the end of the century entails a construction job similar in scope to that accomplished since the Middle Ages. And what about the task of providing work for the 350 million able-bodied men and women currently underemployed or unemployed, the one billion or more new jobs that will be needed for children now being born?

Finally, while people are worried about the depletion of nonrenewable resources, the so-called renewable ones face more imminent dangers: the rapid degradation of the tropical rain forests, the advance of desertification, and an accelerating extinction of animal and plant wildlife. If these processes are not halted, we are bound to lose drastically in terms of health, habitat, and quality of life.

THE WORLD SYSTEM

I submit that neither the convergence in time of global problems, nor the commonality of their nature and scope are accidental. Although they seem to be products of a chaotic amalgamation of factors, processes and phenomena, there is a certain logic in their appearance, manifestations, and magnitude. I think they actually inform us about something fundamental taking place in the very system of international relations: the emergence of the world system.

Here I must point out that there are various approaches to studying the world system and the timing of its appearance. Immanuel Wallerstein, in a monumental work, relates it to the expansion of capitalism, starting with the fifteenth century, when the origins and early conditions of the world system, then exclusively European, appeared.[3] Other authors stress the role of great powers (starting with Portugal) in the formation of the world system since 1500. Although I agree with Wallerstein's focus on the role of capitalism in the formation of the world economy, I consider that political developments did not necessarily parallel the economic ones, as illustrated by the Absolutist State—the maker of modern nation-states in Europe. What followed was essentially a state system, then exclusively European, extending only lately to all continents.

I suggest that the watershed in the creation of a global system encompassing the whole world and functioning with sufficient regularity to impose certain recognizable patterns of behavior on all its subsystems is primarily related to the scientific-technological revolution. It is this revolution that has made communication universal, information instantaneous, transportation supersonic, and modern weaponry planetary, and that has allowed for a global sphere of multilevel interdependencies to emerge and function with a unifying and integrating force. Therefore, I place the appearance of the world system at the middle of the twentieth century, when major breakthroughs in science started to be applied on a large enough scale to become consequential in world politics. Previously, large sections of the world had remained isolated and practically unaffected by central events—even by the two world wars.

The important point is that 'world system' is the conceptualization best suited to explain the new global problems that have arisen in recent decades. Certainly, development, ecological equilibrium, nuclear proliferation, or the energy crisis cannot be dealt with adequately in the context of the "world system of the 1500s" or, for that matter, of the 1800s, for the very simple reason that they were not world problems then. And they were not problems then because there was no world system to account for their global scope.

As I mentioned earlier, what distinguishes the world system from the present international state system is to be found in the relationship between the two levels of systemic motion—the national and the world level. The first level covers the nation-state as the basic political unit of the international system; the second takes the world system and global dynamics as its starting point. To be sure, there is constant interaction between the two. But, whereas in the present international system, the nation-state is still the prime mover whose decisions and performances eventually produce the functioning principles and prevailing patterns of behavior, in the world system, it is the reverse.

A typical effect of the world system upon nation-states is being felt in military policy. Since nuclear missile weapons are planetary both in destruction and delivery capability, nuclear policy acquires a global scope that transcends alliances and overrides all other considerations, including ideological ones. Globalism has led the U.S. and the USSR to stubbornly preserve their monopoly of basic decisions on war and on nuclear strategic weapons. The two nuclear treaties (test-ban and nonproliferation) jointly drafted by American and Soviet experts, as well as SALT I and II, reflect this basic policy. China's advocacy of a strong Western European defense is also inspired by the nuclear logic and the power game it regulates.

The global power rivalry, continuously fed by the arms race, makes for a war system with a drive of its own. This may well explain why the nuclear arms race goes on and on in spite of the fact that already, in the late 1960s, the arsenals of the superpowers were sufficient to destroy the world and kill everybody many times over. The overall effect of the world system is apparent in the active participation in the nuclear arms race of all great powers, irrespective of their domestic system, and in the tendency it generates in other ambitious nations—some of which are still in a preindustrial stage—to go nuclear.

It is in international economic relations and activities that the world system is at its best in influencing nation-states. International trade has been converted from an exclusive club of the big exporting nations into a real world activity. The rate of growth of world exports is rising faster than the growth rate of either production or average GNP. Thus, national economies are increasingly dependent on foreign sources of raw materials and modern technology, and on foreign outlets for their products. The energy crisis highlighted the dependence of most powerful states on oil imports; indeed, interdependence is the law of the world.

The globalization process powered by modern technology is a basic feature of international economic relations. It is a factor so strong that it overpowers even ideological prejudices: joint ventures between socialist states and multinational corporations are cropping up every day. The current economic and financial disorder is truly global with all nations, including socialist ones, feeling its effect.

The attempt of the industrial states to plan their economic development (OECD Scenario for 1980) as well as the strategy set by the regular summit meetings of the seven rich have both ended in complete failure, proving once more that the industrial nations cannot overcome . . . crises by planning in a closed circuit. Equally self-defeating are the barriers raised by these countries against industrial goods of developing nations; thus, the very purchasing power of the latter for buying industrial equipment from the West is reduced. Only by global planning could the present crises be overcome. Gone are the days when economic policies of nations were decided inside; now even major industrial nations, such as Great Britain and Italy, have to develop their annual budget in accordance with the instructions of the International Monetary Fund. Outside factors are now integral to the major economic policies of all governments.

Briefly, in both the military and economic domains, the world system causes nation-states to make adaptive decisions that they would not make in response only to domestic wants. The impact of the world system upon its basic units, the nation-states, is thus felt in all major areas of foreign policy, and, as far as we can tell, the tendency of these external stimuli in determining the behavior of nations is going to grow.

A NEW SYSTEM—A NEW INSTITUTION

Historically, the case for a world authority rests on the emergence of the world system eroding the present international state system. It logically follows that a new system of international relations requires an adequate institution to establish its corresponding world order and secure its smooth functioning during the long transition period from the old system to the new one. To be explicit in what we are talking about, by *world order* I mean a pattern of power relations among states capable of ensuring the functioning of various international activities according to a set of rules—written and unwritten.

Thus far, the discussion of a new international or world order has been dominated by moral, religious, ideological, and, lately, juridical and economic principles and values. Surely, none of these criteria should be overlooked since each provides some of the motivations underlying large-scale human actions so essential to such an undertaking. What is still lacking is conceptual clarity and scientific groundwork, particularly in bringing into focus the fulcrum of politics which is and remains decisive in settling the issue of world order.

A serious intellectual effort is required to fill this gap. Here are my suggestions regarding the directions of such research work and how to go about it.

1. Since the issue involved is chiefly the management of power in international society, I submit that the first thing that must be worked out is the ways and means for the establishment of an international institution wielding power of its own. In practical terms, this means that a transfer of power—a partial and gradual one, to be sure—would have to take place from nation-states to the new institution. The transfer of power to the World Authority being assumed to be gradual, it follows that during the transition period world order will be maintained by a duality of power: the nation-state retaining most of its sovereign prerogatives and the World Authority exercising power in international affairs to the extent of its delegated authority and competence.

2. The concept of World Authority is different from that of world government. The latter presupposes the dissolution of nation-states and the creation, instead, of a single governing body designed to run the whole world, whereas the World Authority requires the nation-state to be maintained with only a partial transfer of power to the new institution so as to enable it to operate effectively within its limited area of competence.

3. It is assumed that the World Authority will be initially entrusted with two major tasks: peace maintenance with a view to enforcing general disarmament and eventually abolishing war, and the restructuring of international economic relations with a view to overcoming the present economic crisis and eliminating the glaring inequality between the developed and developing nations. Securing peace actually means break-

ing the war system by halting the arms race—its specific form of movement—and reversing its momentum. This also involves the gradual dismantling of military forces and organizations parallel with the establishment of a world police force and a world tribunal, which are needed to make sure that the decisions of the World Authority are enforced, to intervene whenever the law is violated, and for the peaceful settlement of disputes.

4. The choice of government, of its economic, social, and political system will remain the inalienable right of each nation. The World Authority will see to it that no foreign power interferes with such internal affairs of member-states. As the existence of a national police force does not prevent citizens from exercising their constitutional rights, so will the World Authority and police force not prevent nation-states from exercising their sovereignty in all spheres of domestic activity, nor will they be able to interfere with the struggle of exploited classes or oppressed minorities for a better society. Briefly, it is only the use of force in interstate relations that will fall within the competence of the World Authority.

5. While we live at a time when nationalism is stronger than ever and nations are extremely sensitive about their sovereign rights, experience shows that nations are nevertheless prepared to transfer some of their prerogatives, provided they are impressed by the advantages deriving therefrom. Recognizing that it is in their best interests that foreign airplanes should fly over their territory and across their frontiers, national governments have accepted the establishment of the International Civil Aviation Organization, and have abided strictly by its rules. Also, such activities as weather control, shipping, control of contagious diseases, have been entrusted to international organizations wielding some power of their own. Therefore, a thorough study should be undertaken to examine the kind of requirements to be met before governments would be willing to hand over national prerogatives to the World Authority in such activities as peace maintenance and economic relations. Since we are dealing with nations having conflicting views, both as to objectives and as to methods, such a study must find compromise solutions to accommodate everyone.

6. Confidence-building measures are essential in the case of a supranational institution, particularly on matters of national security, disarmament, and a world police force—where fears and suspicions reach their highest intensity.

7. Economics of a warless world: The question of conversion to a peace economy must be reexamined in the context of the present economic crisis and strategy of development.

8. Politics of a warless world: What kind of restrictions and pressures are necessary to apply to the nation-states, particularly great powers, in

order to prevent them from using force, and eventually to abolish war? Given the dynamics of power politics, how can the World Authority contain and control it?

9. The law of a warless world: A totally new legal framework must be formulated, keeping in mind the conceptual novelty of a supranational institution and allowing for a gradual process toward that goal. The new constitution must spell out clearly what kind of authority and power and over what substantive areas, will be entrusted to the World Authority; also what kind of safeguards will be necessary to prevent organs of the new institution from encroaching upon areas remaining under the authority of nation-states. Finally, the jurists will also have to examine the creation of a world tribunal to establish ways and means for settling disputes.

10. The new institutions: The World Authority with its enforcement agencies must be conceived and spelled out functionally in terms of membership, structure, organizations, distribution of power and representation, deliberative and executive bodies, secretariat, rules of procedure, etc. Here the authors will have to devise the new institutions in such a way as to allay the fears that the World Authority once constituted may abuse its powers and become a Frankenstein monster that will terrorize us while we are unable to control it. This issue is paramount in terms of political feasibility; for, unless we assure people that they need not fear abuses from the World Authority, the political will for establishing the new institution is not likely to be forthcoming.

Equally important in this respect is to convey the feeling that in the organization of the World Authority there will be fair and equal opportunities for all nations, irrespective of size, power, and wealth. Experience has implanted in the small and poor nations fear and suspicions against misuse and manipulation of international organizations by the powerful and rich nations. A fair system of representation and distribution of power should allay such fears.

In practical terms, the UN could be instrumental in the initiation phase of the new institution, providing the proper forum for discussion of its principles, organization, and structure. What is more, the new institution will probably have to make use of the experienced staff and vast facilities of the UN, once the latter would cease to exist.

CONCLUSION

Let me frankly admit that a world authority, however rational its establishment, and however persuasive its historical case, is far ahead of present political and ideological realities and, therefore, its very idea is bound to encounter formidable resistance. Paradoxically, those who need it most, fear it most.

In fact, the changes that require the setting up of such an institution have come so rapidly in international life—quicker than a generation's span of time—that political thought and practice have been left well behind. In no other domain is there a contrast so great between the speed of change and the nature of problems, on the one hand, and the political institutions supposed to deal with them, on the other hand. And yet, horrendous problems are piling up, threatening our jobs, the peace we cherish, the air we breathe, the cities we live in, the planes we fly in, and, in the last analysis, our very existence as human beings.

In a world divided by power, wealth, and ideology, probably the most difficult assignment will be the building of a model for the World Authority equally attractive and reassuring for all nations. While the citizens of great and developed nations should look at the World Authority as the safest way of avoiding a nuclear catastrophe, the citizens of the Third World should look at it as the best way of building a more democratic and equitable world order. As for the socialist nations, who are interested in both the maintenance of peace and the establishment of a more equitable economic order, surely "peaceful coexistence," however noble a principle, is still an "armed peace," and as such is no guarantee whatever against the outbreak of wars—not even among socialist nations themselves. It is only a world authority that can provide such a guarantee. For a Marxist, it should be clear enough that imperialism will never give up its privileged positions without resorting to the "biggest bang" at its disposal, nor will the advanced capitalist states willingly renounce their commanding positions on the world market. What could socialism mean on a radiated planet?

Apparently, with the emergence of the world system, everybody must think anew and act anew.

Notes

1. Stanley Hoffmann, *Organisations Internationales et Pouvoir Politique des Etats* (Paris: Armand Colin, 1954), p. 412.

2. George Ball, "Slogans and Realities," *Foreign Affairs* 47.4 (July 1969): 625.

3. Immanuel Wallerstein, *The Modern World-System* (New York: Academic Press, 1974), Vol. 1, Introduction.

Questions

1. What is the purpose of a "working hypothesis"? Do you think that the author succeeds in his purpose? Why or why not?

2. Do you think that the world is in transition from the nation-state to some form (even limited) of world authority? Give your reasons.

3. Has the U.N. reached its "historical limits"? State several reasons pro and con.

4. Who, or what, is responsible for the failure of the U.N. to live up to the high hopes of its founders in 1945?

5. What obstacles lie in the path of even a partial transfer of power to a World Authority? Does this mean that the idea should be shelved? Why, or why not?